MostUsedWords.com presents

Spanish Frequency Dictionary

Intermediate Vocabulary

2501 - 5000 Most Common Spanish Words

Book 2

First Printing, 2018

MostUsedWords.com

www.MostUsedWords.com

Contents

Why This Book?

Hello, dear reader.

Thank you for purchasing this book. We hope it serves you well on your language learning journey.

Not all words are created equal. The purpose of this frequency dictionary is to list the most common Spanish words in descending order, so you can learn this language as fast and efficiently as possible.

First, we would like to illustrate the value of a frequency dictionary. For the purpose of example, we have combined frequency data from various languages (mainly Romance, Slavic and Germanic languages) and made it into a single chart.

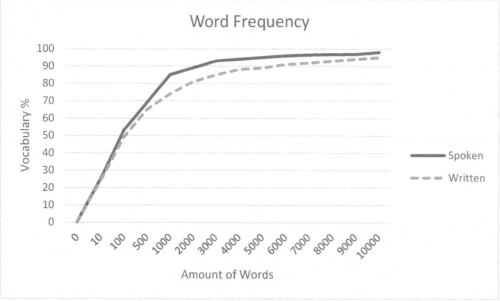

The sweet spots, according to the data seem to be:

Amount of Words	Spoken	Written
• 100	53%	49%
• 1.000	85%	74%
• 2.500	92%	82%
• 5.000	95%	89%
• 7.500	97%	93%
• 10.000	98%	95%

Above data corresponds with Pareto´s law.

Pareto's law, also known as the 80/20 rule, states that, for many events, roughly 80% of the effects come from 20% of the causes.

In language learning, this principle seems to be on steroids. It seems that just 20% of the 20% (95/5) of the most used words in a language account for roughly all the vocabulary you need.

To put this further in perspective: The Collins Spanish Dictionary (August 2016 edition) lists over 310.000 words in current use, while you will only need to know 1.62% (5000 words) to achieve 95% and 89% fluency in speaking and writing. Knowing the most common 10.000 words, or just 3.25%, will net you 98% fluency in spoken language and 95% fluency in written texts.

Keeping this in mind, the value of a frequency dictionary is immense. Study the most frequent words, build your vocabulary and progress quickly. One more frequency asked question needs to be answered.

Well, how many words do you need to know for varying levels of fluency?

While it's important to note that it is impossible to pin down these numbers and statistics with 100% accuracy, these are a global average of multiple sources.

According to research, this is the amount of vocabulary needed for varying levels of fluency.

1. 250 words: the essential core of a language. Without these words, you cannot construct any meaningful sentences.
2. 750 words: are used every single day by every person who speaks the language.
3. 2500 words: should enable you to express everything you could possibly want to say, although some creativity might be required.
4. 5000 words: the active vocabulary of native speakers without higher education.
5. 10,000 words: the active vocabulary of native speakers with higher education.
6. 20,000 words: the amount you need to be able to recognize passively to read, understand, and enjoy a work of literature such as a novel by a notable author.

Caveats & Limitations.

1. **A frequency list is never "The Definite Frequency List."**

Depending on the source material analyzed, you may get different frequency lists. A corpus on spoken word differs from source texts based on a written language.

That is why we chose subtitles as our source, because, according to science, subtitles cover the best of both worlds: they correlate with both spoken and written language.

The frequency list is based on analysis of roughly 20 gigabytes of Spanish subtitles.

Visualize a book with almost 16 million pages, or 80.000 books of 200 pages each, to get an idea of the amount words that have been analyzed for this book.

If you were to read the source text used for this book, it would take you around 100 years of reading 24/7. A large base text is absolutely vital in order to develop an accurate frequency list.

Since 100 years of simply reading and then trying to process the text is a bit much for one person, we have called in additional power to help us establish the frequency rankings.

The raw data included over 1 million entries, or different "words". The raw data has been lemmatized; words are given in their dictionary form.

2. **Creating a accurate frequency list is more complicated than it seems.**

Above mentioned method of classification does come with it´s own complications. Take for example, the word

- **poder(se)**-*vb; m* – be able; power

Obviously, **poder** is most often used as a verb. However, you will see the word rank highly as one of the most common nouns. With our current methods, it is impossibe to determine exactly how often **poder** is used as a noun as opposed to the verb.

But while we developped an accurate method of estimating the correct position of "**poder**-*m* – power", (around the 500th most common word in Spanish), we decided we don't want duplicate entries in our frequency dictionaries. Why?

Poder is a single dictionary entry, and it's choosing between either "hey, you have duplicate entries, your list sucks." and "hey, **poder** isn't the #9 most common noun, your list sucks." (actual customer feedback, paraphrased.)

Because instances like **poder** are very few and inbetween, we kindly ask you to use your common sense while using this dictionary. Decide for yourself on not wether you should learn a translation or not.

Another difficulty are the conjugated verbs. Some conjugated vers can be classified as multiple parts of speech. Take for example **dicho**. It originally ranked somewhere around the 147th most common Spanish word.

As a conjugated verb, **dicho** is the past participle of "**decir**-*vb* – to say" and translates as "said", while as a noun it means "saying, expression".

No way, José, that "saying, expression" is the most 147th most used Spanish word. As previously stated, our words are lemmatized, and **decir** is already listed at place 77.

(Please refer to our upcoming book on Spanish verbs for detailed verb information, all regular and irregular conjugations and bilingual text example sentences.)

We did develop a method to accurately estimate the occurrence of **dicho** as a noun. By the time of writing "**dicho**-*m* – saying, expression" hoovers around the 11.702th place of the most common Spanish words. It is very unlikely that it will enter the 10.000 most common Spanish words, and thus will be out of the scope of our frequency dictionary series.

3. Nouns

We tried our best to keep out proper nouns, such as "**James**, **Ryan**, **Alice** as well as "**Rome**, **Washington**" or "the **Louvre**". Names of countries are an exception to the rule, and are included.

Some common proper nouns have multiple translations. For the ease of explanation, the following example is given in English.

"**Jack**" is a very common first name, but also a noun (a jack to lift up a vehicle) and a verb (to steal something). So is the word "**can**" It is a conjugation of the verb "to be able" as well as a noun (a tin can, or a can of soft drink).

With the current technology, it is unfortunately not possible to precisely identify the correct frequency placements of above words. We came up with a method to accurately estimate the correct placement of these words.

In example, a ~~well known, long running dictionary company~~ competitor's frequency dictionary on the English language listed the noun "**can**", like a can of coke, as the 247th most used word in the English language. Our methods would list it around the 3347th most used word. While not perfect, I *can* tell you that our method is more accurate than theirs.

4. This word doesn't belong there!

Some entries you might find odd in their respective frequency rankings. We were surprised a couple of times ourselves while creating this series. Keep in mind that the frequency list is compiled from a large amount of text, and may include words you wouldn't use yourself. But you might very well encounter them.

In our opinion, it is important you do know these words. Store them somewhere in your passive vocabulary, instead of trying to integrate them into your active vocabulary. But in the end, it's up to you wether you think you should learn a word, or skip it.

5. This is not a Spanish word!

You might find non-Spanish loanwords in this dictionary. We decided to include them, because if they're being used in subtitle translation, it is safe to assume the word has been integrated into the Spanish general vocabulary.

6. Vulgarities

We also decided to keep out vulgarities, even though these are rather common in daily speech. We wanted to keep this book appropriate for readers of all ages. We tried to image what a modern-day middle American woman would take offense to, and drew the line there.

At the same time, some words absolutely needed to be clarified. In rare occasions, the usage of vocabulary items can differ severely between Spanish spoken in Latin America and Spanish spoken in Europe. It could lead to pretty awkward situations if you were not aware of these differences.

These words have been censored in way that one can still deduce their meaning, if one is already in the know. Kids, ask your parents. In example:

- **coger**-*vb* - to take, f*ck (LA)

7. Parallel text example sentences

Some sentences are easy, some are more difficult. Some are a direct translation, some are more loosely translated. Some mimic spoken language, some mimic written language. Some are more high-brow, some are more collequial. In short, we tried to include a mix of different types of language, just like you would encounter in real life.

Example sentences are great, because they show you Spanish word usage in context. You get to learn extra vocabulary from the sentences, since they're in parallel text. And since you'll encounter important, common words over and over again, you will ingrain those words faster in your long term memory.

8. Final thoughts

We are pretty confident our frequency ranking is as solid as it can be, keeping above pitfalls in mind. Still, this frequency list includes 25 extra words to compensate for any irregularities you might encounter. Or you might disagree with the addition of non-Spanish loanwords. So instead of the 2501 – 5000 most common words, you actually get the 2501-5025 most common words.

And one more thing.

The big secret to learning language is this: build your vocabulary, learn basic grammar and go out there and speak. Make mistakes, have a laugh and then learn from your mistakes. Wash, rinse, repeat..

We hope you enjoy this frequency dictionary and that it helps you in your journey of learning Spanish.

How To Use This Dictionary

abbreviation	*abr*	prefix	*pfx*
adjective	*adj*	preposition	*prp*
adverb	*adv*	pronoun	*prn*
article	*art*	suffix	*sfx*
auxiliary verb	*av*	verb	*vb*
conjunction	*con*	verb (reflexive)	*vbr*
contraction	*contr*	singular	*sg*
interjection	*int*	plural	*pl*
noun	*f(eminine), m(asculine)*	(coll)	*colloquial language*
numeral	*num*	(se)	*reflexive verb marker*
particle	*part*	(ES)	*European Spanish*
phrase	*phr*	(LA)	*Latin America Spanish*

Verbs

Some verbs can be used reflexively. Verbs that can be used reflexively are marked by "**(se)**". Only when the verb has a different meaning when used reflexively, we added the qualifier "**vbr**" to indicate the meaning of the reflexive verb.

Word Order

Different parts of speech are divided by "**;**".

Translations

We made the decision to give the most common translation(s) of a word, and respectively the most common part(s) of speech. It does, however, not mean that this is the only possible translations or the only part of speech the word can be used for.

International Phonetic Alphabet (IPA)

The pronunciation of foreign vocabulary can be tricky. To help you get it right, we added IPA entries for each entry. If you already have a base understanding of the pronunciation, you will find the IPA pronunciation straightforward. For more information, please visit www.internationalphoneticalphabet.org

Spanish English Frequency Dictionary

Rank	Spanish	English Translation(s)
	Part of Speech	Spanish Example Sentences
	[IPA]	-English Example Sentences

2501 episodio — **episode**
m
[e.pi.ˈso.ðjo]
Gracias por este episodio.
-Thank you for this episode.

2502 durar — **last**
vb
[du.ˈrar]
No sé cuánto más podré durar.
-I'm not sure how much longer I can last.

2503 organizar — **organize**
vb
[or.ɣa.ni.ˈsar]
Acabo de organizar mi escritorio.
-I just organized my desk.

2504 ligero — **light**
adj
[li.ˈxɛ.ro]
Tengo un ligero dolor de cabeza en estos momentos.
-I have a slight headache now.

2505 músculo — **muscle**
m
[ˈmus.ku.lo]
¡Ya llegan! No muevas un músculo o arruinarás la sorpresa.
-They're coming! Don't move a muscle or you'll ruin the surprise.

2506 misil — **missile**
m
[mi.ˈsil]
La integridad estructural del misil parece estar intacta.
-The structural integrity of the missile appears to be intact.

2507 obispo — **bishop**
m
[o.ˈβis.po]
He ofrecido mi resignación al obispo.
-I've tendered my resignation with the bishop.

2508 herencia — **heritage, inheritance**
f
[ɛ.ˈrẽn.sja]
Digamos que estoy apostando mi herencia.
-You could say I'm gambling my inheritance.

2509 monje — **monk**
m
[ˈmõɲ.xe]
Pedimos la liberación del monje.
-We call for the release of the monk.

2510 atravesar — **cross**
vb
[a.tra.βe.ˈsar]
Sin autorización legal, nadie puede atravesar la frontera.
-Without legal permission, no one is allowed to cross the borderline.

2511 valioso — **valuable**
adj
[ba.ˈljo.so]
Este instrumento es demasiado importante y valioso como para desaprovecharlo.
-This instrument is too important, and too valuable, to squander.

2512 tiroteo — **gunfire**
m
[ti.ro.ˈte.o]
Vi un tiroteo aquí, en la estación.
-I saw a firefight here on the station.

2513 cordero — **lamb**
m
[kor.ˈðɛ.ro]
Ana tenía un cordero cuya lana era blanca como la nieve.
-Ana had a little lamb whose fleece was white as snow.

2514 sellar — **seal, stamp**
vb
[se.ˈjar]
Tenemos que sellar la entrada.
-We have to seal the entrance.

2515 **aplauso**
m
[aˈp.ˈlau̯.so]

applause
Caballeros, un caluroso aplauso para la encantadora Ana.
-Gentlemen, a warm applause for the lovely Ana.

2516 **píldora**
f
[ˈpil̪.do.ra]

pill
Le aconsejé que se tomara la píldora.
-I advised her to go on the pill.

2517 **puño**
m
[ˈpu.ɲo]

fist
Llevas una hora apretando el puño.
-You've been clenching that fist for the last hour.

2518 **marea**
f
[ma.ˈre.a]

tide
Dicen que la marea arrastró los cuerpos.
-They say that the tide washed away the bodies.

2519 **estimar**
vb
[ɛs.ti.ˈmar]

estimate, respect
No fue posible estimar los costes de estas actividades.
-It was not possible to estimate the costs for these activities.

2520 **disfraz**
m
[ˈdis.fras]

costume
Se puso un disfraz de pirata para Halloween.
-He wore a pirate costume for Halloween.

2521 **navaja**
f
[na.ˈβa.xa]

knife
Los detectives encontraron una navaja vieja debajo de la casa.
-The detectives found an old knife under the house.

2522 **indicar**
vb
[ĩn̪.di.ˈkar]

indicate
Indica a tu pareja dónde quieres que pise.
-Indicate to your partner where you want her to step.

2523 **fracasar**
vb
[fra.ka.ˈsar]

fail
Ya no tenemos derecho a fracasar.
-We no longer have the right to fail.

2524 **injusto**
adj
[ĩŋ.ˈxus.to]

unfair
Estás siendo muy injusto conmigo.
-You're being very unfair to me.

2525 **tremendo**
adj
[tre.ˈmẽn̪.do]

tremendous
El Vicepresidente Kinnock pone un entusiasmo tremendo en todo lo que hace.
-Vice-President Kinnock has tremendous enthusiasm for everything he does.

2526 **jungla**
f
[ˈxũŋ.gla]

jungle
Mientras tanto, seguimos caminando a través de esta jungla.
-In the meantime, we continue to march through this jungle.

2527 **espectacular**
adj
[ɛs.pek̚.ta.ku.ˈlar]

spectacular
Y cuando lo entienda, descubrirá algo espectacular.
-And when you understand it, you will discover something spectacular.

2528 **confesar(se)**
vb
[kõm.fe.ˈsar]

confess
También tengo que confesar una tercera motivación.
-I must confess, there's kind of a third motivation as well.

2529 **bobo**
adj; m
[ˈbo.βo]

silly; fool
Es muy importante no ser un bobo.
-It's very important not to be a fool.

2530 **descubrimiento**

discovery

	m	El descubrimiento de la electricidad cambió nuestra historia.
	[dɛs.ku.βri.ˈmjẽn̪.to]	-The discovery of electricity changed our history.
2531	**mosca**	**fly**
	f	Es difícil aplastar una mosca con las manos desnudas.
	[ˈmos.ka]	-It's hard to swat a fly with your bare hands.
2532	**pretender**	**pretend**
	vb	Sería absurdo pretender que la mundialización es la causa de la desigualdad.
	[prɛ.tẽn̪.ˈdɛr]	-It would be absurd to claim that globalization created inequality.
2533	**derrotar**	**defeat**
	vb	Pero primero déjanos intentar derrotarla.
	[dɛ.ro.ˈtar]	-But first, let us try to defeat her.
2534	**heredero**	**heir**
	m	La reina Isabel no tuvo ningún heredero directo.
	[ɛ.re.ˈðɛ.ro]	-Queen Elizabeth did not have any direct heir.
2535	**cortina**	**curtain**
	f	Corre la cortina y toma asiento.
	[kor.ˈti.na]	-Pull back the curtain and take your seat.
2536	**tonelada**	**ton**
	f	Tenemos una tonelada de juguetes que descargar detrás.
	[to.ne.ˈla.ða]	-We've got a ton of toys to unload in the back.
2537	**adolescente**	**teenager; teenage**
	m/f; adj	La actriz adolescente tiene bastantes seguidores.
	[a.ðo.lɛs.ˈsẽn̪.te]	-The teenage actress has quite a few fans.
2538	**azar**	**fate**
	m	Estos acontecimientos no son ni aislados ni producto del azar.
	[a.ˈsar]	-These events are neither isolated nor a product of chance.
2539	**postal**	**postal; postcard**
	adj; f	Ella me envió una tarjeta postal que decía que odia el olor de los animales.
	[pos.ˈtal]	-She sent me a postcard that said she hates the smell of animals.
2540	**hamburguesa**	**burger**
	f	Tienes otros 10 minutos para digerir esa hamburguesa.
	[ãm.bur.ˈɣe.sa]	-You've got another 10 minutes to digest that burger.
2541	**propietario**	**owner**
	m	Él reiteró que era el propietario del negocio.
	[pro.pjɛ.ˈta.rjo]	-He reiterated that he was the owner of the business.
2542	**ficción**	**fiction**
	f	No somos personajes de una ficción.
	[fik.ˈsjõn]	-We're not characters in a fictional thing.
2543	**recto**	**straight**
	adj	Siéntate recto y no lo interrumpas.
	[ˈrek̚.to]	-Sit up straight, and don't interrupt him.
2544	**contratar**	**hire**
	vb	No quiero contratar a otro asociado nunca más.
	[kõn̪.tra.ˈtar]	-I don't want to hire another associate ever again.
2545	**pirata**	**pirate; pirated**
	m/f; adj	Mi hermano pequeño quiere hacerse pirata.
	[pi.ˈra.ta]	-My little brother wants to become a pirate.
2546	**lidiar**	**deal with**

vb
[li.ˈðjar]

Siempre supe lidiar con bravucones.
-I've always known how to handle bullies.

2547 goma rubber

f
[ˈgo.ma]

La cubierta de esta aguja contiene goma natural.
-The needle cover of this syringe contains natural rubber.

2548 obrero worker

m
[o.ˈβɾɛ.ɾo]

Me van a ascender a obrero especializado.
-They're going to promote me to specialized worker.

2549 encendido on; ignition

adj; m
[ɛ̃n.sɛ̃n̪.ˈdi.ðo]

Podrías esperar fuera con el motor encendido.
-You could wait outside with the engine running.

2550 tapa cover

f
[ˈta.pa]

Levanté la tapa y ahí estaba.
-I lifted the lid, and there it was.

2551 avergonzar(se) embarrass

vb
[a.βɛɾ.ɣõn.ˈsar]

Perdona que siempre te haya hecho bromas e intentado avergonzar.
-I'm sorry I always teased you and tried to embarrass you.

2552 lotería lottery

f
[lo.tɛ.ˈri.a]

Yo también quiero analizar la lotería.
-I want to look into the lottery too.

2553 automóvil car

m
[au̯.to.ˈmo.βil]

Sus cadáveres aparecieron en un automóvil al día siguiente.
-The following day, their bodies were discovered in a car.

2554 garantizar guarantee

vb
[ga.ɾãn̪.ti.ˈsar]

Es sumamente importante para garantizar la competitividad.
-It will be very important to guarantee competition.

2555 corear chant

vb
[ko.ɾe.ˈar]

Estoy escuchando a miles de personas corear tu nombre al unísono.
-I'm hearing thousands of people chant your name in unison.

2556 satélite satellite

m
[sa.ˈte.li.te]

El cohete puso un satélite de comunicaciones en órbita.
-The rocket put a communications satellite into orbit.

2557 perfil profile

m
[pɛɾ.ˈfil]

He estado un par de minutos creando su perfil.
-I spent a couple of minutes setting up your profile.

2558 veredicto verdict

m
[bɛ.ɾe.ˈðik̚.to]

Ya ni siquiera fingimos respetar el veredicto del pueblo.
-No more are we even pretending to respect the verdict of the people.

2559 manta blanket

f
[ˈmãn̪.ta]

Al menos déjame traerte otra manta.
-At least let me get you another blanket.

2560 polo pole

m
[ˈpo.lo]

Este país es un polo de estabilidad en el continente.
-This country is a pole of stability on the continent.

2561 grabar record

vb
[gra.ˈβar]

Puedes grabar el vídeo independientemente del audio. -You can record the video independently of the audio.

2562 mansión mansion

f
[mãn.ˈsjõn]
Estamos yendo a mi mansión, donde te daré comida y descanso.
-We are going into my mansion, where I'll give you rest and food.

2563 **pena**　　**pity, punishment**
f
[ˈpe.na]
Siempre fue tratado humanamente mientras cumplía su pena.
-He had always been treated humanely while serving his sentence.

2564 **espléndido**　　**splendid**
adj
[es.ˈplẽn.di.ðo]
Hizo algo espléndido que encendería otros corazones.
-He did something splendid that would set other hearts on fire.

2565 **envidia**　　**envy**
f
[ẽm.ˈbi.ðja]
Cuando oyó que ellos eran tan felices, y tan ricos, la envidia y el odio se levantaron en su corazón y la dejaron sin paz, y no pensó en nada más que en cómo podría llevarlos de nuevo a la desgracia.
-When she heard that they were so happy, and so well off, envy and hatred rose in her heart and left her no peace, and she thought of nothing but how she could bring them again to misfortune.

2566 **privilegio**　　**privilege**
m
[pri.βi.ˈle.xjo]
He tenido el privilegio de visitarle en Camboya.
-I have had the privilege of visiting him in Cambodia.

2567 **vago**　　**vague, lazy; slacker**
adj; m
[ˈba.ɣo]
Este hombre vago e ignorante es mi secretario.
-This ignorant and lazy man is my secretary.

2568 **aguja**　　**needle**
f
[a.ˈɣu.xa]
Deseche la aguja de forma responsable.
-Dispose of the needle in a responsible manner.

2569 **tortuga**　　**tortoise**
f
[tor.ˈtu.ɣa]
Nos estamos refugiando del calor, al igual que la tortuga.
-We are taking shelter from the heat just as the tortoise is.

2570 **obligación**　　**obligation**
f
[o.βli.ɣa.ˈsjõn]
Nuestra obligación es seguir por este camino.
-It is our obligation to continue on this course.

2571 **árabe**　　**Arabian; Arab**
adj; m/f
[ˈa.ra.βe]
Compré un póster árabe en París e hice que me lo enmarcaran.
-I bought an Arab poster in Paris and I had it framed.

2572 **cohete**　　**rocket**
m
[ko.ˈɛ.te]
Ojalá tuviésemos un cohete más grande.
-I wish we had a bigger rocket.

2573 **llover**　　**rain**
vb
[ʎo.ˈβɛr]
Vámonos, va a ponerse a llover.
-Let's go, it's going to pour.

2574 **hilo**　　**thread**
m
[ˈi.lo]
Todo lo que necesitas es una aguja e hilo.
-All you need is a needle and thread.

2575 **química**　　**chemistry**
f
[ˈki.mi.ka]
Esta composición química garantiza la calidad tradicional del producto.
-This chemical composition values ensure the traditional quality of the product.

2576 **bandido**　　**bandit**
m
[bãn.ˈdi.ðo]
Es la bandida y proscrita más famosa de América.
-She is the most notorious bandit and outlaw in America.

2577 curar(se) — **heal**
vb
[ku.ˈrar]
Nosotros podemos curar el mundo.
-We can heal the world.

2578 conflicto — **conflict**
m
[kõɱ.ˈflik̬.to]
Los problemas se han intensificado por el conflicto.
-The problems have been exacerbated by the conflict.

2579 corresponder — **be appropriate, return**
vb
[ko.rɛs.põn̪.ˈdɛr]
El número de investigadores adicionales debería corresponder a las necesidades reales y los recursos disponibles.
-The number of investigators added should correspond to actual needs and available resources.

2580 telefónico — **telephonic**
adj
[te.le.ˈfo.ni.ko]
Me sentía un poco culpable por mi juego telefónico virtual.
-I was feeling a little guilty about my virtual phone game.

2581 conjunto — **combination; joint**
m; adj
[kõŋ.ˈxũn̪.to]
He estado pensando en esto por nuestro pasado conjunto.
-I've been thinking about this because of our history together.

2582 huésped — **guest**
m/f
[ˈwɛs.pɛð]
Estará escondiéndose en esa casa de huéspedes para evitar a los paparazzi.
-She will be hiding in that guest house to avoid the paparazzi.

2583 admirar — **admire**
vb
[að.mi.ˈrar]
Preferiría admirar desde la distancia.
-I'd much rather admire from afar.

2584 especialista — **specialist**
m/f
[ɛs.pe.sja.ˈlis.ta]
Habla muchos idiomas y es especialista en cifras.
-He speaks many languages and he's an expert with ciphers.

2585 forense — **forensic; forensic surgeon**
adj; m/f
[fo.ˈr̃ɛn.se]
Hablé con el forense que realizó las pruebas.
-I spoke to the forensic examiner who ran the tests.

2586 salvador — **savior**
m
[sal.βa.ˈðor]
Creímos que serías el próximo salvador.
-We believed you would be the next savior.

2587 candidato — **candidate**
m
[kãn̪.di.ˈða.to]
Esperaba identificar al candidato seleccionado en unas semanas.
-He expects to identify the selected candidate in a few weeks.

2588 literatura — **literature**
f
[li.tɛ.ra.ˈtu.ra]
A Ana le gusta leer literatura inglesa.
-Ana likes reading English literature.

2589 rincón — **corner**
m
[r̃ĩŋ.ˈkõn]
Inmortalizaré un rincón de nuestra gran morada.
-I'll immortalize one corner of our great dwelling.

2590 cerebral — **cerebral**
adj
[sɛ.re.ˈβral]
Tengo que proteger sus funciones cerebrales.
-I've got to protect their brain functions.

2591 volante — **steering wheel, referral (ES); flying**
m; adj
[bo.ˈlãn̪.te]
Necesito limpiar las huellas de este volante.
-I need to dust the prints off this wheel.

2592 solicitud — **request**

f — La compañía rechazó su solicitud de una transferencia.
[so.li.si.ˈtuð] — -The company rejected his request for a transfer.

2593 marino — **marine; sailor**
adj; m — Jim quiere ser biólogo marino.
[ma.ˈri.no] — -Jim wants to be a marine biologist.

2594 febrero — **February**
m — Este monumento se erigió en febrero de 1985.
[fe.ˈβrɛ.ro] — -This monument was erected in February 1985.

2595 brigada — **squad**
f — En julio comenzará a adiestrarse una cuarta brigada.
[bri.ˈɣa.ða] — -The training of a fourth brigade will begin in July.

2596 aleluya — **hallelujah**
int — Hay iglesias por todo el estado predicando días felices y aleluya.
[a.le.ˈlu.ja] — -There are churches all over the state spreading happy days and hallelujah.

2597 proponer(se) — **suggest; decide**
vb; vbr — Esa es una primera alternativa que nos gustaría proponer.
[pro.po.ˈnɛr] — -That is a first alternative that we would like to propose.

2598 impresionar(se) — **impress**
vb — Tiene ideas nuevas para deslumbrar e impresionar a sus compañeros
[ĩm.pre.sjo.ˈnar] — gobernantes.
— -He has new ideas to dazzle and impress his fellow rulers.

2599 velada — **soiree**
f — Espero que tenga una velada agradable.
[be.ˈla.ða] — -I trust you'll have a most pleasant evening.

2600 certificado — **certificate; registered**
m; adj — ¿Necesita usted un certificado médico?
[sɛr.ti.fi.ˈka.ðo] — -Do you need a doctor's certificate?

2601 excitante — **exciting**
adj — Puedo decirles que esto fue realmente excitante.
[ɛk.si.ˈtãn̪.te] — -I can say this was really exciting.

2602 homosexual — **homosexual; homosexual**
adj; m/f — Promovemos una imagen positiva de personas homosexuales.
[o.mo.sɛk.ˈswal] — -We foster a positive image of homosexual people.

2603 vital — **vital**
adj — Es vital que reciba este mensaje.
[bi.ˈtal] — -It's critical that he gets this message.

2604 euro — **euro**
m — Andorra podrá utilizar el euro como moneda oficial.
[ˈeu̯.ro] — -Andorra shall be entitled to use the euro as its official currency.

2605 descuidar(se) — **neglect; not worry**
vb; vbr — No debemos descuidar los medios tradicionales.
[dɛs.kwi.ˈðar] — -We should not overlook the traditional media.

2606 adelantar(se) — **overtake**
vb — Me moví a la izquierda para adelantar a un minibus.
[a.ðe.lãn̪.ˈtar] — -I moved to the left lane to overtake a minibus.

2607 vestuario — **wardrobe, locker room**
m — Ella se dirige al vestuario.
[bɛs.ˈtwa.rjo] — -She's headed to the locker room.

2608	**ajedrez**	**chess**
	m	Parece una pieza de ajedrez y funciona admirablemente.
	[a.ˈxe.ðres]	-It looks a bit like a chess piece and it functions brilliantly.
2609	**perspectiva**	**perspective**
	f	Desde esta perspectiva, respaldo todas las enmiendas propuestas.
	[pɛrs.pekˈti.βa]	-From this perspective, I support all of the proposed amendments.
2610	**músico**	**musician; musical**
	m; adj	Según esta revista, mi actriz favorita se casará con un músico de jazz la próxima primavera.
	[ˈmu.si.ko]	-According to this magazine, my favorite actress will marry a jazz musician next spring.
2611	**semilla**	**seed**
	f	Cuidamos la semilla porque es la herencia para nuestros hijos.
	[se.ˈmi.ja]	-We take care of the seed because it is the inheritance for our children.
2612	**reto**	**challenge**
	m	No debemos subestimar la magnitud del reto.
	[ˈrɛ.to]	-We should not underestimate the size of the challenge.
2613	**traducir**	**translate**
	vb	¿Los ordenadores pueden traducir obras literarias?
	[tra.ðu.ˈsir]	-Can computers translate literary works?
2614	**descripción**	**description**
	f	El informe incluye una breve descripción del sistema.
	[dɛs.krip.ˈsjõn]	-A brief description of the system was provided in the report.
2615	**célula**	**cell**
	f	El porcentaje de carbohidratos en las células animales es de aproximadamente el seis por ciento.
	[ˈse.lu.la]	-The percentage of carbohydrates in animal cells is approximately 6 percent.
2616	**sábana**	**bed sheet**
	f	Estoy usando una sábana como servilleta.
	[ˈsa.βa.na]	-I'm using a blanket as a napkin.
2617	**decepcionar(se)**	**disappoint**
	vb	No podemos decepcionar a los niños.
	[de.sɛp.sjo.ˈnar]	-The children mustn't be disappointed.
2618	**inocencia**	**innocence**
	f	Una característica del racismo es la inocencia de la víctima que lo sufre.
	[i.no.ˈsɛ̃n.sja]	-One characteristic of racism was the innocence of the person subjected to it.
2619	**timbre**	**ring**
	m	Llamé al timbre pero no hubo respuesta.
	[ˈtĩm.bre]	-I rang the bell, but there was no answer.
2620	**récord**	**record**
	m	Su récord es un nuevo récord mundial en la carrera de cien metros.
	[ˈre.korð]	-His record is a new world record in the 100-meter dash.
2621	**posesión**	**possession**
	f	Portugal ha despenalizado la posesión de drogas para consumo personal.
	[po.se.ˈsjõn]	-Portugal has decriminalized drug possession for personal uses.
2622	**ballet**	**ballet**
	m	Voy a bailar mi último ballet.
	[ba.ˈjɛt]	-I'm going to dance my last ballet.
2623	**provisión**	**provision**

f
[pro.βi.ˈsjõn]
Estoy segura de que tengo una provisión personal.
-I'm sure I have a personal supply.

2624 ayuntamiento — **local government**
m
[a.jũn̪.ta.ˈmjẽn̪.to]
Teníamos un concierto en el ayuntamiento.
-We had a concert at the City Hall.

2625 soga — **rope**
f
[ˈso.ɣa]
No necesito una soga para hacer este trabajo.
-I don't need a rope to do this job.

2626 jazz — **jazz**
m
[ˈxass]
He estado escuchando jazz durante mucho tiempo.
-I've been listening to jazz for so long.

2627 atar — **tie**
vb
[a.ˈtar]
Podría enrollarlo y atar un lazo alrededor.
-I could roll it up and tie a bow around it.

2628 sensacional — **sensational**
adj
[sẽn.sa.sjo.ˈnal]
Acabamos de diseñar una campaña sensacional.
-We've just mapped out a sensational campaign.

2629 cafetería — **coffee shop**
f
[ka.fɛ.tɛ.ˈri.a]
Compartimos un aparcamiento y una cafetería con ellos.
-We share a parking lot and a cafeteria with them.

2630 reunir(se) — **get together**
vb
[reu̯.ˈnir]
A veces lleva meses reunir y verificar información sobre determinados acontecimientos.
-Sometimes it takes months to gather and to check information about specific events.

2631 agotar(se) — **exhaust**
vb
[a.ɣo.ˈtar]
Estás empezando a agotar mi paciencia.
-You're starting to exhaust my patience.

2632 producir — **produce**
vb
[pro.ðu.ˈsir]
Seguirá siendo más barato producir una bombilla ecológica.
-It will still be cheaper to produce an environmentally-friendly light bulb.

2633 rudo — **rough, rude**
adj
[ˈru.ðo]
Jim era rudo, pero también era un tipo gracioso.
-Jim was rude, but he was a funny guy too.

2634 tallar — **engrave**
vb
[ta.ˈjar]
Me han encargado tallar la estatua principal de nuestro templo.
-I was entrusted to carve the main statue for our temple.

2635 versar — **be about**
vb
[bɛr.ˈsar]
Las ideas innovadoras deben versar sobre la prevención y sobre la lucha contra la violencia.
-Innovative ideas must focus on combating as well as preventing violence.

2636 destrozar — **shatter**
vb
[dɛs.tro.ˈsar]
Deberíamos volver y destrozar el sitio.
-We should go back and wreck the place.

2637 pila — **battery, sink, stack**
f
[ˈpi.la]
Me agarró mientras miraba una pila de cartas.
-He grabbed me while I was looking through a stack of mail.

2638 cráneo — **skull**

	m	Anoche alguien me golpeó el cráneo.
	['kra.ne.o]	-Someone last night bashed me on the skull.
2639	**habitante**	**inhabitant**
	m/f	Había sido un habitante del campamento de refugiados.
	[a.βi.ˈtãn̪.te]	-He had been a resident of the refugee camp.
2640	**volumen**	**volume**
	m	Este volumen de etanol no puede disolver completamente 0,5 g del sólido blanco.
	[bo.ˈlu.mẽn]	-This volume of ethanol cannot completely dissolve 0.5 g of the white solid.
2641	**girar(se)**	**turn**
	vb	Bebí demasiado y el suelo parecía girar bajo mis pies.
	[xi.ˈrar]	-I drank too much and the ground seemed to spin under my feet.
2642	**tardar(se)**	**be late**
	vb	Siento haber tardado tanto en devolverle la llamada.
	[tar.ˈðar]	-I'm sorry that it took so long to get back to you.
2643	**romano**	**Roman; Roman person**
	adj; m	Usted lleva años detrás del romano.
	[ro.ˈma.no]	-You've been after the Roman for years.
2644	**pobreza**	**poverty**
	f	Erradicar la pobreza es nuestra responsabilidad moral.
	[po.ˈβre.sa]	-The eradication of poverty is our moral duty.
2645	**pulmón**	**lung**
	m	Él tiene un pulmón perforado.
	[pul.ˈmõn]	-He's suffered a punctured lung.
2646	**hueco**	**space; empty**
	m; adj	Ahora mirad como salgo de este hueco.
	[ˈwe.ko]	-Now watch me get out of this hole.
2647	**hembra**	**female**
	f	Teníamos una hembra ahí con él.
	[ˈẽm.bra]	-We had a female in there with him.
2648	**inusual**	**unusual**
	adj	Parece inusual que no sepamos aprovechar esa oportunidad.
	[i.nu.ˈswal]	-It seems unusual that we failed to grasp that opportunity.
2649	**suicidarse**	**commit suicide**
	vbr	No creía que uno se pudiese suicidar de esa forma.
	[swi.si.ˈðar.se]	-I wouldn't believe you could commit suicide that way.
2650	**quinta**	**country house (ES); mansion (LA)**
	f; f	El albergue tiene en frente una quinta con arboles frutales.
	[ˈkĩn̪.ta]	-The hostel overlooks a country house with fruit trees.
2651	**brillo**	**brightness**
	m	Veamos primero el brillo de vuestra moneda.
	[ˈbri.jo]	-Let's see the shine of your coin first.
2652	**organizado**	**tidy**
	adj	No soy intenso, solo soy sumamente organizado.
	[or.ɣa.ni.ˈsa.ðo]	-I'm not intense, just extremely organized.
2653	**gorra**	**cap**
	f	Esa gorra que tienes es muy bonita.
	[ˈgo.ra]	-That's a nice hat you got there.

2654 **renta**
f
['rɛ̃n.ta]

rent, income
Si usted no paga la renta en cinco días, será desalojado.
-If you don't pay the rent in five days, you'll be evicted.

2655 **educar**
vb
[e.ðu.ˈkar]

educate
Debes educar a tu lengua a distinguir el buen café del malo.
-You must educate your tongue to distinguish good coffee from bad.

2656 **turista**
adj; m/f
[tu.ˈris.ta]

tourist; tourist
Como turista, podrá permanecer en México 180 días.
-As a tourist, you will be able to remain in Mexico for 180 days.

2657 **beca**
f
['be.ka]

scholarship
Tengo que hablar contigo sobre tu beca.
-I need to speak with you about your grant.

2658 **novato**
m; adj
[no.ˈβa.to]

trainee; rookie
Eres parte de la familia ahora, novato.
-You're part of the family now, rookie.

2659 **ascenso**
m
[as.ˈsɛ̃n.so]

rise, promotion
¿Oíste acerca del ascenso de Jim?
-Did you hear about Jim's promotion?

2660 **incómodo**
adj
[ĩŋ.ˈko.mo.ðo]

uncomfortable
Estoy muy incómodo en esta habitación.
-I'm very uncomfortable in this room.

2661 **facultad**
f
[fa.kul̪.ˈtað]

faculty
Hace poco asistí a la boda de un amigo chino. La novia y el novio habían sido compañeros en la universidad, ambos se graduaron en la facultad china. Ya llevan cinco años juntos.
-Recently I attended the wedding of a Chinese friend. The bride and groom had been classmates at university, and both graduated from the Chinese faculty. They've already been together for five years.

2662 **portero**
m
[por.ˈtɛ.ro]

doorman, goalkeeper
Mostré mi billete al portero y entré al teatro.
-I showed my ticket to the doorman and went into the theatre.

2663 **dinamita**
f
[di.na.ˈmi.ta]

dynamite
Manipular dinamita puede ser peligroso.
-Handling dynamite can be dangerous.

2664 **similar**
adj
[si.mi.ˈlar]

similar
El patrón es similar al que usan los carnívoros para acechar grandes presas.
-The pattern is similar to ones that carnivores use to stalk large prey.

2665 **equilibrio**
m
[e.ki.ˈli.βrjo]

balance
Ellos pueden restablecer el equilibrio en las políticas mundiales.
-They can restore balance in global policies.

2666 **insistir**
vb
[ĩn.sis.ˈtir]

insist
Tengo derecho a insistir en ser escuchada.
-I have a right to insist on being heard.

2667 **corte**
m
['kor.te]

cut, court
Mi responsabilidad es entregarlo a la corte.
-My responsibility is to deliver him to the court.

2668 **multar**
vb
[mul̪.ˈtar]

fine
Va muy deprisa y lo van a multar.
-He's going really fast and he's going to get a ticket.

2669	**signo** m ['siɣ.no]	**sign** Un fantasma es un signo visible externo de un miedo interno. -A ghost is an outward and visible sign of an inward fear.	

2669 signo
m
['siɣ.no]
sign
Un fantasma es un signo visible externo de un miedo interno.
-A ghost is an outward and visible sign of an inward fear.

2670 intercambio
m
[ĩn.tɛr.'kãm.bjo]
exchange
Necesitamos innovaciones, un intercambio de buenas experiencias y financiación adicional.
-We need innovations, an exchange of good experiences and additional funding.

2671 divertir(se)
vb
[di.βɛr.'tir]
amuse
Vamos a divertirnos con esto.
-We're going to have fun with this.

2672 bañera
f
[ba.'ɲɛ.ra]
bathtub
La bañera rebosó mientras ella hablaba por teléfono.
-The bathtub overflowed while she was talking on the phone.

2673 conservar
vb
[kõn.sɛr.'βar]
keep
Si queremos conservar las agencias, tenemos que cambiarlas.
-If we want to retain the agencies, we need to change them.

2674 novedad
f
[no.βe.'ðað]
novelty
Esa es una novedad que acojo con satisfacción.
-That is an innovation and I welcome it.

2675 individuo
m
[ĩn.di.'βi.ðwo]
individual
A pesar de tener un sistema reproductor masculino y femenino, la lombriz necesita de otro individuo para que la fecundación ocurra.
-Even though it has a masculine and feminine reproductive system, the earthworm requires another individual to bring forth fecundation.

2676 cómico
adj; m
['ko.mi.ko]
comical; comedian
Espero que no estés planeando convertirte en cómico.
-I hope you're not planning on becoming a comedian.

2677 retroceder
vb
[rɛ.tro.se.'ðɛr]
go back
Tú debes avanzar, no retroceder.
-You should go forward, not back.

2678 vientre
m
['bjɛ̃n.tre]
belly
Dijo que su vientre sobresalía como una montaña.
-He said that her belly stuck out like a mountain.

2679 gol
m
['gol]
goal
Metemos un gol y luego aguantamos.
-We kick one goal and then shut out.

2680 inversión
f
[ĩm.bɛr.'sjõn]
investment
El descenso de la inversión podría relacionarse con varios factores.
-The decline in investment could be associated with a number of factors.

2681 cuñado
m
[ku.'ɲa.ðo]
brother-in-law
Su cuñado no parece gustarle mucho.
-His brother-in-law didn't seem to like him much.

2682 raya
f
['ra.ja]
line
Tiene una raya fina negra en su aleta dorsal.
-He's got a thin, black stripe on his dorsal fin.

2683 ansioso
adj
[ãn.'sjo.so]
eager, worried
Estamos ansioso de volver a nuestros hogares.
-We're anxious to get back to our homeland.

2684 **fotógrafo** — **photographer**
m
[fo.ˈto.ɣɾa.fo]
Yo soy fotógrafo profesional.
-I am a professional photographer.

2685 **occidental** — **western; westerner**
adj; m/f
[ok.si.ðɛ̃n̪.ˈtal]
La frontera occidental también permaneció tranquila.
-The western border has been quiet too.

2686 **crítico** — **critical; critic**
adj; m
[ˈkɾi.ti.ko]
Comparto el tono crítico del informe.
-I share the critical tone of the report.

2687 **bruto** — **brutal; brute**
adj; m
[ˈbɾu.to]
No me quedaré ni un minuto más con semejante bruto.
-I won't stay a minute more with such a brute.

2688 **cortesía** — **courtesy**
f
[koɾ.te.ˈsi.a]
Les dejé terminar esa canción como cortesía profesional.
-I let you finish that song as a professional courtesy.

2689 **plataforma** — **platform**
f
[pla.ta.ˈfoɾ.ma]
Esperábamos poder convertirlo en una buena plataforma de entrenamiento.
-We'd hoped it might build into a good training platform.

2690 **malentender** — **misunderstand**
vb
[ma.lɛ̃n̪.tɛ̃n̪.ˈdɛɾ]
Parecía malentender la naturaleza de nuestra relación.
-He seemed to misunderstand the nature of our relationship.

2691 **probabilidad** — **probability**
f
[pɾo.βa.βi.li.ˈðað]
Tiene una buena probabilidad de recuperar la movilidad.
-He's got a good chance of recovering mobility.

2692 **torta** — **cake, sandwich (LA)**
f
[ˈtoɾ.ta]
Primero necesitamos decidir quién traerá torta a la próxima reunión.
-First, we need to work out who's bringing cake to the next meeting.

2693 **vergonzoso** — **shameful**
adj
[bɛɾ.ɣõn.ˈso.so]
Resulta difícil imaginar un acuerdo más vergonzoso.
-It is hard to imagine a more shameful deal.

2694 **cal** — **lime**
f
[ˈkal]
Mi abuelo solía decir que nunca tienes suficiente cal.
-You can never have enough whitewash, as my grandfather used to say.

2695 **cirujano** — **surgeon**
m
[si.ɾu.ˈxa.no]
Mi padre es un cirujano experto.
-My father is an expert surgeon.

2696 **tela** — **fabric**
f
[ˈte.la]
El vestido está hecho de una tela fina.
-The dress is made of a thin fabric.

2697 **furia** — **fury**
f
[ˈfu.rja]
El odio y la furia oscurecieron mi tinta.
-Hate and fury blackened my ink.

2698 **siesta** — **nap**
f
[ˈsjɛs.ta]
Íbamos a prepararla durante tu siesta.
-We were going to set it up during your nap.

2699 **entusiasmo** — **enthusiasm**
m
[ɛ̃n.tu.ˈsjaṣ.mo]
Parece haber perdido el entusiasmo por encontrarlo.
-She seems to have lost her zeal to find him.

2700	**coco**	**coconut**
	m	Las principales especies arbóreas son el coco y el banyan.
	[ˈko.ko]	-The major tree species are coconut and banyan.
2701	**afueras**	**outskirts**
	fpl	Jim vive en una casa de tres dormitorios en las afueras de Boston.
	[a.ˈfwɛ.ras]	-Jim lives in a three-bedroom house on the outskirts of Boston.
2702	**ferrocarril**	**railway**
	m	El ferrocarril no necesita nuestra tierra.
	[fɛ.ro.ka.ˈril]	-The railroad doesn't need our land.
2703	**costo**	**cost**
	m	¿Puedes calcular el costo total del viaje?
	[ˈkos.to]	-Can you work out the total cost of the trip?
2704	**margen**	**margin**
	m	Escribió sus comentarios al margen de la redacción.
	[ˈmar.xẽn]	-He wrote his comments in the margin of the composition.
2705	**falda**	**skirt**
	f	Es una falda normal plisada con rayas.
	[ˈfal̪.da]	-It's a regular short pleated skirt with stripes on it.
2706	**competir**	**compete**
	vb	Dicen que no pueden competir con los bajos precios de los productos extranjeros.
	[kõm.pɛ.ˈtir]	-They say they cannot compete with low-priced foreign products.
2707	**etapa**	**stage**
	f	Existen numerosos métodos disponibles para cada etapa del proceso.
	[ɛ.ˈta.pa]	-There are numerous methods available for each step of the process.
2708	**audición**	**hearing, audition**
	f	Quiero que hagas una audición ahora.
	[au̯.ði.ˈsjõn]	-I want you to do an audition now.
2709	**mecánico**	**mechanical; mechanic**
	adj; m	El mecánico arregló la avería sin demora.
	[me.ˈka.ni.ko]	-The mechanic repaired the damage without delay.
2710	**esencia**	**essence**
	f	Esa es la esencia del asunto.
	[e.ˈsẽn.sja]	-That is the essence of the matter.
2711	**inicio**	**beginning**
	m	Quería que tuviera un nuevo inicio.
	[i.ˈni.sjo]	-I wanted him to have a fresh start.
2712	**cruce**	**crossing**
	m	Tendremos que encontrar otro cruce.
	[ˈkru.se]	-We'll have to find another crossing.
2713	**aliado**	**ally; allied**
	m; adj	Podría resultar ser un aliado muy poderoso.
	[a.ˈlja.ðo]	-He could prove to be a very powerful ally.
2714	**choque**	**crash**
	m	El choque ocurrió cuando estaba de servicio.
	[ˈtʃo.ke]	-The crash happened when I was away on duty.
2715	**inevitable**	**inevitable**

adj
[i.ne.βi.ˈta.βle]

Esta es una evolución tanto inevitable como deseable.
-This is a development that is both inevitable and desirable.

2716 tierno   **tender**

adj
[ˈtjɛr.no]

Esto es un tierno asado de cerdo con salsa de manzanas.
-This is a tender roast of pork with applesauce.

2717 inyección   **injection**

f
[ĩn̪.t͡ʃɛk.ˈsjõn]

La inyección de esteroides es otra opción de tratamiento.
-Steroid injection is another treatment option.

2718 hechizo   **spell**

m
[e.ˈt͡ʃi.so]

La bruja le lanzó un hechizo al niño travieso.
-The witch cast a spell on the naughty boy.

2719 escopeta   **shotgun**

f
[ɛs.ko.ˈpɛ.ta]

Compró una escopeta de dos cañones.
-He bought a double-barreled shotgun.

2720 sexto   **sixth**

num
[ˈsɛks.to]

Vivimos en el sexto piso.
-We live on the sixth floor.

2721 gallo   **rooster**

m
[ˈga.jo]

Tienen que deshacerse del gallo.
-They have to get rid of the rooster.

2722 bárbaro   **savage; Barbarian**

adj; m
[ˈbar.βa.ro]

Esta muestra de comportamiento bárbaro era inaceptable hasta en su época.
-This display of barbaric behavior was unacceptable even in your time.

2723 arder   **burn**

vb
[ar.ˈðɛr]

Necesitas arder... Para renacer de las cenizas.
-You need to burn... So you can rise from the ashes.

2724 recorrer   **go across, run your eyes over**

vb
[re.ko.ˈrɛr]

Algunos tienen que recorrer largas distancias.
-Some of them have to travel long distances.

2725 caballería   **cavalry**

f
[ka.βa.jɛ.ˈri.a]

La caballería enemiga cruzó el río por un vado desconocido.
-The enemy cavalry crossed the river by an unknown ford.

2726 femenino   **female**

adj
[fe.me.ˈni.no]

Solo estoy intentando explorar mi lado femenino.
-I'm just trying to tap into my feminine side.

2727 arriesgar(se)   **risk**

vb
[a.rjɛs̠.ˈɣar]

Mis instrucciones fueron ayudarte, no arriesgar mi cobertura.
-My instructions were to help you, not jeopardize my cover.

2728 perseguir   **chase**

vb
[pɛr.se.ˈɣir]

Este es un objetivo que debemos perseguir consistentemente.
-This is an objective that we should consistently pursue.

2729 retirar(se)   **remove**

vb
[rɛ.ti.ˈrar]

El demandante podrá retirar su reclamación en cualquier momento.
-The applicant may withdraw his or her appeal at any time.

2730 apuntar   **make a note, aim**

vb
[a.pũn̪.ˈtar]

No puedes apuntar tu telescopio directo al sol.
-You can't point your telescope straight at the sun.

2731 linterna   **lantern**

f
[lĩn̪.ˈtɛr.na]
Nosotros no necesitamos la linterna.
-We don't need the lantern.

2732 almohada — **pillow**
f
[al.mo.ˈa.ða]
Dormiría mejor si tuviera una almohada.
-I'd sleep better if I had a pillow.

2733 vagina — **vagina**
f
[ba.ˈxi.na]
Eso no es arte. Eso es una vagina con dientes.
-That is not art. That is a vagina with teeth.

2734 etc. — **etc.**
adv
[ˈɛt̚k.]
Visitó ciudades del interior, establecimientos penitenciarios, etc.
-He visited towns in the interior of the country, prisons, etc.

2735 rama — **branch**
f
[ˈra.ma]
La rama se dobló pero no se rompió.
-The branch bent but did not break.

2736 bodega — **cellar**
f
[bo.ˈðe.ɣa]
También te propusimos una degustación en nuestra bodega.
-We also proposed you a tasting in our cellar.

2737 ebrio — **drunk**
adj
[ˈe.βrjo]
Estaba muy ebrio, ni siquiera me acuerdo.
-I was so drunk, I don't even remember.

2738 relacionar — **connect**
vb
[re.la.sjo.ˈnar]
Intentaban relacionar su muerte con tu gobierno.
-They were trying to connect his death to your government.

2739 guardián — **guardian**
m
[gwar.ˈðjãn]
Peleó una vez contra Cancerbero, el guardián de tres cabezas del inframundo, con nada más que su sombrero.
-He once fought Cerberus, the three-headed guardian of the underworld, with nothing but his hat.

2740 gratitud — **gratitude**
f
[gra.ti.ˈtuð]
Aceptaste esa responsabilidad con entusiasmo y gratitud.
-You accepted that responsibility with enthusiasm and gratitude.

2741 entierro — **burial**
m
[ẽn̪.ˈtjɛ.ro]
Estábamos llevando los cuerpos para un entierro.
-We were taking the bodies back for a burial.

2742 invasión — **invasion**
f
[ĩm.ba.ˈsjõn]
Este libro trata de la invasión de los Romanos.
-This book deals with the invasion of the Romans.

2743 conveniente — **convenient**
adj
[kõm.be.ˈnjẽn̪.te]
Sería muy conveniente poder censurar esta clase de comentarios.
-It'd be very convenient if we could censor this kind of comments.

2744 emocional — **emotional**
adj
[e.mo.sjo.ˈnal]
Estoy teniendo una crisis emocional ahora mismo.
-I'm having an emotional crisis right now.

2745 escudo — **shield**
m
[ɛs.ˈku.ðo]
El escudo está colapsando rápidamente.
-The shield is collapsing rapidly.

2746 masaje — **massage**

m
[ma.'sa.xe]

El masaje ayuda tanto física como emocionalmente.
-Massage is found to be helpful both physically and emotionally.

2747 lejano — **distant**

adj
[le.'xa.no]

Parece venir de un lugar lejano.
-You seem to come from a distant place.

2748 caber — **fit**

vb
[ka.'βɛr]

Si pudieras caber sería increíble.
-If you could fit, that would be awesome.

2749 césped — **lawn**

m
['ses.peð]

Estaba cortando el césped en mi barrio.
-He was mowing a lawn in my neighborhood.

2750 lana — **wool**

f
['la.na]

Las ovejas son criadas por su lana y por su carne.
-Sheep are raised for their wool and meat.

2751 emocionar(se) — **thrill**

vb
[e.mo.sjo.'nar]

No estoy seguro de que se vaya a emocionar.
-I'm not optimistic she'll be thrilled.

2752 paisaje — **landscape**

m
[pai̯.'sa.xe]

El impacto en el paisaje sería grave.
-The impact on the landscape would be grave.

2753 observación — **observation**

f
[oβ.sɛr.βa.'sjõn]

Permanecerá en observación durante la duración del experimento.
-She'll remain under observation for the duration of the experiment.

2754 depresión — **depression**

f
[de.pre.'sjõn]

Pueden ayudarte a aliviar la depresión o la ansiedad.
-They can help ease your depression or anxiety.

2755 artillería — **artillery**

f
[ar.ti.je.'ri.a]

Utilizaron artillería de largo alcance, además de otras armas.
-Long-range artillery, in addition to other weapons, has been employed.

2756 gemelo — **twin; twin**

adj; m
[xe.'me.lo]

Él pretendía ser su propio gemelo.
-He was pretending to be his own twin.

2757 voluntario — **voluntary; volunteer**

adj; m
[bo.lũn̪.'ta.rjo]

Voy a elegir al voluntario perfecto.
-I shall select the perfect volunteer.

2758 fallo — **failure**

m
['fa.jo]

Supongo que lo que tenemos aquí es un fallo de comunicación.
-I guess what we have here is a failure to communicate.

2759 respetar — **respect**

vb
[rɛs.pɛ.'tar]

El personal deberá respetar normas estrictas de confidencialidad.
-The staff will be required to respect strict rules of confidentiality.

2760 cubo — **cube, bucket**

m
['ku.βo]

Este es un cubo de hielo.
-This is an ice cube.

2761 bus — **bus (coll)**

m
['bus]

Ella miraba a los pasajeros bajarse del bus.
-She watched the passengers get off the bus.

2762 esencial — **essential**

adj
[e.sẽn.ˈsjal]

Lo más importante en los Juegos Olímpicos no es ganar, sino participar, al igual que la cosa más importante en la vida no es el triunfo, sino la lucha. Lo esencial no es haber vencido, sino haber luchado bien.
-The most important thing in the Olympic Games is not to win but to take part, just as the most important thing in life is not the triumph but the struggle. The essential thing is not to have conquered but to have fought well.

2763	**mariscal**	**marshal**
	m/f	Déjame pasar, quiero hablar con el mariscal.
	[ma.ris.ˈkal]	-Let me through, I want to talk with the Marshal.
2764	**caravana**	**caravan**
	f	Nadie atacará una caravana de esta dimensión.
	[ka.ra.ˈβa.na]	-No one will attack a caravan of this dimension.
2765	**radiación**	**radiation**
	f	Emitió además una gran cantidad de radiación.
	[ra.ðja.ˈsjõn]	-It also emitted a great deal of radiation.
2766	**ácido**	**sour; acid**
	adj; m	El pH va de ácido a ligeramente ácido.
	[ˈa.si.ðo]	-The pH ranges from acidic to slightly acidic.
2767	**identificar**	**identify**
	vb	El consejero ayudó a los pacientes a identificar las circunstancias personales que afectaban a su rutina de medicamentos.
	[i.ðẽn.ti.fi.ˈkar]	-The counselor helped patients identify personal circumstances that disrupt their medication schedule.
2768	**respetable**	**respectable**
	adj	Eran de una familia respetable del norte de Inglaterra.
	[rɛs.pɛ.ˈta.βle]	-They were of a respectable family in the north of England.
2769	**propinar**	**inflict**
	vb	Ya conoce el castigo que le podemos propinar.
	[pro.pi.ˈnar]	-He already knows the punishment we can hand out.
2770	**bicho**	**bug**
	m	Estabas buscando un bicho muy importante.
	[ˈbi.tʃo]	-You were looking for a very important bug.
2771	**ubicación**	**location**
	f	La ubicación de este capítulo se determinará posteriormente.
	[u.βi.ka.ˈsjõn]	-The location of this chapter will be determined at a later stage.
2772	**sugerencia**	**suggestion**
	f	¡Esa es una sugerencia constructiva!
	[su.xɛ.ˈrẽn.sja]	-That's a constructive suggestion!
2773	**tomate**	**tomato**
	m	¿El tomate es una fruta o un vegetal?
	[to.ˈma.te]	-Is a tomato a fruit or a vegetable?
2774	**prever**	**foresee**
	vb	Es necesario prever un sistema que aborde estos problemas.
	[pre.ˈβɛr]	-It is necessary to provide for a system which would counter these problems.
2775	**prioridad**	**priority**
	f	Solo abordaré algunos aspectos a los que concedemos prioridad.
	[prjo.ri.ˈðað]	-I will touch only on a few issues to which we attach priority.
2776	**estable**	**stable**

adj

[ɛsˈta.βle]

Esto nos permitirá tener un avance continuado y estable.
-This will allow us to make continuous and steady progress.

2777 mear(se)   **piss**

vb

[meˈar]

No tienes una maceta donde mear.
-You haven't got a pot to piss in.

2778 arrogante   **arrogant**

adj

[a.roˈɣãn̪.te]

Esa chica es arrogante debido a su belleza.
-That girl is arrogant because of her beauty.

2779 sentimental   **sentimental**

adj

[sɛ̃n̪.ti.mɛ̃n̪ˈtal]

No me gustaría retrasarte por ponerme sentimental.
-I wouldn't want to slow you down by being emotional.

2780 cagar(se)   **shit (coll); be terrified**

vb; vbr

[kaˈɣar]

Disculpe, jefe, voy a cagar.
-Boss, sorry, I am going to shit.

2781 expedición   **expedition**

f

[ɛks.pe.ði.ˈsjõn]

Las cintas de esta expedición serán incineradas.
-The tapes from this expedition are going in the fire.

2782 avance   **advance**

m

[aˈβãn.se]

Desde entonces ha habido bastante avance.
-A great deal of progress has been achieved since then.

2783 sostener   **hold**

vb

[sos.teˈnɛr]

Podría sostener esta linterna o bajar el calentador.
-You could hold this flashlight or turn down the heat.

2784 escondite   **hiding place, hide-and-seek**

m

[ɛs.kõn̪ˈdi.te]

Él es el que opera desde un escondite secreto.
-He is the one operating from a secret hideout.

2785 basar(se)   **base on**

vb

[baˈsar]

Debo basar mis decisiones en hechos.
-I have to base my decisions on facts.

2786 mojar   **wet**

vb

[moˈxar]

Este chico está a punto de mojar los pantalones.
-This kid's about to wet his pants.

2787 respiro   **rest**

m

[rɛsˈpi.ro]

Necesitas sentarte y tomarte un respiro.
-You need to sit down, take a breath.

2788 atraer   **attract**

vb

[a.traˈɛr]

Si me quedara solo en el ascensor a las cuatro de la madrugada, gritaría para atraer la atención de los vecinos.
-If I was left alone on the elevator at four in the morning, I'd shout to attract the neighbors' attention.

2789 jamón   **ham**

m

[xaˈmõn]

Tenemos jamón... O podemos hacer espaguetis.
-We have ham... Or we can make spaghetti.

2790 insecto   **insect**

m

[ĩnˈsek̚.to]

Puedo identificar cualquier insecto y arácnido del planeta.
-I can identify every insect and arachnid on the planet.

2791 triunfo   **triumph**

m
['trjũɱ.fo]
Ambas películas capturan el espíritu verdadero del triunfo humano.
-Both of those films capture the true spirit of human triumph.

2792 manicomio   **asylum**
m
[ma.ni.ˈko.mjo]
Vino al manicomio cuando fue capturada.
-She came to the asylum when she got caught.

2793 amabilidad   **kindness**
f
[a.ma.βi.li.ˈðað]
Le agradezco su cooperación y su amabilidad.
-I thank you for your cooperation and kindness.

2794 cicatriz   **scar**
f
[si.ˈka.tris]
Jim tiene una cicatriz en el brazo.
-Jim has a scar on his arm.

2795 pipa   **pipe, seed**
f
[ˈpi.pa]
Ciertamente recordaría si he fumado o no en pipa.
-I'd certainly remember whether or not I'd ever smoked a pipe.

2796 asistir   **attend**
vb
[a.sis.ˈtir]
Jim no pudo asistir a la reunión por un compromiso previo.
-Jim couldn't attend the meeting because of a previous engagement.

2797 universal   **universal**
adj
[u.ni.βɛr.ˈsal]
La música es el lenguaje universal de la humanidad — la poesía, su pasatiempo y deleite universales.
-Music is the universal language of mankind — poetry their universal pastime and delight.

2798 marrón   **brown**
adj
[ma.ˈrõn]
Hay barro marrón saliendo de las duchas.
-There's brown sludge coming out of the showers.

2799 traicionar   **betray**
vb
[trai̯.sjo.ˈnar]
No quiero volver a traicionar su confianza.
-I don't want to betray his trust anymore.

2800 expresar(se)   **express**
vb
[ɛks.pre.ˈsar]
No existen palabras para expresar lo increíble que eres.
-No words can express how amazing you are.

2801 estreno   **premiere**
m
[ɛs.ˈtre.no]
No queríamos molestarte antes del estreno.
-We didn't want to disturb you before the premiere.

2802 entrenar(se)   **train**
vb
[ẽn.tre.ˈnar]
Simplemente no tienes tiempo para trabajar y entrenar mucho.
-You just don't have the time to work and train a lot.

2803 peste   **plague**
f
[ˈpɛs.te]
Lo que dijiste de la peste fue espantoso.
-What you said about the plague was horrible.

2804 supervivencia   **survival**
f
[su.pɛr.βi.ˈβɛn.sja]
Esta medicina aumentará la tasa de supervivencia de los pacientes.
-This medicine will increase the survival rate of the patients.

2805 sierra   **mountains, saw**
f
[ˈsjɛ.ra]
Ella tomó prestada una sierra del granjero.
-She borrowed a saw from the farmer.

2806 granero   **barn**

m
[gra.ˈnɛ.ro]

El granero lleva destruido 6 meses.
-The barn's been destroyed for six months.

2807 coartar — **restrict**

vb
[ko.ar.ˈtar]

No puedes coartar nuestra libertad.
-You cannot restrict our freedom.

2808 ambición — **ambition**

f
[ãm.bi.ˈsjõn]

Vuestra ambición no suena muy patriótica.
-Your ambition does not sound to be so very patriotic.

2809 declarar — **declare**

vb
[de.kla.ˈrar]

Debo declarar un interés personal en este asunto.
-I have to declare a personal interest in this matter.

2810 celebración — **celebration**

f
[se.le.βra.ˈsjõn]

Espero que sea una celebración del fútbol.
-I hope it will be a celebration of football.

2811 senado — **senate**

m
[se.ˈna.ðo]

Dele tiempo al senado para pensar en ello.
-Give the Senate time to think about it.

2812 melodía — **melody**

f
[me.lo.ˈði.a]

Intenté aprenderme la melodía de memoria.
-I tried to learn the melody by heart.

2813 SIDA — **AIDS**

m
[ˈsi.ða]

SIDA significa "Síndrome de InmunoDeficiencia Adquirida".
-AIDS means "Acquired Immune Deficiency Syndrome".

2814 baúl — **trunk**

m
[ba.ˈul]

Supongo que mi tío también envió el baúl.
-I suppose my uncle sent the chest too.

2815 consejero — **counselor**

m
[kõn.se.ˈxɛ.ro]

Era buen consejero para esos niños.
-He was a good counselor to those kids.

2816 demostración — **demonstration**

f
[de.mos.tra.ˈsjõn]

Fíjense en esta demostración de fuerza.
-Watch this demonstration of power.

2817 concernir — **concern**

vb
[kõn.sɛr.ˈnir]

Nuestra segunda respuesta debe concernir al futuro de la energía nuclear en su totalidad.
-Our second response should concern the future of nuclear power as a whole.

2818 avanzar — **advance**

vb
[a.βãn.ˈsar]

Solo cuando se aborden esas cuestione será posible avanzar.
-Only when those issues were tackled would it be possible to advance.

2819 puñado — **handful**

m
[pu.ˈɲa.ðo]

Todo lo que tengo es mi cuerpo herido y un puñado de malos recuerdos.
-All I have is my wounded body and a handful of bad memories.

2820 batallón — **battalion**

m
[ba.ta.ˈjõn]

El batallón se entregó al enemigo.
-The battalion surrendered to the enemy.

2821 coñac — **cognac**

m
[ko.ˈɲak]

Tráeme un coñac cuádruple y una gaseosa.
-Get me a quadruple cognac and a cola back.

2822 inspiración — **inspiration**

f
[ĩns.pi.ra.ˈsjõn]

Deberían servirnos de inspiración a todos nosotros.
-They should serve as an inspiration to all of us.

2823 vicepresidente — **vice-president**

m
[bi.se.pre.si.ˈðẽn̪.te]

Sigo siendo vicepresidente de esta empresa.
-I'm still vice-president of this company.

2824 insoportable — **unbearable**

adj
[ĩn.so.por.ˈta.βle]

El calor se está haciendo insoportable.
-The heat is getting unbearable.

2825 vagón — **carriage of a train**

m
[ba.ˈɣõn]

Queremos atacar el vagón de transporte y rescatarlo.
-We want to attack the transport wagon and rescue him.

2826 mochila — **backpack**

f
[mo.ˈʧi.la]

Ella lleva una mochila a su espalda.
-She is carrying a backpack on her back.

2827 atracción — **attraction**

f
[a.trak.ˈsjõn]

Cuando era joven, experimenté una atracción emocional hacia una mujer.
-When I was a young man, l experienced an emotional attraction toward a woman.

2828 yen — **yen**

m
[ˈɟ̠jẽn]

Tengo 10 yenes en el bolsillo.
-I have 10 yen in my pocket.

2829 apuro — **trouble**

m
[a.ˈpu.ro]

Con el apuro, olvidé los anteojos.
-I forgot my glasses in the hurry.

2830 cometa — **comet; kite**

m; f
[ko.ˈmɛ.ta]

Es su cumpleaños, puede elegir la cometa que quiera.
-It's his birthday, he can have any kite he wants.

2831 guardaespaldas — **bodyguard**

m/f
[gwar.ða.ɛs.ˈpal̪.das]

Estaría bien trabajar de guardaespaldas o algo parecido.
-A job as a bodyguard or something similar would be nice.

2832 asistencia — **assistance**

f
[a.sis.ˈtẽn.sja]

Hoy en día seguimos recibiendo esa asistencia.
-We continue to receive that assistance to this day.

2833 manejo — **use**

m
[ma.ˈne.xo]

Redactaré una queja sobre su manejo de este caso.
-I'm going to file a complaint about your handling of this case.

2834 banquete — **banquet**

m
[bãŋ.ˈkɛ.te]

No había rastro de ninguna invitación al banquete.
-There was no trace of any invitation to the banquet.

2835 establecer — **establish**

vb
[ɛs.ta.βle.ˈsɛr]

Debemos establecer una fecha y conservarla.
-We have to set a date and keep to it.

2836 oculto — **hidden**

adj
[o.ˈkul̪.to]

Tu email permanecerá oculto al público.
-Your email will remain hidden to the public.

2837 **fórmula**   **formula**

f

['for.mu.la]

En realidad no hay una fórmula para la perfección.
-There's really no formula for perfection.

2838 **aprovechar**   **take advantage of**

vb

[a.pro.βe.ˈtʃar]

Tenemos que aprovechar la fuerza de estas comunidades.
-We have to take advantage of the strength of these communities.

2839 **vena**   **vein**

f

[ˈbe.na]

Nunca debe inyectarse en una vena.
-It should never be injected into a vein.

2840 **especialidad**   **specialty**

f

[ɛs.pe.sja.li.ˈðað]

¡Pidamos la langosta! He oído decir que es la especialidad de aquí.
-Let's order the lobster! I've heard that's the specialty dish here.

2841 **convención**   **convention**

f

[kõm.bẽn.ˈsjõn]

Los expertos determinaron que esa convención tendría algunas ventajas.
-Some advantages of such a convention were identified by the experts.

2842 **oriental**   **eastern; Asian**

adj; m

[o.rjẽn.ˈtal]

Una filosofía oriental habría sido buena para ellos.
-An Eastern philosophy would have been good for them.

2843 **álbum**   **album**

m

[ˈal.βũm]

Su álbum debut se llama ¡Bravo!
-Their debut album is called Bravo!

2844 **ahorrar**   **save**

vb

[a.o.ˈrar]

Él trabajó incansablemente para ahorrar más dinero.
-He worked hard so as to save more money.

2845 **mediante**   **through**

prp

[me.ˈðjãn.te]

Queremos afrontar estas cuestiones mediante el diálogo.
-We want to address these issues through dialogue.

2846 **confidencial**   **confidential**

adj

[kõɱ.fi.ðẽn.ˈsjal]

Obviamente, trataré cualquier información como confidencial.
-Obviously, I'll treat any information as confidential.

2847 **flecha**   **arrow**

f

[ˈfle.tʃa]

La flecha dio en el blanco.
-The arrow hit the target.

2848 **virtud**   **virtue**

f

[bir.ˈtuð]

Requiere paciencia, una virtud que necesito mucho.
-It requires patience, a virtue of which I have great need.

2849 **curva**   **curve**

f

[ˈkur.βa]

La sonrisa es la curva más bella del cuerpo de una mujer.
-A smile is the most beautiful curve on a woman's body.

2850 **limón**   **lemon**

m

[li.ˈmõn]

Añade la ralladura de limón y la canela.
-Add the lemon zest and cinnamon.

2851 **lamentable**   **unfortunate, pathetic**

adj

[la.mẽn.ˈta.βle]

Sería lamentable que esta colaboración se viera afectada por obstáculos administrativos.
-It would be regrettable if this partnership were to be hampered by administrative difficulties.

2852 **inferior**   **lower; subordinate**

adj; m/f
[ĩm.fɛ.ˈrjor]

No quería que te sintieras inferior.
-I didn't want you to feel inferior.

2853 **imperial**   **imperial**

adj
[ĩm.pɛ.ˈrjal]

César necesita tranquilidad para apreciar su imperial reflejo.
-Caesar needs peace to admire his imperial reflection.

2854 **asilo**   **asylum**

m
[a.ˈsi.lo]

La familia pidió asilo político.
-The family applied for political asylum.

2855 **desesperación**   **despair**

f
[de.sɛs.pɛ.ra.ˈsjõn]

La gente sentía ira y desesperación.
-People felt a sense of anger and despair.

2856 **poseer**   **possess**

vb
[po.se.ˈɛr]

El individuo deberá poseer los conocimientos lingüísticos necesarios.
-The individual would need to possess the appropriate linguistic skills.

2857 **ángulo**   **angle**

m
[ˈãŋ.gu.lo]

No estamos seguros del ángulo exacto.
-We're not sure of the exact angle.

2858 **reparar**   **repair**

vb
[re.pa.ˈrar]

Debería quedarme aquí, reparar los conectores.
-I should stay here, fix the connectors.

2859 **cancelar**   **cancel**

vb
[kãn.se.ˈlar]

Tenemos que cancelar nuestro viaje a Japón.
-We have to cancel our trip to Japan.

2860 **soltar**   **free, drop**

vb
[sol̪.ˈtar]

Lo que necesita es soltar mi brazo.
-What you need to do is let go of my arm.

2861 **irlandés**   **Irish; Irish person**

adj; m
[ir.lãn̪.ˈdes]

Es correcto y adecuado respetar el voto irlandés.
-It is right and proper to respect the Irish vote.

2862 **castigar**   **punish**

vb
[kas.ti.ˈɣar]

Cuéntale como querías castigar a Ana por rechazarte.
-Tell her how you wanted to punish Ana for rejecting you.

2863 **terrorismo**   **terrorism**

m
[tɛ.ro.ˈris̪.mo]

Debemos analizar las causas del terrorismo.
-We must look at the causes of terrorism.

2864 **frito**   **fried**

adj
[ˈfri.to]

Mi cerebro está frito después de ese examen de inglés.
-After that English exam, my brain is fried.

2865 **ano**   **anus**

m
[ˈa.no]

La gonorrea también puede afectar al ano y la garganta.
-Gonorrhea can also affect the anus and the throat.

2866 **rodaje**   **filming**

m
[ro.ˈða.xe]

Nos estamos acercando al final del rodaje.
-We're getting close to the end of the filming.

2867 **che**   **hey, dude (LA)**

int
[ˈʧe]

Mira che, publicaron tu artículo.
-Dude, look, they published your article.

2868 **desesperar**   **despair**

	vb	Pienso que esto no es una razón suficiente para desesperar y menguar nuestros esfuerzos.
	[de.ses.pe.ˈrar]	-I think that this is not sufficient reason to lose hope and weaken our efforts.
2869	**fenomenal**	**phenomenal**
	adj	Tenerlo a usted dirigiendo este departamento sería fenomenal.
	[fe.no.me.ˈnal]	-Having you run this department, that would be phenomenal.
2870	**garantía**	**guarantee**
	f	Ello será garantía de un futuro sin violencia.
	[ga.rãn̯.ˈti.a]	-That will be a guarantee of a future without violence.
2871	**carnicero**	**butcher**
	m	No dejaría que ese carnicero me cortara el pelo.
	[kar.ni.ˈse.ro]	-I wouldn't let that butcher cut my hair.
2872	**asumir**	**assume**
	vb	Corresponde a los políticos asumir sus responsabilidades.
	[a.su.ˈmir]	-It is up to the politicians to assume their responsibilities.
2873	**alborotar**	**disturb**
	vb	No es nada sobre lo que alborotar.
	[al.βo.ro.ˈtar]	-It's nothing to fuss about.
2874	**salchicha**	**sausage**
	f	Pidamos la pizza con salchicha y cebollas.
	[sal̯.ˈʧi.ʧa]	-Let's get the pizza with sausage and onions.
2875	**boxeo**	**boxing**
	m	Me gustan tales deportes como el boxeo y el hockey.
	[bok.ˈse.o]	-I like such sports as boxing and hockey.
2876	**intelectual**	**mental; intellectual**
	adj; m/f	Esto ha intensificado la vida política e intelectual del país.
	[ĩn̯.te.lek̚.ˈtwal]	-This has intensified the political and intellectual life of the country.
2877	**rana**	**frog**
	f	No soy capaz de distinguir una rana de un sapo.
	[ˈra.na]	-I can't tell a frog from a toad.
2878	**inventar**	**invent**
	vb	Mi afición: inventar formas irregulares de verbos.
	[ĩm.bẽn̯.ˈtar]	-My hobby: inventing irregular forms of verbs.
2879	**bienestar**	**comfort**
	m	Esto da sensación de fuerza y bienestar.
	[bje.nes.ˈtar]	-This gives a feeling of strength and wellbeing.
2880	**taberna**	**tavern**
	f	Estudias aquí, en una taberna ruidosa.
	[ta.ˈβer.na]	-You're studying here, in a rowdy tavern.
2881	**impulso**	**impulse**
	m	Tenemos un impulso y lo seguimos.
	[ĩm.ˈpul.so]	-We have an impulse and we act on it.
2882	**comprometer(se)**	**implicate; get engaged**
	vb; vbr	No puedo comprometer mi integridad porque estemos en una relación.
	[kõm.pro.me.ˈter]	-I can't compromise my integrity because we're in a relationship.
2883	**obedecer**	**obey**
	vb	Siempre traté de obedecer la ley.
	[o.βe.ðe.ˈser]	-I've always tried to obey the law.

2884 ritual
adj; m
[ri.ˈtwal]

ritual; ritual
Sé que no completó el ritual.
-I know he didn't complete the ritual.

2885 fijo
adj
[ˈfi.xo]

fixed
Me encantaría tenerte en cuenta para el empleo fijo.
-I'd be happy to consider you for the permanent position.

2886 atento
adj
[a.ˈtẽn̪.to]

attentive
Soy un padre atento, centrado y responsable.
-I'm an attentive, focused, and responsible father.

2887 perfección
f
[pɛr.fɛk.ˈsjõn]

perfection
Este nivel de perfección no existe realmente.
-This level of perfection doesn't really exist.

2888 ejecutivo
adj; m
[e.xe.ku.ˈti.βo]

executive; manager
El poder ejecutivo también experimenta dificultades.
-The executive branch, too, is experiencing difficulties.

2889 cuna
f
[ˈku.na]

cradle
Terminarás de construir aquella cuna como me prometiste.
-You'll finish building that crib as you promised.

2890 dispositivo
m
[dis.po.si.ˈti.βo]

device
Dejé el dispositivo de rastreo debajo del guardabarros delantero.
-I stuck the tracking device underneath the front fender.

2891 conectar
vb
[ko.nek̚.ˈtar]

connect
Solo tienes que conectar estas cositas atrás.
-You just have to hook up these little things in the back.

2892 cómplice
m/f
[ˈkõm.pli.se]

accomplice
Quizás tenía un cómplice que decidió eliminarlo.
-Maybe he had an accomplice who decided to take him out.

2893 caca
f
[ˈka.ka]

poop (coll)
Admiro tus esfuerzos por recoger toda la caca abandonada.
-I admire your effort to pick up all the abandoned poop.

2894 sesenta
num
[se.ˈsẽn̪.ta]

sixty
Añada sesenta gramos de queso rallado.
-Add sixty grams of grated cheese.

2895 sinvergüenza
m/f; adj
[sĩm.bɛr.ˈɣwẽn.sa]

wretch; rascal
Resulta que solo eres un sinvergüenza insignificante.
-Turns out you're just a petty crook.

2896 capturar
vb
[kap̚.tu.ˈrar]

capture
La cámara también puede capturar vídeo clips con sonido.
-The camera is also able to capture video clips with sound.

2897 brisa
f
[ˈbɾi.sa]

breeze
Una cálida y dulce brisa sopla por los planos e interminables campos.
-A warm, lazy breeze wafts across the flat, endless fields.

2898 violín
m
[bjo.ˈlĩn]

violin
Jim pensó que su violín era Stradivarius porque el nombre Stradivarius estaba en la etiqueta dentro del violín.
-Jim thought his violin was a Stradivarius because the name Stradivarius was on the label inside his violin.

2899 menú

menu

	m	Pídale el menú a la camarera.
	[me.'nu]	-Ask the waitress for the menu.

2900 conquistar — **conquer**

vb
[kõŋ.kis.'tar]

Los romanos no habrían tenido tiempo suficiente para conquistar el mundo si primero hubieran tenido que estudiar latín.
-The Romans would never have had enough time for conquering the world if they had first been required to study Latin.

2901 tirador — **shooter**

m
[ti.ra.'ðor]

Fue abatido por un tirador desconocido.
-He was taken out by an unknown shooter.

2902 confuso — **confusing**

adj
[kõɱ.'fu.so]

Un jurado definitivamente lo encontraría confuso.
-A jury would definitely find it confusing.

2903 factura — **invoice**

f
[fak.'tu.ra]

No aparece en ninguna otra factura.
-It doesn't appear on any other invoice.

2904 ardiente — **burning**

adj
[ar.'ðjẽṇ.te]

Solo está celoso de nuestro ardiente amor.
-He's just jealous of our burning love.

2905 billetera — **wallet**

f
[bi.ʝɛ.'tɛ.ra]

Encontré su billetera y quería devolverla.
-I found your wallet and I wanted to return it.

2906 combatir — **combat**

vb
[kõm.ba.'tir]

Es importante que combatamos y aliviemos el hambre.
-It is important that we combat and alleviate starvation.

2907 madrugar — **rise early**

vb
[ma.ðru.'ɣar]

Además, tengo que madrugar mañana.
-Besides, I've got to be up early tomorrow.

2908 síntoma — **symptom**

m
['sĩṇ.to.ma]

No hablo de un nuevo síntoma.
-I'm not talking about a new symptom.

2909 deprimir(se) — **depress**

vb
[de.pri.'mir]

No te deprimas por tener que descansar.
-Don't get depressed about having to rest.

2910 terremoto — **earthquake**

m
[tɛ.re.'mo.to]

La guerra no es una catástrofe natural como un terremoto o un tsunami. No viene sin aviso.
-War is not a natural disaster like an earthquake or a tsunami. It does not come without warning.

2911 marqués — **marquis**

m
[mar.'kes]

El arruinado marqués se casó con ella.
-The ruined marquis married her.

2912 bata — **robe**

f
['ba.ta]

Hasta preparó mi bata y pantuflas.
-She even laid out my robe and slippers.

2913 satisfacción — **satisfaction**

f
[sa.tis.fak.'sjõn]

Un bocado de satisfacción en cada trozo.
-A mouthful of satisfaction in every bite.

2914 pacto — **pact**

	m		Mientras el pacto prevalezca, habrá poca ayuda disponible.
	['pak.to]		-As long as the pact prevails, there is little help to be found.
2915	**apagado**	**off**	
	adj		El número que ha marcado está apagado.
	[a.pa.'ɣa.ðo]		-The number you've dialed is switched off.
2916	**temblar**	**shake**	
	vb		Empecé a temblar como una hoja.
	[tẽm.'blar]		-I started to shake like a leaf.
2917	**ignorante**	**ignorant; ignoramus**	
	adj; m		Estás mintiendo o eres un ignorante espectacular.
	[iɣ.no.'rãn̪.te]		-You are either lying or spectacularly ignorant.
2918	**supremo**	**supreme**	
	adj		Nos podría llevar al tribunal supremo.
	[su.'pre.mo]		-It could get us to the supreme court.
2919	**navegar**	**sail**	
	vb		Es muy agradable navegar estas aguas.
	[na.βe.'ɣar]		-It is very pleasant to sail these waters.
2920	**categoría**	**category**	
	f		Esa segunda categoría parece muy significativa.
	[ka.te.ɣo.'ri.a]		-That second category is highly significant.
2921	**bastón**	**cane**	
	m		Necesitamos su bastón como prueba.
	[bas.'tõn]		-We need to take your cane into evidence.
2922	**luchador**	**fighter**	
	m		Él es oficialmente un luchador profesional.
	[lu.tʃa.'ðor]		-He is officially a professional fighter.
2923	**rencor**	**resentment**	
	m		Puede no haber tenido un rencor específico.
	[rẽŋ.'kor]		-He might not have had a specific grudge.
2924	**zapatilla**	**slipper**	
	f		Pareces un cachorro con una zapatilla.
	[sa.pa.'ti.ja]		-You look like a puppy with a slipper.
2925	**caramelo**	**candy**	
	m		Cuando quieras fumar, chupa un caramelo.
	[ka.ra.'me.lo]		-When you want to smoke, suck a candy.
2926	**apretar**	**tighten**	
	vb		Cuando eso ocurra, solo tienes que apretar el gatillo.
	[a.prɛ.'tar]		-When that happens, you just got to pull the trigger.
2927	**liberado**	**free**	
	adj		Está ahí sentado, esperando ser liberado.
	[li.βɛ.'ra.ðo]		-He's sitting there, waiting to be released.
2928	**establo**	**barn**	
	m		Sabemos que la producción de carne comienza en el establo.
	[ɛs.'ta.βlo]		-We know that meat production begins in the stall.
2929	**fan**	**fan**	
	m/f		Incluso soy fan del trueque matutino.
	['fãn]		-I'm even a fan of morning bartering.
2930	**batir**	**beat, whip**	

vb
[ba.'tir]
Vamos a batir el récord mundial.
-We are going to beat the world record.

2931 invento — **invention**
m
[ĩm.'bẽn̪.to]
La lavadora es un invento maravilloso.
-The washing machine is a wonderful invention.

2932 comparar — **compare**
vb
[kõm.pa.'rar]
En este ejercicio tenéis que comparar las dos fracciones dadas.
-In this exercise, you have to compare the two given fractions.

2933 aumentar — **increase**
vb
[au̯.mẽn̪.'tar]
¡Ella quería que aumentara los impuestos!
-She wanted me to raise the taxes!

2934 supermercado — **supermarket**
m
[su.pɛr.mɛr.'ka.ðo]
Jim fue al supermercado a comprar unos huevos.
-Jim went to the supermarket to buy some eggs.

2935 autorizar — **authorize**
vb
[au̯.to.ri.'sar]
No puedo autorizar que entres.
-I can't allow you to go inside.

2936 cuidadoso — **careful**
adj
[kwi.ða.'ðo.so]
Me prometió que sería más cuidadoso en el futuro.
-He promised me that he would be more careful in the future.

2937 promedio — **average**
m
[pro.'me.ðjo]
Ambas categorías trabajaban, en promedio, más de 50 horas a la semana.
-Both categories worked, on average, more than 50 hours a week.

2938 interrogatorio — **interrogation**
m
[ĩn̪.tɛ.ro.ɣa.'to.rjo]
El maestro o psicólogo firmará también las actas del interrogatorio.
-The teacher or psychologist will also sign the minutes of the interrogation.

2939 mito — **myth**
m
['mi.to]
Algunas personas piensan que es más que un simple mito.
-Some people believe it's more than just a myth.

2940 crucero — **cruise**
m
[kru.'sɛ.ro]
He trabajado para pagar este crucero.
-I worked to pay for this cruise.

2941 independencia — **independence**
f
[ĩn.de.pẽn̪.'dẽn.sja]
Desempeñan sus funciones con total independencia.
-They carried out their work in complete independence.

2942 crío — **child**
m
['kri.o]
Es solo un crío sin experiencia.
-He's just a child with no experience.

2943 perla — **pearl**
f
['pɛr.la]
Robar la perla, esa es la parte fácil.
-Stealing the pearl, that's the easy part.

2944 portada — **cover**
f
[por.'ta.ða]
Lo están boicoteando por la portada.
-They're boycotting it because of the cover.

2945 contactar — **contact**
vb
[kõn̪.tak̚.'tar]
Para más información contactar con el coordinador, por favor.
-For more information, please contact the coordinator.

2946 chistoso — **funny**

adj
[ʧis.ˈto.so]
Alguien se ve chistoso sin su barba.
-Someone looks funny without his beard.

2947 relámpago
m
[re.ˈlãm.pa.ɣo]
lightning
Lo terminó tan rápido como un relámpago.
-He finished it as quick as lightning.

2948 tinto
adj
[ˈtĩn̪.to]
red wine
Prefiero el vino tinto al blanco.
-I like red wine better than white.

2949 set
m
[ˈsɛt]
set
El set incluye un recetario para inspirarte.
-The set includes a recipe booklet to inspire you.

2950 baloncesto
m
[ba.lõn.ˈsɛs.to]
basketball
Nuestro equipo de baloncesto está reclutando muchachos altos.
-Our basketball team is recruiting tall boys.

2951 centímetro
m
[sɛ̃n̪.ˈti.mɛ.tro]
centimeter
Estamos un centímetro y medio fuera.
-We're a centimeter and a half off here.

2952 guay
adj; int
[ˈgwaj]
great; great (ES) (coll)
Siempre dijimos que haríamos algo guay.
-We always said we'd do something cool.

2953 leña
f
[ˈle.ɲa]
firewood
La leña mojada no arde bien.
-Wet firewood doesn't burn well.

2954 ahorros
mpl
[a.ˈo.ros]
savings
Me temo que me gustaría retirar todos mis ahorros.
-I'm afraid I'd like to withdraw all of my savings.

2955 autopsia
f
[au̯.ˈtop.sja]
autopsy
La ausencia de una autopsia perjudicó seriamente la investigación.
-The absence of an autopsy caused serious damage to the investigation.

2956 amo
m
[ˈa.mo]
owner
Estamos honrados de servirle, joven amo.
-We're honored to serve you, young master.

2957 cuerno
m
[ˈkwɛr.no]
horn
Estabas intentando quitarme el cuerno cuando me escapé.
-They were trying to take my horn when I ran away.

2958 flotar
vb
[flo.ˈtar]
float
Estos barcos no fueron diseñados para flotar del revés.
-These ships weren't designed to stay afloat upside down.

2959 doncella
f
[dõn.ˈse.ja]
maid
Ellos usarán su doncella como rehén.
-They will use your maid as a hostage.

2960 tradicional
adj
[tra.ði.sjo.ˈnal]
traditional
El sake es una bebida alcohólica tradicional japonesa.
-Sake is a traditional Japanese alcoholic drink.

2961 renuncia
f
[re.ˈnũn.sja]
resignation
La junta ha decidido no aceptar su renuncia.
-The board has decided not to take up your resignation.

2962 estallar
burst

vb
[ɛs.ta.ˈjar]
Esta cosa podría estallar en cualquier momento.
-This thing could blow up at any second.

2963 **masacre** — massacre
f
[ma.ˈsa.kre]
Algunos sostienen que participaron en la masacre.
-Some people maintain that they took part in the massacre.

2964 **visual** — visual
adj
[bi.ˈswal]
He llegado a creer que el trabajo visual verdaderamente imaginativo es extremadamente importante para la sociedad.
-I've come to believe that truly imaginative visual work is extremely important in society.

2965 **lava** — lava
f
[ˈla.βa]
El volcán explota en erupciones gigantes de lava.
-The volcano blasts out in gigantic eruptions of lava.

2966 **colocar** — put
vb
[ko.lo.ˈkar]
Dinos donde tenemos que colocar las cosas.
-Tell us where do we have to place the stuff.

2967 **soplar** — blow
vb
[sop̚.ˈlar]
No te olvides de soplar el silbato antes.
-Don't forget to blow a whistle first.

2968 **altar** — altar
m
[al̪.ˈtar]
Colocaré tu armadura delante del altar.
-I will set your armor before the altar.

2969 **pis** — piss (coll)
m
[ˈpis]
Trataba de no hacerme pis en los pantalones.
-I was trying not to pee in my pants.

2970 **ocupación** — occupation
f
[o.ku.pa.ˈsjõn]
Continuarán mientras siga la ocupación.
-They will continue as long as the occupation continues.

2971 **confirmar** — confirm
vb
[kõɱ.fir.ˈmar]
Quisiera confirmar que este informe está disponible.
-I should like to confirm that this report is available.

2972 **infarto** — heart
m
[ĩɱ.ˈfar.to]
Creo que Ana tendrá un infarto.
-I think Ana will have a heart attack.

2973 **prudente** — prudent
adj
[pru.ˈðẽn̪.te]
Tales desafíos requieren que procedamos de forma prudente y responsable.
-Such challenges require us to proceed in a prudent and businesslike manner.

2974 **triple** — triple; triple
adj; m
[ˈtrip̚.le]
Ahora desearía hacer un triple llamamiento.
-I should now like to launch a triple appeal.

2975 **contenido** — contents; reserved
m; adj
[kõn̪.te.ˈni.ðo]
La etiqueta advierte que el contenido de la caja es frágil.
-The label warns that the contents of the box are fragile.

2976 **galaxia** — galaxy
f
[ga.ˈlak.sja]
Cuando salen suficientes estrellas, crean una galaxia.
-When enough stars come out, they create a galaxy.

2977 **eco** — echo

	m		Si gritas desde el borde de un precipicio, puedes oír el eco de tu voz.
	[ˈe.ko]		-If you shout from the top of a cliff, you can hear the echo of your voice.

2978 debatir — discuss

vb
[de.βa.ˈtir]

Es difícil debatir directrices estratégicas en la oscuridad.
-It is difficult to debate strategic guidelines in the dark.

2979 continente — continent

adj
[kõn̯.ti.ˈnẽn̯.te]

Es una oportunidad histórica de unir todo el continente.
-It is a historic opportunity to unite the whole continent.

2980 claridad — clarity

f
[kla.ri.ˈðað]

Creo que hemos logrado claridad y transparencia.
-I do believe that we have achieved clarity and transparency.

2981 desaparición — disappearance

f
[de.sa.pa.ri.ˈsjõn]

Mi familia ni siquiera denunció mi desaparición.
-My family didn't even report me missing.

2982 encajar — fit

vb
[ẽn̯.ka.ˈxar]

Llevo intentando encajar en dos mundos toda mi vida.
-My whole life, I've been trying to fit into two worlds.

2983 difunto — deceased

m
[di.ˈfũn̯.to]

Necesito hablar con los familiares del difunto.
-I need to talk to the deceased's family.

2984 insignificante — insignificant

adj
[ĩn.siɣ.ni.fi.ˈkãn̯.te]

Siempre me hace sentir pequeño e insignificante.
-He's always making me feel small and insignificant.

2985 añadir — add

vb
[a.ɲa.ˈðir]

Debo añadir también que estas dos mujeres son valientes.
-I must also add that these are two women who are courageous.

2986 ilusionar(se) — inspire hope

vb
[i.lu.sjo.ˈnar]

¿Pensabas que se iban a ilusionar más?
-Did you think they'd be more excited?

2987 cacería — hunting

f
[ka.sɛ.ˈri.a]

Cuando vuelvas haremos la cacería.
-When you come back, we'll do the hunt.

2988 mozo — lad

m
[ˈmo.so]

El mozo me ha dicho que subiera.
-The porter told me to come up.

2989 matrícula — license plate, enrollment

f
[ma.ˈtri.ku.la]

Estamos preparados para pagar su matrícula entera.
-We are prepared to pay his entire tuition.

2990 rendir(se) — perform; surrender

vb; vbr
[rẽn̯.ˈdir]

Estos esfuerzos empiezan a rendir frutos.
-These efforts are starting to pay off.

2991 muñeco — doll

m
[mu.ˈɲe.ko]

Él y su muñeco también la buscaban.
-He and his dolly were looking for her too.

2992 mayordomo — butler

m
[ma.jor.ˈðo.mo]

Suena como si estuviera entrenándote para ser un mayordomo inglés.
-It sounds like I'm training you to be an English butler.

2993 antepasado — ancestor

	m	Resulta que tenemos un mismo antepasado.
	[ãn̪.te.pa.ˈsa.ðo]	-It turns out we have a common forefather.
2994	**soda**	**soda**
	f	Alguien derramó soda por detrás del amplificador.
	[ˈso.ða]	-Someone spilled soda down the back of the amplifier.
2995	**automático**	**automatic**
	adj	También puede emplearse un inyector automático.
	[au̯.to.ˈma.ti.ko]	-An automatic injector can be used as well.
2996	**solucionar**	**solve**
	vb	Debemos adoptar medidas decisivas para impedir y solucionar tales
	[so.lu.sjo.ˈnar]	conflictos.
		-We need to take decisive steps to prevent and resolve such conflicts.
2997	**revelar**	**reveal**
	vb	Ni siquiera quiero revelar su nombre.
	[re.βe.ˈlar]	-I don't even want to reveal his name.
2998	**líquido**	**liquid; liquid**
	adj; m	La vacuna es un líquido amarillo.
	[ˈli.ki.ðo]	-The vaccine is a yellow liquid.
2999	**mudo**	**mute**
	adj	Es un cantante mudo que domina la expresión y el gesto.
	[ˈmu.ðo]	-He is a silent singer who has mastered expression and mime.
3000	**trece**	**thirteen**
	num	Yo huí de casa cuando tenía trece años.
	[ˈtre.se]	-I ran away from home when I was thirteen.
3001	**protector**	**protective; protector**
	adj; m	Él es nuestro protector y guardián.
	[pro.tek̚.ˈtor]	-He's our protector and guardian.
3002	**casamiento**	**marriage**
	m	No olviden invitarme al casamiento.
	[ka.sa.ˈmjẽn̪.to]	-Don't forget to invite me to the wedding.
3003	**manar**	**flow**
	vb	¿Qué pasaría cuando el agua deje de manar?
	[ma.ˈnar]	-What would happen when the water stopped flowing?
3004	**refrigerador**	**refrigerator**
	m	Tengo que sacar unos huevos del refrigerador.
	[re.fri.xɛ.ra.ˈðor]	-I have to get some eggs out of the cooler.
3005	**persecución**	**persecution**
	f	Ha habido mucha persecución en la comunidad.
	[pɛr.se.ku.ˈsjõn]	-There's been a lot of persecution of the community.
3006	**apartar**	**set aside**
	vb	Estoy intentando apartar mis sentimientos.
	[a.par.ˈtar]	-I'm trying to set aside my feelings.
3007	**protesta**	**protest**
	f	Me gustaría unirme a esta protesta.
	[pro.ˈtɛs.ta]	-I would like to join this protest.
3008	**montaje**	**assembly**
	m	Estos motivos son un montaje de fotos.
	[mõn̪.ˈta.xe]	-These motifs are a photo montage.

3009	**formal**	**formal**
	adj	Ella no solicitó una audiencia formal.
	[for.ˈmal]	-She did not request a formal oral hearing.

3010	**excepcional**	**exceptional**
	adj	Debe considerarse excepcional y de carácter complementario.
	[ɛk.sɛp.sjo.ˈnal]	-It should be considered exceptional and supplementary in nature.

3011	**cuadra**	**stable, block (LA)**
	f	Estaba perfectamente bien hasta hace una cuadra.
	[ˈkwa.ðra]	-He was perfectly fine until about a block from here.

3012	**crecimiento**	**growth**
	m	La taza de crecimiento en China es la más rápida de la historia humana.
	[kre.si.ˈmjẽ̯.to]	-China's growth rate is the fastest in human history.

3013	**obsesión**	**obsession**
	f	Mi obsesión por Ana empezó a ser un tormento para los dos.
	[oβ.se.ˈsjõn]	-My obsession with Ana became a torment to us both.

3014	**institución**	**institution**
	f	El mundo ya tiene una institución encargada de mantener la paz.
	[ĩns.ti.tu.ˈsjõn]	-The world already has a peace-maintaining institution.

3015	**mulo**	**mule**
	m	Este mulo no puede llevar más carga.
	[ˈmu.lo]	-This mule can't carry a heavier load.

3016	**aprobación**	**approval**
	f	Tu aprobación es importante para mí.
	[a.pro.βa.ˈsjõn]	-Your approval is important to me.

3017	**frágil**	**fragile**
	adj	Él siempre ha sido un niño frágil.
	[ˈfra.xil]	-He'd always been a frail kid.

3018	**mariposa**	**butterfly**
	f	Estás revoloteando como una mariposa.
	[ma.ri.ˈpo.sa]	-You're flitting around like a butterfly.

3019	**lunar**	**lunar; mole**
	adj; m	Le está saliendo sangre del lunar.
	[lu.ˈnar]	-There's blood pouring out of her mole.

3020	**paloma**	**dove**
	f	No puedes camuflarte como una paloma.
	[pa.ˈlo.ma]	-You can't camouflage yourself as a pigeon.

3021	**sudor**	**sweat**
	m	Sécate el sudor de la frente.
	[su.ˈðor]	-Wipe the sweat from your brow.

3022	**trágico**	**tragic**
	adj	Este año ha resultado ser particularmente trágico.
	[ˈtra.xi.ko]	-This year has proved to be a particularly tragic one.

3023	**inicial**	**beginning; initial**
	adj; f	Debemos seguir aprovechando ese éxito inicial.
	[i.ni.ˈsjal]	-We must all continue to build on that initial success.

3024	**web**	**web**
	f	En esta web encontrará toda la información oficial sobre él.
	[ˈwɛβ]	-In this website, you will find all the official information about him.

3025	**costilla**	**rib**
	f	Espero no haberme roto una costilla.
	[kos.ˈti.ja]	-I do hope I haven't cracked a rib.

3026	**vestíbulo**	**lobby**
	m	Te veo en el vestíbulo a las tres.
	[bɛs.ˈti.βu.lo]	-I'll meet you in the lobby at three.

3027	**fundación**	**foundation**
	f	Me encantaría escuchar más sobre cómo funciona tu fundación.
	[fũn̪.da.ˈsjõn]	-I'd love to hear more about how your foundation works.

3028	**ingreso**	**entry, deposit**
	m	No tienes ningún ingreso propio.
	[ĩŋ.ˈgre.so]	-You have no income of your own.

3029	**mutuo**	**mutual**
	adj	Esperamos que continúe este fortalecimiento mutuo de objetivos comunes.
	[ˈmu.two]	-We hope that this mutual reinforcement of common goals will continue.

3030	**enfermería**	**infirmary**
	f	Ni siquiera quería que estudiara enfermería.
	[ẽɱ.fɛr.mɛ.ˈri.a]	-He never even wanted me to go into nursing.

3031	**traficante**	**trafficker**
	m/f	Hablé con un traficante que estuvo preso.
	[tra.fi.ˈkã̯n̪.te]	-I talked to this dealer who'd been busted.

3032	**terraza**	**terrace**
	f	Siempre nos hacen sentarnos en la terraza.
	[tɛ.ˈra.sa]	-They're always making us sit on the balcony.

3033	**sirena**	**siren**
	f	Esa sirena significa que no tiene elección.
	[si.ˈre.na]	-That siren means you don't have a choice.

3034	**judicial**	**judicial; police officer**
	adj; m	Nos agrada comunicar algunas novedades en nuestra labor judicial.
	[xu.ði.ˈsjal]	-We are pleased to report some new developments in our judicial work.

3035	**sirviente**	**servant**
	m	Pareces ser un verdadero sirviente del diablo.
	[sir.ˈβjẽn̪.te]	-You appear to be a true servant of evil.

3036	**escritura**	**writing**
	f	Plasmaré cómo me siento hoy en mi escritura.
	[ɛs.kri.ˈtu.ra]	-I'll put the way I'm feeling today into my writing.

3037	**periodo**	**term**
	m	Estamos atravesando un periodo de cambios y desafíos económicos agudos.
	[pɛ.ˈrjo.ðo]	-We are going through a period of acute economic changes and challenges.

3038	**etiqueta**	**label**
	f	Encontré al fabricante que diseñó la etiqueta.
	[ɛ.ti.ˈkɛ.ta]	-I found the manufacturer who designed the tag.

3039	**peso**	**weight**
	m	El bambú se está doblando con el peso de la nieve.
	[ˈpe.so]	-The bamboo is bending with the weight of the snow.

3040	**religioso**	**religious; priest**
	adj; m	El hombre religioso siguió arrodillado durante horas.
	[re.li.ˈxjo.so]	-The religious man remained kneeling for hours.

3041 **repartir**
vb
[re.par.'tir]

distribute
Tienes que repartir esos contactos, Michael.
-You are required to hand out those leads, Michael.

3042 **resfriado**
adj; m
[rɛs.'frja.ðo]

have a cold; cold
Tardaré mucho tiempo en recuperarme de mi resfriado.
-It will take me a long time to get over my cold.

3043 **sumo**
m; adj
['su.mo]

sumo; supreme
Las antiguas tradiciones del sumo se han convertido en parte del creciente movimiento de la globalización.
-Ancient sumo traditions are becoming part of the growing movement of globalization.

3044 **delincuente**
m/f; adj
[de.lĩŋ.'kwẽn.te]

criminal; delinquent
Jim es un delincuente juvenil.
-Jim is a juvenile delinquent.

3045 **zar**
m
['sar]

tsar
Él se enamoró del zar.
-He fell in love with the Tsar.

3046 **cargado**
adj
[kar.'ɣa.ðo]

strong
Ningún mosquete será cargado hasta que despleguemos para la batalla.
-No muskets are to be loaded until we deploy for battle.

3047 **barriga**
f
[ba.'ri.ɣa]

belly
Tiéndete un momento sobre la barriga.
-Lay over on your tummy for a moment.

3048 **ofender**
vb
[o.fẽn.'dɛr]

offend
Todo el mundo puede ofender a un boxeador, pero no todo el mundo tiene tiempo para pedir disculpas.
-Everyone can offend a boxer, but not everyone has time to apologize.

3049 **cerradura**
f
[sɛ.ra.'ðu.ra]

lock
La cerradura de esa puerta de abajo está rota.
-The lock on that door downstairs is busted.

3050 **pendiente**
m; f; adj
[pẽn.'djẽn.te]

earring; slope; pending
Tendré que buscar tu pendiente luego.
-I will have to look for your earring later.

3051 **barrera**
f
[ba.'rɛ.ra]

barrier
Los necesitábamos para atravesar la barrera.
-We needed you to get us through the barrier.

3052 **postura**
f
[pos.'tu.ra]

posture
No pedimos disculpas por nuestra postura.
-We make no apologies for our stance.

3053 **provecho**
m
[pro.'βe.ʧo]

benefit
Nadie puede acusarte de sacar ningún provecho personal.
-No one can accuse you of making any personal profit.

3054 **aprisa**
adv
[a.'pri.sa]

quickly
Ana, échame una mano, aprisa.
-Ana, give me a hand, quick.

3055 **convento**
m
[kõm.'bẽn.to]

convent
Hoy trabajas en un convento.
-Today you're working in a monastery.

3056 **infantería**

infantry

f
[ĩɱ.fã̠n.ˈtɛ.ri.a]
Nuestras órdenes son esperar a la infantería.
-Our orders are to wait for the infantry.

3057 artificial
adj
[ar.ti.fi.ˈsjal]
artificial
Para este ensayo se utiliza suelo artificial.
-For this test, an artificial soil is used.

3058 doler
vb
[do.ˈlɛr]
hurt
Eso tuvo que doler un poco.
-That's got to sting a bit.

3059 lavandería
f
[la.βã̠n.ˈdɛ.ri.a]
laundry
Será que traen mis calcetines y ropa interior de la lavandería.
-That must be my socks and underwear coming back from the laundry.

3060 arroyo
m
[a.ˈro.jo]
stream
El arroyo solía estar por aquí.
-The stream used to be right around here.

3061 aconsejar
vb
[a.kõn.se.ˈxar]
advise
Decidí estudiar y aconsejar al paciente.
-I decided to study and counsel the patient.

3062 reserva
f
[re.ˈsɛr.βa]
reserve
Respetaremos la decisión y mantendremos nuestra reserva.
-We will respect the decision and maintain our reservation.

3063 colorado
adj
[ko.lo.ˈra.ðo]
red
Normalmente no me pongo colorado al beber.
-I usually don't get red drinking.

3064 cavar
vb
[ka.ˈβar]
dig
Estoy tan avergonzado que podría cavar un agujero y arrastrarme en su interior.
-I'm so embarrassed I could dig a hole and crawl into it.

3065 desprecio
m
[dɛs.ˈpre.sjo]
disdain
Una vez más, Jim rechazó la propuesta con sumo desprecio.
-Again, Jim, with the utmost scorn, rejected the proposal.

3066 plagar
vb
[pla.ˈɣar]
infest
La casa está plagada de bichos.
-The house is infested with bugs.

3067 aló
int
[a.ˈlo]
hello (LA)
Aló, ¿a dónde te fuiste?
-Hallo, where did you go?

3068 separación
f
[se.pa.ra.ˈsjõn]
separation
Es imprescindible obtener una separación similar.
-It is essential to obtain a similar separation.

3069 regalar
vb
[re.ɣa.ˈlar]
gift
No tienes que regalar ningún sucio diamante.
-You don't have to give any dirty diamonds.

3070 escoltar
vb
[ɛs.kol̠.ˈtar]
escort
Yo quiero escoltar al prisionero.
-I want to escort the prisoner.

3071 peinado
m
[pei̯.ˈna.ðo]
hairstyle
Yo nunca entenderé ese peinado.
-I will never understand that hairstyle.

3072	**marcar**	**mark**
	vb	He tardado años en marcar estas tarjetas.
	[mar.ˈkar]	-It's taken me ages to mark these cards.
3073	**capilla**	**chapel**
	f	La Capilla Sixtina es una extensa capilla construida dentro del Palacio Vaticano en 1473.
	[ka.ˈpi.ja]	-The Sistine Chapel is a vast chapel built inside the Vatican Palace in 1473.
3074	**agradecimiento**	**gratitude**
	m	A todos ellos quisiera expresar nuestro profundo agradecimiento.
	[a.ɣra.ðe.si.ˈmjẽn̪.to]	-To all of them, I should like to express our deep gratitude.
3075	**interpretación**	**interpretation**
	f	Mi país no desea apoyar esa interpretación.
	[ĩn̪.tɛr.prɛ.ta.ˈsjõn]	-My country does not wish to support that interpretation.
3076	**cepillo**	**brush**
	m	¿Dónde puedo comprar un cepillo de dientes?
	[se.ˈpi.ʝo]	-Where can I buy a toothbrush?
3077	**hábito**	**habit**
	m	Tengo el hábito de salir a pasear cada día.
	[ˈa.βi.to]	-I am in the habit of taking a walk every day.
3078	**muro**	**wall**
	m	En nuestro edificio tenemos un muro honorífico.
	[ˈmu.ro]	-We have a wall of honor in our building.
3079	**consulta**	**inquiry**
	f	Simplemente envíenos su consulta y nosotros nos atendremos a sus deseos.
	[kõn.ˈsul̪.ta]	-Simply send us your inquiry and we will attend to your request.
3080	**anunciar**	**announce**
	vb	Además, quisiera anunciar las actividades siguientes.
	[a.nũn.ˈsjar]	-In addition, I should like to announce the following activities.
3081	**anual**	**annual**
	adj	El presupuesto anual responderá a los principios de la transparencia.
	[a.ˈnwal]	-The annual budget shall be in compliance with the principles of transparency.
3082	**constitución**	**constitution**
	f	Él tiene una constitución fuerte.
	[kõns.ti.tu.ˈsjõn]	-He has a strong constitution.
3083	**televisor**	**television**
	m	Intenté encender el televisor, pero no funciona.
	[te.le.βi.ˈsor]	-I tried to turn on the television, but it's not working.
3084	**pillar**	**catch up**
	vb	Quizás pueda pillar algo en el aeropuerto.
	[pi.ˈʝar]	-Maybe I can just grab something at the airport.
3085	**despegue**	**takeoff**
	m	Trabajará en el avión hasta su despegue.
	[dɛs.ˈpe.ɣe]	-He will be working on the aircraft until takeoff.
3086	**varón**	**male**
	m	Su deseo era haber nacido varón.
	[ba.ˈrõn]	-Her wish was to have been born a boy.
3087	**halcón**	**hawk**

	m	
	[al.ˈkõn]	Debió ocurrir cuando ese halcón se chocó conmigo. -Must have happened when that falcon smashed into me.
3088	**fino**	**fine**
	adj	Este bambú es demasiado fino para soportar mucho peso.
	[ˈfi.no]	-This bamboo is too thin to bear much weight.
3089	**culto**	**worship; educated**
	m; adj	No hay diferencia entre un culto y una religión.
	[ˈkul̦.to]	-There's no difference between a cult and a religion.
3090	**merced**	**mercy**
	f	Esta vez los tenemos a nuestra merced.
	[mɛr.ˈsɛð]	-This time we have them at our mercy.
3091	**calzón**	**shorts, knickers (LA)**
	m	El chaleco y el calzón también son de seda.
	[kal.ˈsõn]	-The jacket and breeches are also made of silk.
3092	**argumento**	**argument**
	m	Este argumento es pura retórica.
	[ar.ɣu.ˈmẽn̦.to]	-This argument is pure rhetoric.
3093	**barril**	**barrel**
	m	Recorrí las cataratas en un barril.
	[ba.ˈril]	-I went over the falls in a barrel.
3094	**concreto**	**specific**
	adj	Puedo daros un ejemplo muy concreto.
	[kõŋ.ˈkrɛ.to]	-I can give you a very specific example.
3095	**timón**	**rudder**
	m	La próxima vez recordaré purgar el timón.
	[ti.ˈmõn]	-Next time I'll remember to purge the rudder.
3096	**brutal**	**brutal**
	adj	Esa agresión brutal causó grandes daños materiales.
	[bru.ˈtal]	-That barbaric aggression caused great material damage.
3097	**posar**	**pose**
	vb	Tengo que posar para mi estatua.
	[po.ˈsar]	-I have to pose for a statue.
3098	**ballena**	**whale**
	f	El cachalote es la ballena con dientes más grande.
	[ba.ˈje.na]	-A sperm whale is the biggest toothed whale.
3099	**hacienda**	**estate**
	f	Lo encontré cuando adquirí la hacienda.
	[a.ˈsjẽn̦.da]	-I found him when I bought the estate.
3100	**órgano**	**organ**
	m	Nunca tendremos el órgano a tiempo.
	[ˈor.ɣa.no]	-We'd never get the organ in time.
3101	**rechazar**	**reject**
	vb	No quiero rechazar esta demanda.
	[re.tʃa.ˈsar]	-I do not want to reject this claim.
3102	**socialismo**	**socialism**
	m	El thatcherismo surgió como la alternativa más aceptable al socialismo de estado.
	[so.sja.ˈliș.mo]	-Thatcherism emerged as the most plausible alternative to state socialism.

3103	**autógrafo**	**autograph**
	m	Nadie quería mi autógrafo, así que entré y ya.
	[au̯.ˈto.ɣra.fo]	-Nobody wanted my signature, so I just walked in.

3104	**víbora**	**viper**
	f	Es imposible que una víbora regenere tanto veneno tan rápido.
	[ˈbi.βo.ra]	-There's no way a viper regenerates that much venom that quickly.

3105	**anteojos**	**glasses**
	mpl	Jim ni siquiera traía puestos sus anteojos.
	[ãn̪.te.ˈo.xos]	-Jim didn't even have his glasses on.

3106	**transferencia**	**transfer**
	f	Ambas oficinas están cooperando estrechamente para asegurar una transferencia armoniosa.
	[trãns.fɛ.ˈrẽn.sja]	-The two offices are working closely together to ensure a smooth transfer.

3107	**despegar**	**take off**
	vb	Tu carrera está a punto de despegar en Londres.
	[dɛs.pe.ˈɣar]	-Your career's about to take off in London.

3108	**alquilar**	**rent**
	vb	El quince por ciento de las viviendas serán de bajo costo, para que las familias de bajos ingresos puedan comprar o alquilar casas en la zona.
	[al.ki.ˈlar]	-Fifteen percent of the housing will be affordable so that low-income families will be able to buy or rent homes in the area.

3109	**reportero**	**reporter**
	m	Solo soy un pobre aunque honesto reportero.
	[re.por.ˈtɛ.ro]	-I'm only a poor, but honest reporter.

3110	**intimidad**	**privacy**
	f	Piensa en lo divino que será volver a tener intimidad.
	[ĩn̪.ti.mi.ˈðað]	-Think of how divine it'll be to have privacy again.

3111	**séptimo**	**seventh**
	num	India es el séptimo país más grande del mundo.
	[ˈsep̚.ti.mo]	-India is the seventh largest country in the world.

3112	**tentación**	**temptation**
	f	No necesito este tipo de tentación.
	[tẽn̪.ta.ˈsjõn]	-I don't need this kind of temptation.

3113	**haz**	**beam**
	m	El haz de luz asomó entre las copas de los árboles.
	[ˈas]	-The beam of light loomed through the treetops.

3114	**desconocido**	**unknown; stranger**
	adj; m	Estaba en el parque jugando en los columpios cuando se le acercó un desconocido y le ofreció caramelos.
	[dɛs.ko.no.ˈsi.ðo]	-He was playing on the swing in the park when a stranger came by and offered him caramels.

3115	**fallecer**	**die**
	vb	El paciente puede fallecer en cualquier momento.
	[fa.je.ˈsɛr]	-The patient may pass away at any moment.

3116	**técnica**	**technique**
	f	Nunca podrías con mi técnica impecable.
	[ˈtek̚.ni.ka]	-You could never keep up with my flawless technique.

| 3117 | **denuncia** | **complaint** |

	f	No indica el resultado de esta denuncia.
	[de.ˈnũn.sja]	-He does not provide the outcome of this complaint.
3118	**intenso**	**powerful**
	adj	Fue un poco intenso y divertido al mismo tiempo.
	[ĩn̯.ˈtẽn.so]	-It was kind of intense and fun at the same time.
3119	**farmacia**	**pharmacy**
	f	¿Dónde hay una farmacia cerca?
	[far.ˈma.sja]	-Where is a nearby pharmacy?
3120	**secuestrado**	**kidnapped**
	adj	Usted piensa que ha sido secuestrado por extraterrestres.
	[se.kwɛs.ˈtra.ðo]	-You think you've been abducted by aliens.
3121	**gancho**	**hook**
	m	Sería un gran gancho de marketing.
	[ˈgãn̯.ʧo]	-It would be a really great marketing hook.
3122	**furgoneta**	**van**
	f	Había una furgoneta grande y negra aquí.
	[fur.ɣo.ˈnɛ.ta]	-There was a big, black van here.
3123	**recuperación**	**recovery**
	f	Desafortunadamente, la recuperación ha resultado ser muy difícil.
	[re.ku.pɛ.ra.ˈsjõn]	-Unfortunately, the recovery has turned out to be very difficult.
3124	**salido**	**protruding; horny (coll)**
	adj; m	Deberías haber salido media hora antes.
	[sa.ˈli.ðo]	-You should have left half an hour earlier.
3125	**hondo**	**deep**
	adj	El ataque abrió un cráter hondo.
	[ˈõn̯.do]	-The attack left behind a deep crater.
3126	**marcial**	**martial**
	adj	El segundo cómplice sería un artista marcial fuerte pero simple.
	[mar.ˈsjal]	-The second accomplice was to be a strong but simple-minded martial artist.
3127	**adicto**	**addict**
	m	Él es adicto a la heroína.
	[a.ˈðikʾ.to]	-He is a heroin addict.
3128	**soviético**	**Soviet; Soviet**
	adj; m	Soy un ciudadano soviético, solicito asilo político.
	[so.ˈβjɛ.ti.ko]	-I'm a Soviet citizen, I demand political asylum.
3129	**armadura**	**armor**
	f	Su armadura está compuesta de una aleación de titanio y platino.
	[ar.ma.ˈðu.ra]	-Its armor is comprised of a titanium-platinum alloy.
3130	**marcado**	**noticeable; dialing (LA)**
	adj; m	El texto marcado aparecerá en rojo.
	[mar.ˈka.ðo]	-The marked text will be displayed in red.
3131	**describir**	**describe**
	vb	Me gustaría describir las actividades.
	[dɛs.kri.ˈβir]	-I would like to describe the activities.
3132	**embarazo**	**pregnancy**
	m	La justificación para esto es la posibilidad de un embarazo.
	[ẽm.ba.ˈra.so]	-The justification for this is the possibility of a pregnancy.
3133	**medicamento**	**medicine**

m
[me.ði.ka.ˈmɛ̃n̯.to]
Tome este medicamento después de cada comida.
-Take this medicine after each meal.

3134 ansiedad — **anxiety**
f
[ãn.sje.ˈðað]
Espero curar mi ansiedad social un día.
-I hope to cure my social anxiety one day.

3135 cachorro — **puppy**
m
[ka.ˈʧo.ro]
El cachorro la miró con ojos muy tristes.
-The puppy looked at her with very sad eyes.

3136 arquitecto — **architect**
m
[ar.ki.ˈtek̚.to]
Ese arquitecto construye casas muy modernas.
-That architect builds very modern houses.

3137 lecho — **bed**
m
[ˈle.ʧo]
Fui tras las rocas y subí por el lecho del rio.
-I went behind the rocks and I worked my way up that riverbed.

3138 pausa — **pause**
f
[ˈpau̯.sa]
En realidad pensaba en darle una pequeña pausa.
-I'm actually thinking about giving it a bit of a break.

3139 orinar — **urinate**
vb
[o.ri.ˈnar]
No necesitas el bolso para orinar.
-You don't need the bag to urinate.

3140 tijeras — **scissors**
fpl
[ti.ˈxɛ.ras]
Intenté apuñalarlo con unas tijeras.
-I tried to stab him with scissors.

3141 cartero — **postman**
m
[kar.ˈtɛ.ro]
Nunca pensé que sería descubierto por nuestro cartero.
-I never thought I'd be caught out by our postman.

3142 desperdiciar — **waste**
vb
[dɛs.pɛr.ði.ˈsjar]
No tenemos mucho tiempo para desperdiciar.
-We don't have a lot of time to waste.

3143 iniciar — **start**
vb
[i.ni.ˈsjar]
Lo importante es que podamos iniciar nuestros trabajos.
-What is important is that we can start our work.

3144 latín — **Latin**
m
[la.ˈtĩn]
Pablo habla latín. Solía ser un sacerdote.
-Pablo speaks Latin. He used to be a priest.

3145 verdura — **vegetable**
f
[bɛr.ˈðu.ra]
Desde que era niña hay una verdura que odio: los guisantes.
-Since I was a child there has been one vegetable that I hate: peas.

3146 morder(se) — **bite**
vb
[mor.ˈðɛr]
Sigue siendo peligroso y puede morder.
-It's still dangerous and it can bite.

3147 hábil — **skilled**
adj
[ˈa.βil]
Mi padre es un hábil pescador.
-My father is a skilled fisherman.

3148 donar — **donate**
vb
[do.ˈnar]
Mi padre está de acuerdo en donar tu corazón.
-My father agrees to donate your heart.

3149 registrar — **register**

vb
[re.xis.'trar]

Ana, quiero registrar esa declaración.
-Ana, I want to record that statement.

3150 exigir — **require**

vb
[ɛk.si.'xir]

Dichas autoridades pueden exigir una traducción de un certificado.
-The said authorities may require a translation of a certificate.

3151 tronco — **trunk**

m
['trõŋ.ko]

Parece que lleve un tronco sobre los hombros.
-It looks like she's carrying a log across her shoulders.

3152 activo — **active; assets**

adj; m
[ak̚.'ti.βo]

Adoro la tecnología, pero como la mayoría de la gente, nunca he jugado un rol activo en su desarrollo.
-I love technology, but like most people, I've never played an active role in its development.

3153 abuso — **abuse**

m
[a.'βu.so]

Opinamos que esto un abuso.
-We believe that this is an abuse.

3154 católico — **Catholic; Catholic**

adj; m
[ka.'to.li.ko]

Eso no significa que no sea un buen católico.
-Doesn't mean I'm not a good Catholic.

3155 entrever — **glimpse**

vb
[ẽn̪.tre.'βɛr]

También nos han dejado entrever un nuevo y posible camino hacia delante.
-They've also provided a glimpse of a potential new path forward.

3156 hormiga — **ant**

f
[or.'mi.ɣa]

Tienes la inteligencia de una hormiga.
-You've got the intelligence of an ant.

3157 interno — **internal**

adj
[ĩn̪.'tɛr.no]

Podemos monitorizarlo con un rastreador interno.
-We can monitor him with an internal tracker.

3158 rival — **rival; opponent**

adj; m/f
[ri.'βal]

Las brujas no serán rival para un héroe de guerra.
-Witches will be no match for a war hero.

3159 asado — **roast; roast**

adj; m
[a.'sa.ðo]

Iré abajo a empezar el asado.
-I'll go downstairs and start the roast.

3160 profeta — **prophet**

m/f
[pro.'fɛ.ta]

El profeta vendrá a rescatarte.
-The prophet will come to your rescue.

3161 inspección — **inspection**

f
[ĩns.pɛk.'sjõn]

La inspección se realizará en un plazo razonable.
-The inspection shall be performed within a reasonable time frame.

3162 armonía — **harmony**

f
[ar.mo.'ni.a]

Tal vez esté ayudando a llevar la armonía entre las personas con mi música.
-I may be helping to bring harmony between people through my music.

3163 paraguas — **umbrella**

m
[pa.'ra.ɣwas]

¿No vas a sacudir el agua de tu paraguas antes de dejarlo?
-Aren't you going to shake the water off your umbrella before you put it down?

3164 doscientos — **two hundred**

num
[dos.ˈsjẽn.tos]
Me he gastado doscientos en un televisor.
-I spent a couple of hundred on a TV.

3165 **bandeja** **tray**
f
[bãn.ˈde.xa]
¿Quieres una bandeja con eso?
-Do you want a tray with that?

3166 **aterrador** **frightening**
adj
[a.tɛ.ra.ˈðor]
Debemos continuar nuestros esfuerzos por eliminar este fenómeno aterrador.
-We need to continue our efforts to eliminate this terrifying phenomenon.

3167 **explorar** **explore**
vb
[ɛks.plo.ˈrar]
Se recomienda explorar escenarios alternativos adicionales.
-It is recommended to explore additional alternative scenarios.

3168 **podrido** **rotten**
adj
[po.ˈðri.ðo]
No necesitamos acercarnos, desde aquí hueles a podrido.
-We don't need to get closer, you smell rotten from here.

3169 **sendero** **path**
m
[sẽn.ˈdɛ.ro]
No encontrarás la granja si sigues por este sendero.
-You won't find the farm if you keep going down this path.

3170 **mudar(se)** **move**
vb
[mu.ˈðar]
Él debería mudar su oficina aquí.
-He should move his office in here.

3171 **contraseña** **password**
f
[kõn.tra.ˈse.ɲa]
Por favor, elija una contraseña más segura.
-Please choose a more secure password.

3172 **corrupción** **corruption**
f
[ko.rup.ˈsjõn]
No ha habido corrupción generalizada como temíamos.
-There has not been widespread corruption as was feared.

3173 **polaco** **Polish; Polish person**
adj; m
[po.ˈla.ko]
Condeno la declaración del ministro polaco.
-I condemn the statement made by the Polish Minister.

3174 **kilogramo** **kilogram**
m
[ki.lo.ˈɣra.mo]
La dosis semanal recomendada está entre 75 y 300 por kilogramo.
-The recommended weekly dose is between 75 and 300 per kilogram.

3175 **generador** **generator**
m
[xe.nɛ.ra.ˈðor]
Probablemente solo sea el combustible del generador.
-It's probably just the gas in the generator.

3176 **matanza** **killing**
f
[ma.ˈtãn.sa]
No basta con denunciar enérgicamente la matanza de víctimas inocentes.
-It is not enough to vigorously denounce the killing of innocent victims.

3177 **brindar** **toast, provide**
vb
[brĩn.ˈdar]
Deben brindar la asistencia necesaria.
-They must provide the necessary assistance.

3178 **paja** **stalk, masturbation (ES)**
f
[ˈpa.xa]
Debemos, por lo tanto, separar el grano de la paja.
-We must, therefore, separate the wheat from the chaff.

3179 **abeja** **bee**
f
[a.ˈβe.xa]
Una abeja salió por la ventana.
-A bee flew out of the window.

3180 **infección** **infection**

f
[ĩɱ.fɛk.ˈsjõn]

No conocemos el agente causante de esta infección viral.
-We do not know the causative agent of this viral infection.

3181 lata — **can**

f
[ˈla.ta]

Jim bebió un sorbo de su lata de cerveza.
-Jim took a sip from his beer can.

3182 envidiar — **envy**

vb
[ẽm.bi.ˈðjar]

Empiezo a envidiar al ratón muerto.
-I'm starting to envy the dead mouse.

3183 demora — **delay**

f
[de.ˈmo.ra]

Pido disculpas por la demora en enviar la agenda.
-I apologize for the delay in sending the agenda.

3184 referencia — **reference**

f
[re.fɛ.ˈrẽn.sja]

Somos incapaces de entender la referencia.
-We are unable to understand the reference.

3185 alba — **dawn**

m
[ˈal.βa]

Tenéis una hora hasta el alba.
-You have an hour until morning.

3186 pólvora — **gunpowder**

f
[ˈpol.βo.ra]

No vinieron con la pólvora y nos enteramos.
-They didn't come with the powder and we found out.

3187 inmortal — **immortal**

adj
[ĩm.mor.ˈtal]

En realidad no es inmortal, sabes.
-He's not really immortal, you know.

3188 coordenada — **coordinate**

f
[ko.or.ðe.ˈna.ða]

Bien, esta es la última coordenada.
-All right, this is the last coordinate.

3189 zoológico — **zoological; zoo**

adj; m
[so.o.ˈlo.xi.ko]

Llevamos un zoológico de mascotas junto a la interestatal.
-We run a petting zoo by the interstate.

3190 paracaídas — **parachute**

m
[pa.ra.ka.ˈi.ðas]

No debería ir a esquiar sin un paracaídas.
-I just shouldn't go skiing without a parachute.

3191 peluca — **wig**

f
[pe.ˈlu.ka]

Tendremos su peluca lista, señora.
-We'll have your wig ready then, ma'am.

3192 despreciable — **despicable**

adj
[dɛs.pre.ˈsja.βle]

No facilitaré este ejercicio despreciable con mi voto.
-I will not facilitate this despicable exercise with my vote.

3193 pabellón — **pavilion**

m
[pa.βe.ˈjõn]

Podrá accederse a este pabellón durante el horario oficial de la conferencia.
-This pavilion will be accessible during regular conference hours.

3194 borrar — **delete**

vb
[bo.ˈrar]

El sistema dice que no tengo los permisos necesarios para borrar la carpeta.
-The system says I do not have the necessary permissions to delete the folder.

3195 congelar — **freeze**

vb
[kõŋ.xe.ˈlar]

Se me van a congelar las orejas si no entro.
-My ears are going to freeze if I don't go in.

3196	**hacer cosquillas**	**tickle**

vb
[a.ˈsɛr kos.ˈki.jas]

Si te quedas aquí, te voy a hacer cosquillas.
 -If you stay here, I'll tickle you.

3197 chao — **ciao**

int
[ˈtʃa.o]

De repente, un "chao" ya no era suficiente.
 -Suddenly one "ciao" was not enough.

3198 silencioso — **silent**

adj
[si.lẽn.ˈsjo.so]

Es silencioso, pero vale mucho.
 -He is quiet, but he's of real value.

3199 botín — **loot**

m
[bo.ˈtĩn]

Lo decidiremos cuando tengamos el botín.
 -We'll decide that when we get the loot.

3200 insulto — **insult**

m
[ĩn.ˈsul̪.to]

Aprovecharé esta oportunidad perfecta para borrar su insulto.
 -I will take this perfect opportunity to erase his insult.

3201 cifra — **figure**

f
[ˈsi.fra]

Esta cifra incluye 400 viviendas que han sido compradas en la región.
 -This figure includes 400 houses that have been purchased in the region.

3202 natal — **native**

adj
[na.ˈtal]

Centenares de miles de refugiados han regresado a su tierra natal.
 -Hundreds of thousands of refugees have returned to their native land.

3203 localizar — **locate**

vb
[lo.ka.li.ˈsar]

No pudimos localizar a Jim.
 -We could not locate Jim.

3204 garra — **claw**

f
[ˈga.ra]

Es más como una especie de garra.
 -It is more like some sort of claw.

3205 exhibición — **display**

f
[ɛk.si.βi.ˈsjõn]

Soy demasiado modesto para tal exhibición.
 -I'm far too modest for such a display.

3206 detención — **detention**

f
[dɛ.tẽn.ˈsjõn]

Varios testimonios mencionaron la detención de hombres.
 -A number of reports noted the detention of men.

3207 trueno — **thunder**

m
[ˈtrwe.no]

He escuchado el trueno de sus cascos.
 -I have heard the thunder of his hooves.

3208 sobrio — **sober**

adj
[ˈso.βrjo]

Continuaremos esta conversación cuando este sobrio.
 -We will continue this conversation when you are sober.

3209 contador — **counter, accountant**

m
[kõn̪.ta.ˈðor]

Todos creen que soy un contador aburrido.
 -They all think that I'm this boring accountant.

3210 labor — **work**

f
[la.ˈβor]

Están comprometidas a participar en esa labor.
 -They are committed to engaging in that work.

3211 trigo — **wheat**

m
[ˈtri.ɣo]

Los precios del trigo han subido durante los últimos seis meses debido a las malas cosechas.

-Because of the poor harvest, wheat prices have gone up in the last six months.

3212 cooperación — **cooperation**
f
[ko.o.pɛ.ra.ˈsjõn]
La cooperación en la seguridad nuclear también es importante.
-Nuclear safety cooperation is also important.

3213 evolución — **evolution**
f
[e.βo.lu.ˈsjõn]
Debe reconocerse que se está produciendo una evolución importante.
-It must be acknowledged that there is an important evolution taking place.

3214 surgir — **appear**
vb
[sur.ˈxir]
Este problema puede surgir de la falta de recursos suficientes.
-This problem may arise from a lack of adequate resources.

3215 entretenimiento — **entertainment**
m
[ẽn.trɛ.te.ni.ˈmjẽn.to]
Después del entretenimiento, habrá sándwiches.
-After the entertainment, there'll be sandwiches.

3216 seno — **breast, core**
m
[ˈse.no]
Vale, empezaremos con tu seno izquierdo.
-Okay, we'll start with your left breast.

3217 impaciente — **impatient**
adj
[ĩm.pa.ˈsjẽn.te]
Yo también estaba impaciente por conocerle.
-I was eager to meet him, too.

3218 régimen — **regime**
m
[ˈre.xi.mẽn]
Ese problema se heredó del régimen anterior.
-That issue had been inherited from the former regime.

3219 regular — **regulate**
vb
[re.ɣu.ˈlar]
Durante el tiempo caluroso, sudar ayuda al hombre a regular su temperatura corporal.
-During warm weather, sweating helps man regulate his body temperature.

3220 mexicano — **Mexican; Mexican person**
adj; m
[me.xi.ˈka.no]
Un consorcio mexicano ha producido el primer chicle biodegradable.
-A Mexican consortium has produced the first ever biodegradable chewing gum.

3221 marido — **husband**
m
[ma.ˈri.ðo]
Tu marido me dijo dónde encontrarte.
-Your husband told me where to find you.

3222 bombardeo — **bombing**
m
[bõm.bar.ˈðe.o]
Ha sido así desde el bombardeo.
-It's been like this since the bombing.

3223 vigilante — **attentive; guard**
adj; m/f
[bi.xi.ˈlãn.te]
Podría conseguir un trabajo de vigilante.
-I could find a job as a watchman.

3224 reflejo — **reflection; reflex**
m; adj
[re.ˈfle.xo]
Cuando recuperé el sentido, me pareció que me había crecido pelo en los dedos y en las rodillas. Cuando hubo un poco más de luz, miré mi reflejo en un manantial de la montaña y me di cuenta de que me había convertido en un tigre.
-When I regained my senses, it seemed that fur had grown on my fingers and knees. When it became slightly brighter, I looked at my reflection in a mountain stream, and I realized that I had become a tiger.

3225 freno — **brake**

	m [ˈfre.no]	La tercera luz de freno pasó de estar prohibida a ser obligatoria. -The third brake light went from being prohibited to being required.
3226	**lazo** m [ˈla.so]	**bow, rope** He decidido romper mi lazo matrimonial. -I have decided to break my marriage bond.
3227	**maduro** adj; adv [ma.ˈðu.ro]	**ripe; mature** Sería preferible alguien un poco más maduro que Jim. -Someone a little more mature than Jim would be preferable.
3228	**plomo** m [ˈplo.mo]	**lead** Puede encontrarse plomo en las pinturas y el plástico blando de los juguetes. -Lead may be found in toys´ paints and softened plastic.
3229	**catorce** num [ka.ˈtor.se]	**fourteen** Mi hermano Jim tiene catorce años. -My brother Jim is fourteen years old.
3230	**rabino** m [ra.ˈβi.no]	**rabbi** Escuche, rabino, me gustaría hacerle una pregunta. -Listen, rabbi, I'd like to ask you a question.
3231	**matón** m [ma.ˈtõn]	**thug** Me hubiera gustado ver al matón derrotado. -I would like to have seen the bully defeated.
3232	**boxeador** m[bok.se.a.ˈðor]	**boxer** Jim tiene el menor número de derrotas que cualquier boxeador en la liga. -Jim has the fewest losses of any boxer in the league.
3233	**recado** m [re.ˈka.ðo]	**message** Dale el recado cuando él vuelva. -Give him the message when he comes back.
3234	**resumir** vb [re.su.ˈmir]	**summarize** En lugar de eso, propongo resumir mis comentarios en cuatro puntos. -What I propose to do instead is to summarize my remarks in four points.
3235	**apoyar** vb [a.po.ˈjar]	**support** Estas son cosas que deberíamos apoyar conjuntamente. -These are things that we should all in fact jointly support.
3236	**mascota** f [mas.ˈko.ta]	**pet** Ni siquiera tienen una buena mascota. -They don't even have a good mascot.
3237	**provocar** vb [pro.βo.ˈkar]	**provoke** Esto podría, efectivamente, provocar una reacción. -This could, in fact, provoke a reaction.
3238	**mantenimiento** m [mãn̪.te.ni.ˈmjẽn̪.to]	**maintenance** La educación favorecerá la comprensión, la tolerancia y la amistad entre todas las naciones y todos los grupos étnicos o religiosos, y promoverá el desarrollo de las actividades de las Naciones Unidas para el mantenimiento de la paz. -Education shall promote understanding, tolerance, and friendship among all nations, racial or religious groups, and shall further the activities of the United Nations for the maintenance of peace.
3239	**chatarra** f [tʃa.ˈta.ra]	**scrap** Está permitido transportar la chatarra recolectada al dueño. -It's allowed to transport gathered scrap to the owner.
3240	**Pascua**	**Easter**

f
['pas.kwa]
Quiero que tengamos una Pascua maravillosa.
-I want us to have a wonderful Easter.

3241 ofensivo — offensive
adj
[o.fɛ̃n.ˈsi.βo]
Habría encontrado un comentario como ese altamente ofensivo.
-I would've found a remark like that highly offensive.

3242 balcón — balcony
m
[bal.ˈkõn]
Moveré el panel solar del balcón al techo en su debido momento.
-I'll move the solar panel from the balcony to the roof in due course.

3243 acelerar — accelerate
vb
[a.se.lɛ.ˈrar]
Es importante utilizar ese foro para acelerar las conversaciones.
-It is important to use that forum to accelerate the discussions.

3244 privacidad — privacy
f
[pri.βa.si.ˈðað]
Lo hicieron incluso a costa de invadir su privacidad.
-They did it even at the cost of disruption to their privacy.

3245 formidable — formidable
adj
[for.mi.ˈða.βle]
Sería formidable si lo publicaran.
-It would be great if they published it.

3246 barca — small boat
f
[ˈbar.ka]
Necesito coger una barca a Londres.
-I need to get on a boat to London.

3247 investigador — researcher
m
[ĩm.bɛs.ti.ɣa.ˈðor]
No puedo evitarlo, me contrataron como químico investigador.
-I can't help it, I was hired as a research chemist.

3248 norteamericano — North American; North American person
adj; m
[nor.te.a.mɛ.ri.ˈka.no]
Tengo que presentarle a algunas personas al embajador norteamericano.
-I have to introduce some people to the American Ambassador.

3249 chicle — gum
m
[ˈtʃi.kle]
Casi no puede ni caminar y mascar chicle.
-The guy can hardly walk and chew gum.

3250 supervisor — supervisor
m
[su.pɛr.βi.ˈsor]
El supervisor quiere hablar contigo.
-The supervisor wants to talk to you.

3251 cobertura — coverage
f
[ko.βɛr.ˈtu.ra]
Ha habido un incremento sustancial de la cobertura educativa en Perú.
-There has been a substantial expansion of educational coverage in Peru.

3252 manga — manga; sleeve
m/f; f
[ˈmãŋ.ga]
Tienes demasiadas cartas en la manga.
-You got too many cards up your sleeve.

3253 velo — veil
m
[ˈbe.lo]
Lleva puesto un velo para ocultar sus heridas.
-She wears a veil to hide her wounds.

3254 empacar — pack (LA)
vb
[ɛ̃m.pa.ˈkar]
Tenemos que empacar primero, Ana.
-We've got to pack first, Ana.

3255 completar — complete
vb
[kõm.plɛ.ˈtar]
Solo nos llevó quince minutos completar la labor.
-It only took us fifteen minutes to complete the job.

3256 argentino — Argentinian; Argentinian person

adj; m
[ar.xẽn.ˈti.no]

Voy a correr contra el argentino.
-I'm going to race against the Argentinean.

3257 **industrial**

industrial; industrialist

adj; m
[ĩn.dus.ˈtrjal]

Preveía un plan industrial separado para este centro.
-It envisaged a separate industrial plan for this site.

3258 **comprensión**

understanding

f
[kõm.prẽn.ˈsjõn]

Estos números van más allá de la comprensión humana.
-These figures are beyond human understanding.

3259 **ring**

ring

m
[ˈrĩŋg]

Estoy lanzando mi sombrero al ring.
-I'm throwing my hat in the ring.

3260 **nomás**

just (LA)

adv
[no.ˈmas]

Nomás tu hermano está con él.
-Only your brother's with him.

3261 **estropear**

spoil

vb
[ɛs.tro.pe.ˈar]

No quisieras estropear tu delicada vestimenta.
-You wouldn't want to spoil your pretty clothes.

3262 **fruto**

fruit

m
[ˈfru.to]

Son fruto de intervenciones políticas decisivas.
-They are the result of decisive political interventions.

3263 **ensayar**

rehearse

vb
[ẽn.sa.ˈjar]

Creo que deberías ensayar con esos titulares.
-I think you should rehearse with those headlines.

3264 **aroma**

scent

m
[a.ˈro.ma]

Esta rosa silvestre desprende un aroma dulce.
-This wild rose gives off a sweet scent.

3265 **perímetro**

perimeter

m
[pɛ.ˈri.mɛ.tro]

Revisaré el perímetro y dispararé a los guardias.
-I'll work the perimeter and nail the guards.

3266 **grandeza**

greatness

f
[grãn.ˈde.sa]

Juntos podremos devolver la grandeza a nuestro pueblo.
-Together, we can lead our people to greatness again.

3267 **delantero**

front; forward

adj; m
[de.lãn.ˈtɛ.ro]

Esperaba que estuviera en tu bolsillo delantero.
-I was hoping it was in your front pocket.

3268 **propaganda**

advertising

f
[pro.pa.ˈɣãn.da]

Ha llegado la hora de dejar de gastar dinero en propaganda ridícula.
-It is time to stop wasting money on ridiculous propaganda.

3269 **yate**

yacht

m
[ˈɟja.te]

Ella traerá el yate mañana.
-She's bringing the yacht down tomorrow.

3270 **ingenioso**

witty

adj
[ĩn.xe.ˈnjo.so]

Tienes que reconocer que ha sido ingenioso.
-You've got to admit that it was clever.

3271 **atardecer**

twilight; get dark

m; vb
[a.tar.ðe.ˈsɛr]

Es vital que despegue al atardecer.
-It is vital you take off at sunset.

3272 **consideración**

consideration

f
[kõn.si.ðɛ.ra.ˈsjõn]

Por consideración a la industria de la cría de cerdos, el nombre de 'gripe porcina' ha sido cambiado a 'gripe A(H1N1)'.
-Out of consideration to the pig farming industry the name 'pig influenza' has been changed into 'influenza A(H1N1)'.

3273 palmar
vb
[pal.ˈmar]

die (ES) (coll)
Voy a palmar en dos días igualmente.
-I'll croak in two days anyway.

3274 interpretar
vb
[ĭn.tɛr.prɛ.ˈtar]

play, perform
Ana podrá interpretar tu papel.
-Ana will get to play your part.

3275 rezo
m
[ˈre.so]

prayer
Todos podéis uniros a mí en un rezo silencioso.
-You may all join me in a silent prayer.

3276 molino
m[mo.ˈli.no]

mill
Esta es una preciosa foto de un molino de madera. -This is a gorgeous shot of a lumber mill.

3277 cuan
adv
[ˈkwãn]

as
Sé cuan solo te has sentido, cuan asustado.
-I know how alone you've felt, how scared.

3278 refugiar(se)
vb
[re.fu.ˈxjar]

shelter
La obligación del árbol es refugiar.
-It's the tree's duty to shelter.

3279 verificar
vb
[bɛ.ri.fi.ˈkar]

verify
Estos son los procedimientos para verificar la entrada y el análisis de los datos.
-These are the procedures to verify data entry and analysis.

3280 cargamento
m
[kar.ɣa.ˈmẽn.to]

shipment
Mañana, un cargamento de nitroglicerina saldrá en tren.
-Tomorrow, a shipment of nitro will depart by train.

3281 bloqueo
m
[blo.ˈke.o]

block
No pensaron que podría burlar el bloqueo.
-They didn't think you'll manage to force the blockade.

3282 atascar
vb
[a.tas.ˈkar]

jam
Esta munición barata se va a atascar.
-This cheap ammo's going to jam.

3283 jeep
m
[xe.ˈɛp]

jeep
No podría dejar el jeep aquí.
-I couldn't leave the jeep here.

3284 bando
m
[ˈbãn.do]

side
El bando ganador habría pagado mucho mejor.
-The winning side would've paid much better.

3285 litro
m
[ˈli.tro]

liter
Debe de haber un litro de agua aquí.
-There's got to be a liter of water in here.

3286 sobreviviente
m/f; adj
[so.βre.βi.ˈβjẽn.te]

survivor; surviving
Ella va a enseñarme cómo ser un sobreviviente.
-She is going to teach me how to be a survivor.

3287 chaleco

vest

m
[ʧa.ˈle.ko]
Este chaleco de montar se infla cuando te caes.
-This riding vest inflates when you fall.

3288 cualidad — **quality**
f
[kwa.li.ˈðað]
Supongo que todos tenemos al menos una cualidad redentora.
-I guess everyone has at least one redeeming quality.

3289 viviente — **living**
adj
[bi.ˈβjẽn̪.te]
Es una reliquia viviente del pasado lejano.
-It's a living relic of the distant past.

3290 provincia — **province**
f
[pro.ˈβĩn.sja]
Te enviaré a otra provincia, escógela tú mismo.
-I'll deploy you to another province, choose it yourself.

3291 mocoso — **snuffly; brat**
m; adj
[mo.ˈko.so]
Ella le puso mi nombre a ese mocoso.
-She named that brat after me.

3292 circuito — **circuit**
m
[sir.ˈkwi.to]
Cada circuito incluirá un despegue y aterrizaje.
-Each circuit shall include a take-off and a landing.

3293 atajar — **take a shortcut, tackle**
vb
[a.ta.ˈxar]
Era primordial atajar las verdaderas causas de la crisis.
-It was essential to address the root causes of the conflict.

3294 juntar — **put together**
vb
[xũn̪.ˈtar]
Debemos juntar el arroz y esconderlo.
-We must collect the rice and hide it.

3295 examinar — **examine**
vb
[ɛk.sa.mi.ˈnar]
Es imprescindible examinar la estructura actual del comercio.
-It is essential to examine the current structure of trade.

3296 pedo — **fart**
m
[ˈpe.ðo]
Pensaba que su pedo en el elevador iba a ser silencioso.
-He thought his fart in the elevator was going to be silent.

3297 alabar — **praise**
vb
[a.la.ˈβar]
Estamos aquí para alabar al Señor.
-We are here to praise the Lord.

3298 reducir — **reduce**
vb
[re.ðu.ˈsir]
Debemos tratar de reducir su complejidad.
-We have to try to reduce its complexity.

3299 tobillo — **ankle**
m
[to.ˈβi.jo]
Solo necesitamos liberar su tobillo de la polea.
-We just need to free her ankle from the pulley.

3300 jinete — **rider**
m/f
[xi.ˈnɛ.te]
Tienes que seguir al jinete ahora.
-You have to go after the horseman now.

3301 tango — **tango**
m
[ˈtãŋ.go]
Este es el sitio correcto donde aprender tango.
-This is the right place to learn to tango.

3302 implicar(se) — **involve**
vb
[ĩm.pli.ˈkar]
Necesitamos implicar a las personas y convencerlas.
-We need to involve the people and convince them.

3303 billar — **billiards**

m
Solía ganarle en todo, desde el billar hasta el póquer.
[bi.ˈʝar]
-I used to beat him at everything, from pool to poker.

3304 **nevada**
snowfall
f
La fuerte nevada retrasó al tren durante varias horas.
[ne.ˈβa.ða]
-Heavy snow delayed the train for several hours.

3305 **buque**
vessel
m
El buque debía entregarse hoy.
[ˈbu.ke]
-The vessel was to be delivered today.

3306 **descuento**
discount
m
¿Hay descuento por ser estudiante?
[dɛs.ˈkwẽ̃.to]
-Is there a student discount?

3307 **angustia**
anguish
f
Es incalculable la angustia y el sufrimiento causados.
[ãŋ.ˈgus.tja]
-The anguish and suffering caused is incalculable.

3308 **cuervo**
crow
m
Esto es absolutamente ridículo, oficiar un funeral para un cuervo.
[ˈkwɛr.βo]
-This is absolutely ridiculous, holding a funeral for a crow.

3309 **documental**
documentary; documentary
adj; m
Ese documental acerca de la crisis medioambiental me hizo abrir los ojos.
[do.ku.mẽ̃.ˈtal]
-That documentary about the environmental crisis was a real eye-opener.

3310 **consistir**
consist
vb
¿En qué consistirían estas medidas de intervención?
[kõn.sis.ˈtir]
-What would these intervention measures look like?

3311 **pos(t)**
post
pfx
Tengo trastorno de estrés postraumático.
[ˈpost)]
-I have post-traumatic stress disorder.

3312 **estancia**
stay
f
Me gustaría extender mi estancia hasta el domingo.
[ɛs.ˈtãn.sja]
-I'd like to extend my stay through Sunday.

3313 **creador**
creator
m
Solamente el creador de una reunión puede editarla.
[kre.a.ˈðor]
-Only the creator of a meeting may edit it.

3314 **operar**
work
vb
Necesitan operar en un ambiente claramente definido.
[o.pɛ.ˈrar]
-They need to operate in a clearly defined environment.

3315 **bloque**
block
m
Estuvimos alrededor de este bloque muchas veces.
[ˈblo.ke]
-We've been around this block so many times.

3316 **emboscar**
ambush
vb
Eso explicaría por qué ha podido emboscar a nuestras flotas.
[ẽm.bos.ˈkar]
-That would explain how he's been able to ambush our fleets.

3317 **exceso**
excess
m
El exceso de democracia no mata a la paz.
[ɛk.ˈse.so]
-Too much democracy does not kill peace.

3318 **pulgar**
thumb
m
Jim atrapó un mosquito entre su pulgar y su índice.
[pul.ˈɣar]
-Jim caught a mosquito between his thumb and first finger.

3319 **vil**
vile

	adj	Pronto serás curada de esta vil mutación.

adj
['bil]

Pronto serás curada de esta vil mutación.
-Soon you will be cured of this vile mutation.

3320 terminal — **terminal; terminal**
adj; m/f
[tɛr.mi.ˈnal]

Para otros programas, seguirá necesitando utilizar el terminal.
-For other programs, you will still need to use the terminal.

3321 celestial — **celestial**
adj
[se.lɛs.ˈtjal]

También necesitaremos un evento celestial.
-We'll also need a celestial event.

3322 ciclo — **cycle**
m[ˈsi.klo]

El ciclo de vida de los anfibios consta de tres etapas: huevo, larva y adulto. -
The life cycle of an amphibian consists of three stages: egg, larva, and adult.

3323 determinar — **determine**
vb
[dɛ.tɛr.mi.ˈnar]

Sería importante determinar las modalidades adecuadas de esa participación.
-It would be important to determine the appropriate modalities for that participation.

3324 cesar — **cease**
vb
[se.ˈsar]

Mientras la guerra sea considerada como perversa, siempre tendrá su fascinación. Cuando se considere vulgar, cesará de ser popular.
-As long as war is regarded as wicked, it will always have its fascination. When it is looked upon as vulgar, it will cease to be popular.

3325 década — **decade**
f
[ˈde.ka.ða]

Hemos avanzado mucho en la última década.
-We have made much progress in the last decade.

3326 colapso — **collapse**
m
[ko.ˈlap.so]

Causaría el colapso completo del proceso.
-It would cause the complete collapse of the process.

3327 mejora — **improvement**
f
[me.ˈxo.ra]

Hay algunos ámbitos que son susceptibles de mejora.
-There are areas that are open to improvement.

3328 chantaje — **blackmail**
m
[ʧãn̩.ˈta.xe]

Usted robó informes confidenciales como chantaje para vengarse.
-You stole confidential reports as blackmail for revenge.

3329 turco — **Turkish; Turk**
adj; m
[ˈtur.ko]

El gobierno turco debe realizar nuevos esfuerzos en ese sentido.
-Further efforts must be made in this regard by the Turkish Government.

3330 eminencia — **eminence**
f
[e.mi.ˈnɛ̃n.sja]

Perdone, majestad, buscan a su eminencia.
-Excuse me, your Majesty, they're looking for his Eminence.

3331 golfo — **gulf; scoundrel**
m; adj
[ˈgol.fo]

Llegó envuelta en hielo desde el golfo.
-Came packed in ice, all the way from the gulf.

3332 horizonte — **horizon**
m
[o.ri.ˈsõn̩.te]

Ningún candidato en el horizonte parece poder detenerla.
-No candidate on the horizon seems able to stop her.

3333 pálido — **pale**
adj
[ˈpa.li.ðo]

Me molestaban por ser tan pálido.
-They gave me a hard time for being all pale.

3334 anochecer — **dusk; get dark**

m; vb
Volverá antes del anochecer, espero.
[a.no.tʃe.ˈsɛr]
-She'll be back before dark, I hope.

3335 obsesionar(se)   **obsess**
vb
No te empieces a obsesionar con eso.
[oβ.se.sjo.ˈnar]
-Don't let yourself get obsessed with it.

3336 reno   **reindeer**
m
Este es un pequeño reno con un sombrero puesto.
[ˈre.no]
-This one's a little reindeer wearing a hat.

3337 harina   **flour**
f
Solo haz comida que no necesite harina.
[a.ˈri.na]
-Just make food which does not require flour.

3338 sensual   **sensual**
adj
Empezaremos por una mirada más sensual.
[sɛ̃n.ˈswal]
-We will start with a more sensual look.

3339 cardenal   **cardinal**
m
Llamaré al cardenal tan pronto como hayamos terminado.
[kar.ðe.ˈnal]
-I'll put in a call to the cardinal as soon as we're done.

3340 hermandad   **brotherhood**
f
Su sentimiento de hermandad había trascendido los límites del odio y la
[ɛr.mãn̪.ˈdað]
violencia.
-Their sisterhood had transcended the boundaries of hatred and violence.

3341 tejido   **tissue, fabric**
m
También puede haber inflamación del tejido muscular.
[te.ˈxi.ðo]
-There may also be inflammation in the muscle tissue.

3342 escocés   **Scotch; Scot**
adj; m
Uno de los que fueron detenidos es escocés.
[ɛs.ko.ˈses]
-One of those who were detained is Scottish.

3343 publicar   **publish**
vb
El tribunal decidió publicar sus fallos de forma regular.
[pu.βli.ˈkar]
-The tribunal decided to publish its judicial decisions on a regular basis.

3344 carreta   **wagon**
f
Coge una carreta y acuéstale detrás.
[ka.ˈrɛ.ta]
-Get a wagon and lay him down in back.

3345 reportaje   **article**
m
Por eso necesitaba tanto el reportaje.
[re.por.ˈta.xe]
-That's why I needed the story so bad.

3346 representación   **representation**
f
Quizá sea la representación inversa del símbolo.
[re.pre.sɛ̃n̪.ta.ˈsjõn]
-It is perhaps the inverse representation of the symbol.

3347 CD   **CD**
m
Disolvimos el grupo después del quinto CD.
[kð]
-We dissolved the group after the fifth CD.

3348 estelar   **stellar**
adj
Seguiré intentando ser tu alumna estelar.
[ɛs.te.ˈlar]
-I will keep trying to be your star pupil.

3349 nana   **granny; lullaby**
f; f
Este pequeñín está con su nana ahora.
[ˈna.na]
-This little one is with his nana now.

3350	**dibujar**	**draw**
	vb	Es muy difícil dibujar el límite entre amor y amistad.
	[di.βu.ˈxar]	-It is very difficult to draw the boundary between love and friendship.
3351	**histórico**	**historical**
	adj	Creo que estamos ante un acuerdo histórico.
	[is.ˈto.ri.ko]	-I believe we are dealing with a historic agreement.
3352	**pellejo**	**skin**
	m	He pensado en una forma para que puedas salvar el pellejo.
	[pe.ˈje.xo]	-I've thought of a way for you to save your skin.
3353	**valentía**	**courage**
	f	Estaba intentando demostrarle a esta enfermera mi valentía.
	[ba.lẽn̪.ˈti.a]	-I was trying to prove to this nurse that I'm brave.
3354	**baile**	**dance**
	m	Todavía faltan tres semanas para el baile.
	[ˈbai̯.le]	-There's still three weeks before the ball.
3355	**afectado**	**affected; victim**
	adj; m	Dicho traslado de fábrica habría afectado a muchos trabajadores.
	[a.fek̚.ˈta.ðo]	-A lot of employees would have been affected by such factory relocation.
3356	**dominio**	**domain**
	m	Debe introducir primero un nombre de dominio.
	[do.ˈmi.njo]	-You must first enter a domain name.
3357	**confundido**	**confused**
	adj	Estoy algo confundido con ese punto.
	[kõm.fũn̪.ˈdi.ðo]	-I am a little confused on that point.
3358	**tambor**	**drum**
	m	Obtiene unos resultados magníficos solo con un tambor.
	[tãm.ˈbor]	-He gets some wonderful results with just a drum.
3359	**mail**	**email (coll)**
	m	Acabo de leer este mail y pienso que podría interesarte.
	[ˈmai̯l]	-I just read this email and I thought it may interest you.
3360	**refresco**	**soda**
	m	Cómprame un refresco y estaremos en paz.
	[re.ˈfrɛs.ko]	-Buy me a soda and we're even.
3361	**eventualmente**	**occasionally**
	adv	Y eventualmente, se comen todos los maníes.
	[e.βẽn̪.twal.ˈmẽn̪.te]	-And eventually, they eat up all the peanuts.
3362	**quienquiera**	**whoever**
	prn	Me gustaría muchísimo conocer a quienquiera que fue responsable de su muerte.
	[kjẽŋ.ˈkjɛ.ra]	-I should very much like to meet whoever was responsible for his death.
3363	**crueldad**	**cruelty**
	f	Lo condenaron por su crueldad a los animales.
	[krwɛl̪.ˈdað]	-They condemned him for his cruelty to animals.
3364	**pala**	**shovel**
	f	Tendré que comprar una pala.
	[ˈpa.la]	-I'll have to buy a shovel.
3365	**instalación**	**installation**

f
[ĩns.ta.la.ˈsjõn]
Solo utilizamos esta instalación para congelar carbón.
-We only use this facility for carbon freezing.

3366 mérito — merit
m
[ˈmɛ.ri.to]
Puedo vislumbrar algún mérito artístico.
-I can see the possibility of some artistic merit.

3367 admirador — fan
m
[að.mi.ra.ˈðor]
Lo que tengo que decirte es sobre tu admirador.
-What I have to tell you is about your admirer.

3368 dondequiera — wherever
adv
[dõn.de.ˈkjɛ.ra]
El terrorismo es inaceptable dondequiera y cuandoquiera que ocurra.
-Terrorism is unacceptable anywhere, at any time.

3369 nevera — fridge
f
[ne.ˈβɛ.ra]
Hasta tengo soda en la nevera.
-I've even got soda in the fridge.

3370 veloz — fast
adj
[ˈbe.los]
La vida es corta y el tiempo pasa veloz.
-Life is short and time is swift.

3371 setenta — seventy
num
[sɛ.ˈtẽn.ta]
Había unos setenta músicos en total.
-There were around seventy performers in all.

3372 infiel — unfaithful; infidel
adj; m/f
[ĩm.ˈfjɛl]
Quizás no fuera el único infiel.
-Perhaps he wasn't the only unfaithful one.

3373 discreción — discretion
f
[dis.kre.ˈsjõn]
Esto debería dejarse a discreción del tribunal.
-That would be at the discretion of the court.

3374 ajo — garlic
m
[ˈa.xo]
¿Comer un diente de ajo al día es beneficioso para la salud?
-Is eating a clove of garlic every day beneficial to your health?

3375 remoto — distant
adj
[re.ˈmo.to]
Esto bloquea la señal del detonador remoto de la bomba.
-This blocks the remote detonator signal to the bomb.

3376 integridad — integrity
f
[ĩn.te.ɣri.ˈðað]
De esta forma se mantendría su integridad.
-In that way, their integrity would be maintained.

3377 inesperado — unexpected
adj
[i.nɛs.pɛ.ˈra.ðo]
Eso fue muy guay e inesperado.
-That was really cool and very unexpected.

3378 revisión — review
f
[re.βi.ˈsjõn]
La comisión opina que no debemos prejuzgar esta revisión.
-The commission thinks that we should not prejudge this review.

3379 amenazar — threaten
vb
[a.me.na.ˈsar]
Jim dijo que oyó a Ana amenazar con matar a John.
-Jim said he heard Ana threaten to kill John.

3380 santuario — sanctuary
m
[sãn.ˈtwa.rjo]
Él construyó este santuario para estas reliquias sagradas.
-For these holy relics he built this sanctuary.

3381 corporación — corporation

f
[kor.po.ra.ˈsjõn]
Desacuerdos departamentales llevaron a que la corporación se dividiera en cinco compañías separadas.
-Departmental disagreements led the corporation to split into five separate companies.

3382 gripe — **flu**

f
[ˈɡri.pe]
Tengo gripe y estoy cansado.
-I have the flu and I'm tired.

3383 patear — **kick**

vb
[pa.te.ˈar]
En un mes recuperará el sentido común y se pateará a sí misma.
-In a month she'll come to her senses and kick herself.

3384 órbita — **orbit**

f
[ˈor.βi.ta]
Dentro de treinta segundos habremos perdido nuestra órbita.
-In 30 seconds, we'll have missed our orbit.

3385 agarre — **grip**

m
[a.ˈɣa.re]
Normalmente tiene muy buen agarre.
-Normally, it's got a very good grip.

3386 opuesto — **opposite**

adj
[o.ˈpwɛs.to]
Mi delegación siempre se ha opuesto a ello.
-My delegation has always been opposed to it.

3387 tránsito — **transit**

m
[ˈtrãn.si.to]
Se han concertado y aprobado para su aplicación varios acuerdos regionales y subregionales de facilitación del tránsito.
-A number of regional and subregional transit facilitation agreements have been concluded and adopted for implementation.

3388 fugitivo — **fugitive; fugitive**

adj; m
[fu.xi.ˈti.βo]
Tenemos un fugitivo huyendo con mucha ventaja.
-We got a fugitive on the run with a pretty big lead.

3389 calendario — **calendar**

m
[ka.lẽn̪.ˈda.rjo]
El calendario está colgado en la pared.
-The calendar is hanging on the wall.

3390 pañal — **diaper**

m
[pa.ˈɲal]
Necesitará un pañal limpio pronto.
-She will need a clean diaper soon.

3391 cemento — **cement**

m
[se.ˈmẽn̪.to]
Este es un búnker subterráneo fortificado con bloques de cemento de 12 pulgadas.
-This is an underground bunker fortified with 12-inch cement blocks.

3392 morgue — **morgue**

f
[ˈmor.ɣe]
El cuerpo está en una morgue.
-The body's at a mortuary.

3393 no obstante — **however**

con
[ˈno oβs.ˈtãn̪.te]
Queda, no obstante, más margen para la flexibilidad.
-There is, however, more room for flexibility.

3394 cancha — **court**

f
[ˈkãn̪.tʃa]
Estabas encantada de volver a esa cancha.
-You were thrilled to be back out there on that court.

3395 fusión — **fusion**

f
[fu.ˈsjõn]
Nuestros controles meteorológicos y sistemas de fusión son de hace un siglo.
-Our weather controls and fusion systems are a century old.

3396 basurero — **garbage dump, garbageman**
m
[ba.su.ˈrɛ.ro]
Encontré un gato en mi basurero.
-I found a cat in my dumpster.

3397 suministro — **supply**
m
[su.mi.ˈnis.tro]
El apoyo en materia de suministro de agua y saneamiento sigue siendo insuficiente.
-Water supply and sanitation support remain insufficient.

3398 calibre — **caliber**
m
[ka.ˈli.βre]
Las armas se enumeran por orden ascendente según calibre o carga explosiva.
-Weapons are listed in ascending order by caliber or explosive content.

3399 protocolo — **protocol**
m
[pro.to.ˈko.lo]
Debe observarse que Jim no pretendía cambiar la configuración del protocolo de comunicaciones.
-It should be noted that Jim did not intend to change the configuration of the communication protocol.

3400 agresión — **aggression**
f
[a.ɣre.ˈsjõn]
En 2009 fue arrestado por agresión.
-In 2009, he was arrested for assault.

3401 camello — **camel**
m
[ka.ˈme.jo]
Ella y el camello vendrán conmigo.
-She and the camel will come with me.

3402 selección — **selection**
f
[se.lɛk.ˈsjõn]
Encontrará al lado una selección de varios artículos.
-Opposite, you will find a selection of several items.

3403 ancho — **width; wide**
m; adj
[ˈãn̪.ʧo]
El escenario era ancho, con mucha profundidad.
-The soundstage was broad, with a lot of depth.

3404 pijama — **pajamas**
m
[pi.ˈxa.ma]
Ana estaba resfriada y la hiciste quitarse su pijama para la foto.
-Ana had a cold and you made her change out of her pajama's for the picture.

3405 comunicar — **communicate**
vb
[ko.mu.ni.ˈkar]
Jim finalmente logró comunicar sus pensamientos en japonés.
-Jim was finally able to communicate his thoughts in Japanese.

3406 hospitalidad — **hospitality**
f
[os.pi.ta.li.ˈðað]
Nos conmueve su hospitalidad y abnegación.
-We are moved by their hospitality and selflessness.

3407 burla — **taunt**
f
[ˈbur.la]
Supongo que habla con ánimo de burla.
-I assume you speak in a spirit of mockery.

3408 captura — **capture**
f
[kapʼ.ˈtu.ra]
Nos prometió parte de su captura.
-He's promised us some of his catch.

3409 urgencia — **urgency**
f
[ur.ˈxɛ̃n.sja]
Me dijo que tenía un urgencia en el trabajo.
-He told me he was dealing with a work emergency.

3410 mara — **gang (LA)**
f
[ˈma.ra]
El tatuaje indica la mara a la que pertenecen.
-The tattoo identifies the gang they belong to.

3411 acondicionar(se) — **prepare**

vb
[a.kõn̪.di.sjo.ˈnar]

Es innecesario acondicionar el espécimen o efectuar los análisis en una atmósfera acondicionada.
-It is unnecessary to condition the specimen or to conduct analyses in a conditioned atmosphere.

3412 cálido — **warm**
adj
[ˈka.li.ðo]

Propongo que lo recibamos con un cálido aplauso.
-I propose that we greet him with a warm round of applause.

3413 ignorar — **ignore**
vb
[iɣ.no.ˈrar]

Aprendí a no ignorar mi dolor.
-I learned not to ignore my pain.

3414 nuez — **nut**
f
[ˈnwes]

Es el doble de grande que una nuez normal.
-It's twice as big as a normal walnut.

3415 láser — **laser**
m
[ˈla.sɛr]

Para tu información, hay muchos adultos que disfrutan jugando a batallas láser.
-For your information, there are many adults that enjoy playing laser tag.

3416 test — **test**
m
[ˈtest]

El test dice que fui rey en mi vida anterior.
-The test says I was a king in my previous life.

3417 protestar — **protest**
vb
[pro.tɛs.ˈtar]

Quiero protestar enérgicamente contra esto.
-I want to protest very strongly about this.

3418 niñez — **childhood**
f
[ˈni.ɲes]

No puedo hablarte de mi niñez.
-I can't tell you about my childhood.

3419 presuponer — **assume**
vb
[pre.su.po.ˈnɛr]

No podemos presuponer otra cosa a menos que tengamos pruebas.
-We can't assume otherwise unless there's evidence.

3420 abandono — **neglect, desertion**
m
[a.βãn̪.ˈdo.no]

El abandono y el maltrato infantil se consideran delitos penales.
-Child neglect and abuse are considered to be criminal offenses.

3421 jardinero — **gardener**
m
[xar.ði.ˈnɛ.ro]

El jardinero poda las matas con tijeras y el césped con una hoz.
-The gardener cuts back the bushes with shears and the grass with a scythe.

3422 destinar — **destine**
vb
[dɛs.ti.ˈnar]

Era necesario destinar más recursos a esas áreas.
-It was necessary to channel more resources to those areas.

3423 facilidad — **ease**
f
[fa.si.li.ˈðað]

Pero me gusta fingir que fluye con facilidad.
-But I like to pretend that it comes with ease.

3424 dominar — **master**
vb
[do.mi.ˈnar]

Lleva años dominar un idioma extranjero.
-It takes years to master a foreign language.

3425 yarda — **yard**
f
[ˈɟ͡ʝar.ða]

No me moveré una yarda más en esta cosa.
-I'm not moving another yard on this thing.

3426 banquero — **banker**

m	Jim es un banquero de inversiones.
[bãŋ.ˈkɛ.ro]	-Jim is an investment banker.

3427 creencia — **belief**

f
[kre.ˈɛ̃n.sja]

Jim estaba obsesionado con la creencia de que, uno por uno, todos los que le rodeaban eran abducidos y reemplazados por extraterrestres.
-Jim was obsessed by the belief that, one by one, everyone around him was being abducted and replaced by aliens.

3428 sólido — **solid; solid**

adj; m
[ˈso.li.ðo]

Sé que tenemos un caso sólido.
-I know we have a strong case.

3429 extraterrestre — **alien; alien**

adj; m/f
[ɛks.tra.tɛ.ˈrɛs.tre]

No es más extraterrestre que tú.
-He is no more extraterrestrial than you are.

3430 ficha — **chip, ticket**

f
[ˈfi.tʃa]

Esa ficha te permite ver el futuro.
-That chip allows you to see the future.

3431 hipoteca — **mortgage**

f
[i.po.ˈte.ka]

Algunas familias deben hacer frente a pagos de hipoteca particularmente altos.
-Some households face particularly heavy mortgage payments.

3432 estricto — **strict**

adj
[ɛs.ˈtrik.to]

Mi padre es muy estricto conmigo.
-My father is very strict with me.

3433 conforme — **in agreement; just as**

adj; adv
[kõŋ.ˈfor.me]

Podemos actuar conforme al procedimiento que usted propone.
-We can do it in accordance with the procedure that you propose.

3434 cebolla — **onion**

f
[se.ˈβo.ja]

Probablemente tenga una cebolla en el bolsillo.
-He's probably got an onion in his pocket.

3435 poste — **post**

m
[ˈpos.te]

Bebí demasiado y me choqué contra un poste.
-I drank too much, and I bumped into a pole.

3436 honestidad — **honesty**

f
[o.nɛs.ti.ˈðað]

Hemos demostrado nuestra honestidad de propósito.
-We have demonstrated our sincerity of purpose.

3437 rebaño — **flock**

m
[re.ˈβa.ɲo]

Experimentábamos con un rebaño de ovejas.
-We were experimenting with a flock of sheep.

3438 acontecimiento — **event**

m
[a.kõ̃n.te.si.ˈmjẽ̞n.to]

Han transcurrido dos meses desde este trágico acontecimiento.
-Two months to the day have elapsed since that tragic event.

3439 financiero — **financial; financier**

adj; m
[fi.nãn.ˈsjɛ.ro]

Mi supuesto asesor financiero acaba de llamar.
-My so-called financial advisor just rang.

3440 excursión — **excursion**

f
[ɛk.sur.ˈsjõn]

Los chicos tenían ganas de que llegara la excursión.
-The boys were looking forward to the trip.

3441 primario — **primary**

adj
[pri.ˈma.rjo]

Pensé que si cambiaba su microprocesador primario, podría arreglarlo.
-I thought if I changed his primary microprocessor, I could fix it.

3442 mejilla   **cheek**

f
[me.ˈxi.ʝa]

Tienes algo de crema en la mejilla.
-You've got some cream on your cheek.

3443 gasolinera   **gas station**

f
[ga.so.li.ˈnɛ.ra]

Pondría esa gasolinera contra mi negocio en esta ciudad.
-I would put that gas station up against any business in this town.

3444 uy   **whoah, ouch**

int
[ˈwi]

Uy, creo que la máquina me ha dado el cheque de otra persona.
-Oopsies, I think the machine gave me someone else's paycheck.

3445 psicología   **psychology**

f
[si.ko.lo.ˈxi.a]

Actualmente carecemos de programas de psicología clínica.
-At present we do not have programmes for clinical psychology.

3446 seguidor   **follower**

m
[se.ɣi.ˈðor]

Para bloquear a un seguidor lo tendrás que hacer desde tu perfil.
-To block a follower you must do this from your profile.

3447 palanca   **lever**

f
[pa.ˈlãŋ.ka]

Casi necesito una palanca para separarlos.
-I practically needed a crowbar to pry them apart.

3448 flaco   **skinny**

adj
[ˈfla.ko]

Es más cortés decir delgado que flaco.
-It's more polite to say thin than skinny.

3449 perpetuo   **perpetual**

adj
[pɛr.ˈpɛ.two]

Su movimiento perpetuo no se puede detener.
-Its perpetual movement cannot be stopped.

3450 nudo   **knot**

m
[ˈnu.ðo]

Ella sabría cómo hacer un buen nudo.
-She'd know how to tie a good knot.

3451 iniciativa   **initiative**

f
[i.ni.sja.ˈti.βa]

En ausencia de una iniciativa internacional radical, se enfrentan a un futuro muy sombrío.
-In the absence of a radical international initiative, they face a very grim future.

3452 usual   **usual**

adj
[u.ˈswal]

Probablemente esto no sea posible si seguimos con nuestro procedimiento usual.
-It is probable that this is simply not possible if we continue with our usual procedure.

3453 clavo   **nail**

m
[ˈkla.βo]

Imaginen un clavo atravesando la palma de las manos de este hombre.
-Imagine a nail piercing the palm of this man's hands.

3454 universitario   **university; undergraduate**

adj; m
[u.ni.βer.si.ˈta.rjo]

Las mujeres continúan constituyendo la mayoría del alumnado universitario.
-Women continue to form the majority of students at university level.

3455 cultural   **cultural**

adj
[kul̪.tu.ˈral]

Aun así pienso que esto no es una diferencia cultural enorme.
-I still don't think this a huge cultural difference.

3456 alterar   **alter**

	vb	Creo que él necesita alterar su estilo de vida.
	[al̪.tɛ.ˈrar]	-I think he needs to alter his lifestyle.
3457	**núcleo**	**core**
	m	Jim entonces transmitirá la localización exacta del núcleo.
	[ˈnu.kle.o]	-Jim will then transmit the exact location of the core.
3458	**anfitrión**	**host**
	m	La habitación será limpiada regularmente por su anfitrión.
	[ãɱ.fi.ˈtrjõn]	-The room will be cleaned regularly by your host.
3459	**hipócrita**	**hypocritical; hypocrite**
	adj; m/f	Deberías remarcar lo hipócrita que es eso.
	[i.ˈpo.kri.ta]	-You should point out the hypocrisy of that.
3460	**rehabilitación**	**rehabilitation**
	f	Esta es una aplicación del enfoque de la autosuficiencia para la rehabilitación de viviendas.
	[re.a.βi.li.ta.ˈsjõn]	-This is a self-help approach for rehabilitation of dwellings.
3461	**chile**	**chili**
	m	Solo quería dejarles algo de mi chile.
	[ˈtʃi.le]	-I just want to leave you some of my chili.
3462	**digital**	**digital**
	adj	Permitidme que hable de la revolución digital.
	[di.xi.ˈtal]	-Allow me to turn to the digital revolution.
3463	**codo**	**elbow**
	m	Se lastimó su codo cuando se cayó.
	[ˈko.ðo]	-She hurt her elbow when she fell down.
3464	**ladrillo**	**brick**
	m	Todos estos edificios están hechos de concreto reforzado y ladrillo.
	[la.ˈðri.jo]	-All of these buildings are made out of reinforced concrete and brick.
3465	**anteriormente**	**previously**
	adv	Me gustaría reiterar lo que he dicho anteriormente.
	[ãn̪.tɛ.rjor.ˈmẽn̪.te]	-I would like to reiterate what I said earlier.
3466	**tensar(se)**	**tense**
	vb	Tiene que tensar los músculos.
	[tẽn.ˈsar]	-You've got to tense the muscles.
3467	**amuleto**	**amulet**
	m	Los indígenas tenían cada uno un amuleto que consideraban su verdadero corazón.
	[a.mu.ˈlɛ.to]	-The natives each had an amulet, which they considered their true heart.
3468	**revolucionario**	**revolutionary; revolutionary**
	adj; m	Cuando el entendimiento fue anunciado pareció un paso revolucionario.
	[re.βo.lu.sjo.ˈna.rjo]	-When the understanding was announced it looked like a revolutionary step.
3469	**alrededores**	**surroundings**
	m	Todos estamos teniendo que hacer algunos ajustes a nuestros nuevos alrededores físicos.
	[al.re.ðe.ˈðo.res]	-We are all having to make some adjustments to our new physical surroundings.
3470	**frijol**	**bean**
	m	Esa ensalada de frijol negro suena bien.
	[fri.ˈxol]	-That black bean salad sounds good.
3471	**modesto**	**modest**

adj
[mo.ˈðɛs.to]

Siguen buscándose recursos para este proyecto experimental relativamente modesto.
-Resources for this relatively modest pilot project are still being sought.

3472 **cuaderno**

m
[kwa.ˈðɛr.no]

notebook

Cuando vuelva, quiero ver ese cuaderno.
-When I get back, I want to see that notebook.

3473 **rebelión**

f
[re.βe.ˈljõn]

rebellion

Él dijo que la única solución era una rebelión de esclavos.
-He said the only answer was a slave rebellion.

3474 **distinguir**

vb
[dis.tĩŋ.ˈgir]

distinguish

Es importante distinguir entre la empresa y sus directivos.
-It is important to distinguish between the company and its directors.

3475 **huracán**

m
[u.ra.ˈkãn]

hurricane

A pesar del huracán el barco llegó al puerto.
-In spite of the hurricane, the ship reached port.

3476 **sinceridad**

f
[sĩn.sɛ.ri.ˈðað]

sincerity

Su sinceridad se ganó la confianza de todos.
-His sincerity gained the confidence of everyone.

3477 **masculino**

adj
[mas.ku.ˈli.no]

masculine

Cada sustantivo en portugués es masculino o femenino.
-Every noun in Portuguese is either masculine or feminine.

3478 **ancestro**

m
[ãn.ˈsɛs.tro]

ancestor

Heredamos este plan de un ancestro común.
-We inherited this scheme from a common ancestor.

3479 **mecanismo**

m
[me.ka.ˈniş.mo]

mechanism

Estaríamos muy agradecidos si se pudiera hallar tal mecanismo.
-We would be very grateful if such a mechanism could be found.

3480 **cera**

f
[ˈsɛ.ra]

wax

También puede lanzar cera contra su oponente.
-He can also throw wax at his opponent.

3481 **estanque**

m
[ɛs.ˈtãŋ.ke]

pond

Han encontrado una sandalia en el estanque.
-They found a sandal in the pond.

3482 **infinito**

adj; m
[ĩɱ.fi.ˈni.to]

infinite; infinity

Hay un suministro infinito de bodegas.
-There's an endless supply of empty warehouses.

3483 **alojamiento**

m
[a.lo.xa.ˈmjẽn̪.to]

accommodation

Algunos de los refugiados reciben alojamiento y protección provisional.
-Some of the refugees are provided with temporary shelter and protection.

3484 **bono**

m
[ˈbo.no]

bonus, pass

Por favor, compruebe el bono y la confirmación para evitar cualquier posible malentendido.
-Please check the voucher and confirmation in order to avoid any possible misunderstanding.

3485 **artístico**

adj
[ar.ˈtis.ti.ko]

artistic

Alguien que tiene esa clase de potencial artístico merece mucho más.
-Someone who has that kind of artistic potential deserves so much more.

3486 **rechazo**

rejection

m
[re.ˈʧa.so]
Recomendamos el rechazo de esta petición.
-We recommend the rejection of this request.

3487 comerciante — **merchant**
m
[ko.mɛr.ˈsjã̠n.te]
El comerciante sobornó al político.
-The merchant bribed the politician.

3488 blues — **blues**
m
[ˈblwes]
La música aquí es una combinación tranquila de jazz, blues y soul.
-The music here is a chilled combination of jazz, blues, and soul.

3489 generosidad — **generosity**
f
[xe.nɛ.ro.si.ˈðað]
Hubo muchos actos de valor y generosidad.
-There were many acts of bravery and kindness.

3490 entorno — **environment**
m
[ẽ̠n.ˈtor.no]
Nos enfrentamos audazmente a ellos para construir un entorno de paz y estabilidad en nuestra región.
-We are facing them boldly to build an environment of peace and stability in our region.

3491 tramar — **plot**
vb
[tra.ˈmar]
No le creo capaz de tramar una venganza complicada.
-I don't think he's capable of an intricate revenge plot.

3492 admirable — **admirable**
adj
[að.mi.ˈra.βle]
Turquía ha realizado un admirable esfuerzo histórico de aproximación a Europa.
-Turkey has made an admirable effort to move towards Europe.

3493 cintura — **waist**
f
[sĩ̠n.ˈtu.ra]
Esto debería ajustarse mejor a tu cintura ahora.
-This should fit you better around the waist now.

3494 cálculo — **calculation**
m
[ˈkal.ku.lo]
Detrás de la descortesía puede haber un cálculo estratégico más amplio.
-Behind the unpleasantness may lie a broader strategic calculation.

3495 ignorancia — **ignorance**
f
[iɣ.no.ˈrãn.sja]
Para triunfar en la vida necesitas dos cosas: ignorancia y confianza.
-To succeed in life, you need two things: ignorance and confidence.

3496 consentimiento — **consent**
m
[kõn.sẽ̠n.ti.ˈmjẽ̠n.to]
Deberá obtenerse el consentimiento de las comunidades afectadas.
-The consent of the affected communities must be obtained.

3497 apreciar — **appreciate**
vb
[a.pre.ˈsjar]
No aprecia los buenos aviones.
-He doesn't appreciate a good airplane.

3498 fundamental — **fundamental**
adj
[fũ̠n.da.mẽ̠n.ˈtal]
La participación de los musulmanes en la política es de una importancia fundamental para la sociedad.
-The participation of Muslims in politics is of fundamental importance to society.

3499 ochenta — **eighty**
num
[o.ˈʧẽ̠n.ta]
La mujer tiene más de ochenta años.
-The lady is over eighty.

3500 defensor — **defense; defense attorney**
adj; m
[de.fẽ̠n.ˈsor]
Un acusado tiene el derecho de nombrar un defensor en cualquier momento.
-A defendant has the right to appoint a defender at any time.

3501	**concha**	**shell, pussy (LA) (coll)**
	f	Lo que tengo en mi mano es un fósil de una concha.
	[ˈkõn̪.ʧa]	-What I have in my hand is a fossil seashell.

3502	**yerno**	**son-in-law**
	m	Si quieres ser mi yerno, toma mis bendiciones.
	[ˈɟjɛr.no]	-If you want to be my son-in-law, take my blessings.

3503	**tripa**	**intestine, belly**
	f	Mi tripa sigue teniendo el mismo tamaño.
	[ˈtri.pa]	-My belly still has the same size.

3504	**puerco**	**pig; disgusting**
	m; adj	Asé el puerco porque era tu cumpleaños.
	[ˈpwɛr.ko]	-I roasted the pig because it was your birthday.

3505	**espuma**	**foam**
	f	Mi latte no tiene espuma extra.
	[ɛs.ˈpu.ma]	-There's no extra foam in my latte.

3506	**taxista**	**taxi driver**
	m/f	Nuestro taxista decidió pasar la mañana con nosotros.
	[tak.ˈsis.ta]	-Our taxi driver decided to hang out with us this morning.

3507	**ausente**	**absent; absentee**
	adj; m/f	Lamento que ella esté ausente de la conferencia.
	[au̯.ˈsɛn̪.te]	-I am sorry that she is absent from the conference.

3508	**despido**	**dismissal**
	m	El despido ilegal se podrá impugnar ante un tribunal.
	[dɛs.ˈpi.ðo]	-Unlawful dismissal may be challenged in court.

3509	**ingeniería**	**engineering**
	f	La nanotecnología es la ciencia de la ingeniería molecular.
	[ĩn.xe.njɛ.ˈri.a]	-Nanotechnology is the science of molecular engineering.

3510	**expulsar**	**expel**
	vb	Los jóvenes han vuelto para expulsar a los viejos.
	[ɛks.pul.ˈsar]	-The children have returned to expel their elders.

3511	**adelanto**	**advance**
	m	El adelanto y la potenciación de la mujer eran prioridades nacionales en Indonesia.
	[a.ðe.ˈlãn̪.to]	-The advancement and empowerment of women were national priorities in Indonesia.

3512	**asamblea**	**assembly**
	f	Debe reconocerse una asamblea constitucional de estado.
	[a.sãm.ˈble.a]	-Recognition of a constitutional status assembly should be accorded.

3513	**diputado**	**deputy**
	m	Un diputado solamente no podrá pertenecer a más de un grupo político.
	[di.pu.ˈta.ðo]	-A member may not belong to more than one political group.

3514	**agregar**	**add**
	vb	Tan solo quisiera agregar algunas observaciones.
	[a.ɣre.ˈɣar]	-I would only like to add a few points.

3515	**descarga**	**discharge**
	f	No tenemos mucho tiempo para la descarga.
	[dɛs.ˈkar.ɣa]	-We don't have much time for the download.

| 3516 | **diálogo** | **dialogue** |

m
['dja.lo.ɣo]

El diálogo y el compromiso aliviarán las tensiones mejor que el aislamiento.
-Dialogue and engagement will defuse tensions better than isolation.

3517 stop

m
['s.top]

stop sign

No me gusta ese signo de stop.
-I don't like that stop sign.

3518 documentación

f
[do.ku.mɛ̃n̪.ta.'sjõn]

documentation

Ella está en proceso de obtener la documentación necesaria.
-She is in the process of obtaining the relevant documentation.

3519 administrador

m
[að.mi.nis.tra.'ðor]

administrator

Hemos investigado al administrador del hospital.
-We have been checking on the hospital administrator.

3520 sillón

m
[si.'jõn]

armchair

Este sillón es cómodo.
-This armchair is comfortable.

3521 faro

m
['fa.ro]

lighthouse

Solíamos jugar junto al faro cuando éramos niños.
-We used to play out by the lighthouse when we were kids.

3522 enlace

m
[ẽn.'la.se]

link

¿Podrías escribir el enlace al sitio?
-Would you be able to write down the link to the site?

3523 semestre

m
[se.'mɛs.tre]

semester

El fin del semestre llegará pronto.
-The end of the semester will come soon.

3524 oposición

f
[o.po.si.'sjõn]

opposition

Me gustaría expresar mi clara oposición a tales acciones.
-I would like to express my clear opposition to such actions.

3525 alambre

m
[a.'lãm.bre]

wire

Puedo abrirla si encuentro un alambre.
-I can open it if I find some wire.

3526 envolver

vb
[ẽm.bol.'βɛr]

wrap

Ni siquiera puedes envolver un trozo de pizza.
-You can't even wrap a piece of pizza.

3527 participación

f
[par.ti.si.pa.'sjõn]

participation

Sin su participación, habría todavía menos progreso.
-Without their participation, there would be even less progress.

3528 químico

adj; m
['ki.mi.ko]

chemical; chemist

El químico disuelve rápidamente los cálculos de colesterol.
-The chemical rapidly dissolves cholesterol stones.

3529 atrasar(se)

vb
[a.tra.'sar]

delay

No podemos atrasar más esta presentación.
-We can't delay this presentation any longer.

3530 pésimo

adj
['pe.si.mo]

awful

Yo soy un mentiroso pésimo.
-I am a terrible liar.

3531 baba

f
['ba.βa]

slime

Encontraron un poco de esa baba rosada.
-They found a little of that pink slime.

3532 económico

economic

adj
[e.ko.ˈno.mi.ko]

¿Qué es más importante, el desarrollo económico o la protección medio ambiental?
-Which is more important, economic development or environmental protection?

3533 abismo

m
[a.ˈβiş.mo]

abyss

No mires al abismo. Si no, el abismo te mirará a ti.
-Don't look into the abyss. Otherwise, the abyss will gaze into you.

3534 feroz

adj
[ˈfɛ.ros]

fierce

Tiene ese apego feroz a su cámara.
-He's got this fierce attachment to his camera.

3535 blusa

f
[ˈblu.sa]

blouse

Ana, déjame comprarte una blusa.
-Ana, let me buy you a blouse.

3536 violar

vb
[bjo.ˈlar]

violate

No deseamos violar tu privacidad al no consultarte antes.
-We did not wish to violate your privacy by not consulting you first.

3537 evacuación

f
[e.βa.kwa.ˈsjõn]

evacuation

Hemos decidido llevar a cabo la evacuación.
-We have decided to go ahead with the evacuation.

3538 ético

adj
[ˈɛ.ti.ko]

ethical

¿Sería ético sacrificar a una persona para salvar a muchas?
-Would it be ethical to sacrifice one person to save many?

3539 fascista

adj; m/f
[fas.ˈsis.ta]

fascist; fascist

No sé porque eres un fascista.
-I don't know why you are a fascist.

3540 au

int
[ˈau̯]

ouch

¡Au! ¿Acabas de darme una patada?
-Ouch! Did you just kick me?

3541 pescador

m
[pɛs.ka.ˈðor]

fisherman

Digamos que soy pescador y agricultor.
-Let's say I'm a fisherman and a farmer.

3542 apertura

f
[a.pɛr.ˈtu.ra]

opening

He estado trabajando en mi apertura.
-I've been working on my opening.

3543 tomo

m
[ˈto.mo]

volume

Añade un tomo de poesía, por si acaso necesitas una siesta rápida.
-Put in one volume of poetry, in case you need a quick nap.

3544 caña

f
[ˈka.ɲa]

cane, rod

Compré una caña de pescar para ti.
-I bought a fishing pole for you.

3545 pecador

m; adj
[pe.ka.ˈðor]

sinner; sinful

Jim es un pecador impenitente.
-Jim is an unrepentant sinner.

3546 suegro

m
[ˈswe.ɣro]

father-in-law

Tengo un respeto tremendo por mis suegros.
-I have tremendous respect for my father-in-law.

3547 nuca

neck

f
Estaba haciendo esto, como si tuviera la nuca rígida.
['nu.ka]
-He was doing this like he had a stiff neck.

3548 valla   **fence**
f
Una valla separa el jardín del camino.
['ba.ja]
-A fence separates the garden from the lane.

3549 convincente   **convincing**
adj
El grupo no considera convincente esta explicación.
[kõm.bĩn.'sẽn̪.te]
-The group does not consider this explanation to be convincing.

3550 aborto   **abortion**
m
El estrés añadido de la cirugía ha provocado un aborto espontáneo.
[a.'βor.to]
-The added stress of surgery caused a spontaneous miscarriage.

3551 funcionario   **public worker**
m
No soy un funcionario del gobierno.
[fũn.sjo.'na.rjo]
-I'm not a government official.

3552 dramático   **dramatic**
adj
Todo ello sucede en un contexto económico dramático.
[dra.'ma.ti.ko]
-All this is taking place against a dramatic economic background.

3553 top   **top**
m
Al menos podrías quitarte el top.
['top]
-The least you could do is take your top off.

3554 mostrador   **counter**
m
Vamos hacia el mostrador de la tienda.
[mos.tra.'ðor]
-Let's go over to the shop counter.

3555 deprimente   **depressing**
adj
Es muy deprimente tener que mirarlo.
[de.pri.'mẽn̪.te]
-It's so depressing having to look at it.

3556 cobre   **copper**
m
El cobre conduce bien la electricidad.
['ko.βre]
-Copper conducts electricity well.

3557 lote   **set**
m
Este es mi nuevo lote de catálogos orientados a los jóvenes.
['lo.te]
-This is my new batch of youth-oriented catalogs.

3558 oportuno   **timely**
adj
El debate también es oportuno y de interés actual.
[o.por.'tu.no]
-The debate is also timely and topical.

3559 prohibido   **prohibited**
adj
La inyección de salmuera en la carne está prohibida.
[pro.i.'βi.ðo]
-The injection of brine into the meat is prohibited.

3560 atómico   **atomic**
adj
Estoy arrancando el generador atómico de vapor.
[a.'to.mi.ko]
-I am starting up the atomic steam generator.

3561 defecto   **defect**
m
Ustedes van a verificar si esta cámara tiene algún defecto.
[de.'fek.to]
-You guys will check whether there is a defect is in this camera.

3562 proceder   **come from, proceed**
vb
Debemos proceder con cautela y flexibilidad.
[pro.se.'ðer]
-We have to proceed with caution and with flexibility.

3563 bóveda   **vault**

	f	Conocían los túneles y la bóveda.
	['bo.βe.ða]	-They knew about the tunnels and the vault.

3564 casero
adj; m
[ka.'sɛ.ro]

home-made; landlord
Cuando el casero no está, los inquilinos juegan a juegos.
-When the landlord's away, the tenants play games.

3565 chulo
adj; m
['ʧu.lo]

cocky (ES) (coll), great (ES) (coll); scumbag (coll)
Tengo algo muy chulo que enseñarles.
-I have something really cool to show you guys.

3566 agresivo
adj
[a.ɣre.'si.βo]

aggressive
Es un tipo de cáncer inusualmente agresivo.
-It's an unusually aggressive type of cancer.

3567 anormal
adj
[a.nor.'mal]

unusual
Es anormal tener el corazón en el lado derecho.
-It is abnormal to have the heart on the right side.

3568 nativo
adj; m
[na.'ti.βo]

local; native
Un niño que es hablante nativo normalmente sabe muchas cosas acerca de su lengua que un hablante no nativo que lo haya estado estudiando durante muchos años no sabe todavía y que quizá no sabrá nunca.
-A child who is a native speaker usually knows many things about his or her language that a non-native speaker who has been studying for years still does not know and perhaps will never know.

3569 estrado
m
[ɛs.'tra.ðo]

podium
El estrado está definitivamente muy alto.
-The podium is definitely too high.

3570 aficionar
vb
[a.fi.sjo.'nar]

become interested
¡Quizás se debería aficionar a algo, como yo!
-Maybe you should take up a hobby, like me!

3571 éxtasis
m
['ɛks.ta.sis]

ecstasy
Quiere más tiempo para pagar el éxtasis.
-He wants more time to pay for the ecstasy.

3572 iluminación
f
[i.lu.mi.na.'sjõn]

lighting
Carecen totalmente de ventilación y tienen poca iluminación.
-There is absolutely no ventilation and the lighting is dim.

3573 explorador
m
[ɛks.plo.ra.'ðor]

explorer
Quizá deberíamos enviar a un segundo explorador, para estar seguros.
-Maybe we should send in a second scout, to be safe.

3574 colchón
m
[kol.'ʧõn]

mattress
Ana levantó el colchón para cambiar las sábanas.
-Ana raised the mattress in order to change the sheets.

3575 lavabo
m
[la.'βa.βo]

sink, restroom
Fue al lavabo y no volvió.
-He went to the bathroom and never returned.

3576 forastero
m; adj
[fo.ras.'tɛ.ro]

stranger; foreign
Me ignoraste bajo tu propio riesgo, forastero.
-You ignore me at your peril, stranger.

3577 naval
adj
[na.'βal]

naval
Primero, necesitamos romper el bloqueo naval.
-First, we need to break the naval blockade.

3578 sensato

sensible

adj
[sɛ̃.ˈsa.to]
Decidimos que sería sensato vigilarte.
-We decided it might be wise to keep a watch on you.

3579 **campus** **campus**
m
[ˈkãm.pus]
Todo el mundo en este campus está loco.
-Everyone on this campus is nuts.

3580 **alias** **alias**
m
[ˈa.ljas]
Es muy raro hacer negocios con un alias.
-It is so awkward doing business with an alias.

3581 **distante** **distant**
adj
[dis.ˈtã.te]
Parecíamos un organismo intrascendente, distante y poco efectivo.
-We seemed to be an irrelevant, distant, and ineffective body.

3582 **gobernar** **rule**
vb
[go.βɛr.ˈnar]
Querían gobernar mediante la represión.
-They meant to rule by means of repression.

3583 **doblar** **bend, double**
vb
[do.ˈβlar]
Yo solía doblar a John Wayne.
-I used to dub John Wayne.

3584 **votación** **vote**
f
[bo.ta.ˈsjõn]
No habrá votación en esta casa.
-There'll be no voting in this household.

3585 **inconveniente** **problem; inconvenient**
m; adj
[ĩŋ.kõm.be.ˈnjɛ̃n.te]
Lo siento si ha habido algún inconveniente.
-I'm sorry if there's been any inconvenience.

3586 **apodo** **nickname**
m
[a.ˈpo.ðo]
Es difícil imponer un apodo.
-It's hard to force a nickname.

3587 **rapidez** **speed**
f
[ra.ˈpi.ðes]
Considero muy importante la rapidez del proceso.
-In my opinion, the speed of the process is particularly significant.

3588 **ternura** **tenderness**
f
[tɛr.ˈnu.ra]
Todo este arte inocente refleja mucha ternura.
-All this innocent art shows a lot of tenderness.

3589 **lodo** **mud**
m
[ˈlo.ðo]
Qué tan dentro del lodo nos podemos sumergir.
-How deep into the muck we can immerse ourselves.

3590 **yacer** **lie**
vb
[ɟja.ˈsɛr]
Estaría bien si pudiera yacer aquí un rato.
-I'll be okay if I could just lie here a little.

3591 **catástrofe** **catastrophe**
f
[ka.ˈtas.tro.fe]
Una catástrofe ha sido impedida.
-A catastrophe has been averted.

3592 **precisión** **precision**
f
[pre.si.ˈsjõn]
Ana está sentada en su escritorio y traduce una novela. Está rodeada de pilas de voluminosos diccionarios. Ana necesita todos porque traduce con una precisión casi fanática.
-Ana is sitting at her desk and translating a novel. She's surrounded by heaps of big dictionaries. Ana needs all of them as she is translating with an almost fanatic precision.

3593 **embarazoso** **embarrassing**

adj
[ẽm.ba.ra.'so.so]

Debe ser embarazoso y un poco triste.
-It's got to be embarrassing, and a little upsetting.

3594 profecía

f
[pro.fe.'si.a]

prophecy

Nuestro reto es refutar esa terrible profecía.
-It is our challenge to disprove that dire prophecy.

3595 pulgada

f
[pul.'ɣa.ða]

inch

Patrullas armadas tienen cada pulgada del perímetro bajo vigilancia.
-Armed patrols have every inch of the perimeter under observation.

3596 provenir

vb
[pro.βe.'nir]

proceed

El resultado final de estos servicios tendrá que provenir del mercado.
-The ultimate delivery of these services will have to come from the marketplace.

3597 normalidad

f
[nor.ma.li.'ðað]

normalcy

Habrá un par de días en los que todo será raro y luego todo volverá a la normalidad.
-There'll be a couple days of awkwardness and then everything will go back to normal.

3598 retorno

m
[rɛ.'tor.no]

return

La razón de mi retorno es que la gente de Chile es extremadamente amable.
-The reason for my return is that the people of Chile are extraordinarily amiable.

3599 chupar

vb
[tʃu.'par]

suck, absorb (coll)

Tiene la costumbre de chupar el lápiz.
-He has a habit of sucking his pencil.

3600 preparación

f
[pre.pa.ra.'sjõn]

preparation

Como preparación para pintar un retrato, mi amigo toma muchas fotografías con el fin de estudiar el tema en profundidad.
-In preparation for painting a portrait, my friend takes many photographs in order to study the subject closely.

3601 cadera

f
[ka.'ðɛ.ra]

hip

La familia quiere que haga una cirugía de cadera.
-The family wants me to do a hip surgery.

3602 repentino

adj
[re.pẽn.'ti.no]

sudden

Cualquier movimiento repentino y te mato.
-Any sudden moves and I'll kill you.

3603 contrabando

m
[kõn.tra.'βãn.do]

smuggling

Se debe combatir el contrabando de tabaco, la falsificación y otras prácticas ilegales.
-Tobacco smuggling, counterfeiting, and other illegal practices should be combated.

3604 lloro

m
['ʝjo.ro]

crying

Escuché tu lloro y vine a ver cómo estabas.
-I heard your cry and I came to check on you.

3605 forzado

adj
[for.'sa.ðo]

forced

Me veo forzado a preguntarme esto.
-I am forced to ask myself this question.

3606 luto

m
['lu.to]

mourning

Hoy es un día de luto para la nación entera.
-Today is a day of mourning for the whole nation.

3607 musulmán

Muslim; Muslim

adj; m
[mu.sul.ˈmãn]

Es seglar, pero musulmán devoto.
-He is secular, but a devout Muslim.

3608 servidor — **server, servant**

m
[sɛr.βi.ˈðor]

No puedo leer mi correo. El servidor está caído.
-I can't check my mail. The server is down.

3609 en torno a — **about**

prp
[ɛ̃n ˈtor.no a]

El debate de hoy gira en torno a eso.
-That is what today's debate is about.

3610 extender — **extend**

vb
[ɛks.tɛ̃n.ˈdɛr]

Me gustaría extender su misión seis meses.
-I would like to extend your mission six months.

3611 exclusivo — **exclusive**

adj
[ɛks̺.lu.ˈsi.βo]

Nosotros tenemos el derecho exclusivo de venderlos.
-We have the exclusive right to sell them.

3612 desarrollar — **develop**

vb
[de.sa.ro.ˈjar]

Desarrollar conciencia política toma tiempo.
-Developing political awareness takes time.

3613 veinticinco — **twenty-five**

num
[bei̯n.ti.ˈsĩn.ko]

Hay veinticinco estudiantes en el salón de actos.
-There are twenty-five students in the assembly hall.

3614 fanático — **fan; fanatic**

adj; m
[fa.ˈna.ti.ko]

Es un fanático del proyecto piloto.
-He's a fan of the pilot project.

3615 gramo — **gram**

m
[ˈgra.mo]

Un gramo de uranio radiactivo puede estar millones de años haciendo daño.
-One gram of radioactive uranium can cause damage for millions of years.

3616 fax — **fax**

m
[ˈfaks]

Necesito enviar un fax a Vancouver.
-I need to send a fax to Vancouver.

3617 aprobar — **approve**

vb
[a.pro.ˈβar]

Absolutamente no puedo aprobar la proposición.
-I absolutely cannot approve the proposition.

3618 frasco — **jar**

m
[ˈfras.ko]

He encontrado un frasco con ciento veinte dólares dentro.
-I found a jar with a hundred and twenty dollars in it.

3619 interruptor — **switch**

m
[ĩn.te.ruṕ.ˈtor]

Parece como si alguien lo hubiera apagado con un interruptor.
-Looks like somebody turned it off with a switch.

3620 glorioso — **glorious**

adj
[glo.ˈrjo.so]

Ahora hablaré del glorioso país.
-Now I will speak about the glorious country.

3621 finca — **ranch**

f
[ˈfĩŋ.ka]

Ana había pedido visitar la finca durante meses.
-Ana had been requesting to visit the estate for months.

3622 esclavitud — **slavery**

f
[ɛs.kla.βi.ˈtuð]

Nadie estará sometido a esclavitud ni a servidumbre, la esclavitud y la trata de esclavos están prohibidas en todas sus formas.

-No one shall be held in slavery or servitude; slavery and the slave trade shall be prohibited in all their forms.

3623	**precaución** f [pre.kau̯.ˈsjõn]	**caution** La confidencialidad de estos procedimientos constituye una medida de precaución básica. -The confidentiality of such proceedings represents a basic precaution.
3624	**correspondencia** f [ko.rɛs.põn̯.ˈdẽn.sja]	**correspondence** Nunca presto ninguna atención a la correspondencia. -I never pay any attention to the mail.
3625	**lila** adj; f [ˈli.la]	**lilac; lilac** Voy a pintar mi apartamento de color lila. -I am going to paint my apartment lilac.
3626	**latir** vb [la.ˈtir]	**beat** Sentí mi corazón latir fuertemente. -I felt my heart beating violently.
3627	**ciervo** m [ˈsjɛr.βo]	**deer** Llevo kilómetros detrás de este ciervo. -I've been tracking this deer for miles.
3628	**optimista** adj; m/f [op̚.ti.ˈmis.ta]	**optimistic; optimist** Los monjes irlandeses podrían tener una visión optimista de la naturaleza humana. -Irish monks could have an upbeat view of human nature.
3629	**gimnasia** f [xĩm.ˈna.sja]	**physical exercise** Deberá hacer gimnasia durante un mes. -You'll have to exercise for a month.
3630	**trofeo** m [tro.ˈfe.o]	**trophy** Él levantó el trofeo a lo alto. -He held the trophy up high.
3631	**conceder** vb [kõn.se.ˈðɛr]	**grant** No creo que la comisión deba conceder más preferencias. -I do not think the commission should grant any more preferences.
3632	**villano** m; adj [bi.ˈja.no]	**villain; villain** Al ladrón no le agrada la luz de la luna, al villano no le agrada un buen hombre. -A thief doesn't like the moonlight, a villain doesn't like a good man.
3633	**monumento** m [mo.nu.ˈmẽn̯.to]	**monument** Se erigió un inmenso monumento en honor al eminente filósofo. -An immense monument was erected in honor of the eminent philosopher.
3634	**obstáculo** m [oβs.ˈta.ku.lo]	**obstacle** Debemos superar ese obstáculo si queremos progresar finalmente. -We need to overcome that obstacle if we are finally to make progress.
3635	**reunido** adj [reu̯.ˈni.ðo]	**gathered** Necesitamos revaluar cada trozo de información que hayamos reunido. -We need to re-evaluate every piece of information we've collected.
3636	**reja** f [ˈre.xa]	**bar** Hay un montón de admiradores en la reja. -There's a bunch of fans out at the gate.
3637	**cuarentena**	**quarantine**

f
Como indudablemente habrá escuchado, está bajo cuarentena.
[kwa.rɛ̃n.ˈte.na]
-As you've doubtless heard, it's under quarantine.

3638 **gabinete** **cabinet**
m
Dicen que el gabinete renunciará.
[ga.βi.ˈnɛ.te]
-They say the cabinet will resign.

3639 **software** **software**
m
Los juegos de computadora son ejemplos de software multimedia porque
[sof.ˈtwa.re]
combinan texto, imágenes, animación, video y sonido.
-Computer games are examples of software multimedia because they
combine text, images, animation, video, and sound.

3640 **lema** **motto**
m
Este será su primer lema.
[ˈle.ma]
-This will be your first slogan.

3641 **cangrejo** **crab**
m
El cangrejo resultó ser muy bueno.
[kã̃ŋ.ˈgre.xo]
-The crab turned out to be very good.

3642 **porcentaje** **percentage**
m
El portugués es hablado por un porcentaje muy pequeño de la población.
[por.sɛ̃n.ˈta.xe]
-Portuguese is spoken by a very small percentage of the population.

3643 **cocodrilo** **crocodile**
m/f
Es imposible que un cocodrilo hubiera hecho esto.
[ko.ko.ˈðri.lo]
-There's no way a crocodile could do this.

3644 **llanto** **crying**
m
Mi experiencia ha sido mucho llanto.
[ˈʎã̃n.to]
-My experience has been a lot of crying.

3645 **compadre** **godfather, buddy (coll)**
m
Debería sepultarte aquí mismo, compadre.
[kõm.ˈpa.ðre]
-I ought to bury you right here, compadre.

3646 **invertir** **invest**
vb
Debemos invertir más energía política para lograr progresos importantes.
[ĩm.bɛr.ˈtir]
-We need to invest more of our political energy in order to make substantial
progress.

3647 **amoroso** **loving**
adj
Una relación es un vínculo amoroso entre dos personas.
[a.mo.ˈro.so]
-A relationship is a loving bond between two people.

3648 **contable** **accountant; accounting**
m/f; adj
Hace una referencia necesaria al marco jurídico contable existente.
[kõn.ˈta.βle]
-It makes the necessary reference to the existing accounting legal framework.

3649 **cardíaco** **cardiac**
adj
Se le diagnosticó al nacer un defecto cardíaco congénito.
[kar.ˈði.a.ko]
-He was diagnosed at birth with a congenital heart defect.

3650 **dieciséis** **sixteen**
num
En español seis no lleva acento, pero dieciséis sí.
[dje.si.ˈseɪ̯s]
-In Spanish six has no accent, but sixteen has one.

3651 **árbitro** **referee**
m/f
El árbitro sopló su silbato para terminar el partido.
[ˈar.βi.tro]
-The referee blew his whistle to end the match.

3652 **creativo** **creative; copywriter**

adj; m
[kre.a.ˈti.βo]

La crisis económica mundial hace más difícil financiar el sector creativo.
-The global economic crisis makes it more difficult to finance the creative sector.

3653 **arca**

f
[ˈar.ka]

ark

Si tuvieras un arca, tendrías dónde meterlos.
-If you had an ark, you'd have a place to put them all.

3654 **pasto**

m
[ˈpas.to]

pasture

¿Tenés una cortadora de pasto para prestarme?
-Do you have a lawnmower I could borrow?

3655 **arbusto**

m
[ar.ˈβus.to]

bush

Encontró varios fajos de billetes de mil dólares bajo un arbusto y los puso en su cesta.
-She found several stacks of thousand-dollar bills under a bush and put them in her basket.

3656 **esperma**

m
[es.ˈper.ma]

sperm

Estoy inyectando un solo esperma en tu óvulo.
-I am injecting a single sperm into your egg.

3657 **exagerar**

vb
[ek.sa.xe.ˈrar]

exaggerate

Parece tener una tendencia a exagerar las cosas.
-He seems to have a tendency to exaggerate things.

3658 **bordar**

vb
[bor.ˈðar]

embroider, do excellently (coll)

Ni siquiera sabes cómo bordar.
-You don't even know how to embroider.

3659 **ahogar(se)**

vb
[a.o.ˈɣar]

drown

Unos van al bar a pasárselo bien y otros a ahogar sus penas.
-Some go to a bar to have a good time and others to drown their sorrows.

3660 **subterráneo**

adj
[suβ.te.ˈra.ne.o]

underground

El aparcamiento privado subterráneo ofrece un servicio eficiente y complementario de aparcacoches.
-The private underground car park offers an efficient, complimentary valet parking service.

3661 **masivo**

adj
[ma.ˈsi.βo]

massive

El rápido y masivo crecimiento y desarrollo urbano también han dado lugar a importantes problemas ambientales y de salud.
-The rapid and massive urban growth and development have also given rise to significant environmental and health problems.

3662 **legar**

vb
[le.ˈɣar]

bequeath

La intolerancia estaba convirtiéndose velozmente en la más siniestra ideología que el siglo XX pueda legar al futuro.
-Intolerance was rapidly emerging as the most sinister ideology that the twentieth century would bequeath to the future.

3663 **buzón**

m
[bu.ˈsõn]

mailbox

Lamento no haber venido al buzón últimamente.
-Sorry I haven't made it to the mailbox lately.

3664 **fusil**

m
[fu.ˈsil]

rifle

Había un fusil saliendo de cada ventana.
-Every window had a rifle sticking out of it.

3665 **sutil**

adj
[su.ˈtil]

subtle

Hay una sutil diferencia entre las dos palabras.
-There is a subtle difference between the two words.

3666 incorrecto — **incorrect**

adj
[ĩŋ.ko.ˈrek̚.to]

Estuvimos aterradoramente cerca de la órbita del sol porque despegamos desde el lado incorrecto de Mercurio.
-We came fearfully close to the Sun's orbit because we launched from the wrong side of Mercury.

3667 aburrimiento — **boredom**

m
[a.βu.ri.ˈmjẽn̯.to]

Cualquiera moriría de aburrimiento leyendo tu lista.
-A person will die of boredom by reading your list.

3668 yanqui — **Yankee (coll); Yankee (coll)**

m/f; adj
[ˈɟjãŋ.ki]

Avísame cuando se aburra, yanqui.
-Let me know when you get bored, yank.

3669 acostar(se) — **lay down**

vb
[a.kos.ˈtar]

Mi madre estaba tan cansada que se fue a acostar temprano. -My mum was so tired that she went to bed early.

3670 jet — **jet**

m
[ˈxɛt]

Tomó un jet privado esta tarde.
-He took a private jet out this afternoon.

3671 capataz — **foreperson**

m/f
[ka.ˈpa.tas]

Su padre era el capataz de la finca.
-His father was the farm foreman.

3672 sastre — **tailor**

m/f
[ˈsas.tre]

Hace mucho tiempo vivía un sastre que tenía tres hijos pero solo una cabra.
-A long time ago, there lived a tailor who had three sons, but only one goat.

3673 África — **Africa**

f
[ˈa.fri.ka]

En África hay importantes diferencias subregionales y nacionales.
-Within Africa, there are significant subregional and country differences.

3674 trucar — **rig**

vb
[tru.ˈkar]

¿Puedes trucar una luz de emergencia para amplificar su potencia?
-Can you rig an emergency light to amplify its output?

3675 injusticia — **injustice**

f
[ĩŋ.xus.ˈti.sja]

Simplemente están equivocados y es una injusticia.
-You're just wrong and it's an injustice.

3676 penal — **criminal; prison**

adj; m
[pe.ˈnal]

Se inició una investigación penal en relación con este incidente.
-A criminal inquest was instituted regarding this incident.

3677 sincronizar — **synchronize**

vb
[sĩŋ.kro.ni.ˈsar]

Quieren comparar notas y sincronizar relojes.
-They want to compare notes and synchronize watches.

3678 subastar — **auction**

vb
[su.βas.ˈtar]

Una de las primeras medidas fue subastar dos licencias de telecomunicaciones móviles.
-One of the first steps was to auction two mobile telecommunications licenses.

3679 nombrar — **name**

vb
[nõm.ˈbrar]

Su educación fue tan básica que ni siquiera podía nombrar los ocho planetas de nuestro sistema solar.
-Her education was so minimal that she could not even name the eight planets of our Solar System.

3680 inofensivo — **harmless**

adj
[i.no.ˈfẽn.ˈsi.βo]

Mírale, ahí sentado, pretendiendo ser inofensivo.
-Look at him sitting there, pretending to be so harmless.

3681 **hostil**

adj
[os.ˈtil]

hostile

Pareces ponerte muy hostil y agresiva.
-You seem to get very hostile and aggressive.

3682 **definición**

f
[de.fi.ni.ˈsjõn]

definition

Sugirió que se modificara y aclarara la definición.
-He suggested that the definition should be changed and clarified.

3683 **táctica**

f
[ˈtak̚.ti.ka]

tactic

Su táctica fácilmente podría tener un efecto contraproducente.
-His tactic could easily backfire.

3684 **portal**

m
[por.ˈtal]

portal

Somos un portal de reservas de hotel que ofrece reservas en tiempo real.
-We are a hotel reservation portal offering real-time reservations.

3685 **moreno**

adj
[mo.ˈre.no]

dark skinned, brunette

Viendo lo moreno que estás, parece que has pasado la mayor parte de tus vacaciones en la playa.
-Judging by that great tan, it looks like you spent most of your vacation on the beach.

3686 **competición**

f
[kõm.pɛ.ti.ˈsjõn]

competition

La competición en sí misma no es ni buena ni mala.
-Competition is neither good nor evil in itself.

3687 **langosta**

f
[lãŋ.ˈgos.ta]

lobster

¿Comes langosta en Navidad? ¿En serio?
-Do you eat lobster for Christmas? Are you serious?

3688 **olla**

f
[ˈo.ja]

pot

La olla roja está hirviendo.
-The red pot is boiling over.

3689 **tolerar**

vb
[to.lɛ.ˈrar]

tolerate

No deberíamos tolerar más esa parálisis.
-We should not tolerate this paralysis any longer.

3690 **diseñar**

vb
[di.se.ˈɲar]

design

Estas observaciones ayudarán a diseñar el próximo programa mundial.
-These observations will assist in the design of the next Global Programme.

3691 **legítimo**

adj
[le.ˈxi.ti.mo]

legitimate

¿Cuál príncipe es el legítimo sucesor al trono?
-Which prince is the legitimate heir to the throne?

3692 **Atlántico**

m
[aṱ.ˈlãn̪.ti.ko]

Atlantic

El Canal de Panamá conecta el Atlántico con el Pacífico.
-The Panama Canal connects the Atlantic with the Pacific.

3693 **ingenio**

m
[ĩŋ.ˈxe.njo]

wit, ingenuity

La naturaleza la invistió con ingenio y belleza.
-Nature endowed her with wit and beauty.

3694 **recomendación**

f
[re.ko.mẽn̪.da.ˈsjõn]

recommendation

La recomendación de mi jefe fue sumamente importante.
-The recommendation from my boss made all the difference.

3695 **decepción**

disappointment

f
[de.sɛp.ˈsjõn]
Ella indicó su decepción respecto a este problema.
-She has indicated her disappointment with regard to this problem.

3696 **librería** **bookshop**
f
[li.βɾɛ.ˈri.a]
Jim fue a la librería este fin de semana.
-Jim went to the bookstore this weekend.

3697 **variar** **vary**
vb
[ba.ˈrjar]
Cada uno de estos puede variar según el país.
-Each of these can vary by country.

3698 **racista** **racist person; racist**
m/f; adj
[ra.ˈsis.ta]
Recordemos que nadie nace siendo racista.
-Let us remember that no one is born a racist.

3699 **sustancia** **substance**
f
[sus.ˈtãn.sja]
El monóxido de carbono es una sustancia venenosa formada a partir de la combustión incompleta de compuestos de carbono.
-Carbon monoxide is a poisonous substance formed by the incomplete combustion of carbon compounds.

3700 **hongo** **fungus**
m
[ˈõŋ.go]
Encontramos un hongo con un nombre raro.
-We found a fungus called something strange.

3701 **ambicioso** **ambitious; greedy**
adj; m
[ãm.bi.ˈsjo.so]
Jim es un joven ambicioso.
-Jim is an ambitious young man.

3702 **discreto** **discreet**
adj
[dis.ˈkɾɛ.to]
Ella siempre ha actuado de forma tan eficaz como discreta.
-She has always acted in a manner both effective and discreet.

3703 **protagonista** **protagonist**
m/f
[pro.ta.ɣo.ˈnis.ta]
Es mucho mejor con nuestra nueva protagonista.
-It's so much better with our new lead.

3704 **aparición** **appearance, apparition**
f
[a.pa.ri.ˈsjõn]
Hicieron una especie de aparición sorpresa.
-They kind of made an impromptu appearance.

3705 **reglamento** **regulation**
m
[re.ɣla.ˈmẽn.to]
No será posible aplicar este reglamento rápidamente.
-It will not be possible to implement this regulation quickly.

3706 **conserje** **janitor**
m/f
[kõn.ˈsɛr.xe]
Era conserje en el hotel.
-I was a concierge at the hotel.

3707 **homenaje** **tribute**
m
[o.me.ˈna.xe]
Quisiera rendir un homenaje especial al embajador.
-I should like to pay particular tribute to the ambassador.

3708 **ejecutar** **implement, execute**
vb
[e.xe.ku.ˈtar]
Serán necesarios más recursos humanos para ejecutar el programa.
-Additional human resources will be required to implement the programme.

3709 **morfina** **morphine**
f
[mor.ˈfi.na]
A los médicos les queda poca morfina.
-The doctors are running short of morphine.

3710 **juvenil** **youth**

adj
[xu.βe.ˈnil]
¿Hay algún albergue juvenil cerca de aquí?
-Is there a youth hostel near here?

3711 traslado — **move**

m
[traṣ.ˈla.ðo]
La estación de policía para mujeres organizó su traslado a un refugio municipal.
-The women's police station organized her transfer to the municipal shelter.

3712 ejemplar — **model; exemplary**

m; adj
[e.xẽm.ˈplar]
No logrará esto si no consigue mantener una posición ejemplar.
-It will not achieve this if it falls short of maintaining an exemplary position.

3713 solicitar — **request**

vb
[so.li.si.ˈtar]
¿Qué certificados y trámites hacen falta para solicitar un pasaporte para el extranjero?
-What certificates and paperwork are needed to apply for a passport?

3714 ganso — **goose; foolish (ES) (coll)**

m; adj
[ˈgãn.so]
El patito estaría muy contento ahora, si solo el ganso lo tolerara.
-The duckling would be very happy by now, if only the goose would put up with him.

3715 trompeta — **trumpet**

f
[trõm.ˈpɛ.ta]
Estaré aquí mientras tocas esa trompeta.
-I'll be here while you're playing that trumpet.

3716 mostaza — **mustard**

f
[mos.ˈta.sa]
Quiero dos perritos calientes con mostaza y ketchup.
-I'll have two hot dogs with mustard and ketchup.

3717 picante — **spicy; spiciness**

adj; m
[pi.ˈkã̠.te]
Me gustaría poder comer algo picante.
-I wish I could get something spicy to eat.

3718 ingenuo — **ingenuous**

adj
[ĩŋ.ˈxe.nwo]
Él es joven, ingenuo y sin experiencia.
-He's young, naive and inexperienced.

3719 deportivo — **sports**

adj
[de.por.ˈti.βo]
Empecé como periodista deportivo hace años.
-I started as a sports reporter years ago.

3720 maniobra — **maneuver**

f
[ma.ˈnjo.βra]
Durante la maniobra, estarán completamente solos.
-During the maneuver, they are entirely on their own.

3721 hemorragia — **hemorrhage**

f
[e.mo.ˈra.xja]
Iré a por una toalla para parar la hemorragia.
-I'll get a towel to stop the bleeding.

3722 humedad — **moisture**

f
[u.me.ˈðað]
Hay mucha humedad en el aire.
-There's a lot of moisture in the air.

3723 banca — **banking**

f
[ˈbãŋ.ka]
La supervisión de la banca extraterritorial continuó con inspecciones sobre el terreno.
-The supervision of offshore banking was continuing with on-site inspections.

3724 notable — **notable; dignitary**

adj; m
[no.ˈta.βle]
La política de empleo es una excepción notable.
-A notable exception was employment policy.

3725	**múltiple**	**multiple**
	adj	Se trata de un examen de respuestas libres en lugar de selección múltiple.
	[ˈmu̪.tipʼ.le]	-It is a free response exam instead of multiple choice.
3726	**acera**	**sidewalk**
	f	Encontrará sus cosas en la acera.
	[a.ˈsɛ.ra]	-He'll find his things on the sidewalk.
3727	**distracción**	**distraction**
	f	Otra distracción es exagerar la amenaza de la inflación.
	[dis.trak.ˈsjõn]	-Another distraction is exaggerating the threat of inflation.
3728	**estafa**	**scam**
	f	Estáis todos detenidos por robo y estafa.
	[ɛs.ˈta.fa]	-You are all arrested for theft and fraud.
3729	**tesis**	**thesis**
	f	Me gustaría retomar su tesis sobre la función indicativa.
	[ˈte.sis]	-I would like to refer again to her thesis of the signal function.
3730	**pureza**	**purity**
	f	No obstante, el nacionalismo no exigía necesariamente la pureza étnica.
	[pu.ˈre.sa]	-However, nationalism did not necessarily require ethnic purity.
3731	**noventa**	**ninety**
	num	Todo empezó a principios de los noventa.
	[no.ˈβẽn̪.ta]	-It started at the beginning of the nineties.
3732	**monasterio**	**monastery**
	m	Todos los del monasterio se ponen celosos.
	[mo.nas.ˈtɛ.rjo]	-Everybody back at the monastery gets jealous.
3733	**húmedo**	**wet**
	adj	Un clima húmedo es característico en la península.
	[ˈu.me.ðo]	-A humid climate is characteristic of the peninsula.
3734	**burbuja**	**bubble**
	f	Una nueva burbuja reemplazará la anterior.
	[bur.ˈβu.xa]	-A new bubble will replace the old one.
3735	**zumo**	**juice**
	m	Mi hermanastra se acabó el zumo de arándano rojo que quedaba.
	[ˈsu.mo]	-My stepsister finished the last of the cranberry juice.
3736	**empresario**	**businessman**
	m	El empresario se encarga siempre del proceso.
	[ẽm.pre.ˈsa.rjo]	-The businessman is always in charge of the process.
3737	**quebrar**	**break**
	vb	No puedes hacer una tortilla sin quebrar huevos.
	[ke.ˈβrar]	-You can't make an omelet without breaking eggs.
3738	**portar(se)**	**carry; behave**
	vb; vbr	Cada persona debe portar una cinta roja en su muñeca.
	[por.ˈtar]	-Each person should wear a red ribbon around their wrist.
3739	**sacrificar**	**sacrifice**
	vb	No quiero sacrificar a nuestro hijo.
	[sa.kri.fi.ˈkar]	-I don't want to sacrifice our son.
3740	**testificar**	**testify**
	vb	De las víctimas, 250 aceptaron testificar y recibieron ayuda.
	[tɛs.ti.fi.ˈkar]	-Of the victims, 250 agreed to testify and receive assistance.

3741	**margarita**	**daisy**

margarita — **daisy**
f
[mar.ɣa.ˈri.ta]
Has puesto mucha mezcla margarita ahí.
-You put a lot of margarita mix in there.

3742 **himno** — **hymn**
m
[ˈĩm.no]
Señoras y señores, el himno de nuestra corporación.
-Ladies and gentlemen, our corporate anthem.

3743 **tocino** — **bacon**
m
[to.ˈsi.no]
Quiero salchicha y algo de tocino crujiente.
-I want sausage and some good crisp bacon.

3744 **enojo** — **anger**
m
[e.ˈno.xo]
El té de camomila es excelente para el enojo reprimido.
-Chamomile tea is excellent for repressed anger.

3745 **panza** — **belly**
f
[ˈpãn.sa]
El gato está revolcándose, mostrándonos su panza.
-The cat is rolling over, showing us its belly.

3746 **cólera** — **anger**
f
[ˈko.lɛ.ra]
El cólera no es común en Japón.
-Cholera is uncommon in Japan.

3747 **ostra** — **oyster**
f
[ˈos.tra]
La ostra esta protegida sobre un soporte de concha.
-The oyster is secured on a shell stand.

3748 **humillación** — **humiliation**
f
[u.mi.ja.ˈsjõn]
No debieras someterte a esta humillación.
-You shouldn't put up with such humiliation.

3749 **presentir** — **have a feeling**
vb
[pre.sẽn.ˈtir]
A mi edad puedes presentir esas cosas.
-At my age, you can sense these things.

3750 **flora** — **flora**
f
[ˈflo.ra]
Escribió varios libros sobre la flora del subcontinente.
-She'd written several books on the flora of the subcontinent.

3751 **respectar** — **concern**
vb
[rɛs.pekˈ.ˈtar]
Urgimos a todas las partes a respectar sus compromisos.
-We urge all the parties to respect their commitments.

3752 **medicación** — **medication**
f
[me.ði.ka.ˈsjõn]
Aunque sufría dolores, no recibió medicación alguna.
-Although he suffered pain, he did not receive any medication.

3753 **lancha** — **boat**
f
[ˈlãn.tʃa]
Debe de tener una lancha esperándole.
-He's got to have a boat waiting for him.

3754 **uva** — **grape**
f
[ˈu.βa]
Jim compró tres botellas de jugo de uva.
-Jim bought three bottles of grape juice.

3755 **experimentar** — **experiment**
vb
[ɛks.pɛ.ri.mẽn.ˈtar]
Al usar auriculares, los jugadores podrán experimentar todas las partes emocionantes y sorprendentes.
-By wearing headphones, players will experience all the really surprising and moving parts.

3756 **huérfano** — **orphaned; orphan**

adj; m   Nunca me ha molestado ser huérfano.
['wɛr.fa.no]   -I never got upset for being an orphan.

3757 escalar   **climb**

vb   Me gustaría escalar una colina alta.
[ɛs.ka.'lar]   -I would like to climb a tall hill.

3758 excitar   **excite**

vb   Quiero excitar a la muchedumbre.
[ɛk.si.'tar]   -I want to excite the crowd.

3759 muda   **change**

f   La naturaleza no está muda en este conflicto.
['mu.ða]   -Nature is not mute in this conflict.

3760 terrestre   **land; terrestrial**

adj; m   Nada dice no terrestre como un destornillador sónico.
[tɛ.'rɛs.tre]   -Nothing says non-terrestrial like a sonic screwdriver.

3761 género   **gender**

m   El género también da forma al desarrollo de la personalidad.
['xe.nɛ.ro]   -Gender also shapes the development of the self.

3762 afrontar   **face**

vb   Deseamos afrontar estas cuestiones mediante el diálogo.
[a.frõn̪.'tar]   -Our wish is to address these issues through dialogue.

3763 satisfecho   **satisfied**

adj   El maestro estaba lejos de estar satisfecho con el resultado.
[sa.tis.'fe.tʃo]   -The teacher was far from satisfied with the result.

3764 grúa   **crane**

f   Nos secuestró y voló la grúa.
['grwa]   -He kidnapped us and he blew up the crane.

3765 flujo   **flow**

m   Detén el flujo de sangre de la herida.
['flu.xo]   -Stop the flow of blood from the wound.

3766 internar   **send in**

vb   Quiere internar a Jim en un hospital.
[ĩn̪.tɛr.'nar]   -He wants to place Jim in the hospital.

3767 factor   **factor**

m   Un nuevo factor que influye en las reservas de agua es la subida de la
[fak.'tor]   temperatura global.
    -One new factor influencing water supplies is rising global temperature.

3768 complacer   **please**

vb   Aprende rápido y está ansioso por complacer.
[kõm.pla.'sɛr]   -He's quick to learn and eager to please.

3769 tramposo   **trickster; dishonest**

m; adj   No es ilegal engañar a un tramposo.
[trãm.'po.so]   -It's not illegal to cheat a cheater.

3770 motocicleta   **motorcycle**

f   Podría recogerte con mi motocicleta.
[mo.to.si.'klɛ.ta]   -I could pick you up on my bike.

3771 hostia   **blow (coll); damn (coll)**

f; int   Dice que necesitamos una hostia consagrada.
['os.tja]   -He says that we need a consecrated host.

3772	**vulnerable**		**vulnerable**
	adj		Me sentí tan vulnerable como una anciana.
	[bul.nɛ.ˈra.βle]		-I felt as vulnerable as an old lady.
3773	**cooperar**		**cooperate**
	vb[ko.o.pɛ.ˈrar]		Sin embargo, ninguno de ellos quiso cooperar. -However, none of them agreed to cooperate.
3774	**rastrear**		**track**
	vb		No puedo rastrear más que eso.
	[ras.tre.ˈar]		-I can't track any further than that.
3775	**intuición**		**intuition**
	f		Este nivel de intuición es muy importante.
	[ĩn.twi.ˈsjõn]		-This level of intuition is very important.
3776	**chispa**		**spark**
	f		Convertiremos esta chispa en un fuego enfurecido.
	[ˈtʃis.pa]		-We'll turn this spark into a raging fire.
3777	**congresista**		**delegate**
	m/f		El congresista se bebió una taza de café.
	[kõn.gre.ˈsis.ta]		-The congressman drank a cup of coffee.
3778	**aislamiento**		**isolation**
	m		En las ciudades tienen aislamiento especial.
	[ai̯s.la.ˈmjẽn.to]		-In the cities, they have special insulation.
3779	**intervención**		**intervention**
	f		Pondremos fin a la conducta no profesional mediante la prevención y la intervención efectiva.
	[ĩn.tɛr.βẽn.ˈsjõn]		-We will eliminate non-professional conduct through prevention and effective intervention.
3780	**bloquear**		**block**
	vb		La próxima vez, trate de bloquear con su espinilla.
	[blo.ke.ˈar]		-Next time, try blocking with your shin.
3781	**tos**		**cough**
	f		Su hijo presenta una tos perruna.
	[ˈtos]		-Your child's cough has a barking sound.
3782	**cortés**		**courteous**
	adj		Estoy físicamente incapacitado para ser cortés.
	[kor.ˈtes]		-I'm physically incapable of being polite.
3783	**tinieblas**		**darkness**
	fpl		Desata todos tus poderes de las tinieblas.
	[ti.ˈnje.βlas]		-Unleash all your powers of darkness.
3784	**simpatía**		**friendliness**
	f		Su simpatía atraía a las personas, como un imán.
	[sĩm.pa.ˈti.a]		-His friendliness just drew people to him, like a magnet.
3785	**afirmar**		**affirm, maintain**
	vb		Quisiera afirmar que nuestra prioridad sigue siendo el desarme nuclear.
	[a.fir.ˈmar]		-I wish to affirm that our priority remains nuclear disarmament.
3786	**tacto**		**touch**
	m		Tienes mucho que aprender sobre el tacto.
	[ˈtak̚.to]		-You've got a lot to learn about tact.
3787	**específico**		**specific**

adj
[ɛs.pe.ˈsi.fi.ko]

El uso específico del producto debe describirse detalladamente.
-The specific use of the product must be described in detail.

3788 **síndrome**

m
[ˈsĩn.dro.me]

syndrome

Me duelen la muñeca y el antebrazo, pienso que puedo estar padeciendo del síndrome del túnel carpiano. -My wrist and forearm hurt, I think I might be suffering from carpal tunnel syndrome.

3789 **legión**

f
[le.ˈxjõn]

legion

Se alistó en la legión.
-He enlisted in the legion.

3790 **redondo**

adj
[re.ˈðõn̪.do]

round

Dices que había un árbol redondo.
-You say there was a round tree.

3791 **fresa**

f
[ˈfre.sa]

strawberry

Vale, tenemos fresa y chocolate.
-All right, we have strawberry and chocolate.

3792 **asesor**

m; adj
[a.se.ˈsor]

adviser; advisory

Previamente trabajó como asesor especial del ministro.
-Prior to that, he worked as a special adviser to the minister.

3793 **canasta**

f
[ka.ˈnas.ta]

basket

Jim estaba él sólito bajo la canasta.
-Jim was all by himself right under the basket.

3794 **radical**

adj; m/f
[ra.ði.ˈkal]

radical; radical person

Tiene una idea radical para su plato gurmé.
-He has a radical idea for their gourmet dish.

3795 **electrónico**

adj
[e.lek̚.ˈtro.ni.ko]

electronic

Esto es un sensor electrónico de temperatura de la caldera y del tanque de proceso.
-This is an electronic sensor temperature for the boiler and process tank.

3796 **manifestación**

f
[ma.ni.fɛs.ta.ˈsjõn]

manifestation

Conocían el concepto de manifestación pacífica.
-They were aware of the concept of peaceful demonstration.

3797 **veterinario**

m
[bɛ.tɛ.ri.ˈna.rjo]

veterinarian

Mi veterinario no le da de comer a su perro comida de perros comercial.
-My vet won't feed his dog commercial dog food.

3798 **promoción**

f
[pro.mo.ˈsjõn]

promotion

Por favor, compruebe las condiciones y restricciones de cada promoción.
-Please check the conditions and restrictions of each promotion.

3799 **oponente**

m/f; adj
[o.po.ˈnẽn̪.te]

opponent; opposing

También puede lanzar cera contra su oponente para paralizarle.
-He can also throw wax at his opponent to stop them from moving.

3800 **afirmativo**

adj; int
[a.fir.ma.ˈti.βo]

affirmative; sure

Respondemos la pregunta en sentido afirmativo.
-We answer that question in the affirmative.

3801 **pasado**

adj; m
[pa.ˈsa.ðo]

past; past

¿Qué le ha pasado a tu ojo?
-What's happened to your eye?

3802 **suspender**

vb
[sus.pẽn̪.ˈdɛr]

hang, cancel, fail

Alemania no está preparada para suspender estos controles.
-Germany is not prepared to suspend these checks.

3803 **salmón** — **salmon**
m
[sal.ˈmõn]
Parecían dos osos disputándose un salmón.
-Sounded like two grizzlies fighting over a salmon.

3804 **fraternidad** — **fraternity**
f
[fra.tɛr.ni.ˈðað]
Debes pertenecer a una fraternidad para competir.
-You have to be in a fraternity to compete.

3805 **sensibilidad** — **sensitivity**
f
[sɛ̃n.si.βi.li.ˈðað]
En mi materia siempre demostró una gran sensibilidad.
-She's always shown great sensibility in my subject.

3806 **mermelada** — **jam**
f
[mɛr.me.ˈla.ða]
Esta es mi mermelada casera.
-This is my homemade jam.

3807 **puñetazo** — **punch**
m
[pu.ɲɛ.ˈta.so]
Fue noqueado de un puñetazo en el primer asalto.
-He was knocked out by a punch in the first round.

3808 **pimienta** — **pepper**
f
[pi.ˈmjɛ̃n̪.ta]
Agregue sal y pimienta al gusto.
-Add salt and pepper to taste.

3809 **aislar** — **isolate**
vb
[ai̯s̪.ˈlar]
Ese tipo de opinión solo logrará aislar a los hijos únicos de esta sociedad.
-That kind of judgment will just seclude only children in society.

3810 **dorar** — **brown**
vb
[do.ˈrar]
Yo lo doro todo entero.
-I brown the whole thing.

3811 **suéter** — **sweater**
m
[ˈswɛ.tɛr]
Ella le tejió un suéter por su cumpleaños.
-She knit him a sweater for his birthday.

3812 **búfalo** — **buffalo**
m
[ˈbu.fa.lo]
Se hicieron herramientas con huesos de búfalo.
-Buffalo bones were made into tools.

3813 **resaca** — **hangover**
f
[re.ˈsa.ka]
Pero siento que tengo una resaca terrible.
-But I feel that I have a terrible hangover.

3814 **tregua** — **truce**
f
[ˈtre.ɣwa]
Dijo que quería ofrecerme una tregua.
-He said he wanted to offer me a truce.

3815 **vanidad** — **vanity**
f
[ba.ni.ˈðað]
Una persona puede ser orgullosa sin ser vanidosa. El orgullo está más relacionado con nuestra opinión de nosotros mismos, la vanidad con lo que querríamos que los otros pensaran de nosotros.
-A person may be proud without being vain. Pride relates more to our opinion of ourselves, vanity to what we would have others think of us.

3816 **vino** — **wine**
m
[ˈbi.no]
También adoptamos el añadir azúcar al vino.
-We also adopted the addition of sugar to wine.

3817 **leve** — **mild**
adj
[ˈle.βe]
La mayoría de las veces, un esguince leve sanará en 7 a 10 días. -Most of the time, a mild sprain will heal in 7-10 days.

3818 dieciocho   **eighteen**

num

[dje.ˈsjo.tʃo]

Ana ha tenido el mismo novio desde que tenía dieciocho años.
-Ana has had the same boyfriend since she was eighteen.

3819 blando   **soft**

adj

[ˈblã̠n.do]

Temía que te estuvieses volviendo blando.
-I was afraid you might be getting soft.

3820 tumor   **tumor**

m

[tu.ˈmor]

Para un tumor así necesita esteroides.
-For a tumor like this, he needs steroids.

3821 quinientos   **five hundred**

num

[ki.ˈnjẽ̠n.tos]

Bueno, puedo darle quinientos cincuenta pesos.
-Well, I can give you five hundred and fifty pesos.

3822 flanco   **flank**

m

[ˈflã̠n.ko]

El flanco de tu ejército es vulnerable.
-Your army's flank is vulnerable.

3823 imitar   **imitate**

vb

[i.mi.ˈtar]

Solías imitar a personajes del libro.
-You used to imitate characters from the book.

3824 viajero   **traveler**

m

[bja.ˈxɛ.ro]

Nuestro hogar siempre está abierto para el viajero cansado.
-Our home is always open to the weary traveler.

3825 anotar   **write down**

vb

[a.no.ˈtar]

Déjeme anotar la información para usted.
-Let me write down the information for you.

3826 carnaval   **carnival**

m

[kar.na.ˈβal]

Sería ingenuo subestimar los efectos de este carnaval.
-It would be naive to underestimate the effects of this carnival.

3827 holandés   **Dutch; Dutch person**

adj; m

[o.lã̠n.ˈdes]

Un inglés, un belga y un holandés entran a un bar y se sientan en el mostrador. El cantinero dice, "espera, ¿esto es una broma o qué?"
-An Englishman, a Belgian and a Dutchman enter a pub and sit down at the counter. Says the barkeeper, "Wait a minute, is this a joke or what?"

3828 afeitar(se)   **shave**

vb

[a.fei̯.ˈtar]

Voy a afeitar el resto.
-I will shave the rest.

3829 crucial   **crucial**

adj

[kru.ˈsjal]

Es crucial que actúen con integridad.
-It is crucial that they act with integrity.

3830 exitoso   **successful**

adj

[ɛk.si.ˈto.so]

Era un escritor exitoso en una revista prominente.
-He was a successful writer at a prominent magazine.

3831 jurisdicción   **jurisdiction**

f

[xu.riş.ðik.ˈsjõn]

En ese caso, el estado tendría jurisdicción exclusiva.
-In such a case, the state would have exclusive jurisdiction.

3832 comprador   **buyer**

m

[kõm.pra.ˈðor]

Todavía no han encontrado comprador para esa casa. -They still haven't found a buyer for that house.

3833 dañar   **damage**

	vb	Podríamos dañar algo y podrías demandarnos.
	[da.ˈɲar]	-We might damage something and you could sue us.
3834	**escoba**	**broom**
	f	Coge una escoba y ayúdanos a limpiar.
	[ɛs.ˈko.βa]	-Grab a broom and help us clean.
3835	**extensión**	**extension**
	f	Tal extensión requeriría la autorización específica de la asamblea general.
	[ɛks.tẽn.ˈsjõn]	-Such an extension would require the specific authorization of the general assembly.
3836	**comportarse**	**behave**
	vbr	No puedo comportarme como los demás.
	[kõm.por.ˈtar.se]	-I can't behave like everybody else.
3837	**derribar**	**knock down**
	vb	Tenemos pruebas de que intentó derribar dos aviones comerciales.
	[dɛ.ri.ˈβar]	-We have proof that he tried to bring down two commercial airliners.
3838	**calefacción**	**heating**
	f	El proyecto tiene por objeto promover modelos de negocios para aumentar la introducción y expansión de aplicaciones con fines de calefacción y refrigeración basadas en la energía solar en determinados sectores industriales de la India.
	[ka.le.fak.ˈsjõn]	-The project aims to promote business models for increasing penetration and scaling up of solar energy-based heating and cooling applications in selected industrial sectors in India.
3839	**devoción**	**devotion**
	f	Estamos siendo testigos de escenas increíbles sin precedentes de devoción silenciosa.
	[de.βo.ˈsjõn]	-We are witnessing incredible, unprecedented scenes of quiet devotion.
3840	**remolcar**	**tow**
	vb	Quieres eso para remolcar barcos muy rápido.
	[re.mol.ˈkar]	-You want that to tow boats very fast.
3841	**peculiar**	**peculiar**
	adj	Este dinero tiene un olor peculiar.
	[pe.ku.ˈljar]	-This money has a peculiar smell to it.
3842	**colaboración**	**collaboration**
	f	Tu colaboración es importante para todos nosotros.
	[ko.la.βo.ra.ˈsjõn]	-Your collaboration is important for all of us.
3843	**ramo**	**bouquet**
	m	Compré un precioso ramo de amapolas.
	[ˈra.mo]	-I bought a beautiful bouquet of poppies.
3844	**aguante**	**endurance**
	m	No va a tener el aguante.
	[a.ˈɣwãn̪.te]	-He's not going to have the endurance.
3845	**proposición**	**proposition**
	f	Ana, nunca he recibido una proposición tan halagadora, pero no va a funcionar.
	[pro.po.si.ˈsjõn]	-Ana, I've never received a more flattering proposal, but it won't work out.
3846	**pino**	**pine**
	m	Solía haber un gran pino en frente de mi casa.
	[ˈpi.no]	-There used to be a big pine tree in front of my house.
3847	**canadiense**	**Canadian; Canadian person**

adj; m/f
[ka.na.ˈðj̃ẽn.se]

El canadiense taló el árbol con un hacha.
-The Canadian chopped down the tree with an ax.

3848 **mención**

mention

f
[mɛ̃n.ˈsjõn]

La mera mención de la sangre me hace estremecer.
-The mere mention of blood makes me shudder.

3849 **aceptable**

acceptable

adj
[a.sep̚.ˈta.βle]

¿Sería esto aceptable para ti?
-Would this be acceptable to you?

3850 **partícula**

particle

f
[par.ˈti.ku.la]

Ana estaba trabajando para aislar una nueva partícula.
-Ana was working to isolate a new particle.

3851 **genética**

genetics

f
[xe.ˈnɛ.ti.ka]

Una prueba genética puede diagnosticar esta enfermedad.
-Genetic testing can diagnose this disease.

3852 **elevador**

elevator

m
[e.le.βa.ˈðor]

La viste en el elevador al bajar.
-You saw her in the elevator on the way down.

3853 **presionar**

press

vb
[pre.sjo.ˈnar]

No voy a presionar ningún botón.
-I'm not going to press any buttons.

3854 **confirmación**

confirmation

f
[kõɱ.fir.ma.ˈsjõn]

Encontrarás los detalles en el e-mail de confirmación.
-You will find the details in the confirmation email.

3855 **comparación**

comparison

f
[kõm.pa.ra.ˈsjõn]

Los edificios son pequeños en comparación con los rascacielos de Nueva York.
-The buildings are small in comparison to the skyscrapers in New York.

3856 **diagnóstico**

diagnosis; diagnostic

m; adj
[djaɣ.ˈnos.ti.ko]

Mi diagnóstico no estaba claro.
-My diagnosis was not clear.

3857 **trama**

plot

f
[ˈtra.ma]

Tu trama también tiene agujeros.
-Your plot has holes in it, too.

3858 **látigo**

whip

m
[ˈla.ti.ɣo]

Nos interrogaron con el látigo de púas.
-We were interrogated with the barbed whip.

3859 **complicación**

complication

f
[kõm.pli.ka.ˈsjõn]

La principal complicación es lesionarse al caminar dormido.
-The main complication is getting injured while sleepwalking.

3860 **inmenso**

immense

adj
[ĩm.ˈmɛ̃n.so]

Realmente controla su inmenso peso muy bien.
-It really does control its immense weight very well.

3861 **hoguera**

bonfire

f
[o.ˈɣɛ.ra]

Debería arder en la hoguera por amarte.
-I ought to be burned at the stake for loving you.

3862 **domicilio**

address

m
[do.mi.ˈsi.ljo]

La empresa trasladó su domicilio empresarial a Hong Kong con fines tributarios.
-The company moved its corporate domicile to Hong Kong for tax purposes.

3863	**expreso**	**express; express**
	adj; m	He retenido al expreso durante cuatro minutos.
	[ɛks.ˈpre.so]	-I've held the down express for four minutes.
3864	**pelirrojo**	**redheaded; redhead**
	adj; m	Espero que ese pequeño y mimado pelirrojo te esté tratando bien.
	[pe.li.ˈro.xo]	-I hope that spoiled little ginger's treating you all right.
3865	**coser**	**sew**
	vb	Quiero levantarme temprano para coser su vestido de entierro.
	[ko.ˈsɛr]	-I want to get up early and sew her burial dress.
3866	**crítica**	**review**
	f	Ella es una crítica muy severa.
	[ˈkri.ti.ka]	-She is a harsh critic.
3867	**honra**	**honor**
	f	Nadie será objeto de injerencias arbitrarias en su vida privada, su familia, su
	[ˈõn.ra]	domicilio o su correspondencia, ni de ataques a su honra o a su reputación.
		-No one shall be subjected to arbitrary interference with his privacy, family, home or correspondence, nor to attacks upon his honor and reputation.
3868	**consumo**	**consumption**
	m	El consumo de arroz en Japón está bajando.
	[kõn.ˈsu.mo]	-Japan's consumption of rice is decreasing.
3869	**histérico**	**hysterical; hysteric**
	adj; m	Tenemos que sedar al hombre, está histérico.
	[is.ˈtɛ.ri.ko]	-We have to sedate the man, he's hysterical.
3870	**caviar**	**caviar**
	m	Vayamos al restaurante más caro a tomar caviar y champaña.
	[ka.ˈβjar]	-Let's go to the most expensive restaurant and have caviar and champagne.
3871	**sobredosis**	**overdose**
	f	En caso de sobredosis se debe buscar asistencia médica.
	[so.βre.ˈðo.sis]	-In the event of an overdose, medical advice should be sought.
3872	**atracar(se)**	**rob, dock; stuff yourself**
	vb; vbr	Los dos buques no tuvieron permitido atracar hasta hoy.
	[a.tra.ˈkar]	-The two ships were not allowed to dock until today.
3873	**enterar(se)**	**pay (LA); find out**
	vb; vbr	La mayoría de personas se sorprenden al enterarse que la guardia de la prisión es una mujer.
	[ẽn.tɛ.ˈrar]	-It surprises most people to find out that the prison warden is a woman.
3874	**mendigo**	**beggar**
	m	Lo recogí cuando era un mendigo.
	[mẽn.ˈdi.ɣo]	-I picked him up when he was a beggar.
3875	**escalofrío**	**chill**
	m	De verdad, acabo de tener un escalofrío.
	[ɛs.ka.lo.ˈfri.o]	-Honestly, I just got a chill.
3876	**íntimo**	**intimate**
	adj	Fui íntimo amigo de tu padre.
	[ˈĩn.ti.mo]	-I was a close friend of your father.
3877	**superficial**	**superficial**
	adj	Ella es superficial y materialista.
	[su.pɛr.fi.ˈsjal]	-She is materialistic and shallow.
3878	**volcán**	**volcano**

m
[bol.ˈkãn]

El volcán vuelve a estar activo.
-The volcano has become active again.

3879 letrero — **sign**

m
[lɛ.ˈtrɛ.ro]

Deberías traer un letrero colgado del cuello como servicio al público.
-You ought to wear a sign around your neck as a public service.

3880 tercio — **third**

m
[ˈtɛr.sjo]

La comunidad internacional tendrá que generar del tercio restante.
-The remaining third is to be generated by the international community.

3881 epidemia — **epidemic**

f
[e.pi.ˈðe.mja]

Se debe contrarrestar la epidemia mediante una participación amplia.
-The epidemic should be counteracted through a broad set of interventions.

3882 decano — **dean**

m
[de.ˈka.no]

El nuevo decano llega hoy.
-The new dean arrives today.

3883 dimensión — **dimension**

f
[di.mɛ̃n.ˈsjõn]

Esto suma una nueva dimensión de complejidad al problema.
-This adds a new dimension of complexity to the problem.

3884 estándar — **standard; standard**

adj; m
[ɛs.ˈtãn̪.dar]

Esto es un procedimiento de investigación estándar.
-This is a standard investigative procedure, major.

3885 culpabilidad — **culpability**

f
[kul.pa.βi.li.ˈðað]

Era muy difícil demostrar la culpabilidad de un individuo.
-It was very difficult to establish the guilt of an individual.

3886 fichar — **sign, clock in**

vb
[fi.ˈʧar]

Solo tiene que fichar cada dos horas.
-He just has to check in every two hours.

3887 deriva — **drift**

f
[dɛ.ˈri.βa]

La deriva continental ha hecho mucho más que conformar la tierra.
-Continental drift has done much more than shaping the earth.

3888 psiquiátrico — **psychiatric; psychiatric hospital**

adj; m
[si.ˈkja.tri.ko]

Mañana le trasladaremos a un hospital con un servicio psiquiátrico adecuado.
-Tomorrow we'll move you to a hospital with a proper psychiatric department.

3889 acudir — **go to**

vb
[a.ku.ˈðir]

No pudo acudir debido a un compromiso anterior.
-She was unable to attend due to a prior engagement.

3890 trauma — **trauma**

m
[ˈtrau̯.ma]

Dejamos atrás otro año de trauma nacional.
-We are leaving behind another year of national trauma.

3891 negociación — **negotiation**

f
[ne.ɣo.sja.ˈsjõn]

Supongo que esta será una negociación difícil.
-I guess this is going to be a difficult negotiation.

3892 lujuria — **lust**

f
[lu.ˈxu.rja]

Fuiste al hotel para satisfacer tu lujuria.
-You went to the hotel to satisfy your lust.

3893 menta — **mint**

f
[ˈmɛ̃n̪.ta]

No debí comer primero la menta.
-I shouldn't have eaten the mint first.

3894	**confiable**	**reliable**
	adj	Habría encontrado en él un asociado confiable y comprometido.
	[kõm̩.ˈfja.βle]	-She would have found in him a reliable and committed partner.
3895	**altitud**	**altitude**
	f	La altitud máxima es de 305 metros.
	[al̩.ti.ˈtuð]	-The maximum height is 305 meters.
3896	**correa**	**strap**
	f	Tengo un contratiempo con una correa.
	[ko.ˈre.a]	-I'm experiencing a mishap with a strap.
3897	**aspirina**	**aspirin**
	f	Cariño, lo mejor será que te traiga una aspirina.
	[as.pi.ˈri.na]	-Honey, maybe I'd better get you an aspirin.
3898	**finanzas**	**treasury**
	fpl	En finanzas sabemos qué hacer con activos riesgosos.
	[fi.ˈnãn.sas]	-In finance, we know what to do with assets that are risky.
3899	**occidente**	**west**
	m	El occidente está atrapado en una crisis de la deuda.
	[ok.si.ˈðẽn̩.te]	-The west is ensnared in a debt crisis.
3900	**esqueleto**	**skeleton**
	m	Puede que no podamos recuperar un esqueleto completo.
	[es.ke.ˈlɛ.to]	-We might not be able to recover a complete skeleton.
3901	**formulario**	**form**
	m	La empresa cumplimentará el formulario por duplicado.
	[for.mu.ˈla.rjo]	-The undertaking shall complete two copies of the form.
3902	**pianista**	**pianist**
	m/f	Su madre es una pianista excelente.
	[pja.ˈnis.ta]	-Her mother is a wonderful pianist.
3903	**sereno**	**calm; dew**
	adj; m	Algunas personas tienen un temperamento sereno o exudan gentileza.
	[sɛ.ˈre.no]	-Some people have a calm temperament or exude courtesy.
3904	**carpa**	**marquee, carp**
	f	Los peces tales como la carpa o la trucha viven en agua dulce.
	[ˈkar.pa]	-Fish such as carp and trout live in fresh water.
3905	**mandíbula**	**jaw**
	f	Recuerda que tenía la mandíbula rota.
	[mãn̩.ˈdi.βu.la]	-Remember, now, she had a broken jaw.
3906	**aprendiz**	**apprentice**
	m/f	El aprendiz también debe asistir a las sesiones anuales de capacitación teórica.
	[a.ˈprẽn̩.dis]	-The apprentice must also attend theoretical training sessions annually.
3907	**transmitir**	**transmit**
	vb	Solo el consejo de seguridad puede transmitir ese mensaje con credibilidad.
	[trãns̩.mi.ˈtir]	-Only the security council can credibly convey that message.
3908	**padrastro**	**stepfather**
	m	Mi padrastro no era diabético.
	[pa.ˈðras.tro]	-My stepfather was not diabetic.
3909	**encendedor**	**lighter**
	m	No puedes suicidarte con un encendedor.
	[ẽn.sẽn̩.de.ˈðor]	-You can't kill yourself with a lighter.

3910 zoo
m
['so.o]

zoo
Tres chimpancés han conseguido escapar hoy del zoo.
-Three chimpanzees found their way out of the zoo today.

3911 atún
m
[a.'tũn]

tuna
El atún de aleta azul se encuentra en peligro de extinción inmediato.
-Bluefin tuna is in immediate danger of extinction.

3912 potente
adj
[po.'tẽn.te]

powerful
Le dimos un analgésico experimental muy potente.
-We gave you a very powerful experimental painkiller.

3913 intervenir
vb
[ĩn.tɛr.βe.'nir]

take part, operate
Tenemos que intervenir lo antes posible para ayudar a definir las fronteras.
-We need to intervene as swiftly as possible to help define the borders.

3914 ametralladora
f
[a.mɛ.tra.ja.'ðo.ra]

machine gun
Deberías encontrarlo con tu ametralladora.
-You should find it with your machine gun.

3915 hundir(se)
vb
[ũn.'dir]

sink
Mentiste sobre quién estaba intentando hundir la campaña.
-You lied about who was trying to sink the campaign.

3916 suciedad
f
[su.sje.'ðað]

dirt
Sencillamente, no esperábamos ver tanta suciedad en la zona de compras familiar.
-We simply didn't expect to see such filth on the family shopping site.

3917 decencia
f
[de.'sẽn.sja]

decency
Están prohibidos los ritos religiosos contrarios a la decencia pública.
-Religious rites contrary to public decency are prohibited.

3918 maquinar
vb
[ma.ki.'nar]

plot
No voy a maquinar contra ti.
-I'm not going to plot against you.

3919 tutor
m
[tu.'tor]

tutor
Tu tutor asignado es Jim.
-Your assigned tutor is Jim.

3920 agrado
m
[a.'ɣra.ðo]

liking
Aparentemente no le agrado a Jim.
-Apparently, Jim doesn't like me.

3921 retrete
m
[rɛ.'tre.te]

toilet
No había agua potable ni retrete.
-There was no clean water and no toilet.

3922 calentar
vb
[ka.lẽn.'tar]

heat
Necesitas fuego para calentar el cuerpo.
-You need a fire to heat the body.

3923 vale
m; int
['ba.le]

voucher; ok
Eso vale trecientos dólares.
-That's worth three hundred dollars.

3924 disturbio
m
[dis.'tur.βjo]

disturbance
Cualquiera que cause un disturbio será expulsado.
-Anyone who causes a disturbance will be sent out.

3925 interferir

interfere

vb
[ĩn̪.tɛr.fɛ.ˈrir]

Interferir en un funeral es una grave falta de respeto.
-Interfering a funeral it's a great show of disrespect.

3926 gorro **hat**

m
[ˈgo.ro]

Toque este gorro y todos caeremos.
-Touch this hat and we all go down.

3927 tablero **board**

m
[ta.ˈβlɛ.ro]

Tu objetivo es apoderarte del tablero.
-Your aim is to take over the board.

3928 sede **headquarters**

f
[ˈse.ðe]

No visité la sede de tu empresa.
-I didn't visit the headquarters of your company.

3929 noroeste **northwest**

m
[no.ro.ˈɛs.te]

La mezquita está situada al noroeste de las afueras del campamento de Yabalia y próxima a Beit Lahiya.
-The mosque is situated near the north-west outskirts of Jabaliyah camp, close to Beit Lahia.

3930 puntería **aim**

f
[pũn̪.ˈtɛ.ri.a]

No soy realmente conocido por mi puntería.
-I'm not really known for my marksmanship.

3931 topar(se) **run into**

vb
[to.ˈpar]

Me preguntaba si me iba a topar contigo.
-I was wondering if I'd run into you.

3932 caminata **walk**

f
[ka.mi.ˈna.ta]

Daremos una caminata luego de desayunar.
-We're going for a walk after breakfast.

3933 diccionario **dictionary**

m
[dik.sjo.ˈna.rjo]

El diccionario está incompleto. Solo llega a la letra J.
-The dictionary is incomplete. It only goes to the letter J.

3934 amigable **friendly**

adj
[a.mi.ˈɣa.βle]

Solo te estoy dando un consejo amigable.
-I'm just passing on some friendly advice.

3935 agonía **agony**

f
[a.ɣo.ˈni.a]

He sufrido mucho dolor y agonía.
-I have suffered so much pain and agony.

3936 marear(se) **make someone dizzy, annoy (coll)**

vb
[ma.re.ˈar]

Se empieza a marear, se desorienta, le falta el aire.
-He gets dizzy, disoriented, he's out of breath.

3937 calentamiento **heating**

m
[ka.lẽn̪.ta.ˈmjẽn̪.to]

La lucha contra el calentamiento global será larga.
-The fight against global warming will be a long one.

3938 expectativas **expectations**

fpl
[ɛks.pek̚.ta.ˈti.βas]

Lamentablemente, los resultados de ninguna manera justifican las expectativas.
-Unfortunately, the results do not in any way justify the expectations.

3939 horca **gallows**

f
[ˈor.ka]

Fue arrestado por asesino y corre riesgo de horca.
-He was arrested for murder and risks the gallows.

3940 sueco **Swedish; Swedish person**

adj; m
['swe.ko]

He de decir que, como sueco, siento envidia.
-I have to say that, as a Swede, I am rather envious.

3941 reclamar — **demand**
vb
[re.kla.'mar]

Así fue como llegaron a reclamar su humanidad.
-This is how they came to reclaim their humanity.

3942 cobertizo — **shed**
m
[ko.βɛr.'ti.so]

Estaba sacando mis cosas del cobertizo.
-I was getting my things out of the shed.

3943 acompañante — **companion**
m/f
[a.kõm.pa.'ɲãn̪.te]

Él no dijo nada sobre que ibas a traer un acompañante.
-He didn't say anything about you bringing a companion.

3944 variedad — **variety**
f
[ba.rje.'ðað]

Los arrecifes de coral atraen una variedad preciosa de vida marina.
-Coral reefs attract a variety of beautiful marine life.

3945 estrecho — **narrow**
adj
[ɛs.'tre.ʧo]

Tomaremos otro camino, también lo suficientemente estrecho.
-We'll take another path, also narrow enough.

3946 concentrar(se) — **assemble, focus**
vb
[kõn.sɛ̃n̪.'trar]

Ahí es donde debemos concentrar todas nuestras fuerzas inmediatamente.
-That's where we must concentrate all our forces immediately.

3947 armada — **navy**
f
[ar.'ma.ða]

Nuestra armada es necesaria para defender nuestras costas.
-Our navy is needed to defend our own shores.

3948 fiscalía — **district attorney's officer**
f
[fis.ka.'li.a]

A continuación fueron detenidos con autorización de la fiscalía.
-Subsequently, they were arrested, upon the approval of the prosecution.

3949 cebo — **bait**
m
['se.βo]

Pensamos que podríamos conseguir algo de cebo para la mañana.
-We thought we'd get some bait for the morning.

3950 antigüedad — **antiquity**
f
[ãn̪.ti.ɣwe.'ðað]

No ha indicado ni la antigüedad ni el estado del equipo.
-She has not indicated the age or condition of the equipment.

3951 jarra — **mug**
f
['xa.ra]

Él pidió una jarra de cerveza.
-He asked for a glass of beer.

3952 artefacto — **artifact**
m
[ar.te.'fak̚.to]

Ella halló un artefacto en su país.
-She found an artifact in her country.

3953 ordinario — **ordinary**
adj
[or.ði.'na.rjo]

No detectó nada fuera de lo ordinario.
-He didn't detect anything out of the ordinary.

3954 puntual — **punctual; on time**
adj; adv
[pũn̪.'twal]

Esto garantiza que las actividades se realicen de manera puntual.
-This ensures the activities are carried out in a timely manner.

3955 elevado — **high**
adj
[e.le.'βa.ðo]

Su elevado salario le permite vivir cómodamente.
-His higher salary allows him to live comfortably.

3956 adoptar — **adopt**

		vb	Naturalmente, necesitamos adoptar un enfoque común.

vb
[a.ðop̚.ˈtar]
Naturalmente, necesitamos adoptar un enfoque común.
-Of course, we need to adopt a common approach.

3957 alcohólico — **alcoholic; alcoholic person**
adj; m
[al.ko.ˈo.li.ko]
Dijiste en la entrevista que tu padre era alcohólico.
-You said in the interview your father was a drunk.

3958 reventar — **burst**
vb
[re.βɛ̃n.ˈtar]
Bueno, siento reventar tu burbuja.
-Well, I hate to burst your bubble.

3959 penique — **penny**
m
[pe.ˈni.ke]
No me interesa aceptar un penique tuyo.
-I'm not interested in taking a nickel from you.

3960 plegaria — **prayer**
f
[ple.ˈɣa.rja]
Ahora diremos la plegaria del Señor.
-We will now say the Lord's Prayer.

3961 acceder — **agree, access**
vb
[ak.se.ˈðɛr]
Pretendí acceder para sacármelo de encima.
-I pretended to agree to get him off my back.

3962 inestable — **unstable**
adj
[i.nɛs.ˈta.βle]
La situación política fue muy inestable durante los próximos diez años de su reinado.
-The political situation was extremely unstable during the next ten years of his reign.

3963 espiar — **spy**
vb
[ɛs.ˈpjar]
Solo hago esto para espiar al personal.
-I just do this to spy on the help.

3964 entrañar — **involve**
vb
[ɛ̃n.tra.ˈɲar]
Se reconoció también que esas cuestiones podían entrañar objetivos contradictorios de las distintas naciones, regiones y grupos.
-It was also recognized that those issues might involve conflicting goals between nations, regions, and groups.

3965 atleta — **athlete**
m/f
[at̚.ˈlɛ.ta]
Quiero volver a ser una atleta.
-I want to go back to being an athlete.

3966 cantina — **cafeteria**
f
[kã̯n.ˈti.na]
¿Me puede sugerir una buena cantina?
-Can you suggest me a good tavern?

3967 tour — **tour**
m
[ˈtou̯r]
El tour cuenta con traslados y acomodaciones.
-The tour counts with transfers and accommodations.

3968 analizar — **analyze**
vb
[a.na.li.ˈsar]
Queremos analizar tu orina.
-We want to analyze your urine.

3969 determinado — **determined**
adj
[dɛ.tɛr.mi.ˈna.ðo]
Sabes exactamente qué hacer en cualquier momento determinado.
-You know exactly what to do at any given moment.

3970 chisme — **rumor, junk (coll)**
m
[ˈʧiʂ.me]
Ha habido algún chisme, supongo.
-There's been some gossip, I suppose.

3971 corrección — **correction**

f
[ko.rɛk.ˈsjõn]

Al principio pareció una corrección natural.
-Initially, this looked like a natural correction.

3972 **gitano**

adj; m
[xi.ˈta.no]

gypsy; gypsy

Ni siquiera quiere conocer al guitarrista gitano.
-He doesn't ever want to meet the gypsy guitarist.

3973 **invertido**

adj
[ĩm.bɛr.ˈti.ðo]

inverted

He invertido mucho en este activo.
-I've invested a lot in this asset.

3974 **convicto**

adj; m
[kõm.ˈbik.to]

convicted; convict

El convicto fugado está armado y es peligroso.
-The escaped convict is armed and dangerous.

3975 **rol**

m
[ˈrol]

role

Sigue cumpliendo tu rol como mensajera.
-Continue to fulfill your role as a messenger.

3976 **estafador**

m
[ɛs.ta.fa.ˈðor]

swindler

Nunca pensé que fuera un estafador.
-I never thought he was a con man.

3977 **amargo**

adj
[a.ˈmar.ɣo]

bitter

No lo bebas porque es demasiado amargo.
-Don't drink it because it's too bitter.

3978 **jornada**

f
[xor.ˈna.ða]

day

Hay trabajo como para una jornada.
-There's enough for a day's work.

3979 **dental**

adj
[dẽn.ˈtal]

dental

Tuvimos una coincidencia dental al instante.
-We got a dental match in no time.

3980 **cuadrado**

adj; m
[kwa.ˈðra.ðo]

square; square

Cada cuadrado puede contener un único símbolo.
-Each square may hold one and only one symbol.

3981 **veterano**

adj; m
[bɛ.tɛ.ˈra.no]

veteran; veteran

Es un político veterano conocido por ser razonablemente moderado.
-He is a veteran politician known to be reasonably moderate.

3982 **saque**

m
[ˈsa.ke]

kickoff

Tienes que trabajar tu saque.
-You have to work on your serve.

3983 **choza**

f
[ˈtʃo.sa]

hut

A mi amigo le gusta vivir en la ciudad, pero su mujer prefiere vivir en su pequeña choza campestre.
-My friend likes to live in the city, but his wife prefers to live in their little cottage in the country.

3984 **minero**

m
[mi.ˈnɛ.ro]

miner

No necesitas eso para ser un minero.
-You don't need that to be a miner.

3985 **instructor**

m
[ĩns.truk.ˈtor]

instructor

Tenía un enorme talento como instructor militar.
-He had great talent as a military instructor.

3986 **conmovedor**

touching

adj
[kõm.mo.βe.ˈðor]
Eres tan cariñoso. Es conmovedor.
-You're so caring. It's touching.

3987 octavo — **eighth**

num
[ok.ˈta.βo]
La reunión es en el octavo piso.
-The meeting is on the eighth floor.

3988 editar — **edit**

vb
[e.ði.ˈtar]
Puede editar la palabra sugerida o escribir otra palabra.
-You can edit the suggested word or enter another word.

3989 descuidado — **careless**

adj
[dɛs.kwi.ˈða.ðo]
Parece como si le tuviéramos descuidado.
-He looks as if we've neglected him.

3990 aprieto — **predicament**

m
[a.ˈprjɛ.to]
Eso nos pone en un aprieto.
-That puts us on the spot.

3991 rasguñar — **scratch**

vb
[raṣ.ɣu.ˈɲar]
Lamento la interrupción, pero le gusta rasguñar.
-Sorry for the interruption, but she likes to scratch.

3992 buey — **ox**

m
[ˈbwei̯]
Debiste haber estado aquí cuando estaba con el buey.
-You should have been here when I was with the ox.

3993 murciélago — **bat**

m/f
[mur.ˈsje.la.ɣo]
No dijiste nada sobre un murciélago.
-You didn't say anything about a bat.

3994 calabaza — **pumpkin**

f
[ka.la.ˈβa.sa]
No haremos que talles la calabaza.
-We won't make you carve the pumpkin.

3995 irresponsable — **irresponsible**

adj
[i.rɛs.põn.ˈsa.βle]
Sería irresponsable no aprobar este acuerdo.
-It would be irresponsible not to adopt this agreement.

3996 antídoto — **antidote**

m
[ãn̪.ˈti.ðo.to]
La fe es el antídoto perfecto para el miedo.
-Faith is the perfect antidote for fear.

3997 ingresar — **hospitalize, join**

vb
[ĩŋ.gre.ˈsar]
Será un gran desafío ingresar al doctorado.
-Entering the doctorate is going to be a great challenge.

3998 jaleo — **fuss (coll)**

m
[xa.ˈle.o]
No puedo relajarme con todo este jaleo.
-I can't relax with all this racket.

3999 manteca — **butter**

f
[mãn̪.ˈte.ka]
Comí pan con manteca esta mañana.
-I ate bread and butter this morning.

4000 canciller — **chancellor**

m/f
[kãn.si.ˈjɛr]
El canciller en persona lo llamó un hombre de honor.
-The chancellor himself called him a man of honor.

4001 escalón — **step**

m
[ɛs.ka.ˈlõn]
No podía recordar qué escalón estaba suelto.
-I couldn't remember which step was loose.

4002 deliberado — **deliberate**

adj
[de.li.βε.ˈra.ðo]

Esto parece un acto deliberado de humillación.
-This feels like a deliberate act of humiliation.

4003 ternero — calf

m
[tɛr.ˈnɛ.ro]

Yo sé que salvaste al ternero.
-I know you saved the calf.

4004 telón — curtain

m
[te.ˈlõn]

Todo lo que tienes que hacer es subir el telón.
-All you have to do is lift the curtain.

4005 vara — rod

f
[ˈba.ra]

Veo una vara de almendro.
-I see a rod of an almond tree.

4006 carpintero — carpenter

m
[kar.pĩn̪.ˈtɛ.ro]

Acabo de hablar con el carpintero.
-I just talked to the carpenter.

4007 cucaracha — cockroach

f
[ku.ka.ˈra.tʃa]

Hay una cucaracha en el baño.
-There's a cockroach in the bathroom.

4008 arranque — start, outburst

m
[a.ˈrãŋ.ke]

La llave está en el arranque.
-The key is in the ignition.

4009 corral — farmyard

m
[ko.ˈral]

Llegaremos hasta los caballos del corral.
-We'll get to the horses in the corral.

4010 Vaticano — Vatican

m
[ba.ti.ˈka.no]

Temo que sea un espía del Vaticano.
-I fear that he is a spy of the Vatican.

4011 animar — encourage

vb
[a.ni.ˈmar]

Hola Jim, vinimos a animar a tu novio.
-Hello Jim, we came to cheer on your boyfriend.

4012 soporte — support

m
[so.ˈpor.te]

Les estoy agradecida por su atención y soporte.
-I am grateful for your attention and support.

4013 tenedor — fork

m
[te.ne.ˈðor]

No olvides usar el tenedor correcto.
-Don't forget to use the right fork.

4014 cariñoso — affectionate

adj
[ka.ri.ˈɲo.so]

Siempre ha sido muy cariñoso con sus cuñados.
-He's always been very affectionate with his in-laws.

4015 discutido — controversial

adj
[dis.ku.ˈti.ðo]

¿Has discutido alguna vez con tu gerente?
-Have you ever argued with your manager?

4016 sensor — sensor

m
[sɛ̃n.ˈsor]

Desvíe el módulo de intensificación de la señal al sensor principal.
-Reroute the signal enhancement module to the main sensor.

4017 compositor — composer

m
[kõm.po.si.ˈtor]

¿Quién es tu compositor favorito?
-Who is your favorite songwriter?

4018 pasatiempo — pastime

	m	
	[pa.sa.ˈtjẽm.po]	El pasatiempo de mi padre es conducir coches de carreras.
		-My father's hobby is race car driving.
4019	**organismo**	**organism**
	m	
	[or.ɣa.ˈniṣ.mo]	Todo organismo en la superficie morirá en días.
		-Every organism on the surface will be dead within days.
4020	**púrpura**	**purple**
	adj	
	[ˈpur.pu.ra]	Arrojaste ese papel en una basura púrpura.
		-You threw that piece of paper into a purple trashcan.
4021	**morado**	**purple**
	adj	
	[mo.ˈra.ðo]	Debería haber cogido el morado.
		-I should have got the purple one.
4022	**admiración**	**admiration**
	f	
	[að.mi.ra.ˈsjõn]	Los narcisistas son a menudo presuntuosos, menospreciativos, condescendientes con las opiniones de otros, mientras que al mismo tiempo, tienen una abrumadora necesidad de admiración y consuelo.
		-Narcissists are often snobbish, disdainful and patronizing of others' opinions, while, at the same time, having an overwhelming need for admiration and reassurance.
4023	**pilar**	**pillar**
	m	
	[pi.ˈlar]	Es muy importante reforzar su pilar interno.
		-It is very important to strengthen its internal pillar.
4024	**operador**	**operator**
	m	
	[o.pɛ.ra.ˈðor]	Por favor cuelgue y el operador le devolverá la llamada.
		-Please hang up and the operator will call you back.
4025	**espionaje**	**espionage**
	m	
	[ɛs.pjo.ˈna.xe]	Han sido detenidos por las autoridades griegas acusados de espionaje.
		-They have been arrested by the Greek authorities on charges of espionage.
4026	**asignar**	**assign**
	vb	
	[a.siɣ.ˈnar]	Puede asignar un atajo especial de teclado para iniciar su programa.
		-You can assign a special keyboard shortcut to launch your program.
4027	**inauguración**	**opening**
	f	
	[i.nau̯.ɣu.ra.ˈsjõn]	Estoy esperando esta inauguración con inmenso placer.
		-I am looking forward to the inauguration with the greatest pleasure.
4028	**nostalgia**	**nostalgia**
	f	
	[nos.ˈtal.xja]	Lloro de nostalgia por mi patria.
		-I weep out of longing for my homeland.
4029	**sustituto**	**substitute**
	m	
	[sus.ti.ˈtu.to]	Solo tenemos que encontrarte un compañero sustituto.
		-We just need to find you a substitute partner.
4030	**momia**	**mummy**
	f	
	[ˈmo.mja]	Si encontramos la momia ganaremos una fortuna.
		-If we find the mummy, we'll make a fortune.
4031	**conmoción**	**shock**
	f	
	[kõm.mo.ˈsjõn]	Parece que haya sufrido una conmoción.
		-You look as if you've had a shock.
4032	**ría**	**estuary**
	f	
	[ˈri.a]	También es utilizado por pequeñas embarcaciones de pesca que faenan en el interior de la ría.
		-It is also used by small fishing boats which work inside the estuary.

4033	**ceder**	**give**
	vb	Tarde o temprano tendré que ceder.
	[se.ˈðɛɾ]	-Sooner or later I'm going to have to give in.

4034	**evacuar**	**evacuate**
	vb	Va a asegurar o evacuar el lugar.
	[e.βa.ˈkwar]	-He is to secure or evacuate the premises.

4035	**suero**	**serum**
	m	Va a volver a inyectar el suero en las personas.
	[ˈswɛ.ro]	-He is going to inject the serum back into people.

4036	**plantar(se)**	**plant, stand up (coll); stand firm**
	vb; vbr	Después de que terminemos de cavar la trinchera, plantar las flores será fácil.
	[plãn̪.ˈtar]	-After we finish digging the trench, planting the flowers will be easy.

4037	**espina**	**thorn**
	f	Tengo una espina en el dedo y no puedo sacármela.
	[ɛs.ˈpi.na]	-There's a thorn in my finger and I can't get it out.

4038	**determinación**	**determination**
	f	Quiero darle las gracias sinceramente por su determinación.
	[dɛ.tɛr.mi.na.ˈsjõn]	-I should like to thank you sincerely for your determination.

4039	**sapo**	**toad**
	m	Transformaré a esta preciosa princesa en un sapo.
	[ˈsa.po]	-I'll turn this beautiful princess into a toad.

4040	**bah**	**bah**
	int	Y tú estabas como "¡bah! ".
	[ˈba]	-And you were like, "bah!".

4041	**pezón**	**nipple**
	m	Tiene una segunda herida de bala encima del pezón izquierdo.
	[pe.ˈsõn]	-He has a second bullet wound above the left nipple.

4042	**reemplazar**	**replace**
	vb	Se siguen lanzando satélites meteorológicos para reemplazar y ampliar la capacidad existente.
	[re.ẽm.pla.ˈsar]	-Additional meteorological satellites continue to be launched both to replace and to expand existing capabilities.

4043	**navegación**	**navigation**
	f	Puede utilizarse para la navegación y la detección.
	[na.βe.ɣa.ˈsjõn]	-It can be used for navigation and detection.

4044	**filmación**	**shooting**
	f	Jim me invitó a ver la filmación.
	[fil.ma.ˈsjõn]	-Jim invited me to watch some of the filming.

4045	**guardería**	**daycare center**
	f	Va de ese apartamento a la guardería.
	[gwar.ðɛ.ˈri.a]	-She goes from that apartment to the daycare.

4046	**humillante**	**humiliating**
	adj	Es humillante y aparecerá en todos los periódicos.
	[u.mi.ˈjãn̪.te]	-It's humiliating, and it'll be in all of the newspapers.

4047	**eficiente**	**efficient**
	adj	La tecnología de la invención es sencilla y eficiente.
	[e.fi.ˈsjẽn̪.te]	-The technology of the invention is simple and efficient.

| 4048 | **enfermar(se)** | **get sick** |

vb
[ẽɱ.fɛr.ˈmar]

La gente pobre tiene más probabilidades de enfermar.
-People who are poor are more likely to get sick.

4049 **envenenar**

poison

vb
[ẽm.be.ne.ˈnar]

Está intentando envenenar nuestra comida.
-He's trying to poison our food.

4050 **laberinto**

maze

m
[la.βɛ.ˈrĩn̪.to]

Nos sacaron del laberinto y nos trajeron aquí.
-They pulled us off the maze and brought us here.

4051 **pisar**

step

vb
[pi.ˈsar]

Es como si la fueras a pisar.
-It's as if you were going to step on her.

4052 **jaque**

check

m
[ˈxa.ke]

Ana dice que estás en jaque.
-Ana says you're in check.

4053 **madrina**

godmother

f
[ma.ˈðri.na]

La madrina preparó una deliciosa tarta.
-The godmother baked a delicious cake.

4054 **víspera**

eve

f
[ˈbis.pɛ.ra]

Hoy es víspera de Navidad.
-Today it's the day before Christmas.

4055 **Nochebuena**

Christmas Eve

f
[no.ʧe.ˈβwe.na]

Realmente es la única Nochebuena que recuerdo.
-It's actually the only Christmas Eve I remember.

4056 **noción**

notion

f
[no.ˈsjõn]

Perdí la noción del tiempo.
-I've lost the notion of time.

4057 **balsa**

raft

f
[ˈbal.sa]

Tenemos que poder construir y montar esta balsa en unos tres días.
-We ought to be able to build and assemble this raft in about three days.

4058 **tendencia**

trend

f
[tẽn̪.ˈdẽn.sja]

Parece que esta tendencia está extendiéndose.
-It seems this tendency is on the rise.

4059 **estadístico**

statistical; statistician

adj; m
[ɛs.ta.ˈðis.ti.ko]

La preparación del programa estadístico no se realizó aisladamente.
-The development of the statistical programme did not happen in isolation.

4060 **carbono**

carbon

m
[kar.ˈβo.no]

Los fertilizantes químicos por definición no contienen carbono.
-Chemical fertilizers by definition don't have carbon in them.

4061 **bocado**

bite

m
[bo.ˈka.ðo]

Una zanahoria es un bocado saludable.
-A carrot is a healthy snack.

4062 **cóctel**

cocktail

m
[ˈkok̚.tɛl]

El cóctel de gambas estaba delicioso.
-The prawn cocktail was delicious.

4063 **Panamá**

Panama

m
[pa.na.ˈma]

Ella dijo que era de Panamá.
-She said she is from Panama.

4064 **vicio**

vice

	m	Parece que sustituyes un vicio por otro.
	['bi.sjo]	-Seems like you're trading one vice for another.

4065 manguera — **hose**

f
[mãŋ.'gɛ.ra]

Demasiada información se presentó de una sola vez. Asimilarla fue como beber de una manguera para incendios.
-Too much information was presented all at once. Taking it in was like drinking from a fire hose.

4066 disfrazar(se) — **disguise**

vb
[dis.fra.'sar]

Sospecho que es para disfrazar tu hipocresía.
-I suspect it's to disguise your hypocrisy.

4067 antena — **antenna**

f
[ãn̪.'te.na]

¿Han conectado la antena de la radio?
-Have they connected the radio antenna?

4068 presidencial — **presidential**

adj
[pre.si.ðẽn.'sjal]

No tenemos noticias del búnker presidencial.
-We have no word from the presidential bunker.

4069 cabalgar — **ride**

vb
[ka.βal.'ɣar]

Sé cómo cazar y cabalgar sin una silla de montar.
-I know how to hunt and ride without a saddle.

4070 bastar(se) — **be enough; be capable of**

vb; vbr
[bas.'tar]

Normalmente, deberían bastar 20 ml.
-A quantity of 20 ml should normally be sufficient.

4071 astronauta — **astronaut**

m/f
[as.tro.'nau̯.ta]

El astronauta perdió su agarre de la llave y lo único que pudo hacer era mirar consternado como se alejaba flotando.
-The astronaut lost his grip on the wrench and all he could do was watch in dismay as it floated serenely away.

4072 ofertar — **offer**

vb
[o.fɛr.'tar]

¿Qué piensas que deberíamos ofertar?
-What do you think we should offer?

4073 crudo — **raw, tough (ES) (coll)**

adj
['kru.ðo]

A mí me pareció muy crudo.
-I thought it was really raw.

4074 circulación — **circulation**

f
[sir.ku.la.'sjõn]

La sangre es el fluido responsable de la circulación de los nutrientes.
-Blood is the fluid responsible for the circulation of nutrients.

4075 drogadicto — **junkie**

m
[dro.ɣa.'ðik̚.to]

Esto fue escrito por un drogadicto en 1797.
-This was written in 1797 by a junkie.

4076 letal — **lethal**

adj
[lɛ.'tal]

Un incidente de 2011 de intoxicación letal se informó detalladamente.
-One incident of a lethal intoxication from 2011 is reported in detail.

4077 náusea — **nausea**

f
['nau̯.se.a]

Se presenta en una fiebre y náuseas leves.
-It presents in a fever and slight nausea.

4078 soborno — **bribery**

m
[so.'βor.no]

Quiero denunciar un intento de soborno.
-I'd like to report a bribery attempt.

4079 europeo — **European; European**

adj; m — Hemos realizado grandes progresos en el ámbito europeo.
[eu̯.ro.ˈpe.o] — -We have achieved a great deal of progress at the European level.

4080 **sardina** — **sardine**
f
[sar.ˈði.na] — Soñé que era una sardina. -I dreamt I was a sardine.

4081 **decorar** — **decorate**
vb
[de.ko.ˈrar] — Esta es una manera interesante de decorar su bicicleta. -This is an interesting way to decorate your bike.

4082 **igualdad** — **equality**
f
[i.ɣwal̯.ˈdað] — Estos me parecen unos pasos importantes hacia la igualdad. -I believe that these are important steps toward equality.

4083 **maquinaria** — **machinery**
f
[ma.ki.ˈna.rja] — Un viejo trabajador fue encontrado reparando maquinaria en el taller. -An old worker was found repairing machinery in the workshop.

4084 **subtítulo** — **subtitle**
m
[suβ.ˈti.tu.lo] — En la ventana emergente puedes cambiar varias propiedades del subtítulo. -You can change various properties of the subtitle in the window that pops up.

4085 **insensible** — **insensitive**
adj
[ĩn.sẽn.ˈsi.βle] — Es inapropiado e insensible cambiar la interpretación durante la votación. -It is inappropriate and insensitive to change the interpretation during the vote.

4086 **apasionar(se)** — **inspire; be crazy about**
vb; vbr
[a.pa.sjo.ˈnar] — Son las dos peores cosas por las que uno puede apasionarse. -It's like the two worst things to be passionate about.

4087 **reconstruir** — **rebuild**
vb
[re.kõns.ˈtrwir] — La práctica de poner en contacto a los productores locales con los consumidores urbanos podría reconstruir el sistema alimentario local. -Linking local producers with urban consumers could rebuild the local food system.

4088 **pirámide** — **pyramid**
f
[pi.ˈra.mi.ðe] — Están amontonadas en esta gran pirámide. -It's piled up in this great big pyramid.

4089 **convoy** — **convoy**
m
[kõm.ˈboi̯] — Se espera hoy al convoy de las Indias Orientales. -The East India convoy is expected today.

4090 **maní** — **peanut**
m
[ma.ˈni] — Puedes volver cuando quieras y coger un maní. -You can come back anytime and get yourself a peanut.

4091 **fidelidad** — **fidelity**
f
[fi.ðe.li.ˈðað] — Necesito estar seguro de tu fidelidad. -I need to be sure of your fidelity.

4092 **trapo** — **cloth**
m
[ˈtra.po] — Mira a ver si pudieras conseguirme un trapo grueso. -See if you can find me a thick rag.

4093 **arquitectura** — **architecture**
f
[ar.ki.tek.ˈtu.ra] — Es más probable que sea un presupuesto para la arquitectura. -It is more likely to be a budget for architecture.

4094 **preparativos** — **preparations**

mpl
[pre.pa.ra.ˈti.βos]

Nosotros completaremos nuestros preparativos pronto.
-We will soon complete our preparations.

4095 transmisor

m; adj
[trãn̞.mi.ˈsor]

transmitter; transmitting

Vas a tener que llevar este transmisor.
-You're going to have to wear this transmitter.

4096 cumbre

f
[ˈkũm.bre]

summit

Nuestra misión es detener la próxima cumbre.
-Our mission is to stop the upcoming summit meeting.

4097 sudar

vb
[su.ˈðar]

sweat

Ni siquiera sabía que podía sudar tanto.
-I didn't even know that I could sweat this much.

4098 seguido

adj[se.ˈɣi.ðo]

non-stop

La situación ha seguido deteriorándose. -The situation has continued to deteriorate.

4099 inclusive

adv
[ĩŋ.klu.ˈsi.βe]

inclusive

Debemos guardar las apariencias, tú inclusive.
-We need to keep up appearances, even you.

4100 sabroso

adj
[sa.ˈβro.so]

tasty

¡Caramba, qué sabroso se ve eso!
-Wow, that looks really tasty!

4101 patrulla

f
[pa.ˈtru.ja]

patrol

Los merodeadores han estado en patrulla continua.
-The marauders have been on continuous patrol.

4102 reaccionar

vb
[re.ak.sjo.ˈnar]

react

Debemos encontrar maneras de reaccionar rápida y efectivamente.
-We must look for ways to react quickly and effectively.

4103 barbero

m
[bar.ˈβɛ.ro]

barber

Voy a un barbero. Necesito afeitarme.
-I'm going to a barber. I need a shave.

4104 revelación

f
[re.βe.la.ˈsjõn]

revelation

Cuando murió, tuve una revelación.
-When she died, I had a revelation.

4105 lanza

f
[ˈlãn.sa]

spear

Pensó que me había matado con esa lanza mágica... Pero sobreviví.
-He thought he killed me with that magic spear... But I survived.

4106 neumático

m; adj
[neu̯.ˈma.ti.ko]

tire; inflatable

Su muerte no fue causada por un neumático defectuoso.
-His death was not caused by a defective tire.

4107 rap

m
[ˈrap]

rap

Hice un pequeño rap como discurso.
-I did a little rap as my speech.

4108 incumbir

vb
[ĩŋ.kũm.ˈbir]

concern

Este arreglo puede incumbir a la comunidad entera.
-This arrangement can concern the whole community.

4109 africano

adj; m
[a.fri.ˈka.no]

African; African person

El folclore africano es muy interesante.
-African folklore is very interesting.

4110 tranvía

tram

	m	Cuando me canse cogeré el tranvía.
	[trãm.ˈbi.a]	-When I'm tired, I'll catch a tram.

4111 fiar(se) — **sell on credit; trust**

vb; vbr
[ˈfjar]

Ella es una mujer calculadora, traicionera de la que no hay que fiarse.
-She is a scheming, treacherous woman, not to be trusted.

4112 nalga — **buttock**

f
[ˈnal.ɣa]

La inyección será en tu nalga.
-The injection will be in your bottom.

4113 aviación — **aviation**

f
[a.βja.ˈsjõn]

La aviación ha sido durante mucho tiempo una industria privilegiada.
-Aviation has long been a privileged industry.

4114 nobleza — **nobility**

f
[no.ˈβle.sa]

No les importamos a la nobleza.
-The gentry doesn't care for us.

4115 broche — **brooch**

m
[ˈbro.tʃe]

Pensé que estaría bien llevar el broche esta noche.
-I thought it might be nice to wear the brooch tonight.

4116 diecisiete — **seventeen**

num
[dje.si.ˈsjɛ.te]

Costó diecisiete meses y cinco días construirla.
-It took seventeen months and five days to build.

4117 panel — **panel**

m
[pa.ˈnɛl]

Puedo leer los símbolos de su panel.
-I can read the symbols on their panel.

4118 apartado — **section; remote**

m; adj
[a.par.ˈta.ðo]

Este apartado aborda varias cuestiones en cada capítulo.
-This section in each chapter deals with a number of questions.

4119 peluquería — **hairdresser**

f
[pe.lu.kɛ.ˈri.a]

Suelo ir a la peluquería una vez al mes.
-I usually go to the barber once a month.

4120 bocadillo — **sandwich**

m
[bo.ka.ˈði.jo]

Empezaré con el bocadillo de atún.
-I'll open with the tuna sandwich.

4121 bofetada — **slap**

f
[bo.fɛ.ˈta.ða]

Es una bofetada en la cara para todos nuestros jóvenes que quieren labrarse un futuro.
-It is a slap in the face for all our young people who want to build a future for themselves.

4122 talón — **heel**

m
[ta.ˈlõn]

Apagaste el cigarrillo con el talón.
-You put the cigarette out with your heel.

4123 porción — **portion**

f
[por.ˈsjõn]

Faltaba una porción considerable de la tarta.
-A considerable portion of the cake was missing.

4124 acta — **record**

f
[ˈak̚.ta]

Ya hemos solicitado la rectificación del acta.
-We have already asked for the record to be adjusted.

4125 ironía — **irony**

f
[i.ro.ˈni.a]
Pensé que apreciarías la ironía.
-I thought you'd appreciate the irony.

4126 filósofo   **philosopher**

m
[fi.ˈlo.so.fo]
No solo soy filósofo, señor.
-I'm not only a philosopher, sir.

4127 mamar   **nurse**

vb
[ma.ˈmar]
Voy a darle de mamar.
-I'm going to nurse him.

4128 infernal   **infernal**

adj
[ĩɱ.fɛr.ˈnal]
No puedo detener este artefacto infernal yo solo.
-I can't stop this infernal contraption on my own.

4129 escombro   **rubbish**

m
[ɛs.ˈkõm.bro]
Este montón de escombro de aquí es un catre.
-This pile of debris here is a cot.

4130 diplomático   **diplomatic; diplomat**

adj; m
[dip̚.lo.ˈma.ti.ko]
Las malas noticias son que viaja con pasaporte diplomático.
-The bad news is he's traveling on a diplomatic passport.

4131 muslo   **thigh**

m
[ˈmus̠.lo]
En niños pequeños, la inyección puede administrarse en el músculo del muslo.
-In very small children, the injection may be given into the thigh muscle.

4132 exigente   **demanding**

adj
[ɛk.si.ˈxẽn̪.te]
Soy muy exigente con mis empleados.
-I'm very demanding on my employees.

4133 accidental   **accidental**

adj
[ak.si.ðẽn̪.ˈtal]
El descubrimiento de la cura fue casi accidental.
-The discovery of the cure was almost accidental.

4134 lima   **lime, file**

f
[ˈli.ma]
Cariño, bebería gasolina si le pusieras una lima.
-Honey, I'd drink gasoline if you put a lime in it.

4135 espectador   **viewer**

m
[ɛs.pek̚.ta.ˈðor]
Hoy estoy aquí solamente como espectador.
-I'm just here as a spectator today.

4136 diseñador   **designer**

m
[di.se.ɲa.ˈðor]
¿Quién es tu diseñador de moda preferido?
-Who's your favorite fashion designer?

4137 irónico   **ironic**

adj
[i.ˈro.ni.ko]
En un giro cruelmente irónico del destino, algún día Jim será un ejemplo para todos nosotros.
-In a cruelly ironic twist of fate, someday Jim will serve as an example to all of us.

4138 equivocación   **mistake**

f
[e.ki.βo.ka.ˈsjõn]
Creo que sería una equivocación muy grande.
-I believe that would be a very big mistake.

4139 colmar   **fulfill**

vb
[kol.ˈmar]
Se han tomado algunas medidas para colmar estos huecos.
-Some initiatives had been undertaken to fill the gaps.

4140 riñón   **kidney**

	m	Tengo algunos compradores que vienen a mirar mi riñón bueno.
	[ri.ˈɲõn]	-I got some buyers coming over to look at my good kidney.
4141	**asno**	**donkey**
	m	Había elegido como símbolo de su partido al asno.
	[ˈas̞.no]	-He had chosen as the symbol of his party the donkey.
4142	**arrojar**	**throw**
	vb	Dejémosle arrojar palomitas al piso.
	[a.ro.ˈxar]	-Let him throw popcorn on the floor.
4143	**componer**	**compose**
	vb	Podríamos componer himnos en su honor.
	[kõm.po.ˈnɛr]	-We could compose anthems in her honor.
4144	**panda**	**panda**
	m	Ana nunca había visto a un panda gigante.
	[ˈpãn̪.da]	-Ana had never seen a giant panda.
4145	**pertenencia**	**belonging**
	f	Tampoco señaló su pertenencia a una organización terrorista.
	[pɛr.te.ˈnẽn.sja]	-Nor did he indicate his membership in any terrorist organization.
4146	**mineral**	**mineral; mineral**
	adj; m	La amalgamación solo funciona con mineral que contenga oro en estado libre.
	[mi.nɛ.ˈral]	-Amalgamation only works with ore containing free gold.
4147	**cesta**	**basket**
	f	Meteremos nuestras armas en una cesta.
	[ˈsɛs.ta]	-We'll lower our guns in a basket.
4148	**distribución**	**distribution**
	f	La distribución de estos materiales ha beneficiado a siete millones de niños.
	[dis.tri.βu.ˈsjõn]	-Seven million children have benefited from the distribution of these materials.
4149	**destructor**	**destroyer**
	m	No soy un destructor de compañías.
	[dɛs.truk̚.ˈtor]	-I am not a destroyer of companies.
4150	**prosperidad**	**prosperity**
	f	La prosperidad de un país depende de sus ciudadanos.
	[pros.pɛ.ri.ˈðað]	-The prosperity of a country depends upon its citizens.
4151	**contabilidad**	**accounting**
	f	Cada participante se ocupa de su propia contabilidad.
	[kõn̪.ta.βi.li.ˈðað]	-Each partner takes care of her own accounting.
4152	**porro**	**joint**
	m	Estaba fumándome un porro cuando entraron.
	[ˈpo.ro]	-I was smoking a joint when they walked in.
4153	**orientación**	**orientation**
	f	Tengo un malísimo sentido de la orientación.
	[o.rjẽn̪.ta.ˈsjõn]	-I have a really bad sense of direction.
4154	**fluir**	**flow**
	vb	Sintió un nudo en la garganta y lágrimas comenzaron a fluir de sus ojos.
	[ˈflwir]	-She felt a lump in the back of her throat and tears began to well in her eyes.
4155	**prevenir(se)**	**warn; get ready**
	vb; vbr	Los chequeos regulares son necesarios para prevenir la ceguera.
	[pre.βe.ˈnir]	-Regular check-ups are needed to prevent blindness.

4156 comunismo — **communism**
m
[ko.mu.ˈniş.mo]
El capitalismo es la explotación del hombre por el hombre. El comunismo es exactamente lo opuesto.
-Capitalism is the exploitation of man by man. Communism is the exact opposite.

4157 anticuado — **antiquated**
adj
[ãn̪.ti.ˈkwa.ðo]
No entiendo cómo encuentran algo con este sistema anticuado.
-I don't understand how you find anything with this antiquated system.

4158 intensidad — **intensity**
f
[ĩn̪.tẽn.si.ˈðað]
Hay un aumento en la frecuencia e intensidad de los fenómenos meteorológicos extremos.
-There is an increase in the frequency and intensity of extreme weather events.

4159 seminario — **seminary**
m
[se.mi.ˈna.rjo]
No voy a volver al seminario.
-I will not come back to the seminary.

4160 percepción — **perception**
f
[pɛr.sɛp.ˈsjõn]
Esta percepción puede variar con el paso del tiempo.
-This perception can change with the passage of time.

4161 arsenal — **arsenal**
m
[ar.se.ˈnal]
Cavamos un túnel que lleva directo al arsenal.
-We dug a tunnel that leads directly to the stockpile.

4162 contribución — **contribution**
f
[kõn̪.tri.βu.ˈsjõn]
Creo que han hecho una contribución muy buena.
-I believe they have made a very good contribution.

4163 verdugo — **executioner**
m
[bɛr.ˈðu.ɣo]
Tanto el verdugo como su hija fueron generosos y comprensivos.
-Both the hangman and his daughter were generous and sympathetic.

4164 funcionamiento — **functioning**
m
[fũn.sjo.na.ˈmjẽn̪.to]
Los primeros ordenadores electrónicos se pusieron en funcionamiento en 1945.
-The first electronic computers went into operation in 1945.

4165 residente — **resident; resident**
adj; m/f
[re.si.ˈðẽn̪.te]
Ahora me gustaría presentarles a nuestro primer afortunado residente.
-Now I'd like to introduce you to our first lucky resident.

4166 vengar(se) — **avenge**
vb
[bẽŋ.ˈgar]
Él lo mató para vengar a su padre muerto.
-He killed him to avenge his dead father.

4167 cuota — **fee**
f
[ˈkwo.ta]
Esta cuota se calculó utilizando datos verificados.
-This share was calculated on the basis of verified data.

4168 liderazgo — **leadership**
m
[li.ðɛ.ˈraş.ɣo]
Será una contribución importante para garantizar un liderazgo más responsable.
-It will be a major contribution towards ensuring a more responsible leadership.

4169 infame — **dreadful; villain**
adj; m/f
[ĩm.ˈfa.me]
Tú debes ser el infame sheriff Carter.
-You must be the infamous sheriff Carter.

4170 testículo — **testicle**

	m	He escuchado que solo tiene un testículo.
	[tɛs.ˈti.ku.lo]	-I heard he's only got one testicle.

4171 editorial — **editorial; leading article; publishing house**

adj; m; f
[e.ði.to.ˈrjal]

He querido trabajar en una editorial.
-I've wanted to work in a publishing house.

4172 cagado — **wimpy (coll)**

m
[ka.ˈɣa.ðo]

Estás cagado de miedo como lo has estado toda tu vida.
-You're scared to death like you have been all your life.

4173 resurrección — **Resurrection**

f
[re.su.rɛk.ˈsjõn]

Los hechizos de resurrección pueden ser muy complicados.
-Resurrection spells can be very tricky.

4174 brujería — **witchcraft**

f
[bru.xɛ.ˈri.a]

Refutaré todas las acusaciones de brujería.
-I will disprove all the charges of witchcraft.

4175 saliva — **saliva**

f
[sa.ˈli.βa]

Deberíamos hacerle un test de saliva a este tío.
-We ought to give this guy a saliva test.

4176 individual — **single, personal**

adj
[ĩn̪.di.βi.ˈðwal]

El transporte público solo es más rápido que el individual en las zonas urbanas.
-Public transport is only quicker than private transport in urban areas.

4177 bronce — **bronze**

m
[ˈbrõn.se]

Tendrá que conformarse con el bronce.
-He may have to settle for the bronze.

4178 barbacoa — **barbecue**

f
[bar.βa.ˈko.a]

Vendrán algunas personas esta tarde para una barbacoa.
-We're having some people over this afternoon for a barbecue.

4179 tostar — **toast**

vb
[tos.ˈtar]

Ve a tostar la rosca, no te metas.
-Go toast the bagel, mind your own business.

4180 guarida — **hideout**

f
[gwa.ˈri.ða]

Debe estar llevándolos hacia su guarida.
-He must be pushing them towards his lair.

4181 opio — **opium**

m
[ˈo.pjo]

Todo lo que recuerdo es el olor al opio.
-All I remember is the smell of opium.

4182 faraón — **pharaoh**

m
[fa.ra.ˈõn]

Los depósitos del faraón están vacíos.
-The pharaoh's storehouses are empty.

4183 cagada — **shit (coll), screw-up (coll)**

f
[ka.ˈɣa.ða]

Esta ha sido una cagada tras otra.
-This has been one fuck-up after another.

4184 patinar — **skate**

vb
[pa.ti.ˈnar]

Quiero decir, solíamos patinar juntos.
-I mean, we used to skate together.

4185 puré — **purée**

m
[pu.ˈre]

No hay nada anormal en el puré de albahaca.
-There is nothing abnormal about basil puree.

4186 paradero — **whereabouts**

m

[pa.ra.'ðe.ro]

Todavía no se conoce el paradero del sospechoso.
-The whereabouts of the suspect are still unknown.

4187 vínculo — **link**

m

['bĩn.ku.lo]

Este vínculo permite comprobar la calidad de la información recogida.
-This link makes it possible to check the quality of the information collected.

4188 audaz — **bold**

adj

['au̯.ðas]

Decidí hacer un movimiento decisivo y audaz.
-I decided to make a bold and decisive move.

4189 titular(se) — **headline; title; owner**

m; vb; adj

[ti.tu.'lar]

Vuestra hermana no debería venderle por un titular.
-Your sister shouldn't sell him out for a headline.

4190 cerilla — **match**

f

[se.'ri.ja]

Coge una cerilla y enciéndela.
-Take out a match and light it.

4191 utilidad — **utility**

f

[u.ti.li.'ðað]

Tampoco tengo una utilidad para ello.
-I don't have a use for it either.

4192 severo — **stern**

adj

[se.'βe.ro]

El comandante sufrió un severo daño neural.
-The commander suffered severe neural damage.

4193 irrelevante — **irrelevant**

adj

[i.re.le.'βãn̯.te]

Incluso aunque eso fuera cierto, sería irrelevante.
-Even if that were true, it's irrelevant.

4194 aproximar(se) — **bring closer**

vb

[a.prok.si.'mar]

Presidente, me agrada decir que en esta segunda lectura los partidos han trabajado juntos para aproximar sus posiciones.
-President, I am pleased to say that, at this second reading, the parties have worked to bring their positions closer together.

4195 morada — **dwelling**

f

[mo.'ra.ða]

Lamento molestarlo en su hermosa morada.
-I'm very sorry to disturb you at your lovely abode.

4196 creciente — **growing; swelling**

adj; f

[kre.'sjẽn̯.te]

Ana miraba al cielo estrellado, con la luna en cuarto creciente que iluminaba aquella noche otoñal.
-Ana looked at the starry sky, with a quarter moon that illuminated that autumn night.

4197 informante — **informant**

m/f

[ĩm.for.'mãn̯.te]

El informante no está aquí.
-The informant is not here.

4198 relleno — **stuffed; stuff**

adj; m

[re.'je.no]

El lomo está ligeramente relleno con escarola a la parrilla.
-The loin is lightly stuffed with grilled escarole.

4199 forzar — **force**

vb

[for.'sar]

No puedes forzar a los pétalos de una rosa para que se abran antes de tiempo.
-You cannot force open the petals of a rosebud before its time.

4200 enfoque — **approach**

m

[ẽm.'fo.ke]

Este enfoque también se aplica al transporte ferroviario regional.
-This approach also applies to regional rail services.

4201 cartucho — **cartridge**
m
[kar.ˈtu.ʧo]
Por favor sustituya el cartucho vacío de la impresora.
-Please replace the empty printer cartridge.

4202 banana — **banana**
f
[ba.ˈna.na]
Os daré este lubricante de banana gratis.
-I'll throw this banana in for free.

4203 carnicería — **butcher's shop; slaughter**
f; f
[kar.ni.sɛ.ˈri.a]
Ya fui a la carnicería esta mañana.
-I already went to the butcher's shop this morning.

4204 apurado — **rushed**
adj
[a.pu.ˈra.ðo]
Le dije que no estaba apurado.
-I told you I wasn't in a hurry.

4205 caracol — **snail**
m
[ka.ra.ˈkol]
El caracol se refugió en su caparazón.
-The snail retreated into its shell.

4206 vacuna — **vaccine**
f
[ba.ˈku.na]
Debe utilizarse la dosis completa de vacuna recomendada.
-The full recommended dose of the vaccine should be used.

4207 tazón — **bowl**
m
[ta.ˈsõn]
Puedes pasarme ese tazón, querida.
-You can hand me that bowl, dear.

4208 liberal — **liberal**
adj
[li.βɛ.ˈral]
Mi padre era librepensador, un hombre metódico, liberal.
-My father was a free thinker, a methodic man, a liberal.

4209 cápsula — **capsule**
f
[ˈkap.su.la]
Cada cápsula blanda contiene 100 mg.
-Each soft capsule contains 100 mg.

4210 marcador — **marker**
m
[mar.ka.ˈðor]
Tengo mi marcador, los alcanzaré.
-I got my marker, I'll catch up.

4211 bancarrota — **bankruptcy**
f
[bãŋ.ka.ˈro.ta]
Bajo las circunstancias, la bancarrota es inevitable.
-Under the circumstances, bankruptcy is inevitable.

4212 invencible — **invincible**
adj
[ĩm.bẽn.ˈsi.βle]
Jim parece creer que es invencible.
-Jim seems to think that he's invincible.

4213 rompecabezas — **puzzle**
m
[rõm.pe.ka.ˈβe.sas]
Ella le explicó cómo resolver el rompecabezas.
-She explained to him how to solve the puzzle.

4214 federación — **federation**
f
[fe.ðɛ.ra.ˈsjõn]
La federación alemana de la miel se opuso a este registro.
-The German honey production federation opposed this registration.

4215 reposo — **rest**
m
[re.ˈpo.so]
Necesita reposo absoluto y nada de preocupaciones.
-He has to have complete rest and no worries.

4216 interrogar — **question**
vb
[ĩn.tɛ.ro.ˈɣar]
Él sabe cómo interrogar a las personas.
-He knows how to interrogate people.

4217 descenso — **descent**
m
[dɛs.ˈsẽn.so]
Su último vector de velocidad indica un descenso en picado.
-Their last velocity vector indicates a steep descent.

4218 dividir — **divide**
vb
[di.βi.ˈðir]
Tendremos que dividir y conquistar, supongo.
-We'll just have to divide and conquer, I guess.

4219 adopción — **adoption**
f
[a.ðop.ˈsjõn]
Los derechos de adopción de parejas del mismo sexo son una importante cuestión para la comunidad LGBT.
-Same-sex adoption rights are an important issue for the LGBT community.

4220 falla — **fault**
f
[ˈfa.ʝa]
No permitiré otra falla en esta casa.
-I will not permit another failure in this house.

4221 temperamento — **temperament**
m
[tẽm.pɛ.ra.ˈmẽn̪.to]
Hay caballos con mucho temperamento, rapidez y una constancia increíble.
-There are horses with much temper, agility and, an unbelievable perseverance.

4222 exponer — **expose**
vb
[ɛks.po.ˈnɛr]
Él tuvo el valor de exponer el escándalo.
-He had the courage to expose the scandal.

4223 presidencia — **presidency**
f
[pre.si.ˈðẽn.sja]
Su experiencia es garantía de una presidencia útil y fructífera.
-His experience is a guarantee of a useful and fruitful presidency.

4224 intruso — **intruder; out of place**
m; adj
[ĩn̪.ˈtru.so]
Completamos el rastreo en el sistema del intruso.
-We completed the back-trace on the intruder's system.

4225 israelí — **Israeli; Israeli**
adj; m/f
[iş.ra.e.ˈli]
El asentamiento israelí no ha cesado.
-The Israeli settlement has not stopped at all.

4226 bufanda — **scarf**
f
[bu.ˈfãn̪.da]
Compré una corbata para Jim y compraré una bufanda para Ana.
-I bought a tie for Jim and I'll buy a scarf for Ana.

4227 tender(se) — **tend, hang up; lie down**
vb; vbr
[tẽn̪.ˈdɛr]
La decisión del consejo deberá tender a una distribución geográfica racional de las cantidades disponibles.
-The decision of the council shall aim at a rational geographical distribution of the funds made available.

4228 relato — **tale**
m
[re.ˈla.to]
Según el relato oficial, los ocupantes del buque ignoraron una bengala de advertencia.
-According to the official account, the vessel's occupants ignored a warning flare.

4229 noruego — **Norwegian; Norwegian person**
adj; m
[no.ˈrwe.ɣo]
Sería razonable que Dinamarca copiara el modelo noruego.
-It would be reasonable for Denmark to copy the Norwegian model.

4230 flauta — **flute**
f
[ˈflau̯.ta]
Mi hija quiere una flauta para Navidad.
-My daughter wants a flute for Christmas.

4231 suceso — **event**

m
[su.ˈse.so]

Japón se está moviendo hacia adelante para superar ese trágico suceso.
-Japan is now moving forward to overcome that tragic event.

4232 cubierto

adj; m
[ku.ˈβjɛr.to]

covered; piece of cutlery

Mi coche está cubierto de caca de paloma.
-My car is covered with pigeon poop.

4233 vitamina

f
[bi.ta.ˈmi.na]

vitamin

Las naranjas contienen mucha vitamina C.
-Oranges contain a lot of vitamin C.

4234 bombardero

m
[bõm.bar.ˈðɛ.ro]

bomber

Traje un bombardero desde San Francisco.
-I flew a bomber in from San Francisco.

4235 alucinación

f
[a.lu.si.na.ˈsjõn]

hallucination

Ha experimentado una alucinación debido a una liberación de endorfinas.
-You experienced a hallucination due to an endorphin release.

4236 ruptura

f
[rup̚.ˈtu.ra]

rupture

Para los niños de hasta 5 años de edad, la ruptura de la familia puede ser difícil de entender.
-For children up to 5 years old, family breakdown can be difficult to understand.

4237 tractor

m
[trak̚.ˈtor]

tractor

Arruinaron los campos, volcaron un tractor.
-They tore up the fields, turned over a tractor.

4238 inminente

adj
[ĩm.mi.ˈnẽn̪.te]

imminent

Estaba pensando en nuestro osado e inminente escape.
-I was thinking about our imminent and daring escape.

4239 tributo

m
[tri.ˈβu.to]

tribute

Quisiera rendirles mi tributo personal por su determinación.
-I would like to pay my personal tribute to your resolve.

4240 manuscrito

m
[ma.nus.ˈkri.to]

manuscript

El manuscrito del libro debe cumplir con los requisitos obligatorios de distribución.
-The book manuscript must meet the mandatory distribution requirements.

4241 carroza

f
[ka.ˈro.sa]

carriage

Prepararé su carroza, mi señor.
-I'll prepare your chariot, my lord.

4242 biología

f
[bjo.lo.ˈxi.a]

biology

Los ejemplos incluyen aplicaciones de la biología sintética y la nanotecnología.
-Examples include applications of synthetic biology and nanotechnology.

4243 indiferente

adj
[ĩn̪.di.fɛ.ˈrẽn̪.te]

indifferent

A la juventud de nuestro país le es indiferente la política.
-The youth of our country is indifferent to politics.

4244 corporal

adj; m
[kor.po.ˈral]

corporal; corporal

El agua siempre ha sido un símbolo de purificación y renovación, tanto corporal como espiritual.
-Water has always been a symbol of purification and renovation, both corporal and spiritual.

4245 egipcio

adj; m
[e.ˈxip.sjo]

Egyptian; Egyptian person

Esta es una copia de su pasaporte egipcio.
-This is a copy of his Egyptian passport.

4246 ingle
f
['ĩŋ.gle]

groin

Él tuiteó sin querer una foto de su ingle a sus 40.000 seguidores.
-He accidentally tweeted a picture of his groin to 40,000 followers.

4247 fragmento
m
[fraɣ.'mɛ̃n̪.to]

fragment

Este fragmento de la melodía necesita una habilidad real. Tardé años en aprender a tocarlo en el piano.
-This part of the tune needs some real skill. It took me ages to learn how to play it on the piano.

4248 silbato
m
[sil.'βa.to]

whistle

Jim, puedes guardar tu silbato.
-Jim, you can put away your whistle.

4249 delfín
m
[dɛl.'fĩn]

dolphin

Un delfín perdido no es exactamente una alta prioridad.
-A missing dolphin isn't exactly a high priority.

4250 descifrar
vb
[dɛs.si.'fraɾ]

decipher

Desearía poder descifrar cómo derrotar al sistema.
-I wish I could figure out how to beat the system.

4251 burlar(se)
vb; vbr
[buɾ.'laɾ]

evade; mock

Se deben resistir los intentos de burlar el derecho internacional.
-It must resist the attempts to circumvent international law.

4252 eje
m
['e.xe]

shaft

Algo ha mordido las conexiones del eje de utilidad.
-Something chewed through the connections in the utility shaft.

4253 carnet
m
[kaɾ.'nɛt]

license

Tengo carnet, pero soy demasiado agresivo.
-I got a license, but I have too much hostility.

4254 visible
adj
[bi.'si.βle]

visible

Necesita hacerse visible de esta forma.
-It needs to be made visible in this way.

4255 Sudáfrica
f
[su.'ða.fri.ka]

South Africa

La constitución establece la cultura política de una Sudáfrica libre.
-The constitution sets out the political culture of a free South Africa.

4256 racional
adj
[ra.sjo.'nal]

rational

El método de enseñanza Yawara-Jitsu es científico, racional y progresivo.
-Yawara-Jitsu teaching method is scientific, rational and progressive.

4257 acampar
vb
[a.kãm.'paɾ]

camp

Hallamos el lugar perfecto para acampar.
-We've found the perfect place to camp.

4258 psicólogo
m
[si.'ko.lo.ɣo]

psychologist

En algunas comisarías de mujeres, hay un psicólogo de guardia para proporcionar asesoramiento.
-In some women's police stations, there is a psychologist on duty to provide counseling.

4259 estufa
f
[ɛs.'tu.fa]

stove

En varias ocasiones dejó la estufa encendida.
-On several occasions, she left the stove on.

4260 sangriento
adj
[sãŋ.'grjɛ̃n̪.to]

bloody

Nadie puede detener este baño sangriento.
-No one can stop this bath of blood.

4261 directivo — **manager; managerial**

m; adj
[di.rek̚.ˈti.βo]

Un buen número de personal directivo de categoría superior y técnicos competentes han abandonado el país.
-A good number of high-level managerial staff and skilled technicians have left the country.

4262 esfera — **sphere**

f
[ɛs.ˈfɛ.ra]

La Tierra es solo una esfera suspendida en el espacio.
-The Earth is just a sphere suspended in space.

4263 neutral — **neutral; third party**

adj; m/f
[neu̯.ˈtral]

Un país neutral es un país que no vende armas a un país en guerra, excepto si paga en metálico.
-A neutral country is a country that doesn't sell weapons to a warring country, unless you pay cash.

4264 prejuicio — **prejudice**

m
[pre.ˈxwi.sjo]

¿Por qué los japoneses tienen tanto prejuicio contra las lesbianas y los bisexuales?
-Why are Japanese so prejudiced against lesbians and bisexuals?

4265 mezclar — **mix**

vb
[mɛs.ˈklar]

Resulta peligroso mezclar amoníaco con lejía.
-Mixing ammonia and bleach is dangerous.

4266 verso — **verse**

m
[ˈbɛr.so]

No hay nada en Navidad como las fábulas de animales en verso.
-Nothing says Christmas like animal fables in verse.

4267 destacamento — **detachment**

m
[dɛs.ta.ka.ˈmɛ̃n̪.to]

El destacamento está en el gimnasio.
-The task force is in the gym.

4268 piar — **tweet**

vb
[ˈpjar]

Es solo que no lo escuché piar.
-I just didn't hear it chirp.

4269 jarrón — **vase**

m
[xa.ˈrõn]

Hay un jarrón con bolas verdes y grandes.
-There's a vase with big green bubbles.

4270 cofre — **chest**

m
[ˈko.fre]

Alguien tiene que quedarse y cuidar el cofre.
-Someone has to stay and guard the chest.

4271 funerario — **funeral**

adj
[fu.nɛ.ˈra.rjo]

Incluso puedes usarlo como tu retrato funerario.
-You can even use it as your funeral portrait.

4272 grifo — **water tap; curly (LA)**

m; adj
[ˈgri.fo]

El grifo del baño está estropeado.
-The faucet in the bathroom's out of order.

4273 corregir — **correct**

vb
[ko.re.ˈxir]

Yo quiero corregir este artículo.
-I want to correct this article.

4274 abundancia — **abundance**

f
[a.βũn̪.ˈdãn.sja]

Decidió compartir su abundancia con alguien menos afortunado.
-He decided to share his abundance with someone less fortunate.

4275 incumbencia — **incumbency**

f
[ĩŋ.kũm.ˈbɛ̃n.sja]

No es tu incumbencia quien durmió donde.
-It's none of your business who slept where.

4276 **corrupto**

adj; m
[ko.ˈrup̚.to]

corrupt; corrupt person

El canciller no parece ser corrupto.
-The chancellor doesn't appear to be corrupt.

4277 **contexto**

m
[kõn̪.ˈtɛks.to]

context

La paz brinda el contexto más seguro para un desarrollo duradero.
-Peace provides the most secure context for lasting development.

4278 **cónsul**

m/f
[ˈkõn.sul]

consul

Quiero hablar con el cónsul Jim.
-I'd like to speak to Consul Jim.

4279 **libreta**

f
[li.ˈβrɛ.ta]

notebook

Quería enseñarme su libreta de ahorros.
-She wanted to show me her bank book.

4280 **topo**

m
[ˈto.po]

mole

Necesitamos demostrar si Jim es el topo.
-We need to prove whether Jim's the mole.

4281 **interrupción**

f
[ĩn̪.tɛ.rup.ˈsjõn]

interruption

Me avergüenza esta grosera interrupción.
-I'm embarrassed by this rude interruption.

4282 **pistolero**

m
[pis.to.ˈlɛ.ro]

gunman

Para ser pistolero, eres bastante pesimista.
-For a gunman, you're one hell of a pessimist.

4283 **consulado**

m
[kõn.su.ˈla.ðo]

consulate

Mira, puedo llegar al consulado.
-Look, I can make it to the consulate.

4284 **característica**

f
[ka.rak̚.tɛ.ˈris.ti.ka]

feature

Este debate tiene una característica fundamental.
-This debate has one fundamental feature.

4285 **esteroide**

m
[ɛs.tɛ.ˈroi̯.ðe]

steroid

Aparentemente este es su esteroide preferido.
-Apparently, this is his steroid of choice.

4286 **tortilla**

f
[tor.ˈti.ja]

omelette

Podría hacer una tortilla con ensalada.
-I could make an omelet and salad.

4287 **balance**

m
[ba.ˈlãn.se]

balance

Todavía tenemos un balance positivo aquí hoy.
-We still have a positive balance here today.

4288 **Atenas**

f
[a.ˈte.nas]

Athens

Quiero visitar las ruinas de Atenas.
-I want to visit the ruins of Athens.

4289 **irresistible**

adj
[i.re.sis.ˈti.βle]

irresistible

Mesalia es una ciudad con un encanto irresistible.
-Mesalia is a town of irresistible charm.

4290 **antro**

m
[ˈãn̪.tro]

den

Esto no es exactamente un antro de drogadictos.
-This is not exactly a crack den.

4291 **pulga**

flea

f
['pul.ɣa]

Una pulga puede saltar doscientas veces su propio tamaño.
-A flea can jump 200 times its own height.

4292 **establecimiento** **establishment**

m
[ɛs.ta.βle.si.'mjẽn̪.to]

Este es un establecimiento libre de humos.
-This is a non-smoking establishment.

4293 **gelatina** **jelly**

f
[xe.la.'ti.na]

Si tuviéramos gelatina de menta sería fantástico.
-If we had some mint jelly, that would be fabulous.

4294 **estrellar(se)** **crash**

vb
[ɛs.tre.'ʝar]

Soy piloto y puedo asegurarte que no nos vamos a estrellar.
-I'm a pilot, and I can assure you, we're not going to crash.

4295 **periodismo** **journalism**

m
[pɛ.rjo.'ðiṣ.mo]

Pocas personas se dedican al periodismo para engañar deliberadamente al público.
-Few people go into journalism to deliberately mislead the public.

4296 **madrastra** **stepmother**

f
[ma.'ðras.tra]

Dejé el regalo de tu madrastra dentro por accidente.
-I left your stepmother's present inside by accident.

4297 **ceja** **eyebrow**

f
['se.xa]

Levantas la ceja izquierda cuando mientes.
-Your left eyebrow goes up when you lie.

4298 **loro** **parrot**

m
['lo.ro]

Siempre he querido comerme un loro.
-I've always wanted to eat a parrot.

4299 **trayectoria** **trajectory**

f
[tra.jek̚.'to.rja]

Es difícil predecir la trayectoria del progreso tecnológico.
-The trajectory of technological progress is difficult to predict.

4300 **atado** **tied**

adj
[a.'ta.ðo]

Él estará atado a condiciones que debe respetar.
-He'll be bound by conditions that he must respect.

4301 **entusiasmar(se)** **delight; be thrilled**

vb; vbr
[ẽn̪.tu.sjaṣ.'mar]

Gracias por entusiasmar a los de los asientos baratos.
-Thanks for giving the guys in the cheap seats a thrill.

4302 **capricho** **whim**

m
[ka.'pri.tʃo]

No podemos pues considerarlos el resultado de un capricho tecnológico.
-We cannot consider them to be the result of a technological whim.

4303 **póquer** **poker**

m
['po.kɛr]

No sé donde habría aprendido a jugar al póquer.
-I don't know where he would have learned to play poker.

4304 **inquieto** **restless**

adj
[ĩŋ.'kjɛ.to]

Has estado inquieto toda la mañana.
-You've been uneasy all morning.

4305 **válvula** **valve**

f
['bal.βu.la]

Podría haberle hecho lo mismo a la válvula de seguridad.
-It could've done the same thing to the safety valve.

4306 **triunfar** **triumph**

vb
[trjũɱ.'far]

Solamente con este método podemos triunfar.
-It is only through this method that we can succeed.

4307	**oral**	**oral**
	adj	La tradición oral ha existido durante cientos de años.
	[o.ˈral]	-Oral tradition has existed for hundreds of years.
4308	**abordar**	**tackle**
	vb	Reconoció la necesidad de abordar las preocupaciones del sector bancario.
	[a.βor.ˈðar]	-He recognized the need to address the concerns of the banking industry.
4309	**proyección**	**projection**
	f	Acabo de recibir una invitación para tu proyección.
	[pro.jɛk.ˈsjõn]	-I just got an invitation for your screening.
4310	**monitor**	**monitor**
	m	Señor, el monitor sigue mostrando información errónea.
	[mo.ni.ˈtor]	-Sir, the monitor is still giving the wrong information.
4311	**discípulo**	**disciple**
	m	Supongo que Jim podría ser considerado un discípulo.
	[dis.ˈsi.pu.lo]	-I suppose Jim could be considered a disciple.
4312	**narcótico**	**narcotic; narcotic**
	adj; m	Borramos los rastros del narcótico.
	[nar.ˈko.ti.ko]	-We erase the traces of the narcotic.
4313	**evaluación**	**evaluation**
	f	La evaluación se basó en el análisis de la información disponible.
	[e.βa.lwa.ˈsjõn]	-The evaluation involved analyzing available information.
4314	**lector**	**reader**
	m	Un lector atento habría percibido el error.
	[lek.ˈtor]	-A careful reader would have noticed the mistake.
4315	**amistoso**	**friendly**
	adj	Jim es amistoso con todos.
	[a.mis.ˈto.so]	-Jim is friendly to everybody.
4316	**limitado**	**limited**
	adj	Las bombillas solo tienen un limitado impacto medioambiental.
	[li.mi.ˈta.ðo]	-Light bulbs only have a limited impact on the environment.
4317	**adicional**	**additional**
	adj	Cualquier indicio adicional de ocultamiento de documentos sería grave.
	[a.ði.sjo.ˈnal]	-Any further sign of the concealment of documents would be serious.
4318	**arrogancia**	**arrogance**
	f	Estaba bastante alarmado por la arrogancia y la ignorancia mostrada por los estadounidenses.
	[a.ro.ˈɣãn.sja]	-I was quite alarmed at the arrogance and ignorance showed by the Americans.
4319	**agencia**	**agency**
	f	Preguntaremos en una agencia de viajes.
	[a.ˈxɛ̃n.sja]	-We will ask at a travel agency.
4320	**bolígrafo**	**pen**
	m	Si tu bolígrafo fuera rojo, estaría bien.
	[bo.ˈli.ɣra.fo]	-If your pen were red, that would be good.
4321	**milicia**	**militia**
	f	Nuestra milicia es responsable de todas las personas de este vecindario.
	[mi.ˈli.sja]	-Our militia's responsible for all the people in this neighborhood.
4322	**imitación**	**imitation**

f
[i.mi.ta.ˈsjõn]

No tendrás que usar esta imitación barata.
-You won't have to wear this cheap imitation.

4323 **delegación**

delegation

f
[de.le.ɣa.ˈsjõn]

La delegación presentará un informe después de cada reunión.
-A report shall be submitted by the delegation after each meeting.

4324 **catarata**

cataract

f
[ka.ta.ˈra.ta]

Tarde o temprano nos engullirá la catarata.
-Sooner or later, the waterfall will swallow us.

4325 **rabo**

tail

m
[ˈra.βo]

Ese perro tiene el rabo corto.
-That dog has a short tail.

4326 **laguna**

lagoon

f
[la.ˈɣu.na]

La laguna se secó el verano pasado.
-The pond dried up last summer.

4327 **tacaño**

miserly

adj
[ta.ˈka.ɲo]

No puedes llevarme a ningún sitio porque eres tacaño.
-You can't take me anywhere because you're cheap.

4328 **secuestrar**

kidnap

vb
[se.kwɛs.ˈtrar]

Estaban intentando secuestrar a uno de los perros.
-They were attempting to kidnap one of the dogs.

4329 **comprensible**

understandable

adj
[kõm.prẽn.ˈsi.βle]

Es comprensible que quiera volver a casarse.
-I understand that he wants to remarry.

4330 **desmayarse**

faint

vbr
[dɛs̪.ma.ˈjar.se]

El mareo es una sensación como que uno se podría desmayar.
-Light-headedness is a feeling like you might faint.

4331 **exilio**

exile

m
[ɛk.ˈsi.ljo]

Intentaré recordarme eso mientras estoy en el exilio.
-I'll try to remind myself of that while I'm in exile.

4332 **procurar**

attempt

vb
[pro.ku.ˈrar]

Debemos procurar que esta propuesta de directiva modificada se retire.
-We must ensure that this proposal for an amended directive is withdrawn.

4333 **simio**

ape

m
[ˈsi.mjo]

Enséñame también cómo ser un simio, por favor.
-Please teach how me to be an ape, too.

4334 **contaminación**

contamination

f
[kõn̪.ta.mi.na.ˈsjõn]

Organizar los juegos olímpicos en un lugar con mucha contaminación
atmosférica da lugar a un gran riesgo para los atletas.
-Holding the Olympics where there's severe atmospheric pollution gives rise
to a great risk for athletes.

4335 **cultivar**

cultivate

vb
[kul̪.ti.ˈβar]

También comían raíces y vegetales que empezaron a cultivar.
-They also ate roots and vegetables that they started to grow.

4336 **reflexionar**

reflect

vb
[re.flɛk.sjo.ˈnar]

Es hora de reflexionar sobre tu pasado.
-It's time to reflect on your past.

4337 **inaceptable**

unacceptable

	adj	La cifra de diecinueve millones de desempleados es inaceptable.
	[i.na.seṕ.ˈta.βle]	-The figure of 19 million unemployed is quite simply unacceptable.
4338	**leopardo**	**leopard**
	m	Un leopardo y un babuino divagaban libremente por el terreno.
	[le.o.ˈpar.ðo]	-A leopard and baboon wander freely over the grounds.
4339	**homicida**	**killer; murder**
	m/f; adj	El arma homicida no fue hallada.
	[o.mi.ˈsi.ða]	-The murder weapon wasn't found.
4340	**encubrir**	**cover**
	vb	Los funcionarios implicados trataron posteriormente de encubrir el incidente.
	[ẽŋ.ku.ˈβrir]	-The implicated staff members later attempted to cover up the incident.
4341	**alzar**	**raise**
	vb	La comunidad internacional tiene el deber de alzar su voz contra ese peligro.
	[al.ˈsar]	-The international community has a duty to raise its voice against this danger.
4342	**motín**	**riot**
	m	Capitán, quisiera reportar un motín.
	[mo.ˈtĩn]	-Captain, I wish to report a mutiny.
4343	**cereal**	**grain-based; cereal**
	adj; m	En algunas zonas las cosechas de cereal quedaron destruidas por completo.
	[sɛ.re.ˈal]	-In some areas, cereal crops were completely destroyed.
4344	**pulsera**	**bracelet**
	f	No compré una pulsera de 500 dólares.
	[pul.ˈsɛ.ra]	-I didn't buy a bracelet for $500.
4345	**reponer**	**replenish**
	vb	Cada uno de ustedes tiene otra bolsa de arroz para reponer.
	[re.po.ˈnɛr]	-You each have another bag of rice to replenish.
4346	**vómito**	**vomit**
	m	Quería una recompensa por limpiar todo aquel vómito.
	[ˈbo.mi.to]	-He wanted a reward for cleaning up all that puke.
4347	**remo**	**oar**
	m	Alguien me ha golpeado con un remo.
	[ˈre.mo]	-Someone hit me with an oar.
4348	**cordón**	**cord**
	m	Mi cordón se quedó atrapado en la escalera mecánica.
	[kor.ˈðõn]	-My shoelace got caught in the escalator.
4349	**remate**	**ending**
	m	Estoy ansiosa por oír el remate.
	[re.ˈma.te]	-I can't wait to hear the punch line.
4350	**reverencia**	**reverence**
	f	Entre mi gente, un verdadero buscador es tratado con la máxima reverencia.
	[re.βɛ.ˈrẽn.sja]	-Among my people, a true seeker is treated with utmost reverence.
4351	**fósforo**	**match**
	m	Somos un fósforo esperando encenderse.
	[ˈfos.fo.ro]	-We're a match waiting to ignite.
4352	**inmortalidad**	**immortality**
	f	Yo creo en la inmortalidad del alma.
	[ĩm.mor.ta.li.ˈðað]	-I believe in the immortality of the soul.
4353	**vocación**	**vocation**

f
[bo.ka.ˈsjõn]

Nunca elijas una nueva vocación solo porque estás inquieto.
-Never choose a new vocation just because you are restless.

4354 coral

coral

m
[ko.ˈral]

El arrecife de coral es la atracción principal de la región.
-The coral reef is the region's prime attraction.

4355 impecable

impeccable

adj
[ĩm.pe.ˈka.βle]

En cada instancia, la lógica fue impecable.
-In each instance, the logic was impeccable.

4356 recreo

break

m
[re.ˈkre.o]

En este recreo los alumnos pueden jugar, descansar y tomar un refrigerio.
-In this break, students can play, relax and have refreshments.

4357 divorciar(se)

divorce

vb
[di.βor.ˈsjar]

Si pierdes esta oportunidad nunca te podrás divorciar.
-If you lose this chance you'll never be able to divorce.

4358 perverso

wicked

adj
[pɛr.ˈβɛr.so]

Rechazarme te provoca un gusto perverso.
-You take a perverse pleasure in turning me down.

4359 encanto

charm

m
[ẽŋ.ˈkãn̪.to]

El hotel presenta habitaciones acogedoras y tiene un encanto tradicional.
-The hotel provides you with cozy guest rooms and has a traditional charm.

4360 observador

observer; observant

m; adj
[oβ.sɛr.βa.ˈðor]

Lo que quiero es un buen observador.
-What I want is a good observer.

4361 plantación

plantation

f
[plãn̪.ta.ˈsjõn]

Parece capaz de incendiar una plantación.
-She looks like she might burn down a plantation.

4362 prado

meadow

m
[ˈpra.ðo]

Esto está destinado a la creación de un prado de floración permanente.
-This is intended for creating a permanent flowering meadow.

4363 evidenciar

demonstrate

vb
[e.βi.ðẽn.ˈsjar]

La empresa debería evidenciar un compromiso.
-The company should demonstrate a commitment.

4364 violeta

violet; violet

adj; f
[bjo.ˈlɛ.ta]

El otro par es violeta con hebillas rojas y amarillas.
-The other pair is violet with red and yellow trimming.

4365 calificación

qualification

f
[ka.li.fi.ka.ˈsjõn]

Los procedimientos internos de calificación de riesgos no se validaban con métodos estadísticos.
-Internal rating procedures were not validated using statistical methods.

4366 transformación

transformation

f
[trãns.for.ma.ˈsjõn]

La transformación de la energía debe comenzar ahora.
-The energy transformation must begin now.

4367 inspirar

inspire

vb
[ĩns.pi.ˈrar]

Nuestro trabajo es enseñar e inspirar.
-It's our job to instruct and inspire.

4368 cansancio

fatigue

m
[kãn.ˈsãn.sjo]

Su cansancio puede ser un síntoma de enfermedad.
-Your tiredness may in itself be a symptom of illness.

4369 ventilación — **ventilation**
f
[bẽṇ.ti.la.ˈsjõn]
Este producto no debe usarse en condiciones de ventilación insuficiente.
-This product is not to be used under conditions of poor ventilation.

4370 mosquito — **mosquito**
m
[mos.ˈki.to]
Desearía ser un mosquito ahora mismo.
-I wish I was a mosquito right now.

4371 codicia — **greed**
f
[ko.ˈði.sja]
También intervinieron la codicia y la necedad.
-Greed and stupidity had also come into play.

4372 dotar — **supply**
vb
[do.ˈtar]
El acero se utiliza para dotar a los neumáticos de rigidez y solidez.
-Steel is used to provide rigidity and strength to the tires.

4373 póliza — **policy**
f
[ˈpo.li.sa]
Descubrimos lo de esa póliza y le preguntamos.
-We found out about that policy, and we asked her.

4374 laboral — **work**
adj
[la.βo.ˈral]
Esta lista debe estar disponible si un inspector laboral la pide.
-This list must be made available to a labor inspector upon request.

4375 lesión — **injury**
f
[le.ˈsjõn]
El dentista tuvo que informar de la lesión.
-The dentist had to report the injury.

4376 esponja — **sponge**
f
[ɛs.ˈpõŋ.xa]
Tiene un cerebro como una esponja cuántica.
-It's got a brain like a quantum sponge.

4377 bocina — **horn**
f[bo.ˈsi.na]
No necesitamos tocar nuestra propia bocina. -We don't need to blow our own horn.

4378 estofado — **stew; stewed**
m; adj
[ɛs.to.ˈfa.ðo]
Toma algo de este estofado.
-Have some of this stew.

4379 transbordador — **ferry**
m
[trãṣ.βor.ða.ˈðor]
Ella usaba este transbordador continuamente.
-She used this ferry all the time.

4380 portón — **gate**
m
[por.ˈtõn]
No recuerdo que este portón estuviera aquí antes.
-I don't remember this gate being here before.

4381 civilizado — **civilized**
adj
[si.βi.li.ˈsa.ðo]
Siempre ha formado parte del comportamiento civilizado.
-It has always been a part of civilized behavior.

4382 galo — **Gallic**
adj
[ˈga.lo]
Gergovie, un pueblo galo cercano, había sido la aldea fortificada de Vercingétorix, conquistada por Julio César.
-Gergovie, a nearby Gallic town, used to be the fortified town of Vercingétorix, conquered by Julius Caesar.

4383 heno — **hay**
m
[ˈe.no]
Llevemos este fardo de heno hacia abajo.
-Let's get this bale of hay down.

4384 compensación — **compensation**

f
[kõm.pẽn.sa.ˈsjõn]

Según las investigaciones, muchas víctimas preferirían recibir compensación del delincuente.
-According to research, many victims would rather receive compensation from the offender.

4385 compensar — **compensate**

vb
[kõm.pẽn.ˈsar]

Incluso las compañías aéreas económicas deben compensar a sus pasajeros.
-Even budget airlines must compensate their passengers.

4386 cierre — **closing**

m
[ˈsjɛ.re]

Cierre la caja con cola y no con cinta.
-Seal the box with glue, and not with tape.

4387 trío — **trio**

m
[ˈtri.o]

El trío de británicos fue arrestado tres meses después.
-The British trio was arrested three months later.

4388 barbilla — **chin**

f
[bar.ˈβi.ʝa]

Solo quiero mirar tu barbilla.
-I want to just look at your chin.

4389 bachillerato — **A levels**

m
[ba.tʃi.ʝɛ.ˈra.to]

Era la peor perdedora de nuestro bachillerato.
-She was absolutely the biggest loser in our high school.

4390 índice — **index**

m
[ˈĩn̪.di.se]

¿Por qué ha disminuido tan bruscamente el índice de natalidad?
-Why has the birthrate declined so sharply?

4391 mártir — **martyr**

m/f
[ˈmar.tir]

Caeré con gusto como un mártir.
-I will willingly fall as a martyr.

4392 foco — **focus, spotlight**

m
[ˈfo.ko]

Lamentablemente, no están en el foco y están muy oscuras.
-Unfortunately, they are not in focus and too dark.

4393 fastidio — **nuisance**

m
[fas.ˈti.ðjo]

Esta iglesia es un fastidio y nada más.
-This church is a nuisance and nothing more.

4394 reemplazo — **replacement**

m
[re.ẽm.ˈpla.so]

Quizás estoy siendo completamente desagradecido dejándola sin reemplazo.
-Maybe I'm being totally ungrateful leaving her without a replacement.

4395 inscripción — **registration**

f
[ĩns.krip.ˈsjõn]

El equipo siguió vigilando asuntos electorales, incluyendo la inscripción de nuevos votantes.
-The team continued to monitor electoral matters, including the registration of new voters.

4396 adrenalina — **adrenalin**

f
[a.ðre.na.ˈli.na]

La adrenalina vuelve papilla a una mente perfectamente buena.
-Adrenaline turns perfectly good minds to mush.

4397 fabricar — **manufacture**

vb
[fa.βri.ˈkar]

Tendremos que fabricar el antídoto aquí mismo.
-We'll have to manufacture the antidote right here.

4398 hormona — **hormone**

f
[or.ˈmo.na]

Esto podría estar relacionado con el nivel de testosterona, la hormona masculina.
-This may be related to the level of the male hormone testosterone.

4399 herrero — **blacksmith**

m

[ɛ.ˈrɛ.ro]

La práctica hace la perfección, o como dice un refrán francés, el herrero se hace forjando.

-Practice makes perfect or, as the French proverb says, forging makes a blacksmith.

4400 programar — **program**

vb

[pro.ɣra.ˈmar]

Algunas personas no saben programar nada.

-Some people don't know how to program at all.

4401 palestino — **Palestinian; Palestinian person**

adj; m

[pa.lɛs.ˈti.no]

El presidente palestino ha formulado ahora sus condiciones para el diálogo.

-The Palestinian president has now set his conditions for dialogue.

4402 limosna — **alms**

f

[li.ˈmos̱.na]

Lo primero que vieron fue un viejo mendigo, de mirada triste, pidiendo limosna.

-The first thing they saw was an old beggar with a sad expression on his face, asking for alms.

4403 duende — **spirit**

m

[ˈdwẽ̠n.de]

Atrapar a ese duende debe haberte sido complicado.

-Catching that leprechaun must have been hard work.

4404 esquiar — **ski**

vb

[ɛs.ˈkjar]

Me gusta esquiar en junio.

-I like skiing in June.

4405 pegamento — **glue**

m

[pe.ɣa.ˈmẽ̠n.to]

¡No toques mi puente de espaguetis! El pegamento todavía se está secando.

-Don't touch my spaghetti bridge! The glue is still hardening.

4406 prostitución — **prostitution**

f

[pros.ti.tu.ˈsjõn]

Fue arrestado hoy bajo cargos de prostitución y extorsión.

-He was arrested today on prostitution and racketeering charges.

4407 agricultura — **agriculture**

f

[a.ɣri.kul̪.ˈtu.ra]

Los biocombustibles que están subvencionados están desestabilizando enormemente la agricultura.

-Biofuels, which are subsidized, are vastly destabilizing agriculture.

4408 aplastar — **crush**

vb

[ap̚.las.ˈtar]

No puedo aplastar moscas con mi libro.

-I cannot squash flies with my book.

4409 flojo — **loose, slacker**

adj

[ˈflo.xo]

Soy demasiado flojo para levantarme tan temprano.

-I am too lazy to get up that early.

4410 mango — **mango**

m

[ˈmãŋ.go]

Gracias por tu delicioso mango.

-Thank you for your delicious mango.

4411 nuera — **daughter-in-law**

f

[ˈnwɛ.ra]

Había comprado estos brazaletes para mi nuera.

-I had bought these bangles for my daughter-in-law.

4412 chocar — **hit**

vb

[ʧo.ˈkar]

La próxima vez intenta verlo antes de chocarte con ello.

-Next time, try to see it before you hit it.

4413 tasa — **valuation**

f
['ta.sa]
Se prevé que esta tasa seguirá descendiendo.
-It is anticipated that this rate will continue to decline.

4414 reactor — **reactor**
m
[re.ak̚.'tor]
Incluso el reactor más seguro es dirigido por personas.
-Even the safest power station is manned by people.

4415 consultar — **consult**
vb
[kõn.sul̪.'tar]
Deberías consultar a un doctor si los síntomas empeoran.
-You should consult a doctor if the symptoms get worse.

4416 brújula — **compass**
f
['bru.xu.la]
Encontré esta brújula en tu garaje.
-I found this compass in your garage.

4417 cereza — **cherry**
f
[sɛ.'re.sa]
Guardaré esa cereza para después del show.
-I'll save that cherry for after the show.

4418 apelación — **appeal**
f
[a.pe.la.'sjõn]
Presenté apelación ante un tribunal militar.
-I submitted an appeal to a military court.

4419 disgustar — **disgust**
vb
[diʂ.ɣus.'tar]
Nosotros no queremos disgustar a tu preciosa hija nunca más.
-We don't want to upset your beautiful daughter anymore.

4420 despiadado — **ruthless**
adj
[dɛs.pja.'ða.ðo]
Tienes que ser despiadado en estas circunstancias.
-You've got to be ruthless in these circumstances.

4421 natación — **swimming**
f
[na.ta.'sjõn]
Es curioso porque de pequeña odiaba la natación.
-It's odd because, as a child, I hated swimming.

4422 psicológico — **psychological**
adj
[si.ko.'lo.xi.ko]
Todo abuso físico o psicológico está prohibido.
-Any form of physical or psychological abuse is prohibited.

4423 empeorar — **worsen**
vb
[ẽm.pe.o.'rar]
Sin embargo, la situación no deja de empeorar.
-Yet the situation continues to worsen.

4424 circular — **circular; travel**
adj; vb
[sir.ku.'lar]
He recibido una circular del banco.
-I've received a circular from the bank.

4425 arzobispo — **archbishop**
m
[ar.so.'βis.po]
Estamos preparando los papeles del arzobispo para enviarlos.
-We're getting the archbishop's papers ready for shipment.

4426 inventario — **inventory**
m
[ĩm.bẽn̪.'ta.rjo]
Tengo un interés muy particular en este inventario.
-I have a very particular personal interest in this inventory.

4427 honrar — **honor**
vb
[õn.'rar]
Intento honrar su memoria continuando ese trabajo.
-I try to honor his memory by continuing that work.

4428 hervir — **boil**
vb
[ɛr.'βir]
Sé cómo hervir un huevo.
-I do know how to boil an egg.

4429 imprudente — **reckless**

adj
[ĩm.pru.ˈðɛ̃n̪.te]

Esa imprudente y peligrosa conducta no debe continuar.
-This reckless and dangerous pattern of behavior must not continue.

4430 **acelerador**

m; adj
[a.se.lɛ.ra.ˈðor]

accelerator; accelerant

El detonador estaba conectado a un acelerador.
-The detonator was connected to an accelerator.

4431 **ardilla**

f
[ar.ˈði.ja]

squirrel

¿Cuántas orejas tiene una ardilla?
-How many ears does a squirrel have?

4432 **composición**

f
[kõm.po.si.ˈsjõn]

composition

Estoy trabajando en la composición ahora mismo.
-I'm working on the composition right now.

4433 **decoración**

f
[de.ko.ra.ˈsjõn]

decoration

Él estudió decoración de interiores.
-He studied interior decoration.

4434 **peluquero**

m
[pe.lu.ˈkɛ.ro]

hairdresser

Voló hasta aquí con un peluquero.
-He flew up here with a hairdresser.

4435 **eficaz**

adj
[e.ˈfi.kas]

effective

Las escuelas y sus directores necesitan un control disciplinario más eficaz.
-The schools and their heads need more efficient disciplinary control.

4436 **atentar**

vb
[a.tɛ̃n̪.ˈtar]

attack

El terrorista de Chicago ha vuelto a atentar.
-The Chicago bomber has struck again.

4437 **retaguardia**

f
[rɛ.ta.ˈɣwar.ðja]

rearguard

Acaban de atacarnos por la retaguardia.
-We've just been clipped from the rear.

4438 **siniestro**

adj
[si.ˈnjɛs.tro]

sinister

Todo esto puede parecer muy siniestro.
-This can all seem very sinister.

4439 **elegancia**

f
[e.le.ˈɣãn.sja]

elegance

Todas las habitaciones combinan el confort contemporáneo con la elegancia tradicional.
-Each of the rooms is a combination of contemporary comfort and traditional elegance.

4440 **templar**

vb
[tɛ̃m.ˈplar]

cool down

Ella supo templar sus teorías hasta tener pruebas concretas.
-She knew to temper her theories until she had concrete evidence.

4441 **pronunciar**

vb
[pro.nũn.ˈsjar]

pronounce

Mis disculpas a los intérpretes por obligarles a pronunciar este trabalenguas.
-My apologies to the interpreters for forcing them to pronounce this tongue twister.

4442 **roble**

m
[ˈro.βle]

oak

El roble siguió erguido después de la tormenta.
-The oak tree remained standing after the storm.

4443 **inmoral**

adj
[ĩm.mo.ˈral]

immoral

Opino que es inmoral que un ser humano adquiera tanta riqueza.
-I think it's immoral that any human being should acquire that much wealth.

4444 **convencional**

conventional

	adj [kõm.bẽn.sjo.ˈnal]	La amenaza del terrorismo convencional sigue exigiendo toda nuestra atención. -The threat of conventional terrorism continues to require our full and undivided attention.
4445	**zanahoria** f [sa.na.ˈo.rja]	**carrot** Añade la zanahoria rallada al relleno. -Add the shredded carrot to the stuffing.
4446	**masajista** m/f [ma.sa.ˈxis.ta]	**massage therapist** Eres ese masajista del otro día. -You're that masseur from the other day.
4447	**semen** m [ˈse.mẽn]	**semen** Los bancos de semen no catalogan esos rasgos. -Sperm banks don't catalog those traits.
4448	**boletín** m[bo.lɛ.ˈtĩn]	**bulletin** Los nombres de los estudiantes que habían suspendido el examen estaban puestos en el boletín de anuncios. -The names of the students who failed in the examination were posted on the bulletin board.
4449	**enseñanza** f [ɛ̃n.se.ˈɲãn.sa]	**teaching** En casos excepcionales también puede impartirse enseñanza en inglés. -In exceptional cases, teaching can also be carried out in English.
4450	**soberano** adj; m [so.βɛ.ˈra.no]	**sovereign; sovereign** En una democracia el pueblo es el soberano. -In a democracy, it is the people who are sovereign.
4451	**aliviar** vb [a.li.ˈβjar]	**relieve** Muchos consideran que la eutanasia es una forma de aliviar el dolor del paciente. -Many consider that euthanasia is a way to relieve a patient's sufferings.
4452	**Caribe** m [ka.ˈri.βe]	**the Caribbean** Estamos examinando en particular la zona del Caribe. -We are looking particularly at the area of the Caribbean.
4453	**agitar** vb [a.xi.ˈtar]	**shake** Estos son pósteres de propaganda para agitar a las masas. -These are propaganda posters to agitate the masses.
4454	**mudanza** f [mu.ˈðãn.sa]	**move** Puedo darle unos dólares para ayudarle con la mudanza. -I could give you a couple dollars to help you move.
4455	**cursi** adj; m/f [ˈkur.si]	**corny; pretentious** No puedo soportar esta música cursi. -I can't stand this sappy music.
4456	**donación** f [do.na.ˈsjõn]	**donation** Te estoy pidiendo que hagas una donación. -I'm asking you to make a donation.
4457	**suburbio** m [su.ˈβur.βjo]	**suburb** Me mandarán a un suburbio aburrido. -I get shipped off to some boring suburb.
4458	**rajar(se)** vb; vbr [ra.ˈxar]	**slice; back out (coll)** Podría rajar su yugular tan rápido como cualquiera de vosotros podría apretar el gatillo. -I can slit his jugular as quick as any one of you can squeeze off a shot.

4459 disputa — dispute
f
[dis.ˈpu.ta]
Tras mucha negociación, los dos lados de la disputa llegaron a un compromiso.
-After much negotiation, the two sides in the dispute reached a compromise.

4460 resolución — resolution
f
[re.so.lu.ˈsjõn]
La resolución que acabamos de aprobar facilitará tal transformación.
-The resolution we have just adopted will facilitate such a transformation.

4461 coincidir — coincide
vb
[koi̯n.si.ˈðir]
Sus declaraciones verbales deberían coincidir con los hechos.
-The verbal declarations would have to match the facts.

4462 humildad — humility
f
[u.mil̩.ˈdað]
Tienes que tener escepticismo y humildad.
-You've got to have skepticism and humility.

4463 talentoso — talented
adj
[ta.lẽn̩.ˈto.so]
Me han dicho que es muy talentoso.
-I'm told that he's quite talented.

4464 deshacer — undo
vb
[de.sa.ˈsɛr]
No puedo deshacer este nudo.
-I can't untie this knot.

4465 teja — tile
f
[ˈte.xa]
La teja que se cayó del tejado se rompió en pedazos.
-The tile which fell from the roof broke into pieces.

4466 inmigrante — immigrant; immigrant
adj; m/f
[ĩm.mi.ˈɣrãn̩.te]
Óliver descubrió que su nueva novia era una inmigrante ilegal.
-Oliver found out that his new girlfriend is an illegal immigrant.

4467 delegar — delegate
vb
[de.le.ˈɣar]
Sería absurdo delegar la educación y la cultura a un nivel supranacional.
-It would be absurd to delegate education and culture to a supranational level.

4468 corteza — crust
f
[kor.ˈte.sa]
La corteza terrestre también empezará a moverse.
-The earth's crust will also start to move.

4469 avena — oats
f
[a.ˈβe.na]
Cuando las cosas iban mal, tomábamos avena.
-When things were bad, we had porridge.

4470 peludo — hairy
adj
[pe.ˈlu.ðo]
Busco a alguien pequeño y peludo.
-I'm looking for something small and hairy.

4471 seña — sign
f
[ˈse.ɲa]
No te preocupes, nos hará una seña.
-Don't worry about it, she'll give us a signal.

4472 corazonada — hunch
f
[ko.ra.so.ˈna.ða]
Resulta que tu corazonada era acertada.
-It turns out your hunch was right.

4473 buitre — vulture
m
[ˈbwi.tre]
Ahora sí que sueno como un buitre.
-Now I really do sound like a vulture.

4474 remordimiento — remorse

m	No me dejes marcharme con este remordimiento.
[re.mor.ði.ˈmjẽ̠.to]	-Don't let me leave with this remorse.

4475 laurel — **laurel**

m
[lau̯.ˈɾɛl]

Compra algo de laurel para hacer un adobo esta noche.
-Buy some laurel to make a marinade tonight.

4476 descargar — **download**

vb
[dɛs.kar.ˈɣar]

También quiero descargar esas fotos.
-I also want to download those photos.

4477 parroquia — **parish**

f
[pa.ˈro.kja]

Voy a asignarte a una parroquia.
-I'm going to assign you to a parish.

4478 tarifa — **rate**

f
[ta.ˈri.fa]

Tienen una tarifa muy especial para alcaldes.
-They make a very special rate for mayors.

4479 presto — **ready; promptly**

adj; adv
[ˈpɾɛs.to]

Estaré presto para ir en una hora.
-I'll be ready to go in an hour.

4480 peón — **pawn**

m
[pe.ˈõn]

Jim probablemente habría sido considerado el peón.
-Jim would most likely have been considered the pawn.

4481 perdición — **perdition**

f
[pɛr.ði.ˈsjõn]

Un grito vertical perfora el aire nocturno y anuncia la perdición entre las nubes.
-A vertical scream pierces the night air and echoes doom through the clouds.

4482 recurrir — **appeal, resort**

vb
[re.ku.ˈrir]

Puedes enseñarles buenos modales a los niños sin recurrir al castigo.
-You can teach good manners to children without resorting to punishment.

4483 callejero — **stray; street map**

adj; m
[ka.ʝe.ˈxɛ.ro]

Pude rastrearla usando un contacto callejero confiable.
-I was able to track her down using a reliable street contact.

4484 espeluznante — **horrifying**

adj
[ɛs.pe.luṣ.ˈnã̠n.te]

Se la llevaron en su camioneta espeluznante con ventanillas oscuras.
-They took her in their spooky van with the windows all blacked out.

4485 albergue — **hostel**

m
[al.ˈβɛr.ɣe]

Ocasionalmente funciona también como albergue para jóvenes.
-It also functions as a youth hostel from time to time.

4486 impotente — **impotent**

adj
[ĩm.po.ˈtẽ̠n.te]

Me obligaste a anunciarle al mundo que era impotente.
-You forced me to announce to the world that I was impotent.

4487 envejecer — **age**

vb
[ẽm.be.xe.ˈsɛr]

Envejecer es una cosa fascinante. Mientras más envejeces, más quieres envejecer.
-Getting old is a fascination thing. The older you get, the older you want to get.

4488 aula — **classroom**

f
[ˈau̯.la]

Necesito sacar algo de este aula.
-I need to get something out of this classroom.

4489 criterio — **opinion, guideline**

	m	Confío en que los quince compartan este criterio.
	[kri.ˈtɛ.rjo]	-I trust that the fifteen will share this opinion.
4490	**hipótesis**	**hypothesis**
	f	La segunda hipótesis era la correcta.
	[i.ˈpo.te.sis]	-The second hypothesis was the correct one.
4491	**desarmar**	**disarm**
	vb	Eres lo suficientemente bueno como para desarmar a un agente del FBI.
	[de.sar.ˈmar]	-You are good enough to disarm an FBI agent.
4492	**mármol**	**marble**
	m	Los pisos de mármol no son hermosos.
	[ˈmar.mol]	-Marble floors are not beautiful.
4493	**diploma**	**diploma**
	m	Obtendré mi diploma en dos años.
	[dip̚.ˈlo.ma]	-I'll get my diploma in two years.
4494	**anestesia**	**anesthesia**
	f	Se realiza con anestesia supervisada por un médico.
	[a.nɛs.ˈte.sja]	-It is carried out with anesthesia supervised by a doctor.
4495	**joyería**	**jewelry**
	f	Toda mi bella joyería está vendida.
	[xo.ʝɛ.ˈri.a]	-All my beautiful jewelry is sold.
4496	**acertar**	**get right**
	vb	En realidad, no suelo acertar.
	[a.sɛr.ˈtar]	-I don't usually get it right, actually.
4497	**secuestrador**	**kidnapper**
	m	Su único crimen es ser hermano del secuestrador.
	[se.kwɛs.tra.ˈðor]	-His only crime is being fraternally related to the kidnapper.
4498	**denunciar**	**report**
	vb	Permite a la gente denunciar electrónicamente las infracciones cometidas en Internet.
	[de.nũn.ˈsjar]	-It allows people to report violations on the Internet electronically.
4499	**sucesor**	**successor**
	m	Tu sucesor ya ha sido escogido.
	[su.se.ˈsor]	-Your replacement has already been chosen.
4500	**entretenido**	**entertaining**
	adj	Verte la otra noche fue muy entretenido.
	[ẽn.trɛ.te.te.ˈni.ðo]	-Watching you the other night, that was real entertaining.
4501	**intacto**	**intact**
	adj	Seguimos trabajando incansablemente para mantener intacto ese historial intachable.
	[ĩn.ˈtak̚.to]	-We continue to work very hard to keep that exceptional record intact.
4502	**decreto**	**decree**
	m	Este artículo proporciona las definiciones de algunos conceptos clave utilizados en el decreto.
	[de.ˈkrɛ.to]	-This article provides the definitions of a number of key terms used in the decree.
4503	**superviviente**	**survivor**
	m/f	Él es el único superviviente del pueblo.
	[su.pɛr.βi.ˈβjẽn.te]	-He's the only survivor in the village.
4504	**yeso**	**plaster**

m
Ojalá pudiera quitarme este yeso pronto. Me pica un montón.
['ɟʝe.so]
-I wish I could take this cast off soon. It's itching a lot.

4505 peine   **comb**

m
Tengo un peine de madera.
['pei̯.ne]
-I have a wooden comb.

4506 prenda   **garment**

f
Esta prenda tiene las características de un chaleco.
['pɾẽn.da]
-This garment has the characteristics of a waistcoat.

4507 azotea   **rooftop**

f
No debemos marcharnos de esta azotea.
[a.so.'te.a]
-We must not leave this rooftop.

4508 armamento   **armament**

m
Lo que no les daremos será ni nuestra tecnología ni nuestro armamento.
[aɾ.ma.'mẽn.to]
-What we will not provide is any of our technology or weaponry.

4509 grueso   **heavy; thickness**

adj; m
Espero que se haya puesto el suéter grueso.
['gɾwe.so]
-I hope she took her heavy sweater.

4510 foro   **forum**

m
Trataremos sobre ello en el foro adecuado.
['fo.ro]
-We will talk about that in the appropriate forum.

4511 demandar   **sue, demand**

vb
No deberías demandar a Tom.
[de.mãn.'daɾ]
-You should not sue Tom.

4512 capitalismo   **capitalism**

m
El capitalismo tuvo que verse moderado por la caridad.
[ka.pi.ta.'liş.mo]
-Capitalism had to be tempered by charity.

4513 respaldo   **back**

m
Él está apoyándose en el respaldo de la silla.
[rɛs.'pal̪.do]
-He is leaning on the back of the chair.

4514 clavar   **nail**

vb
Puedo usarlos para clavar la operación carnaval invernal.
[kla.'βaɾ]
-I can use it to nail operation winter carnival.

4515 ídolo   **idol**

m/f
El ídolo vale millones para ciertos coleccionistas.
['i.ðo.lo]
-The idol is worth millions to the right collector.

4516 suspiro   **sigh**

m
Dejó salir un suspiro cuando el trabajo fue terminado.
[sus.'pi.ro]
-He let out a sigh when the job was finished.

4517 acre   **acre; acrid**

m; adj
En 1960, un acre de terreno mantenía a una persona.
['a.kre]
-In 1960, one acre of land sustained one person.

4518 mediocre   **mediocre**

adj
Todo parecía tan mediocre y tedioso.
[me.'ðjo.kre]
-Everything just seemed so mediocre and tedious.

4519 contestador   **cheeky, answering machine**

adj
Hice una copia cuando instale el contestador.
[kõn.tɛs.ta.'ðoɾ]
-I made a copy when I installed the answering machine.

4520 ejercer   **practice**

vb
[e.xɛr.ˈsɛr]

La pregunta es si en realidad hay alguien dispuesto a ejercer ese tipo de presión.
-The question is whether anyone is actually willing to exert that sort of pressure.

4521 republicano — **republican**

m
[re.pu.βli.ˈka.no]

Podríamos tener un presidente republicano.
-We could have a Republican president.

4522 exquisito — **exquisite**

adj
[ɛks.ki.ˈsi.to]

Ya sea fresco o maduro, se trata de un producto exquisito.
-Whether fresh or mature, it is an excellent product.

4523 empapar(se) — **soak**

vb
[ẽm.pa.ˈpar]

Dile que vaya a empapar su pelo rojo.
-Tell him to go soak his red hair.

4524 considerable — **considerable**

adj
[kõn.si.ðɛ.ˈra.βle]

Para conseguir ese objetivo será necesaria una ayuda considerable.
-Considerable aid will be required in order to achieve this objective.

4525 caluroso — **hot**

adj
[ka.lu.ˈro.so]

Debe ser horriblemente caluroso en verano.
-It must be terribly hot in the summer.

4526 entendimiento — **understanding**

m
[ẽn̪.tẽn̪.di.ˈmjẽn̪.to]

Jim, intentemos llegar a un entendimiento.
-Jim, let's try to reach an understanding.

4527 quemadura — **burn**

f
[ke.ma.ˈðu.ra]

Reconozco una quemadura química cuando la veo.
-I know a chemical burn when I see one.

4528 graduar(se) — **adjust; graduate**

vb; vbr
[gra.ˈðwar]

Todos en esta clase tienen la oportunidad de graduarse.
-Everyone in this room has a chance to graduate.

4529 lateral — **side**

adj
[la.tɛ.ˈral]

Hay una vista lateral de un pequeño nido.
-There is a side view of a small nest.

4530 enmendar — **amend**

vb
[ẽm.mẽn̪.ˈdar]

Siempre es oportuno enmendar las deficiencias.
-It's always appropriate to correct shortcomings.

4531 taco — **taco, peg**

m
[ˈta.ko]

Jamás he pagado por un taco aquí.
-I have never paid for a taco here.

4532 fracturar(se) — **fracture**

vb
[frak̚.tu.ˈrar]

No te puedes fracturar intencionadamente una clavícula.
-You can't intentionally fracture a clavicle.

4533 jabalí — **wild boar**

m/f
[xa.βa.ˈli]

Iré a por un jabalí.
-I'll go get a boar.

4534 honorario — **honorary**

adj
[o.no.ˈra.rjo]

Fue cónsul honorario de Honduras y las Filipinas.
-He was honorary consul of Honduras and the Philippines.

4535 defensivo — **defensive; defense**

adj; m
[de.fɛ̃n.ˈsi.βo]
Deseo señalar que esta doctrina es de carácter exclusivamente defensivo.
-I want to note that this doctrine is exclusively defensive in nature.

4536 tornar(se) change
vb
[tor.ˈnar]
También puedo tornar su mentira en verdad.
-I can change his lie into the truth, too.

4537 atroz atrocious
adj
[ˈa.tros]
Ella puede soltar la más atroz mentira sin pestañear los ojos.
-She can tell the most outrageous lie without batting an eye.

4538 teatral theatrical
adj
[te.a.ˈtral]
Toda obra teatral es artificiosa por naturaleza.
-Every theatrical performance is a contrivance by its very nature.

4539 rosado rose
adj
[ro.ˈsa.ðo]
Resaltan el rosado de mis mejillas.
-They bring out the rose in my cheeks.

4540 justificar justify
vb
[xus.ti.fi.ˈkar]
Era necesario justificar, reafirmar y reforzar constantemente los derechos humanos.
-There was a need to constantly justify, reaffirm and strengthen human rights.

4541 predecir predict
vb
[pre.ðe.ˈsir]
Nadie podía predecir cuándo ocurriría eso.
-No one could predict when that would happen.

4542 portátil portable; laptop
adj; m
[por.ˈta.til]
He estado intentando localizar nuestro portátil desaparecido.
-I've been trying to locate our missing laptop.

4543 reformar reform
vb
[re.for.ˈmar]
Creemos que queda aún mucho margen para reformar.
-We believe that there is still a great deal of room for reform.

4544 col cabbage
f
[ˈkol]
Finalmente puedo despedirme de la col.
-I can finally say goodbye to the cabbage.

4545 triángulo triangle
m
[ˈtrjãŋ.gu.lo]
Estas tres medidas deben formar un triángulo equilátero.
-These three measures should draw an equilateral triangle.

4546 asma asthma
m
[ˈas̺.ma]
Muchas personas sufren asma y otras afecciones.
-Large numbers of people suffer from asthma and other complaints.

4547 mayonesa mayonnaise
f
[ma.jo.ˈne.sa]
Necesito algo para extender la mayonesa.
-I need something to spread the mayo.

4548 uña nail
f
[ˈu.ɲa]
Ayuda a la uña a crecer sana y fuerte.
-It helps the nail grow strong and healthy.

4549 gen gene
m
[ˈxɛ̃n]
Quizá esto sea algún tipo de gen extraterrestre que todavía no hemos identificado.
-Maybe this is some type of extraterrestrial gene that we still haven't yet identified.

4550 transferir transfer

vb
[trãn.fɛ.ˈrir]

La comunidad decidió libremente transferir sus tierras comunales al nuevo gobierno.
-The community freely decided to transfer its communal land to the new government.

4551 estacionar — **park**

vb
[ɛs.ta.sjo.ˈnar]

Supongo que no me dejaran estacionar aquí.
-I don't suppose they'll let me park here.

4552 creíble — **credible**

adj
[kre.ˈi.βle]

Hemos declarado reiteradamente que solo mantendremos una disuasión mínima creíble.
-We have repeatedly declared that we shall maintain only a minimum credible deterrent.

4553 céntimo — **cent**

m
[ˈsẽn.ti.mo]

Recibirás cada céntimo cuando todo esto acabe.
-You'll get every penny when this is over.

4554 condolencia — **condolence**

f
[kõn.do.ˈlẽn.sja]

Creo que su auténtica condolencia reside ahí.
-I think that's where her real sympathy lies.

4555 charlatán — **fraudster, chatterbox**

m
[tʃar.la.ˈtãn]

Este tipo obviamente es un charlatán.
-This chap is obviously a charlatan.

4556 celeste — **light blue, of heaven**

adj
[se.ˈlɛs.te]

El celeste es el color del cielo, y en consecuencia, también del mar, los lagos y ríos.
-Light blue is the color of the sky and, consequently, is also the color of the sea, lakes, and rivers.

4557 cartón — **cardboard**

m
[kar.ˈtõn]

Las cajas de cartón son frágiles.
-The cardboard boxes are fragile.

4558 comediante — **comedian**

m/f
[ko.me.ˈðjãn.te]

Es el único comediante con ese conjunto.
-He was the only comedian in this outfit.

4559 matrimonial — **matrimonial**

adj
[ma.tri.mo.ˈnjal]

Te llamo porque hemos visto tu anuncio matrimonial.
-I've called you because we saw your matrimonial ad.

4560 piojo — **louse**

m
[ˈpjo.xo]

No asustas ni a un piojo enfermo con eso.
-You can't frighten even a sick louse with that.

4561 consciencia — **consciousness**

f
[kõns.ˈsjẽn.sja]

Le tomó años aclarar su consciencia.
-It took years to make her consciousness clear.

4562 bobada — **nonsense, trifle**

f
[bo.ˈβa.ða]

Pocas veces he leído tanta bobada junta.
-I've rarely read such nonsense.

4563 escupir — **spit**

vb
[ɛs.ku.ˈpir]

Pronto le haré escupir el dinero.
-Soon I will make him spit the money.

4564 vegetal — **vegetal; vegetable**

	adj; m	El polen, aunque sea recolectado por las abejas, es un producto vegetal.
	[be.xɛ.ˈtal]	-Pollen, although harvested by bees, is a vegetal product.
4565	**canguro**	**kangaroo; babysitter**
	m; m/f	El canguro salta muy alto.
	[kãŋ.ˈgu.ro]	-The kangaroo jumps very high.
4566	**vagar**	**wander**
	vb	Puede vagar alrededor del aeropuerto refunfuñando.
	[ba.ˈɣar]	-He can wander around the airport muttering.
4567	**media**	**stocking**
	f	Mire. Es la otra media.
	[ˈme.ðja]	-Look, it's the other stocking.
4568	**transformar(se)**	**transform**
	vb	No importa cuánto grites "¡auuuu!", no te vas a transformar en un lobo.
	[trãns.for.ˈmar]	-Regardless of how loud you scream "Oo-oo!", you won't turn into a wolf.
4569	**módulo**	**module**
	m	Necesitaré un piloto para recuperar el otro módulo.
	[ˈmo.ðu.lo]	-I'll need a pilot to bring the other pod back.
4570	**grieta**	**crack**
	f	Si continúan investigando, encontraran una grieta.
	[ˈgrjɛ.ta]	-If they keep investigating, they will find a crack.
4571	**concejal**	**councilor**
	m	Él era el controlador en jefe, señor.
	[kõn.se.ˈxal]	-He was the head controller, sir.
4572	**amnesia**	**amnesia**
	f	Estos son pacientes con amnesia producto de alguna experiencia traumática.
	[ãm.ˈne.sja]	-These are patients with amnesia, caused by some traumatic experience.
4573	**comodidad**	**comfort**
	f	Antiguamente la sal era una comodidad rara y costosa.
	[ko.mo.ði.ˈðað]	-Salt was a rare and costly commodity in ancient times.
4574	**coreano**	**Korean; Korean person**
	adj; m	Acabo de tener mi primera clase de coreano.
	[ko.re.ˈa.no]	-I just had my first lesson in Korean.
4575	**mero**	**mere**
	adj	La comisión no puede seguir siendo un mero observador.
	[ˈmɛ.ro]	-The commission cannot remain a mere observer.
4576	**aparcamiento**	**parking**
	m	La encontré llorando en el aparcamiento.
	[a.par.ka.ˈmjẽn̪.to]	-I found her crying in the parking lot.
4577	**ofensa**	**offense**
	f	No necesito decirte que esto es una ofensa criminal.
	[o.ˈfẽn.sa]	-I don't need to tell you that this is a criminal offense.
4578	**extinción**	**extinction**
	f	Su extinción significó una pérdida patrimonial importante.
	[ɛks.tĩn.ˈsjõn]	-Their extinction represented a great loss for the natural heritage of the city.
4579	**insultar**	**insult**
	vb	No estoy lo suficientemente borracho como para dejar que me insultes.
	[ĩn.sul̪.ˈtar]	-I'm not drunk enough to let you insult me.
4580	**ticket**	**ticket**

m
[tik̚.ˈkɛt]
Recogeré el ticket en un minuto.
-I'll pick up the ticket in a minute.

4581 **actualidad**
f
[ak̚.twa.li.ˈðað]
currently
La actualidad nos ofrece numerosos ejemplos de tabúes que hay que eliminar.
-There are currently numerous examples of such taboos that need to be lifted.

4582 **cruzado**
adj
[kru.ˈsa.ðo]
cross
Lo detendrás cuando los haya cruzado.
-You'll stop him when he's crossed them.

4583 **taquilla**
f
[ta.ˈki.ʝa]
ticket window
Tienes puntos verdes en tu taquilla.
-You've got green dots in your locker.

4584 **amplio**
adj
[ˈãm.pljo]
spacious
Necesitamos alcanzar un acuerdo ambicioso y amplio en Copenhague.
-We need to reach an ambitious and comprehensive agreement in Copenhagen.

4585 **pizarra**
f
[pi.ˈsa.ra]
blackboard
Tengo una pizarra llena de aviones.
-I've got a board full of planes.

4586 **invadir**
vb
[ĩm.ba.ˈðiɾ]
invade
No debes invadir la privacidad de otros.
-You must not invade the privacy of others.

4587 **preservar**
vb
[pre.sɛɾ.ˈβar]
preserve
Se invirtieron cientos de miles de millones de dólares para preservar estas instituciones disfuncionales.
-Hundreds of billions have been spent to preserve these dysfunctional institutions.

4588 **emisora**
f
[e.mi.ˈso.ɾa]
broadcasting station
Tienes que suscribirte para escuchar esta emisora.
-You need to be a subscriber to listen to this station.

4589 **prefecto**
m
[pre.ˈfek̚.to]
prefect
El nuevo prefecto quiere ser popular entre los ciudadanos.
-The new prefect wants to be popular with the citizens.

4590 **morar**
vb
[mo.ˈɾar]
dwell
Los ancianos dijeron que no deberíamos morar en el pasado.
-The elders said we should not dwell on the past.

4591 **creyente**
m/f
[kre.ˈʝẽn̪.te]
believer
Yo soy el último creyente que queda de la diosa Deméter.
-I am the last remaining worshipper of the goddess Demeter.

4592 **farol**
m
[fa.ˈɾol]
lantern, bluff
Los reguladores no aceptaron su farol y lo obligaron a dimitir.
-The regulators called his bluff and forced him to resign.

4593 **castrar**
vb
[kas.ˈtrar]
castrate
Conocí a un fantasma cuyo asunto pendiente era castrar a su cuñado.
-I knew a ghost whose unfinished business was to castrate her brother-in-law.

4594 **ajuste**
m
[a.ˈxus.te]
adjustment
China debe elegir entre un mayor crecimiento y un ajuste estructural más rápido.
-China must choose between higher growth and faster structural adjustment.

4595 **obsequio**   **gift**
m   No importa que no traigas obsequio.
[oβ.ˈse.kjo]   -It's okay that you didn't get a gift.

4596 **confortable**   **comfortable**
adj   Estamos seguros de que su estancia será muy confortable.
[kõɱ.for.ˈta.βle]   -We are sure that your demurrage will be very comfortable.

4597 **anónimo**   **anonymous**
adj   Prefiere seguir siendo anónimo por ahora.
[a.ˈno.ni.mo]   -He prefers to remain anonymous at this time.

4598 **consultorio**   **office, consultancy**
m   Reúnete conmigo en mi consultorio esta tarde.
[kõn.sul̯.ˈto.rjo]   -Just meet me at my office this afternoon.

4599 **dedicación**   **dedication**
f   Quiero felicitarlos por su nivel de interés y dedicación a este asunto.
[de.ði.ka.ˈsjõn]   -I want to congratulate you on your level of interest and dedication to the subject.

4600 **reflejar(se)**   **reflect**
vb   También parece reflejar una práctica general.
[re.fle.ˈxar]   -It also appears to reflect a general practice.

4601 **tiranía**   **tyranny**
f   Vivir bajo la tiranía a menudo hace a las personas sumisas y temerosas.
[ti.ra.ˈni.a]   -Living under tyranny often renders people submissive and fearful.

4602 **tornillo**   **screw**
m   Un tornillo pasante se ha roto.
[tor.ˈni.jo]   -One through bolt has been torn.

4603 **interferencia**   **interference**
f   No entiendo por qué enviaron toda esa interferencia eléctrica.
[ĩn̯.tɛr.fɛ.ˈrẽn.sja]   -I don't see why they'd send up all that electronic jamming.

4604 **festejar**   **celebrate**
vb   Así no es como acostumbrábamos a festejar.
[fɛs.te.ˈxar]   -This is not how we used to party.

4605 **rosario**   **rosary**
m   Ese era mi rosario favorito.
[ro.ˈsa.rjo]   -That was my favorite rosary.

4606 **metáfora**   **metaphor**
f   Utilizamos un árbol como metáfora para una organización.
[mɛ.ˈta.fo.ra]   -We used a tree as a metaphor for an organization.

4607 **pujar**   **bid**
vb   Vale, tenemos un nuevo objeto para pujar.
[pu.ˈxar]   -Okay, we have a new item up for bid.

4608 **vejez**   **old age**
f   La vejez trae decrepitud al cuerpo.
[ˈbe.xes]   -Old age brings a decrepitude to the body.

4609 **tirano**   **tyrant**
m   Ayudaste a un tirano a esclavizar una nación.
[ti.ˈra.no]   -You helped a tyrant enslave a nation.

4610 **catálogo**   **catalog**

	m	En breve podrás consultar nuestro catálogo completo.
	[ka.ˈta.lo.ɣo]	-You will shortly be able to consult our complete catalog.
4611	**mediana**	**median**
	f	Esta mediana de edades es casi la misma para mujeres de diferentes medios sociales.
	[me.ˈðja.na]	-This median age is virtually the same for women from different backgrounds.
4612	**liebre**	**hare**
	f	La liebre robó una zanahoria del jardín.
	[ˈlje.βre]	-The hare stole a carrot from the garden.
4613	**realeza**	**royalty**
	f	No sabía que había realeza en Arkansas.
	[re.a.ˈle.sa]	-I didn't know they had royalty in Arkansas.
4614	**cascada**	**waterfall**
	f	Técnicamente, no es una cascada normal.
	[kas.ˈka.ða]	-Technically, it's not a normal waterfall.
4615	**comunión**	**communion**
	f	Es una invitación a su comunión.
	[ko.mu.ˈnjõn]	-It is an invitation to his communion party.
4616	**inundación**	**flood**
	f	Ambos quedaron seriamente dañados por la inundación.
	[i.nũn̪.da.ˈsjõn]	-Both of them were severely damaged in the flood.
4617	**rendición**	**surrender**
	f	Parará solo cuando accedas a una rendición total.
	[rẽn̪.di.ˈsjõn]	-It will cease only when you agree to total surrender.
4618	**aplicar**	**apply**
	vb	Resulta relativamente fácil elaborar y aplicar propuestas sobre estos temas.
	[ap̚.li.ˈkar]	-It is relatively easy to draw up and implement proposals on these issues.
4619	**precedente**	**previous; precedent**
	adj; m	Espero que no siente un precedente.
	[pre.se.ˈðẽn̪.te]	-I hope that it does not constitute a precedent.
4620	**instalar**	**install**
	vb	El hombre trató de instalar su propia antena.
	[ĩns.ta.ˈlar]	-The man tried to install his own antenna.
4621	**tubería**	**pipeline**
	f	Esta tubería tiene más percebes que tú.
	[tu.βɛ.ˈri.a]	-This pipe has more barnacles than you do.
4622	**Holanda**	**Holland**
	f	Luego, de repente estábamos en Holanda.
	[o.ˈlãn̪.da]	-Then suddenly we were in Holland.
4623	**mascar**	**chew**
	vb	Dame una de esas gomas de mascar.
	[mas.ˈkar]	-Give me one of those pieces of gum.
4624	**cuadrar**	**square**
	vb	Porque los datos tienen que cuadrar.
	[kwa.ˈðrar]	-Because the facts have to add up.
4625	**cisne**	**swan**

m
['sis̰.ne]

Este cisne no es blanco.
-This swan is not white.

4626 sello — **seal**

m
['se.jo]

Él me dio su sello de aprobación.
-He gave me his stamp of approval.

4627 dinosaurio — **dinosaur**

m
[di.no.'sau̯.rjo]

Estamos interesados en la investigación del doctor sobre un dinosaurio.
-The truth is, we are interested in the doctor's research on a dinosaur.

4628 transportar — **transport**

vb
[trãns.por.'tar]

Estamos aumentando las oportunidades para transportar recursos energéticos.
-We are stepping up opportunities for the transport of energy resources.

4629 grabadora — **recorder**

f
[gra.βa.'ðo.ra]

Esta grabadora no es nueva.
-This tape recorder is not new.

4630 franqueza — **frankness**

f
[frãŋ.'ke.sa]

He manejado mi administración con espíritu de franqueza.
-I have run my administration in a spirit of openness.

4631 compatriota — **compatriot**

m/f
[kõm.pa.'trjo.ta]

El caballero no quiere dejar a su compatriota.
-The gentleman does not want to leave his compatriot.

4632 comprensivo — **understanding, comprehensive**

adj
[kõm.prẽn.'si.βo]

Muchas gracias por ser tan comprensivo.
-Thank you so much for being so understanding.

4633 suposición — **assumption**

f
[su.po.si.'sjõn]

Buena suposición, pero lo tengo bajo control.
-Nice guess, but I've got this.

4634 suspensión — **suspension**

f
[sus.pẽn.'sjõn]

Por favor, devuelva a su farmacéutico el frasco con la suspensión sobrante.
-Please return the bottle containing any leftover suspension to your
pharmacist.

4635 intercambiar — **exchange**

vb
[ĩn̪.tɛr.kãm.'bjar]

Aquí es imposible intercambiar secretos íntimos.
-It's impossible to exchange intimate secrets here.

4636 revancha — **rematch**

f
[re.'βãn̪.t͡ʃa]

Estoy disponible para la revancha cuando gustes.
-I'm around for a rematch anytime you want.

4637 higiénico — **hygienic**

adj
[i.'xje.ni.ko]

Tenemos derecho a un lugar de trabajo seguro e higiénico.
-We are entitled to a safe and hygienic workplace.

4638 turismo — **tourism**

m
[tu.'ris̰.mo]

El turismo sostenible es un enfoque del turismo que integra consideraciones
éticas, sociales y ambientales de forma económicamente viable.
-Sustainable tourism is an approach to tourism that integrates ethical, social
and environmental considerations in an economically viable way.

4639 sable — **saber**

m
['sa.βle]

El tigre dientes de sable se extinguió durante la era de hielo.
-It was during the ice age that the saber-toothed tiger became extinct.

4640 enigma — **enigma**

	m	Intenta descifrar el enigma que soy yo.
	[e.ˈniɣ.ma]	-Try to penetrate the enigma that is me.

4641 calcular — **calculate**

vb
[kal.ku.ˈlar]

Han utilizado las matemáticas para calcular cómo habría sido la formación del universo inmediatamente antes y después del Big Bang.
-Math has been used to calculate how would the universe formation had been just before and after the Big Bang.

4642 accionista — **shareholder**

m/f
[ak.sjo.ˈnis.ta]

Incluso es el único accionista de algunas empresas.
-He is even the sole shareholder in a few companies.

4643 estante — **shelf**

m
[ɛs.ˈtã̠n.te]

Vi esta cámara sobre ese estante ayer.
-I saw this camera sitting up there on the shelf yesterday.

4644 operativo — **operational; operation**

adj; m
[o.pɛ.ra.ˈti.βo]

El presupuesto operativo no basta para financiar estos programas.
-The operational budget is not sufficient to finance these programmes.

4645 arrecife — **reef**

m
[a.re.ˈsi.fe]

Esta es una playa artificial con entrada directa al arrecife.
-This is a man-made beach with direct entrance to the reef.

4646 aluminio — **aluminum**

m
[a.lu.ˈmi.njo]

Hubo una época en la que el aluminio era más caro que el oro.
-There was a time when aluminum was more expensive than gold.

4647 fachada — **facade**

f
[fa.ˈʧa.ða]

El colegio tiene una hermosa fachada.
-The college has a beautiful facade.

4648 torcer(se) — **twist**

vb
[tor.ˈsɛr]

Solo tendré que torcer algunos brazos.
-I'll just have to twist some arms.

4649 colaborar — **collaborate**

vb
[ko.la.βo.ˈrar]

El personal médico que se negaba a colaborar sufría represalias.
-Medical personnel who did not collaborate faced reprisals.

4650 sobretodo — **overcoat**

m
[so.βrɛ.ˈto.ðo]

Necesito algo de dinero para comprarme un sobretodo.
-I need some money to buy a coat.

4651 ruidoso — **noisy**

adj
[rwi.ˈðo.so]

Estoy comiendo en un lugar ruidoso.
-I'm having a bite in a noisy place.

4652 rollo — **roll, bore (coll)**

m
[ˈro.ɟo]

Necesitamos encontrar ese rollo de cinta.
-We need to find that roll of ribbon.

4653 señorito — **young gentleman**

m
[se.ɲo.ˈri.to]

Sube a tu cuarto ahora mismo, señorito.
-You get up to your room right now, mister.

4654 reportar(se) — **bring, report (LA); report in (LA)**

vb; vbr
[re.por.ˈtar]

Tendría que reportar dicha interferencia a la policía.
-I'd have to report such interference to the police.

4655 inquilino — **tenant**

	m	El posible inquilino pertenecía a una minoría étnica.
	[ĩŋ.ki.ˈli.no]	-The would-be tenant was a member of an ethnic minority.
4656	**huerto**	**orchard**
	m	Todo cambió cuando te marchaste del huerto.
	[ˈwɛr.to]	-It was different after you left the orchard.
4657	**celebridad**	**celebrity**
	f	Admites que soy una celebridad.
	[se.le.βri.ˈðað]	-You're admitting I'm a celeb.
4658	**necio**	**fool; stupid**
	m; adj	Quizás haya sido un necio por hacerlo.
	[ˈne.sjo]	-Maybe I have been foolish to do so.
4659	**olfato**	**smell**
	m	Esas pistas pueden también explicar porqué las deficiencias dietéticas de cinc conducen a una pérdida de olfato.
	[ol.ˈfa.to]	-Those clues may also explain why dietary zinc deficiencies lead to a loss of smell.
4660	**moralidad**	**morality**
	f	Si por otro lado continúas aferrándote a tu moralidad equivocada, morirás.
	[mo.ra.li.ˈðað]	-If, on the other hand, you continue to cling to your misguided morality, you die.
4661	**fibra**	**fiber**
	f	Necesitan más fibra en la dieta.
	[ˈfi.βra]	-You need more fiber in your diet.
4662	**cultivo**	**farming**
	m	Para estas personas el cultivo es vital para asegurar la comida.
	[kul̪.ˈti.βo]	-For these people, the crop is vital for food security.
4663	**primitivo**	**primitive**
	adj	Fue algo muy primitivo y más remoto que cualquier otra cosa que haya experimentado antes.
	[pri.mi.ˈti.βo]	-It was very primal and more remote than anything I'd ever experienced before.
4664	**activar**	**activate**
	vb	Necesitará ambos para instalar y activar el producto.
	[ak̚.ti.ˈβar]	-You will need both to install and activate the product.
4665	**alucinante**	**awesome**
	adj	Este lugar es alucinante, Jim.
	[a.lu.si.ˈnãn̪.te]	-This place is amazing, Jim.
4666	**ponche**	**punch**
	m	Va a traer diez galones de ponche.
	[ˈpõn̪.tʃe]	-She's bringing in ten gallons of punch.
4667	**inmersión**	**immersion**
	f	Ella será nuestro oficial de inmersión.
	[ĩm.mɛr.ˈsjõn]	-She's going to be our diving officer.
4668	**preciosidad**	**preciousness**
	f	Ahora mi nuevo amor es esta preciosidad.
	[pre.sjo.si.ˈðað]	-Now my new love is this beauty.
4669	**arrastrar(se)**	**drag**
	vb	Puedes caminar o te puedo arrastrar.
	[a.ras.ˈtrar]	-You could either walk, or I can drag you.

4670	**conservador**	**conservative; conservative**
	adj; m	Eso es lo que realmente significaría ser conservador.
	[kõn.sɛr.βa.ˈðor]	-That's what it would really mean to be conservative.
4671	**paralizar**	**paralyze**
	vb	Esta suspensión ha contribuido a paralizar las investigaciones.
	[pa.ra.li.ˈsar]	-This suspension helped to paralyze the investigations.
4672	**congelado**	**frozen**
	adj	El lago por el que cruzamos estaba congelado.
	[kõŋ.xe.ˈla.ðo]	-The lake where we crossed over was frozen.
4673	**parcial**	**partial**
	adj	Habría sido prematuro e inadecuado que una delegación parcial ofreciera respuestas.
	[par.ˈsjal]	-It would have been premature and inappropriate for a partial delegation to respond.
4674	**juerga**	**good time**
	f	Me apunté cuando terminé la juerga.
	[ˈxwɛr.ɣa]	-I signed up when my bender was over.
4675	**interminable**	**endless**
	adj	La exploración continuará durante todo el atardecer, gracias a la interminable luz del día.
	[ĩn.tɛr.mi.ˈna.βle]	-Exploration will continue all evening thanks to the endless daylight.
4676	**décimo**	**tenth**
	num	En 1994 fue elegido décimo Presidente de Finlandia.
	[ˈde.si.mo]	-In 1994 he was elected the tenth President of Finland.
4677	**librar(se)**	**fight, have free time; escape from**
	vb; vbr	La prevención es clave si queremos librar al planeta de tal flagelo.
	[li.ˈβrar]	-Prevention is key if we want to rid the planet of such a scourge.
4678	**decena**	**ten**
	f	Revisamos cada centímetro del lugar una decena de veces.
	[de.ˈse.na]	-We've checked every inch of the place a dozen times.
4679	**terciopelo**	**velvet**
	m	Llevaba un alegre abrigo de terciopelo de color chocolate, con botones de diamante, y con dos enormes bolsillos que siempre estaban llenos de huesos, dejados allí durante la cena por su cariñosa amante.
	[tɛr.sjo.ˈpe.lo]	-He wore a jaunty coat of chocolate-colored velvet, with diamond buttons, and with two huge pockets which were always filled with bones, dropped there at dinner by his loving mistress.
4680	**reparación**	**repair**
	f	La comunidad internacional reclama reparación y rehabilitación.
	[re.pa.ra.ˈsjõn]	-The international community has called for repair and rehabilitation.
4681	**longitud**	**length**
	f	¿Cómo se calcula la longitud de la circunferencia? Lo he olvidado.
	[lõŋ.xi.ˈtuð]	-How do you calculate the length of the circumference? I've forgotten.
4682	**previo**	**previous**
	adj	Usted menospreció el trabajo previo realizado por otras personas.
	[ˈpre.βjo]	-You underestimated the prior work that had been done by some people.
4683	**telescopio**	**telescope**
	m	Con el telescopio se pueden ver objetos lejanos.
	[te.lɛs.ˈko.pjo]	-We can see distant objects with a telescope.

4684 cordura   **sanity**

f

[kor.ˈðu.ra]

Tú también estás intentando salvar tu cordura.
-You're also trying to save your sanity.

4685 alejado   **remote**

adj

[a.le.ˈxa.ðo]

Necesitabas estar alejado de todo esto.
-You needed to be far away from all of this.

4686 humillar   **humiliate**

vb

[u.mi.ˈjar]

Esas medidas tienen por objeto aterrorizar y humillar a las personas.
-These measures are meant to terrify and humiliate people.

4687 dilema   **dilemma**

m

[di.ˈle.ma]

El Islam se enfrenta ahora a un dilema similar.
-Islam now confronts a similar dilemma.

4688 panadería   **bakery**

f

[pa.na.ðɛ.ˈri.a]

Una vez bajó las escaleras hacia la panadería.
-This one time, he went down the stairs to the bakery.

4689 sexualidad   **sexuality**

f

[sɛk.swa.li.ˈðað]

Yo no tengo problemas con mi sexualidad.
-I don't have any issues with my sexuality.

4690 noveno   **ninth**

num

[no.ˈβe.no]

La educación para la salud se imparte a los alumnos de noveno grado.
-Health education is taught to ninth graders.

4691 distraído   **distracted; scatterbrain**

adj; m

[dis.tra.ˈi.ðo]

Cuando se presentaba, parecía distraído.
-When he did show up, he seemed distracted.

4692 antorcha   **torch**

f

[ãn̪.ˈtor.tʃa]

Cuando se apague tu antorcha, ríndete.
-When your torch goes out, then give up.

4693 improbable   **unlikely**

adj

[ĩm.pro.ˈβa.βle]

Creo que es altamente improbable que Jim vaya a jugar a los bolos.
-I think it's highly unlikely that Jim will go bowling.

4694 vainilla   **vanilla**

f

[bai̯.ˈni.ja]

Estaba pensando en vainilla tradicional con aderezo de fresa.
-I'm thinking traditional vanilla with strawberry drizzle.

4695 camisón   **nightgown**

m

[ka.mi.ˈsõn]

Yo solía odiar ese camisón.
-I used to hate that nightgown.

4696 párrafo   **paragraph**

m

[ˈpa.ra.fo]

El párrafo enfatiza el mensaje.
-The paragraph emphasizes the message.

4697 inmunidad   **immunity**

f

[ĩm.mu.ni.ˈðað]

Por tercera vez, tienes inmunidad.
-For the third time, you have immunity.

4698 ración   **ration**

f

[ra.ˈsjõn]

Se ha observado que estos precios bajan cuando se distribuye la ración íntegra.
-These prices have been found to decline when the full ration is distributed.

4699 seducir   **seduce**

vb
[se.ðu.ˈsir]

Ana trató de seducir a su secretaria.
-Ana tried to seduce her secretary.

4700 agotador — **exhausting**

adj
[a.ɣo.ta.ˈðor]

Era demasiado agotador ocultárselo a ella.
-It was too exhausting keeping it from her.

4701 tic — **tic**

m
[ˈtik]

Discúlpeme. Es un tic nervioso.
-I'm sorry. It's a nervous tic.

4702 escorpión — **scorpion**

m
[ɛs.kor.ˈpjõn]

Debe ser el veneno del escorpión gigante.
-It must be the toxin from the giant scorpion.

4703 dominante — **dominant**

adj
[do.mi.ˈnãn̪.te]

Es una fuerza dominante en Internet.
-It is a dominant force on the Internet.

4704 charla — **chat**

f
[ˈtʃar.la]

Tuvimos una corta e insatisfactoria charla al teléfono.
-We had a brief and unsatisfying chat on the phone.

4705 invención — **invention**

f
[ĩm.bẽn.ˈsjõn]

Esta es una invención que ayudará a liberar a la humanidad.
-This is an invention that will help liberate mankind.

4706 noticiero — **news (LA)**

m
[no.ti.ˈsjɛ.ro]

Trabajaste con Jim en el noticiero nocturno.
-You worked with Jim at the nightly news.

4707 sobrenatural — **supernatural**

adj
[so.βre.na.tu.ˈral]

Está empezando a creer en lo sobrenatural.
-He's starting to believe in the supernatural stuff.

4708 patriota — **patriot; patriotic**

m/f; adj
[pa.ˈtrjo.ta]

Eso es algo que todo patriota quiere.
-That is something that every patriotic want.

4709 aduana — **customs**

f
[a.ˈðwa.na]

El comercio de metales preciosos también está sometido al control de los servicios de aduana.
-Trade in precious metals is also subject to control by customs.

4710 dinastía — **dynasty**

f
[di.nas.ˈti.a]

Eres un miembro de la dinastía.
-You are a member of the dynasty.

4711 trescientos — **three hundred**

num
[trɛs.ˈsjẽn̪.tos]

Hay trescientos solicitantes para una sola posición.
-There are three hundred applicants for only one position.

4712 desempleo — **unemployment**

m
[de.sẽm.ˈple.o]

El desempleo sigue siendo elevado y la demanda interna es muy débil.
-Unemployment remains elevated and domestic demand is anaemic.

4713 formalidad — **formality**

f
[for.ma.li.ˈðað]

La periodicidad y el grado de formalidad de esos documentos varían considerablemente.
-The regularity and formality of these documents varies greatly.

4714 colar(se) — **strain, leak; sneak in**

vb; vbr
[ko.ˈlar]

Tapa el recipiente, déjalo reposar cinco minutos y cuélalo.
-Cover the container, let stand five minutes and strain.

4715 **boludo** — **silly (LA) (coll); moron (LA) (coll)**
adj; m
[bo.ˈlu.ðo]
Como ese boludo que estaba aquí contigo.
-Like that jerk who was here with you.

4716 **discoteca** — **disco**
f
[dis.ko.ˈte.ka]
Estas personas están en la discoteca.
-These people are in the club.

4717 **moribundo** — **dying; dying person**
adj; m
[mo.ri.ˈβũn̪.do]
Estaba moribundo cuando le llevaron al hospital.
-He was dying when they took him to the hospital.

4718 **bancario** — **banking; bank employee**
adj; m
[bãŋ.ˈka.rjo]
Todos ellos solicitaron un préstamo bancario.
-All of them applied for a bank loan.

4719 **detector** — **detector**
m
[dɛ.tekˀ.ˈtor]
Este detector de metales no funciona en absoluto.
-This metal detector is not working at all.

4720 **microondas** — **microwave**
mpl
[mi.kro.ˈõn̪.das]
Veo que tiene un microondas aquí enganchado.
-I see you have a microwave hooked up out here.

4721 **ancla** — **anchor**
f
[ˈãŋ.kla]
El barco echó el ancla en el puerto.
-The ship dropped anchor in the harbor.

4722 **escultura** — **sculpture**
f
[ɛs.kul̪.ˈtu.ra]
Él hizo una escultura de arena.
-He made a sand sculpture.

4723 **empatar** — **tie**
vb
[ɛm.pa.ˈtar]
Su equipo necesita tres puntos para empatar.
-His club needs three points to tie.

4724 **jerez** — **sherry**
m
[ˈxɛ.res]
Champaña después del jerez provoca acidez a tu pancita.
-Champagne after sherry makes tummy grow wary.

4725 **abortar** — **abort**
vb
[a.βor.ˈtar]
Sería lamentable abortar sus intentos a medio camino.
-It would be unfortunate to abort its attempt in mid-course.

4726 **fiero** — **fierce**
adj
[ˈfjɛ.ro]
Pensé que estabais en el frente, luchando contra el fiero enemigo.
-I thought you were at the front, fighting the fierce enemy.

4727 **exploración** — **exploration**
f
[ɛks.plo.ra.ˈsjõn]
Dicha exploración solo será posible bajo condiciones específicas.
-Such an exploration would only be possible under certain conditions.

4728 **alimentación** — **food, supply**
f
[a.li.mɛ̃n̪.ta.ˈsjõn]
Al igual que las personas, los animales necesitan una alimentación equilibrada.
-Just like people, animals need balanced nutrition.

4729 **can** — **hound**
m
[ˈkãn]
Luego de este periodo, el can continua realizando ejercicios físicos y entrenamiento de mantenimiento.
-After this period, the dog continues to engage in physical exercise and maintenance training.

4730 **pradera** — **meadow**

f
[pra.ˈðɛ.ra]

El cañón llega hasta la pradera y todo este verdor atrae a grandes dinosaurios.
-The canyon runs down to the prairie and all this greenery attracts larger dinosaurs.

4731 rublo **ruble**

m
[ˈru.βlo]

Tendré que cobrarte medio rublo más.
-I'll have to charge you half a ruble extra.

4732 limitar(se) **restrict**

vb
[li.mi.ˈtar]

La Unión Europea no puede limitar su acción al control de la inmigración.
-The European Union cannot confine its activities to immigration control.

4733 estudiantil **student (coll)**

adj
[ɛs.tu.ðjã̠n̠.ˈtil]

Este proceso terminará mejorando el rendimiento estudiantil.
-This process will ultimately result in improved student achievement.

4734 oponer(se) **oppose**

vb
[o.po.ˈnɛr]

¿Cómo se pueden oponer activamente a esto?
-How can they actively oppose that?

4735 adversario **adversary**

m
[að.βɛr.ˈsa.rjo]

No me gustaría ser su adversario.
-I wouldn't want to be your opponent.

4736 ajustar **adjust**

vb
[a.xus.ˈtar]

Creo que puedo ajustar nuestros sensores internos para mejorarla.
-I believe I can adjust our internal sensors to improve it.

4737 cimiento **foundation**

m
[si.ˈmjẽ̠n.to]

Sobre este cimiento histórico, construimos nuestra civilización.
-On top of this historical foundation, we build our civilization.

4738 adicción **addiction**

f
[a.ðik.ˈsjõn]

Es una adicción que necesita ser alimentada.
-It's an addiction that needs to be fed.

4739 implacable **relentless**

adj
[ĩm.pla.ˈka.βle]

No puedo entender el odio implacable que todavía siente por su viejo rival.
-I cannot understand the implacable hatred that he still feels for his old rival.

4740 definir **define**

vb
[de.fi.ˈnir]

Definir qué es realmente verdad o no es un tema que ocupa muchas páginas en la historia de la filosofía.
-Distinguishing truth from everything else is a theme filling many pages in the history of philosophy.

4741 donante **donor**

m/f
[do.ˈnã̠n.te]

Cuando renové mi licencia de conductor tuve que decidir si quería ser donante de órganos.
-When I got my driver's license renewed, I had to decide if I wanted to be an organ donor.

4742 moción **motion**

f
[mo.ˈsjõn]

Podrías retirar la moción ahora mismo.
-You could withdraw your motion right now.

4743 paranoia **paranoia**

f
[pa.ra.ˈnoi̯.a]

La paranoia y la rabia homicida eran muy comunes.
-Paranoia and homicidal rage were common.

4744 pender **hang over**

vb
[pẽ̠n.ˈdɛr]

Mi caso podría pender de un hilo.
-My case could hang on a thread.

4745 **programación**
f
[pro.ɣra.ma.ˈsjõn]
programming
Seguía siendo necesario reducir el proceso de programación.
-There was still a need to reduce the programming process.

4746 **esposo**
m
[ɛs.ˈpo.so]
husband
Mi esposo está desempleado y busca trabajo.
-My husband is out of work and looking for a job.

4747 **castaño**
adj; m
[kas.ˈta.ɲo]
brown; chestnut
Tenía una mirada profunda y unos bonitos ojos de color castaño ambarino.
-She had a deep gaze and beautiful amber brown colored eyes.

4748 **redacción**
f
[re.ðak.ˈsjõn]
essay, editorial office
Quitando unos poco errores leves, tu redacción fue excelente.
-Apart from a few minor mistakes, your composition was excellent.

4749 **retener**
vb
[rɛ.te.ˈnɛr]
retain
Quizás pueda retener y llevar estas técnicas al mundo.
-I might be able to retain and bring these techniques to the world.

4750 **estimulante**
adj; m
[ɛs.ti.mu.ˈlã̪n.te]
stimulating; stimulant
Al contrario, es profundamente estimulante.
-On the contrary, it's profoundly stimulating.

4751 **degenerar**
vb
[de.xe.nɛ.ˈrar]
degenerate
Si se permite que continúen, estos conflictos pueden degenerar en genocidio.
-Such conflicts, if allowed to continue, may degenerate into genocide.

4752 **broncear(se)**
vb
[brõn.se.ˈar]
tan
Estaba bronceándome en los lugares equivocados.
-I was getting tan in the wrong places.

4753 **posterior**
adj
[pos.tɛ.ˈrjor]
rear, following
El envío de los productos se realiza un mes posterior al pedido.
-Delivery of goods is done after a month of placing the order.

4754 **motivación**
f
[mo.ti.βa.ˈsjõn]
motivation
Puedes demostrar tu motivación haciendo distintas preguntas durante la entrevista.
-You can prove your motivation by asking different questions during the interview.

4755 **localización**
f
[lo.ka.li.sa.ˈsjõn]
location
La localización del pueblo favorece mucho su aislamiento.
-The location of the village favors much isolation.

4756 **caldo**
m
[ˈkal̪.do]
broth
Pensé que podríamos prepararle un caldo de gallina.
-I thought we could make her some chicken broth.

4757 **guarnición**
f
[gwar.ni.ˈsjõn]
trimming, garnish
Actuarán solo como guarnición, permaneciendo en constante comunicación conmigo.
-You're to act as a garrison only, remaining in constant communication with me.

4758 **complot**
m
[kõm.ˈplot]
conspiracy
He oído que hay un complot para asesinarme.
-I've been told that there's a plot to assassinate me.

4759 **recorte**
m
[re.ˈkor.te]
cutback
Ella nos habló del recorte.
-She told us about the cutback.

4760 **metálico**　　　　　　　**metal; cash**
adj; m
[mɛˈta.li.ko]
El producto está enmarcado con una banda metálica.
-The product is framed with a metal band.

4761 **apocalipsis**　　　　　　**apocalypse**
m
[a.po.kaˈlip.sis]
El apocalipsis ya ocurrió una vez.
-The apocalypse has happened once before.

4762 **entrante**　　　　　　　**entering; appetizer (ES)**
adj; m
[ẽn̯ˈtrã̯n̯.te]
Todo el correo entrante es abierto por mí mismo.
-Any incoming mail gets opened by myself.

4763 **plasmar**　　　　　　　**express**
vb
[plaş.ˈmar]
El proyecto de resolución debería plasmar esos avances.
-The draft resolution should reflect these developments.

4764 **clemencia**　　　　　　**clemency**
f
[kle.ˈmẽn.sja]
Te arrastrarás por el piso pidiéndome clemencia.
-You'll crawl on the floor, begging me for mercy.

4765 **derramar**　　　　　　**spill**
vb
[dɛ.ra.ˈmar]
Trataré de no derramar nada.
-I'll try not to spill anything.

4766 **rocío**　　　　　　　　**dew**
m
[ro.ˈsi.o]
El rocío se evaporó cuando el sol salió.
-The dew evaporated when the sun rose.

4767 **diarrea**　　　　　　　**diarrhea**
f
[dja.ˈre.a]
Puede desarrollarse a consecuencia de la diarrea.
-It may develop as a consequence of diarrhea.

4768 **cargador**　　　　　　**charger**
m
[kar.ɣa.ˈðor]
Cógeme algo de ropa y mi cargador de teléfono.
-Pick me up some clothes and my phone charger.

4769 **vocabulario**　　　　　**vocabulary**
m
[bo.ka.βu.ˈla.rjo]
Su vocabulario es realmente inadecuado.
-His vocabulary is really inadequate.

4770 **mugre**　　　　　　　**grime**
f
[ˈmu.ɣre]
Jim está cubierto de mugre pegajosa.
-Jim is covered in slimy goo.

4771 **embarcar**　　　　　　**embark**
vb
[ẽm.bar.ˈkar]
Estaba intentando embarcar en un vuelo a Venezuela.
-He was trying to board a flight to Venezuela.

4772 **esmeralda**　　　　　　**emerald**
f
[ɛş.mɛ.ˈral̯.da]
Sus ojos eran de un color verde esmeralda espectacular.
-Her eyes were a spectacular emerald green.

4773 **diabólico**　　　　　　**diabolical**
adj
[dja.ˈβo.li.ko]
Pensaré en algo brillante y diabólico.
-I'll come up with something brilliant and diabolical.

4774 **obediencia**　　　　　**obedience**
f
[o.βe.ˈðjẽn.sja]
Llevará más tiempo del que tengo enseñarle obediencia.
-It will take more time than I have to teach her obedience.

4775 **umbral**　　　　　　　**threshold**

m
[ũm.ˈbral]

Muchas tecnologías se encuentran actualmente en el umbral de la viabilidad económica.
-Many technologies are currently at the threshold of economic viability.

4776 iluminar

vb
[i.lu.mi.ˈnar]

illuminate

Una lámpara se quema para iluminar a los demás.
-A lamp burns to enlighten others.

4777 brecha

f
[ˈbre.tʃa]

gap

Necesitamos ampliar la brecha entre nosotros y nuestros agresores.
-We need to widen the gap between us and our aggressors.

4778 acuario

m
[a.ˈkwa.rjo]

aquarium

¿Hay un acuario en este zoológico?
-Is there an aquarium at this zoo?

4779 tropical

adj
[tro.pi.ˈkal]

tropical

Filipinas es un país tropical con unas condiciones climáticas cálidas.
-The Philippines is a tropical country with warm weather conditions.

4780 desertor

m
[de.sɛr.ˈtor]

deserter

Siempre me he preguntado qué sentía un desertor.
-I've often wondered how a deserter might feel.

4781 transición

f
[trãn.si.ˈsjõn]

transition

La justicia de transición es esencial para la reconstrucción y la reconciliación después de un conflicto.
-Transitional justice is essential to post-conflict reconstruction and reconciliation.

4782 frustrar(se)

vb; vbr
[frus.ˈtrar]

hinder; become frustrated

Nos harán responsables y no podemos frustrar sus expectativas.
-They will hold us accountable, and we cannot frustrate their expectations.

4783 acoso

m
[a.ˈko.so]

harassment

Sesenta y cinco denuncias fueron presentadas en relación al acoso.
-Sixty-five complaints were received with respect to harassment.

4784 atropellar

vb
[a.tro.pe.ˈjar]

run over

Alguien acaba de intentar atropellar a Jim.
-Someone just tried to run over Jim.

4785 infectar(se)

vb
[ĩɱ.fek.ˈtar]

infect

Podemos infectar a la colonia.
-We can infect the colony.

4786 magistrado

m
[ma.xis.ˈtra.ðo]

magistrate

Déjalo. Informaré al magistrado más tarde.
-Leave him. I'll inform the magistrate later.

4787 perezoso

adj; m
[pɛ.re.ˈso.so]

lazy; sloth

No logras mucho siendo perezoso.
-You don't get much from just being lazy.

4788 ahorcar(se)

vb
[a.or.ˈkar]

hang

Es el doble de peligroso ahorcar al muchacho.
-It's twice as dangerous to hang the boy.

4789 torturar(se)

vb
[tor.tu.ˈrar]

torture

Ellos no quieren torturarte a ti.
-They do not want to torture you.

4790 guiar

guide

| | vb | Estos son los criterios que deberían guiar las negociaciones regionales. |
| | ['gjar] | -These are the criteria that should guide regional negotiations. |

4791 anhelo **longing**

m
[a.'ne.lo]

Todos nosotros tenemos alguna clase de anhelo.
-All of us have some kind of longing.

4792 hocico **snout**

m
[o.'si.ko]

Había leche por todo su hocico.
-There was milk all over its snout.

4793 jefatura **leadership**

f
[xe.fa.'tu.ra]

Soy gerente asociado en la jefatura corporativa.
-I'm an assistant manager at their corporate headquarters.

4794 caldera **boiler**

f
[kal̪.'dɛ.ra]

Revisaré la caldera. No quiero duchas frías.
-I'll check the boiler. l don't want cold showers.

4795 chivo **kid, young goat**

m
['tʃi.βo]

Un chivo expiatorio perfecto para su incompetencia.
-A perfect scapegoat for their incompetence.

4796 zanjar **dig, settle**

vb
[sãŋ.'xar]

Tenemos una propuesta que ofrecerte para zanjar este asunto.
-We have a proposition to offer you to settle this once and for all.

4797 adjunto **attached; attachment**

adj; m
[að.'xũ̯.to]

Jim era adjunto del comandante de brigada.
-Jim was deputy brigade commander.

4798 sultán **sultan**

m
[sul̪.'tãn]

A nosotros no nos corresponde cuestionar al sultán.
-It is not our place to question the sultan.

4799 frenar **brake**

vb
[fre.'nar]

No es nuestra intención frenar este proceso.
-It is not our intention to stop this process.

4800 pingüino **penguin**

m
[pĩŋ.'gwi.no]

No es diferente, es un pingüino emperador.
-It's not different, it's an emperor penguin.

4801 mandato **mandate**

m
[mãn̪.'da.to]

Su relincho es como el mandato de un monarca.
-His neigh is like the bidding of a monarch.

4802 elevar **raise**

vb
[e.le.'βar]

Necesitamos aprovechar esta oportunidad y elevar nuestras miras.
-We need to take advantage of this opportunity and raise our sights.

4803 sabotaje **sabotage**

m
[sa.βo.'ta.xe]

Se habían producido secuestros y sabotaje de instalaciones gubernamentales y civiles.
-There had been instances of kidnapping and sabotage of Government and civilian facilities.

4804 esplendor **splendor**

m
[ɛs.plẽn̪.'dor]

No había visto esta clase de esplendor desde Bambi.
-I haven't seen this kind of splendor since Bambi.

4805 faz **face**

f
['fas]

Esta tormenta cambiará la faz de nuestro planeta.
-This one storm is going to change the face of our planet.

4806 búho

m
['bu.o]

owl

¿Cuál es la diferencia entre un búho y una lechuza?
-What's the difference between an owl and a barn owl?

4807 enloquecer

vb
[ẽn.lo.ke.'sɛr]

madden

Cualquiera enloquecería en este depósito.
-A person could go crazy in this dump.

4808 empeño

m
[ẽm.'pe.ɲo]

determination, pawn

Estamos trabajando con empeño, decisión y firmeza para lograr ese objetivo.
-We are working with determination, resolve and commitment to achieve that goal.

4809 delicadeza

f
[de.li.ka.'ðe.sa]

delicacy

En ocasiones la delicadeza y la diplomacia son mejores que la coerción.
-Sometimes finesse and diplomacy are better than coercion.

4810 fondos

mpl
['fõn.dos]

funds

Simplemente tenemos que tratar de encontrar fondos suficientes aquí.
-We simply have to try and find sufficient funds here.

4811 matadero

m
[ma.ta.'ðɛ.ro]

slaughterhouse

Los animales serán transportados a un matadero.
-The animals will be transported to a slaughterhouse.

4812 indefenso

adj
[ĩn.de.'fẽn.so]

defenseless

Estás completamente indefenso en un avión.
-You're completely helpless on an airplane.

4813 polar

adj
[po.'lar]

polar

Generalmente me presentan como explorador polar.
-I'm usually introduced as a polar explorer.

4814 trasladar(se)

vb
[tras.la.'ðar]

move

Nos tuvimos que trasladar completamente a su mundo.
-We had to completely transfer ourselves over to their world.

4815 panorama

m
[pa.no.'ra.ma]

landscape

Ese edificio no armoniza con el panorama circundante.
-The building doesn't blend in with its surroundings.

4816 sanatorio

m
[sa.na.'to.rjo]

sanatorium

Sería un poco complicado meterles a todos en un sanatorio.
-It would be a bit tricky to put you all in a sanatorium.

4817 proveedor

m
[pro.βe.e.'ðor]

supplier

La secretaría se reunió con el proveedor de joyas.
-The secretariat met with the jewelry supplier.

4818 mentalidad

f
[mẽn.ta.li.'ðað]

mentality

La misma mentalidad opera hoy en día en un ambiente cada vez más orientado al financiamiento privado.
-The same mentality operates today in an increasingly privatized funding environment.

4819 chequear

vb
[tʃe.ke.'ar]

check

No escanees los registros para chequear enlaces incorrectos.
-Do not scan the rows to check for incorrect links.

4820 prototipo

prototype

m
[pro.to.ˈti.po]

Dice que el prototipo de horno funcionaba como se esperaba.
-He says the prototype furnace functioned as designed.

4821 portugués

adj; m
[por.tu.ˈɣes]

Portuguese; Portuguese person

Escuchar una conversación en portugués es una experiencia irreal.
-Listening to a Portuguese conversation is an unreal experience.

4822 prometedor

adj
[pro.mɛ.te.ˈðoɾ]

promising

Un planteamiento más prometedor es invertir en los propios alumnos.
-A more promising approach is to make investments in the students themselves.

4823 aperitivo

m
[a.pɛ.ɾi.ˈti.βo]

appetizer

Pero podrías pensar en un aperitivo.
-But you might give some thought to an appetizer.

4824 descarado

adj; m
[dɛs.ka.ˈra.ðo]

shameless; insolent person

Es descarado, confiado y organizado.
-He's brazen, confident, and organized.

4825 planchar

vb
[plãn̪.ˈʧaɾ]

iron

No tiene que planchar nuestra ropa.
-You don't have to iron our clothes.

4826 neumonía

f
[neu̯.mo.ˈni.a]

pneumonia

Su neumonía fue curada por medio de un milagro divino.
-His pneumonia was cured through a divine miracle.

4827 cínico

adj; m
[ˈsi.ni.ko]

shameless; shameless person

Pero discúlpeme, soy cínico por naturaleza.
-But forgive me, I'm cynical by nature.

4828 ganga

f
[ˈgãŋ.ga]

bargain

Ella quiere ver qué ganga está recibiendo.
-She wants to see what a bargain she's getting.

4829 siervo

m
[ˈsjɛɾ.βo]

serf

Pedimos que tu siervo Jim nos entrenara.
-We asked your servant Jim to train us.

4830 convicción

f
[kõm.bik.ˈsjõn]

conviction

Una parte de esta convicción está enraizada en mi propia experiencia.
-Part of this conviction is rooted in my own experience.

4831 palco

m
[ˈpal.ko]

box seat

He preparado un palco para ti.
-I have arranged a box for you.

4832 hedor

m
[e.ˈðoɾ]

stench

Emiten el hedor de fruta podrida.
-They give off the stench of rotting fruit.

4833 mercurio

m
[mɛɾ.ˈku.rjo]

mercury

Estas pilas también contienen mercurio pero en una concentración mucho menor.
-These batteries also contain mercury but at a much smaller concentration.

4834 secta

f
[ˈsek̚.ta]

sect

Podría iniciar una secta con esa cosa.
-He could start a cult with that thing.

4835 desacuerdo

m
[de.sa.ˈkwɛɾ.ðo]

disagreement

Esta es la razón por la que estoy en desacuerdo contigo.
-This is the reason I disagree with you.

4836 **excitación** — **excitement**
f
[ɛk.si.ta.ˈsjõn]
No estás lista para tanta excitación.
-You're not ready for so much excitement.

4837 **hidrógeno** — **hydrogen**
m
[i.ˈðro.xe.no]
Para producir hidrógeno se necesita electricidad.
-In order to produce hydrogen one needs electricity.

4838 **jubilación** — **retirement**
f
[xu.βi.la.ˈsjõn]
Le deseo una jubilación muy feliz y próspera.
-I wish him a very happy and prosperous retirement.

4839 **autoestima** — **self-esteem**
f
[au̯.to.ɛs.ˈti.ma]
También deben incluir aspectos psicológicos y de autoestima.
-They should also include psychological aspects and the building of self-esteem.

4840 **directorio** — **directory**
m
[di.rek.ˈto.rjo]
Lo encontrarás en tu directorio actual.
-You'll find it in your current directory.

4841 **vivienda** — **apartment**
f
[bi.ˈβjẽn.da]
También seguirán asignándose fondos internacionales a la vivienda.
-International funds will also continue to be directed into housing.

4842 **rastreo** — **search**
m
[ras.ˈtre.o]
También vamos a ir a los límites de nuestras comunicaciones y rastreos.
-We're also going to go to the limits of our communications and tracking.

4843 **parrilla** — **grill**
f
[pa.ˈri.ʝa]
Quiero que veas mi nueva parrilla.
-I want you to see my new barbecue.

4844 **agudo** — **high-pitched**
adj
[a.ˈɣu.ðo]
Además, está degenerando en un agudo problema social.
-It was degenerating, furthermore, into an acute social problem.

4845 **renacimiento** — **rebirth, Renaissance**
m
[re.na.si.ˈmjẽn.to]
Decidimos llamar a este proceso el renacimiento africano.
-We choose to call this process the African renaissance.

4846 **portaaviones** — **aircraft carrier**
m
[por.ta.a.ˈβjo.nes]
Aquí hay personal suficiente para manejar un portaaviones.
-There's enough staff in here to run an aircraft carrier.

4847 **alérgico** — **allergic; person with allergies**
adj; m
[a.ˈlɛr.xi.ko]
Él es alérgico al polvo del hogar.
-He is allergic to house dust.

4848 **parásito** — **parasite; parasitic**
m; adj
[pa.ˈra.si.to]
¡No eres más que un parásito social!
-You're nothing more than a social parasite!

4849 **sincronización** — **synchronization**
f
[sĩn.kro.ni.sa.ˈsjõn]
No será fácil alcanzar dicha sincronización.
-Such synchronization will not be easy to achieve.

4850 **desafiar** — **challenge**
vb
[de.sa.ˈfjar]
Como padres, deberíamos desafiar a estos tipos.
-As parents, we should challenge these guys.

4851 **resistente** — **resistant**

adj
[re.sis.ˈtẽn̪.te]

No termino de entender por qué es tan resistente.
-I don't fully understand why he's so resistant.

4852 **innecesario**

unnecessary

adj
[ĭn.ne.se.ˈsa.rjo]

Es innecesario decir que una persona experimentada lo hará mejor que una sin experiencia.
-It is needless to say that an experienced person will do better than someone without experience.

4853 **cenicero**

ashtray

m
[se.ni.ˈsɛ.ro]

Dejé uno quemándose en un cenicero.
-I let one burn out in an ashtray.

4854 **superintendente**

superintendent

m/f
[su.pɛ.rĩn̪.tẽn̪.ˈdẽn̪.te]

La versión definitiva del proyecto educativo deberá remitirse al superintendente regional.
-The final version of the educational project should be sent to the regional superintendent.

4855 **senda**

track

f
[ˈsẽn̪.da]

Seguiremos en la senda del desarrollo autóctono.
-We will continue on the path of indigenous development.

4856 **razonar**

reason

vb
[ra.so.ˈnar]

Yo quería hacerles razonar y pensar.
-I wanted to make them reason and think.

4857 **preparatorio**

preparatory; pre-university study

adj; m
[pre.pa.ra.ˈto.rjo]

Vuelvo al hotel para mi debate preparatorio.
-I'm going back to the hotel for my debate prep.

4858 **perturbar(se)**

disturb, disorient

vb
[pɛr.tur.ˈβar]

No quisiera perturbar tus pequeños arreglos.
-I wouldn't want to disturb all your little arrangements.

4859 **sonriente**

smiling

adj
[sõn.ˈrjẽn̪.te]

Cuando despertó, estaba sonriente y hambriento.
-When he woke up, he was smiling and hungry.

4860 **sentenciar**

sentence

vb
[sẽn̪.tẽn.ˈsjar]

Ahora tienes el poder de sentenciar su alma al infierno.
-Now you have the power to sentence his soul straight to hell.

4861 **homosexualidad**

homosexuality

f
[o.mo.sɛk.swa.li.ˈðað]

Siempre escondí mi homosexualidad de mí mismo.
-I always hid my homosexuality from myself.

4862 **intérprete**

interpreter

m/f
[ĩn.ˈter.prɛ.te]

Si la persona inculpada busca a su propio intérprete, eso también está permitido.
-If an accused person arranges his or her own interpreter, that is also permitted as a matter of course.

4863 **pendejo**

asshole (LA) (coll); fool (LA) (coll)

adj; m
[pẽn̪.ˈde.xo]

Probablemente defenderé al pendejo que me disparó.
-I'll probably defend the asshole who shot me.

4864 **señalar**

mark

vb
[se.ɲa.ˈlar]

Dentro del autobús lo puedo entender, pero, ¿realmente es necesario señalar el destino con un altavoz también fuera del autobús?
-In the bus, I can understand, but should the destination also be announced by a loudspeaker outside the bus too?

4865 **pésame**

condolence

m
['pe.sa.me]

Señoras y señores, quisiera empezar agradeciéndoles su pésame y oraciones.
-Ladies and gentlemen, I'd like to start by thanking you for your sympathy and prayers.

4866 romo **blunt**

adj
['ro.mo]

Proceda lentamente hacia con el instrumento romo hasta alcanzar la posición ideal.
-Slowly proceed upwards with the blunt instrument until the ideal position is reached.

4867 popularidad **popularity**

f
[po.pu.la.ri.'ðað]

La ciudad está ganando popularidad como un importante destino turístico.
-The city is gaining popularity as a major tourist destination.

4868 reservación **reservation (LA)**

f
[re.sɛr.βa.'sjõn]

Quisiera confirmar una reservación, por favor.
-I'd like to confirm a reservation, please.

4869 ambulante **traveling**

adj
[ãm.bu.'lãn̪.te]

La chica es una vendedora ambulante de medicinas.
-The girl is a traveling medicine peddler.

4870 penetrar **penetrate**

vb
[pe.nɛ.'trar]

Vuestro cohete será capaz de penetrar sin resistencia.
-Your rocket will be able to penetrate without resistance.

4871 vencedor **winner; winner**

adj; m
[bẽn.se.'ðor]

Veamos quién será el vencedor final.
-Let's see who will be the final winner.

4872 tormento **torment**

m
[tor.'mẽn̪.to]

Puedo entender el tormento que ha sido.
-I can understand what a torment it has been.

4873 folleto **brochure**

m
[fo.'ʝɛ.to]

Registró mi mesa y encontró el folleto.
-He went through my desk and found the brochure.

4874 doctorar(se) **award a doctorate**

vb
[dok̚.to.'rar]

Me voy a doctorar en teología.
-I'm getting my doctorate in theology.

4875 inapropiado **inappropriate**

adj
[i.na.pro.'pja.ðo]

Ni siquiera hay nada en ello que sea inapropiado.
-There's not even anything in it that's inappropriate.

4876 tacón **heel**

m
[ta.'kõn]

Ni siquiera podrías ponértelas, tienen un tacón ortopédico.
-You couldn't even wear them, they have an orthopedic heel.

4877 trinchera **trench**

f
[trĩn̪.'ʧɛ.ra]

Le ordeno retirarse a la segunda trinchera.
-I order you to retreat to the second trench.

4878 destreza **skill**

f
[dɛs.'tre.sa]

Darle un ladrillazo a alguien requiere mucha destreza.
-Hitting someone with a brick takes a lot of skill.

4879 demócrata **democrat**

m/f
[de.'mo.kra.ta]

Ser ciudadano europeo y ser demócrata exige ciertos conocimientos.
-It requires certain knowledge to be a European citizen and to be democratic.

4880 rienda **rein**

f
['rjẽ̃.da]
Sigue escapándose, pero no puedo ponerle una rienda.
-She keeps getting out, but I can't put a bridle on her.

4881 descortés impolite

adj
[dɛs.kor.'tes]
Es descortés mirar fijamente a las personas.
-It's impolite to stare at people.

4882 muchedumbre crowd

f
[mu.tʃe.'ðũm.bre]
Perdimos al hombre entre la muchedumbre.
-We lost sight of the man in the crowd.

4883 insinuar insinuate

vb
[ĩn.si.'nwar]
No sé que estás intentando insinuar.
-I don't know what you're trying to imply.

4884 tibio warm

adj
['ti.βjo]
Quiero un catre tibio y tres comidas diarias.
-I want a warm bunk and three meals a day.

4885 manto mantle

m
['mãn̪.to]
Quizás tenga el manto de invisibilidad.
-Maybe's he's got the cloak of invisibility.

4886 dictadura dictatorship

f
[dik̚.ta.'ðu.ra]
Birmania es gobernado por una dictadura militar.
-Myanmar is ruled by a military dictatorship.

4887 acogedor cozy

adj
[a.ko.xe.'ðor]
Este es un hotel acogedor de carácter familiar y ambiente distendido.
-This is a cozy hotel with a family character and a relaxed atmosphere.

4888 cobra cobra

f
['ko.βra]
Era como mirar a una cobra.
-It was like watching a cobra.

4889 viudo widower; widow

m; adj
['bju.ðo]
Él es un viudo con tres niños pequeños que cuidar.
-He's a widower with three small children to take care of.

4890 credibilidad credibility

f
[kre.ði.βi.li.'ðað]
Creo que deberían acortarse los plazos o perderemos credibilidad.
-I believe that time limits should be reduced, otherwise, we will lose credibility.

4891 especia spice

f
[ɛs.'pe.sja]
Se preocupa más por sus hombres que por la especia.
-He's more concerned over his men than the spice.

4892 aro ring

m
['a.ro]
Al día siguiente instalé el aro de básquet.
-The next day, I put up the basketball hoop.

4893 evangelio gospel

m
[e.βãŋ.'xe.ljo]
Este es el evangelio del Señor.
-This is the gospel of the Lord.

4894 descender descend

vb
[dɛs.sẽn̪.'dɛr]
Podría descender sobre nosotros de repente.
-He could suddenly descend upon us.

4895 horroroso dreadful

adj
[o.ro.'ro.so]
Pasar el rato conmigo es horroroso.
-Hanging out with me is awful.

4896 disgusto

m

[dis̬.ˈɣus.to]

disgust

Es absolutamente correcto que expresemos nuestro disgusto porque tal acción haya tenido lugar.
-It is absolutely right that we voice our displeasure at such an action having taken place.

4897 acercamiento

m

[a.sɛr.ka.ˈmjẽn.to]

approach

Si tomamos un acercamiento sistemático, maximizaremos nuestra eficiencia.
-If we take a systematic approach, we'll maximize our efficiency.

4898 equivalente

adj

[e.ki.βa.ˈlẽn.te]

equivalent

Este libro es el equivalente literario a los dulces: tú solo quieres comerte uno, pero terminas devorando el paquete entero.
-This book is the literary equivalent of sweets: you only want to eat one, but end up devouring the whole packet.

4899 relevante

adj

[re.le.ˈβãn.te]

outstanding

Este era un documento muy interesante y relevante.
-This was a very interesting and relevant document.

4900 emisión

f

[e.mi.ˈsjõn]

emission

Todo el equipo empleado para medir la emisión de los contaminantes también deberá adaptarse.
-All the equipment used to measure the emission of pollutants will also have to be adjusted.

4901 asociar

vb

[a.so.ˈsjar]

associate

Cuando las carteras sean mixtas, se tomarán las medidas oportunas para asociar a las comisiones competentes.
-Appropriate arrangements shall be made to associate relevant committees where portfolios are mixed.

4902 alga

f

[ˈal.ɣa]

seaweed

Se zambulle en el mar helado para recoger alga marina.
-She dives into the freezing sea to harvest seaweed.

4903 atuendo

m

[a.ˈtwẽn.do]

attire

Me gustaría verte con ese atuendo.
-I would like to see you in that attire.

4904 descendiente

m/f

[dɛs.sẽn.ˈdjẽn.te]

descendant

Naturalmente, costará dinero localizar a ese descendiente.
-Naturally, it will take money to trace that descendant.

4905 mareo

m

[ma.ˈre.o]

dizziness

Siento enormemente mencionarlo, pero mi mareo está empeorando.
-I'm terribly sorry to mention it, but the dizziness is getting worse.

4906 asaltar

vb

[a.sal̬.ˈtar]

assault

Intentaron asaltar un banco en Nueva Orleans.
-They tried to rob a bank in New Orleans.

4907 rasgo

m

[ˈras̬.ɣo]

feature

Usted tiene un rasgo genético inusual.
-That's an unusual genetic trait you have.

4908 lagarto

m

[la.ˈɣar.to]

lizard

Un lución es un lagarto sin patas, no una serpiente.
-A slow-worm is a limbless lizard, not a snake.

4909 frontal

adj [frõn.ˈtal]

frontal

Un pedazo de tubería de agua rompió toda la sección frontal. -A piece of water pipe ripped up the whole front section.

4910 lechuga — **lettuce**
f
[le.ˈtʃu.ɣa]
Jim y Ana cultivan lechuga en su jardín.
-Jim and Ana grow leaf lettuce in their garden.

4911 charco — **puddle**
m
[ˈtʃar.ko]
El hielo se fundió y se transformó en un charco de agua.
-The ice melted into a puddle of water.

4912 ojear — **glance over**
vb
[o.xe.ˈar]
Me encantaría ojear el portafolio de patentes detrás de todo esto.
-I would love to browse the patent portfolio behind all this.

4913 mundial — **worldwide**
adj
[mũn̪.ˈdjal]
Está buscando provocar un impacto global, mundial.
-He's looking to make a global, worldwide impact.

4914 histeria — **hysteria**
f
[is.ˈtɛ.rja]
El diagnóstico clínico es histeria pero hay más.
-The clinical diagnosis is hysteria but there's more to it.

4915 balazo — **shot**
m
[ba.ˈla.so]
Hubiera recibido un balazo por él.
-I would have taken a bullet for him.

4916 navío — **ship**
m
[na.ˈβi.o]
Recibí autorización del gobierno de Colombia para dispararle a su navío.
-I received authorization of the government from Colombia to shoot to their ship.

4917 hindú — **Hindu; Hindu person**
adj; m/f
[ĩn̪.ˈdu]
Un hindú nos enseñará a respirar.
-A Hindu will teach us how to breathe.

4918 quirófano — **operating room**
m
[ki.ˈro.fa.no]
Tu paciente salió de quirófano hace un rato.
-Your patient's been out of surgery a while.

4919 fúnebre — **funeral**
adj
[ˈfu.ne.βre]
El tren fúnebre incluirá 11 furgones.
-The funeral train will consist of 11 cars.

4920 manchar — **stain**
vb
[mãn̪.ˈtʃar]
No quiero manchar la alfombra.
-I don't want to stain the carpet.

4921 compás — **compass**
m
[kõm.ˈpas]
Esto es un verdadero compás magnético incorporado.
-This is a built-in genuine magnetic compass.

4922 sublime — **sublime**
adj
[su.ˈβli.me]
Dejé ese placer sublime para ti.
-I've left that sublime pleasure for you.

4923 portador — **carrier**
m
[por.ta.ˈðor]
Causará una reacción en el portador.
-It'll cause a reaction in the carrier.

4924 tempestad — **storm**
f
[tẽm.pɛs.ˈtað]
La mujer acababa de enviudar y su choza había quedado destruida por una tempestad.
-The woman's husband had just died, and her hut had been destroyed by a storm.

4925 heterosexual — **heterosexual**

adj

[ɛ.tɛ.ro.sɛkˈswal]

Necesito a un hombre heterosexual del público.

-I need a straight guy from the audience.

4926 anular(se) — **cancel; destroy**

vb; vbr

[a.nuˈlar]

Obviamente, podrá anular esta autorización cuando usted desee.

-Naturally, you can cancel this authorization at any time.

4927 abusar — **abuse**

vb

[a.βuˈsar]

Uno no debe abusar de los animales.

-One must not abuse animals.

4928 súbdito — **subject**

m

[ˈsuβ.ði.to]

Si fueras mi súbdito, estaría obligada a disciplinarte.

-If you were my subject, I would be forced to discipline you.

4929 ingrediente — **ingredient**

m

[ĩŋ.greˈðjẽn̪.te]

La sal es un ingrediente indispensable para cocinar.

-Salt is an indispensable ingredient for cooking.

4930 reconstrucción — **reconstruction**

f

[re.kõns.trukˈsjõn]

Parece que Ana ha acabado la reconstrucción facial de la víctima.

-Looks like Ana finished the victim's facial reconstruction.

4931 cadete — **cadet**

m/f

[kaˈðɛ.te]

Me asignaron aquí como cadete de vuelo.

-I'm assigned here as a flying cadet.

4932 recuento — **count**

m

[reˈkwẽn̪.to]

Escaparás de noche tras el último recuento.

-You'll escape at night after the last count.

4933 informal — **informal; unreliable person**

adj; m/f

[ĩɱ.forˈmal]

Estoy empezando una conversación informal contigo.

-I'm striking up a casual conversation with you.

4934 alza — **rise**

f

[ˈal.sa]

Todo el mundo espera una alza de los precios.

-The whole world expected a big rise in prices.

4935 compartimento — **compartment**

m

[kõm.par.ti.ˈmẽn̪.to]

Hay algunas almohadas extra en el compartimento superior.

-There are some extra pillows in your overhead compartment.

4936 espectro — **spectrum, ghost**

m

[ɛs.ˈpek̚.tro]

Solo puede leerse en el espectro ultravioleta.

-They can only be read in the ultraviolet spectrum.

4937 pulpo — **octopus**

m

[ˈpul.po]

Tengo una canción sobre un pulpo.

-I've got a song about an octopus.

4938 comuna — **commune**

f

[ko.ˈmu.na]

Mis padres biológicos vivían en una comuna en Pensilvania.

-My birth parents, they lived with this commune in Pennsylvania.

4939 servilleta — **napkin**

f

[sɛr.βi.ˈjɛ.ta]

Dejé de leer cuando arrancaste una de mis páginas y la usaste como servilleta.

-I stopped reading when you tore out one of my pages and used it as a napkin.

4940 porcelana — **porcelain**

f

[por.se.ˈla.na]

Siento que no tengamos porcelana más bella.

-I'm sorry we don't have finer china.

4941	**manipular**	**manipulate**
	vb	Va a manipular las válvulas de presión.
	[ma.ni.pu.ˈlar]	-He's going to tamper with the pressure valves.

4942	**legendario**	**legendary**
	adj	Solo seguimos los últimos deseos de un legendario guerrero.
	[le.xẽn̪.ˈda.rjo]	-We're just following the last wishes of a legendary warrior.

4943	**prójimo**	**neighbor, friend (LA)**
	m	Han traído daño a su prójimo.
	[ˈpro.xi.mo]	-You've brought harm unto your fellow man.

4944	**brutalidad**	**brutality**
	f	La crueldad y la brutalidad de sus actos son inexplicables.
	[bru.ta.li.ˈðað]	-The cruelty and barbarity of their actions are inexplicable.

4945	**ascender**	**ascend**
	vb	Elizabeth tendrá que ascender al trono sin mí.
	[as.sẽn̪.ˈdɛr]	-Elizabeth will have to ascend the throne without me.

4946	**cuestionar**	**question**
	vb	Entonces tendré que cuestionar su inteligencia.
	[kwɛs.tjo.ˈnar]	-Then, I'd have to question your intelligence.

4947	**costero**	**coastal**
	adj	En el informe se destacan los principales problemas y enfoques de interés general para el turismo costero sostenible en África.
	[kos.ˈtɛ.ro]	-The report highlights key issues and approaches of general relevance to sustainable coastal tourism in Africa.

4948	**tolerancia**	**tolerance**
	f	A lo largo de la historia, el islam a demostrado por medio de sus palabras y sus acciones las posibilidades de la tolerancia religiosa y la equidad racial.
	[to.lɛ.ˈrãn.sja]	-Throughout history, Islam has demonstrated through words and deeds the possibilities of religious tolerance and racial equality.

4949	**retorcer**	**twist**
	vb	Me gustaría retorcer tu brazo.
	[rɛ.tor.ˈsɛr]	-I'd like to wring your arm.

4950	**escrúpulo**	**scruple**
	m	Esto fue solo un escrúpulo temporal.
	[ɛs.ˈkru.pu.lo]	-This was just a temporary scruple.

4951	**volador**	**flying**
	adj	Nunca antes había construido una máquina voladora.
	[bo.la.ˈðor]	-I've never built a flying machine before.

4952	**trucha**	**trout**
	f	Eso de la trucha es muy interesante.
	[ˈtru.ʧa]	-That's a very interesting point about trout.

4953	**imaginario**	**imaginary; imaginary**
	adj; m	Lo que le pasó a mi barco no fue imaginario.
	[i.ma.xi.ˈna.rjo]	-What happened to my ship was not imagined.

4954	**soja**	**soy**
	f	El documento ofrece guías para la producción de soja responsable para un desarrollo sostenible.
	[ˈso.xa]	-The document provides guidelines for responsible soy production for a sustainable development.

| 4955 | **aprendizaje** | **learning** |

m
[a.prẽn̪.di.ˈsa.xe]

Promoverán el aprendizaje de idiomas extranjeros.
-They shall promote the learning of foreign languages.

4956 recinto — **enclosure**

m
[re.ˈsĩn̪.to]

Me preocupa la seguridad de nuestro recinto.
-I'm concerned about the safety of our compound.

4957 lavadora — **washing machine**

f
[la.βa.ˈðo.ra]

La lavadora no cabe por la puerta.
-The washer doesn't fit through the door.

4958 ruleta — **roulette**

f
[ru.ˈlɛ.ta]

Jim y Ana jugaron a la ruleta rusa.
-Jim and Ana played a game of Russian roulette.

4959 filtro — **filter**

m
[ˈfil̪.tro]

Decidimos ocultarlo con un filtro impreso.
-We decided to hide it with a printed filter.

4960 superstición — **superstition**

f
[su.pɛrs.ti.ˈsjõn]

Una superstición es una explicación prematura que dura más de lo que cabría razonablemente esperar.
-A superstition is a premature explanation that overstays its time.

4961 Colombia — **Colombia**

f
[ko.ˈlõm.bja]

Ha visitado Colombia, México y Mozambique.
-She has visited Colombia, Mexico, and Mozambique.

4962 capitalista — **capitalist; capitalist**

adj; m/f
[ka.pi.ta.ˈlis.ta]

Jim es un capitalista de riesgo.
-Jim is a venture capitalist.

4963 ligar(se) — **tie, flirt (coll)**

vb
[li.ˈɣar]

No tienen tiempo de ligar con jóvenes sabelotodo.
-They don't have time to flirt with you young wise guys.

4964 arcilla — **clay**

f
[ar.ˈsi.ja]

Todos ustedes serán inmortalizados en arcilla.
-All of you will be immortalized in clay.

4965 enganchado — **hooked (coll)**

adj
[ẽŋ.gãn̪.ˈʧa.ðo]

Al principio solo estaba mirando las oraciones en Francés, pero antes de darme cuenta ya me había enganchado traduciéndolas.
-At first, I was only looking at the French sentences, but before I knew it, I was hooked into translating them.

4966 desvío — **detour**

m
[dɛs̠.ˈβi.o]

Te estoy llevando al aeropuerto con un pequeño desvío.
-I'm taking you to the airport with one quick detour.

4967 fogata — **bonfire**

f
[fo.ˈɣa.ta]

Nunca dejes una fogata desatendida.
-Never leave a campfire unattended.

4968 célebre — **famous**

adj
[ˈse.le.βre]

Serás el cura más célebre de China.
-You'll become the most celebrated priest in China.

4969 anarquía — **anarchy**

f
[a.nar.ˈki.a]

Evitar esa anarquía redunda en beneficio de todos.
-It is in everyone's interest to avoid such anarchy.

4970 monstruoso — **monstrous**

adj
[mõns.ˈtrwo.so]

Era un experimento monstruoso, lleno de tragedia.
-It was a monstrous experiment, full of tragedy.

4971 **lona**

f
[ˈlo.na]

canvas

Solo necesito asegurar esta lona un poquito.
-I just need to secure this tarp a little.

4972 **Mediterráneo**

m
[me.ði.tɛ.ˈra.ne.o]

Mediterranean

Un buque de carga, con rumbo a Atenas, se hundió en el Mediterráneo sin dejar rastro.
-A cargo vessel, bound for Athens, sank in the Mediterranean without a trace.

4973 **criticar**

vb
[kri.ti.ˈkar]

criticize

Considero que criticar es demasiado fácil.
-I believe that it is too easy to criticize.

4974 **flexible**

adj
[flɛk.ˈsi.βle]

flexible

No soy lo suficientemente flexible para sentarme en la posición del loto.
-I'm not flexible enough to sit in the lotus position.

4975 **mafioso**

adj; m
[ma.ˈfjo.so]

mafia; mobster

La familia del mafioso, Lincoln, tiene un largo historial de delincuencia y terrorismo.
-The family of the mobster, Lincoln, has a long history of crime and terrorism.

4976 **holocausto**

m
[o.lo.ˈkau̯s.to]

holocaust

El temor a un holocausto nuclear parece haber terminado con la Guerra Fría.
-Fear of a nuclear holocaust seems to have ended with the Cold War.

4977 **zarpar**

vb
[sar.ˈpar]

set sail

Esta mañana hemos recibido órdenes para que nos preparemos a zarpar.
-We received orders this morning to make ready to sail.

4978 **chorrada**

f
[tʃo.ˈra.ða]

nonsense, knick-knack (ES) (coll)

Los niños siempre están diciendo chorradas.
-Kids are always talking nonsense.

4979 **rugby**

m
[ˈruɣ.βi]

rugby

Será fantástico enseñarte a jugar al rugby.
-It'd be great to teach you how to play rugby.

4980 **constar**

vb
[kõns.ˈtar]

feature, appear

Esta advertencia deberá constar en el acta.
-This notification shall be mentioned in the record.

4981 **útero**

m
[ˈu.tɛ.ro]

uterus

He detectado algunas irregularidades en el útero.
-I have detected some irregularities in the uterus.

4982 **contenedor**

m
[kõn̪.te.ne.ˈðor]

container

Solíamos tardar seis horas en soltar un contenedor.
-It used to take us six hours to release a container.

4983 **adquirir**

vb
[að.ki.ˈrir]

acquire

En el pasado, los hombres se vendían a sí mismos al Diablo para adquirir poderes mágicos. Hoy en día adquieren estos poderes de la ciencia, y se ven forzados a transformarse en demonios.
-In former days, men sold themselves to the Devil to acquire magical powers. Nowadays they acquire those powers from science, and find themselves compelled to become devils.

4984 **acorde**

chord; in accordance with

	m; adj	Acorde al manual, es la única opción.
	[a.ˈkor.ðe]	-According to that manual, it's the only option.
4985	**estatura**	**stature**
	f	Tiene tu estatura, ojos castaños.
	[ɛs.ta.ˈtu.ra]	-She is about your height, brown eyes.
4986	**indispensable**	**indispensable**
	adj	Es indispensable reducir el volumen de papel utilizado.
	[ĩn̪.dis.pẽn.ˈsa.βle]	-It was essential to reduce the amount of paper used.
4987	**auxiliar**	**assistant; assist**
	adj; vb	Dispárame si quieres, pero quiero auxiliar a tu padre.
	[au̯k.si.ˈljar]	-Shoot me if you want, but I mean to help your father.
4988	**noreste**	**northeast**
	m	Jim, tomarás la división noreste.
	[no.ˈrɛs.te]	-Jim, you'll take the northeast division.
4989	**relativo**	**concerning**
	adj	El segundo ámbito, relativo a consideraciones medioambientales, es otra cuestión muy importante.
	[re.la.ˈti.βo]	-The second area, concerning environmental considerations, is another very important question.
4990	**encaje**	**lace, fitting**
	m	El encaje está suave contra mi piel.
	[ẽŋ.ˈka.xe]	-The lace feels soft against my skin.
4991	**vibración**	**vibration**
	f	El ruido del motor y la vibración han sido aislados y significativamente reducidos.
	[bi.βra.ˈsjõn]	-Motor noise and vibration have been isolated and significantly reduced.
4992	**residuo**	**residue**
	m	Deberíamos ser capaces de analizar el residuo.
	[re.ˈsi.ðwo]	-We should be able to analyze the residue.
4993	**camarón**	**prawn**
	m	La acuicultura del camarón también se veía amenazada.
	[ka.ma.ˈrõn]	-Prawn farming will also be threatened.
4994	**seductor**	**seductive; seducer**
	adj; m	Quiero decir, es un seductor.
	[se.ðuk̚.ˈtor]	-I mean, he's a flirt.
4995	**largar(se)**	**tell, give; leave (coll)**
	vb; vbr	Con el debido respeto, me voy a largar de aquí.
	[lar.ˈɣar]	-With all due respect, I'm going to get the hell out of here.
4996	**carecer**	**lack**
	vb	El conocimiento por sí solo puede carecer de los elementos necesarios para fomentar la paz.
	[ka.re.ˈsɛr]	-Knowledge alone may lack the necessary elements to bring about peace.
4997	**rampa**	**ramp**
	f	Estoy pensando en poner una rampa.
	[ˈrãm.pa]	-I'm thinking of putting in a ramp.
4998	**mayor**	**largest, elderly**
	adj	Parece joven, pero de hecho es mayor que tú.
	[ma.ˈjor]	-She looks young, but as a matter of fact, she is older than you are.
4999	**madurar**	**mature**

	vb	Tíos, tenéis que madurar. Aprender a ser independientes.
	[ma.ðu.ˈrar]	-Guys, you need to grow up. Learn to be independent.
5000	**enorgullecer(se)**	**please; feel proud**
	vb; vbr	También podemos enorgullecernos de la contribución que hemos hecho.
	[e.nor.ɣu.je.ˈsɛr]	-We can also take pride in the contribution we have made.
5001	**indicio**	**indication**
	m	El primer indicio de esta tormenta no es un trueno.
	[ĩn̯.ˈdi.sjo]	-The first hint of this storm is not a thunderclap.
5002	**piña**	**pineapple**
	f	Me gusta la piña azul de Jim.
	[ˈpi.ɲa]	-I like Jim's blue pineapple.
5003	**reclutar**	**recruit**
	vb	Esto no es una operación para reclutar partidarios.
	[re.klu.ˈtar]	-This is not an operation to recruit supporters.
5004	**trayecto**	**journey**
	m	Una vez que haya salido de la costa, el trayecto será corto pero muy sinuoso.
	[tra.ˈɟek̚.to]	-Once you have left the coast, the journey is short but very winding.
5005	**linaje**	**lineage**
	m	El presidente nombra a los secretarios basándose en lazos de linaje reconocidos.
	[li.ˈna.xe]	-The president appoints the chiefs based on recognized lineage ties.
5006	**manantial**	**spring**
	m	Los animales no beben del manantial.
	[ma.nã̯n̯.ˈtjal]	-The animals don't drink from the spring.
5007	**numeroso**	**numerous**
	adj	Era rey de un pueblo numeroso.
	[nu.mɛ.ˈro.so]	-He was king over numerous people.
5008	**negligencia**	**negligence**
	f	Entre estos casos se incluyen desde la negligencia hasta agresiones y asesinatos.
	[ne.ɣli.ˈxɛ̃n.sja]	-These cases include everything from negligence to assault and killings.
5009	**coyote**	**coyote**
	m	Parece que ahí entró un coyote.
	[ko.ˈɟo.te]	-Looks like a coyote got in there.
5010	**presenciar**	**witness**
	vb	Es difícil presenciar algo tan abrumador.
	[pre.sɛ̃n.ˈsjar]	-It's difficult to witness something so overwhelming.
5011	**fulano**	**some guy (coll)**
	m	Fulano de Tal es un apelativo para una persona anónima.
	[fu.ˈla.no]	-John Doe is a nickname for an anonymous person.
5012	**milenio**	**millennium**
	m	Pronto ingresaremos al primer siglo del tercer milenio.
	[mi.ˈle.njo]	-We will soon enter the first century of the third millennium.
5013	**experimental**	**experimental**
	adj	Era una estación de energía experimental.
	[ɛks.pɛ.ri.mɛ̃n̯.ˈtal]	-It was an experimental power station.
5014	**encarcelar**	**imprison**
	vb	El régimen ha decidido encarcelar a los oponentes.
	[ɛ̃ŋ.kar.se.ˈlar]	-The regime has chosen to imprison opponents.

5015	**analista**	**analyst**
	m/f	No quiero terminar como analista financiero.
	[a.na.ˈlis.ta]	-I don't want to wind up a financial analyst.
5016	**hermosura**	**beauty**
	f	Si crees que puedes atraerme con tu hermosura, te equivocas y mucho.
	[ɛr.mo.ˈsu.ra]	-If you think you can entice me with your beauty then you are so wrong.
5017	**erupción**	**eruption**
	f	Una erupción apareció en su cuello.
	[ɛ.rup.ˈsjõn]	-A rash broke out on her neck.
5018	**heroico**	**heroic**
	adj	Conociéndole, sería algo bastante heroico.
	[ɛ.ˈroi̯.ko]	-Knowing him, it was something quite heroic.
5019	**marfil**	**ivory**
	m	Quiero usar un vestido marfil con hombros descubiertos.
	[mar.ˈfil]	-I want to wear an ivory gown with bare shoulders.
5020	**malaria**	**malaria**
	f	La malaria tiene graves consecuencias económicas y humanas para África.
	[ma.ˈla.rja]	-Malaria has a serious economic as well as human impact on Africa.
5021	**precipicio**	**cliff**
	m	Debería haberte lanzado por ese precipicio.
	[pre.si.ˈpi.sjo]	-I should've thrown you off that cliff back there.
5022	**hebreo**	**Hebrew; Jew**
	adj; m	Aprenderé hebreo y estudiaré el Talmud.
	[e.ˈβre.o]	-I will learn Hebrew and study the Talmud.
5023	**hipnosis**	**hypnosis**
	f	Le haré volver allí mediante hipnosis.
	[ipˀ.ˈno.sis]	-I'm going to take you back there using hypnosis.
5024	**persiana**	**blind**
	f	Abre esa persiana, unos centímetros.
	[pɛr.ˈsja.na]	-Open that blind, just a few inches.
5025	**nato**	**born**
	adj	Eras un jinete nato, Jim.
	[ˈna.to]	-You were a natural born horseman, Jim.

Adjectives

Rank	Spanish-PoS	Translation(s)
2504	ligero-*adj*	light
2511	valioso-*adj*	valuable
2524	injusto-*adj*	unfair
2525	tremendo-*adj*	tremendous
2527	espectacular-*adj*	spectacular
2529	bobo-*adj; m*	silly; fool
2537	adolescente-*m/f; adj*	teenager; teenage
2539	postal-*adj; f*	postal; postcard
2543	recto-*adj*	straight
2545	pirata-*m/f; adj*	pirate; pirated
2549	encendido-*adj; m*	on; ignition
2564	espléndido-*adj*	splendid
2567	vago-*adj; m*	vague, lazy; slacker
2571	árabe-*adj; m/f*	Arabian; Arab
2580	telefónico-*adj*	telephonic
2581	conjunto-*m; adj*	combination; joint
2585	forense-*adj; m/f*	forensic; forensic surgeon
2590	cerebral-*adj*	cerebral
2591	volante-*m; adj*	steering wheel, referral (ES); flying
2593	marino-*adj; m*	marine; sailor
2600	certificado-*m; adj*	certificate; registered
2601	excitante-*adj*	exciting
2602	homosexual-*adj; m/f*	homosexual; homosexual
2603	vital-*adj*	vital
2610	músico-*m; adj*	musician; musical
2628	sensacional-*adj*	sensational
2633	rudo-*adj*	rough, rude
2643	romano-*adj; m*	Roman; Roman person
2646	hueco-*m; adj*	space; empty
2648	inusual-*adj*	unusual
2652	organizado-*adj*	tidy
2656	turista-*adj; m/f*	tourist; tourist
2658	novato-*m; adj*	trainee; rookie
2660	incómodo-*adj*	uncomfortable
2664	similar-*adj*	similar
2676	cómico-*adj; m*	comical; comedian
2683	ansioso-*adj*	eager, worried
2685	occidental-*adj; m/f*	western; westerner
2686	crítico-*adj; m*	critical; critic
2687	bruto-*adj; m*	brutal; brute
2693	vergonzoso-*adj*	shameful
2709	mecánico-*adj; m*	mechanical; mechanic
2713	aliado-*m; adj*	ally; allied
2715	inevitable-*adj*	inevitable
2716	tierno-*adj*	tender
2722	bárbaro-*adj; m*	savage; Barbarian
2726	femenino-*adj*	female
2737	ebrio-*adj*	drunk
2743	conveniente-*adj*	convenient
2744	emocional-*adj*	emotional
2747	lejano-*adj*	distant
2756	gemelo-*adj; m*	twin; twin
2757	voluntario-*adj; m*	voluntary; volunteer
2762	esencial-*adj*	essential
2766	ácido-*adj; m*	sour; acid
2768	respetable-*adj*	respectable
2776	estable-*adj*	stable
2778	arrogante-*adj*	arrogant
2779	sentimental-*adj*	sentimental
2797	universal-*adj*	universal
2798	marrón-*adj*	brown
2824	insoportable-*adj*	unbearable
2836	oculto-*adj*	hidden
2842	oriental-*adj; m*	eastern; Asian
2846	confidencial-*adj*	confidential
2851	lamentable-*adj*	unfortunate, pathetic
2852	inferior-*adj; m/f*	lower; subordinate
2853	imperial-*adj*	imperial
2861	irlandés-*adj; m*	Irish; Irish person
2864	frito-*adj*	fried
2869	fenomenal-*adj*	phenomenal
2876	intelectual-*adj; m/f*	mental; intellectual
2884	ritual-*adj; m*	ritual; ritual
2885	fijo-*adj*	fixed
2886	atento-*adj*	attentive
2888	ejecutivo-*adj; m*	executive; manager
2895	sinvergüenza-*m/f; adj*	wretch; rascal

2902	**confuso**-*adj*	confusing
2904	**ardiente**-*adj*	burning
2915	**apagado**-*adj*	off
2917	**ignorante**-*adj; m*	ignorant; ignoramus
2918	**supremo**-*adj*	supreme
2927	**liberado**-*adj*	free
2936	**cuidadoso**-*adj*	careful
2946	**chistoso**-*adj*	funny
2948	**tinto**-*adj*	red wine
2952	**guay**-*adj; int*	great; great (ES) (coll)
2960	**tradicional**-*adj*	traditional
2964	**visual**-*adj*	visual
2973	**prudente**-*adj*	prudent
2974	**triple**-*adj; m*	triple; triple
2975	**contenido**-*m; adj*	contents; reserved
2979	**continente**-*adj*	continent
2984	**insignificante**-*adj*	insignificant
2995	**automático**-*adj*	automatic
2998	**líquido**-*adj; m*	liquid; liquid
2999	**mudo**-*adj*	mute
3001	**protector**-*adj; m*	protective; protector
3009	**formal**-*adj*	formal
3010	**excepcional**-*adj*	exceptional
3017	**frágil**-*adj*	fragile
3019	**lunar**-*adj; m*	lunar; mole
3022	**trágico**-*adj*	tragic
3023	**inicial**-*adj; f*	beginning; initial
3029	**mutuo**-*adj*	mutual
3034	**judicial**-*adj; m*	judicial; police officer
3040	**religioso**-*adj; m*	religious; priest
3042	**resfriado**-*adj; m*	have a cold; cold
3043	**sumo**-*m; adj*	sumo; supreme
3044	**delincuente**-*m/f; adj*	criminal; delinquent
3046	**cargado**-*adj*	strong
3050	**pendiente**-*m; f; adj*	earring; slope; pending
3057	**artificial**-*adj*	artificial
3063	**colorado**-*adj*	red
3081	**anual**-*adj*	annual
3088	**fino**-*adj*	fine
3089	**culto**-*m; adj*	worship; educated
3094	**concreto**-*adj*	specific
3096	**brutal**-*adj*	brutal
3114	**desconocido**-*adj; m*	unknown; stranger
3118	**intenso**-*adj*	powerful
3120	**secuestrado**-*adj*	kidnapped
3124	**salido**-*adj; m*	protruding; horny (coll)
3125	**hondo**-*adj*	deep
3126	**marcial**-*adj*	martial
3128	**soviético**-*adj; m*	Soviet; Soviet
3130	**marcado**-*adj; m*	noticeable; dialing (LA)
3147	**hábil**-*adj*	skilled
3152	**activo**-*adj; m*	active; assets
3154	**católico**-*adj; m*	Catholic; Catholic
3157	**interno**-*adj*	internal
3158	**rival**-*adj; m/f*	rival; opponent
3159	**asado**-*adj; m*	roast; roast
3166	**aterrador**-*adj*	frightening
3168	**podrido**-*adj*	rotten
3173	**polaco**-*adj; m*	Polish; Polish person
3187	**inmortal**-*adj*	immortal
3189	**zoológico**-*adj; m*	zoological; zoo
3192	**despreciable**-*adj*	despicable
3198	**silencioso**-*adj*	silent
3202	**natal**-*adj*	native
3208	**sobrio**-*adj*	sober
3217	**impaciente**-*adj*	impatient
3220	**mexicano**-*adj; m*	Mexican; Mexican person
3223	**vigilante**-*adj; m/f*	attentive; guard
3224	**reflejo**-*m; adj*	reflection; reflex
3227	**maduro**-*adj; adv*	ripe; mature
3241	**ofensivo**-*adj*	offensive
3245	**formidable**-*adj*	formidable
3248	**norteamericano**-*adj; m*	North American; North American person
3256	**argentino**-*adj; m*	Argentinian; Argentinian person
3257	**industrial**-*adj; m*	industrial; industrialist
3267	**delantero**-*adj; m*	front; forward
3270	**ingenioso**-*adj*	witty
3286	**sobreviviente**-*m/f; adj*	survivor; surviving

3289	**viviente**-*adj*	living	
3291	**mocoso**-*m; adj*	snuffly; brat	
3309	**documental**-*adj; m*	documentary; documentary	
3319	**vil**-*adj*	vile	
3320	**terminal**-*adj; m/f*	terminal; terminal	
3321	**celestial**-*adj*	celestial	
3329	**turco**-*adj; m*	Turkish; Turk	
3331	**golfo**-*m; adj*	gulf; scoundrel	
3333	**pálido**-*adj*	pale	
3338	**sensual**-*adj*	sensual	
3342	**escocés**-*adj; m*	Scotch; Scot	
3348	**estelar**-*adj*	stellar	
3351	**histórico**-*adj*	historical	
3355	**afectado**-*adj; m*	affected; victim	
3357	**confundido**-*adj*	confused	
3370	**veloz**-*adj*	fast	
3372	**infiel**-*adj; m/f*	unfaithful; infidel	
3375	**remoto**-*adj*	distant	
3377	**inesperado**-*adj*	unexpected	
3386	**opuesto**-*adj*	opposite	
3388	**fugitivo**-*adj; m*	fugitive; fugitive	
3403	**ancho**-*m; adj*	width; wide	
3412	**cálido**-*adj*	warm	
3428	**sólido**-*adj; m*	solid; solid	
3429	**extraterrestre**-*adj; m/f*	alien; alien	
3432	**estricto**-*adj*	strict	
3433	**conforme**-*adj; adv*	in agreement; just as	
3439	**financiero**-*adj; m*	financial; financier	
3441	**primario**-*adj*	primary	
3448	**flaco**-*adj*	skinny	
3449	**perpetuo**-*adj*	perpetual	
3452	**usual**-*adj*	usual	
3454	**universitario**-*adj; m*	university; undergraduate	
3455	**cultural**-*adj*	cultural	
3459	**hipócrita**-*adj; m/f*	hypocritical; hypocrite	
3462	**digital**-*adj*	digital	
3468	**revolucionario**-*adj; m*	revolutionary; revolutionary	
3471	**modesto**-*adj*	modest	
3477	**masculino**-*adj*	masculine	
3482	**infinito**-*adj; m*	infinite; infinity	
3485	**artístico**-*adj*	artistic	

3492	**admirable**-*adj*	admirable	
3498	**fundamental**-*adj*	fundamental	
3500	**defensor**-*adj; m*	defense; defense attorney	
3504	**puerco**-*m; adj*	pig; disgusting	
3507	**ausente**-*adj; m/f*	absent; absentee	
3528	**químico**-*adj; m*	chemical; chemist	
3530	**pésimo**-*adj*	awful	
3532	**económico**-*adj*	economic	
3534	**feroz**-*adj*	fierce	
3538	**ético**-*adj*	ethical	
3539	**fascista**-*adj; m/f*	fascist; fascist	
3545	**pecador**-*m; adj*	sinner; sinful	
3549	**convincente**-*adj*	convincing	
3552	**dramático**-*adj*	dramatic	
3555	**deprimente**-*adj*	depressing	
3558	**oportuno**-*adj*	timely	
3559	**prohibido**-*adj*	prohibited	
3560	**atómico**-*adj*	atomic	
3564	**casero**-*adj; m*	home-made; landlord	
3565	**chulo**-*adj; m*	cocky (ES) (coll), great (ES) (coll); scumbag (coll)	
3566	**agresivo**-*adj*	aggressive	
3567	**anormal**-*adj*	unusual	
3568	**nativo**-*adj; m*	local; native	
3576	**forastero**-*m; adj*	stranger; foreign	
3577	**naval**-*adj*	naval	
3578	**sensato**-*adj*	sensible	
3581	**distante**-*adj*	distant	
3585	**inconveniente**-*m; adj*	problem; inconvenient	
3593	**embarazoso**-*adj*	embarrassing	
3602	**repentino**-*adj*	sudden	
3605	**forzado**-*adj*	forced	
3607	**musulmán**-*adj; m*	Muslim; Muslim	
3611	**exclusivo**-*adj*	exclusive	
3614	**fanático**-*adj; m*	fan; fanatic	
3620	**glorioso**-*adj*	glorious	
3625	**lila**-*adj; f*	lilac; lilac	
3628	**optimista**-*adj; m/f*	optimistic; optimist	
3632	**villano**-*m; adj*	villain; villain	
3635	**reunido**-*adj*	gathered	
3647	**amoroso**-*adj*	loving	

3648	**contable**-*m/f; adj*	accountant; accounting
3649	**cardíaco**-*adj*	cardiac
3652	**creativo**-*adj; m*	creative; copywriter
3660	**subterráneo**-*adj*	underground
3661	**masivo**-*adj*	massive
3665	**sutil**-*adj*	subtle
3666	**incorrecto**-*adj*	incorrect
3668	**yanqui**-*m/f; adj*	Yankee (coll); Yankee (coll)
3676	**penal**-*adj; m*	criminal; prison
3680	**inofensivo**-*adj*	harmless
3681	**hostil**-*adj*	hostile
3685	**moreno**-*adj*	dark skinned, brunette
3691	**legítimo**-*adj*	legitimate
3698	**racista**-*m/f; adj*	racist person; racist
3701	**ambicioso**-*adj; m*	ambitious; greedy
3702	**discreto**-*adj*	discreet
3710	**juvenil**-*adj*	youth
3712	**ejemplar**-*m; adj*	model; exemplary
3714	**ganso**-*m; adj*	goose; foolish (ES) (coll)
3717	**picante**-*adj; m*	spicy; spiciness
3718	**ingenuo**-*adj*	ingenuous
3719	**deportivo**-*adj*	sports
3724	**notable**-*adj; m*	notable; dignitary
3725	**múltiple**-*adj*	multiple
3733	**húmedo**-*adj*	wet
3756	**huérfano**-*adj; m*	orphaned; orphan
3760	**terrestre**-*adj; m*	land; terrestrial
3763	**satisfecho**-*adj*	satisfied
3769	**tramposo**-*m; adj*	trickster; dishonest
3772	**vulnerable**-*adj*	vulnerable
3782	**cortés**-*adj*	courteous
3787	**específico**-*adj*	specific
3790	**redondo**-*adj*	round
3792	**asesor**-*m; adj*	adviser; advisory
3794	**radical**-*adj; m/f*	radical; radical person
3795	**electrónico**-*adj*	electronic
3799	**oponente**-*m/f; adj*	opponent; opposing
3800	**afirmativo**-*adj; int*	affirmative; sure
3801	**pasado**-*adj; m*	past; past
3817	**leve**-*adj*	mild
3819	**blando**-*adj*	soft
3827	**holandés**-*adj; m*	Dutch; Dutch person
3829	**crucial**-*adj*	crucial
3830	**exitoso**-*adj*	successful
3841	**peculiar**-*adj*	peculiar
3847	**canadiense**-*adj; m/f*	Canadian; Canadian person
3849	**aceptable**-*adj*	acceptable
3856	**diagnóstico**-*m; adj*	diagnosis; diagnostic
3860	**inmenso**-*adj*	immense
3863	**expreso**-*adj; m*	express; express
3864	**pelirrojo**-*adj; m*	redheaded; redhead
3869	**histérico**-*adj; m*	hysterical; hysteric
3876	**íntimo**-*adj*	intimate
3877	**superficial**-*adj*	superficial
3884	**estándar**-*adj; m*	standard; standard
3888	**psiquiátrico**-*adj; m*	psychiatric; psychiatric hospital
3894	**confiable**-*adj*	reliable
3903	**sereno**-*adj; m*	calm; dew
3912	**potente**-*adj*	powerful
3934	**amigable**-*adj*	friendly
3940	**sueco**-*adj; m*	Swedish; Swedish person
3945	**estrecho**-*adj*	narrow
3953	**ordinario**-*adj*	ordinary
3954	**puntual**-*adj; adv*	punctual; on time
3955	**elevado**-*adj*	high
3957	**alcohólico**-*adj; m*	alcoholic; alcoholic person
3962	**inestable**-*adj*	unstable
3969	**determinado**-*adj*	determined
3972	**gitano**-*adj; m*	gypsy; gypsy
3973	**invertido**-*adj*	inverted
3974	**convicto**-*adj; m*	convicted; convict
3977	**amargo**-*adj*	bitter
3979	**dental**-*adj*	dental
3980	**cuadrado**-*adj; m*	square; square
3981	**veterano**-*adj; m*	veteran; veteran
3986	**conmovedor**-*adj*	touching
3989	**descuidado**-*adj*	careless
3995	**irresponsable**-*adj*	irresponsible

4002	**deliberado**-*adj*	deliberate	4224	**intruso**-*m; adj*	intruder; out of place
4014	**cariñoso**-*adj*	affectionate	4225	**israelí**-*adj; m/f*	Israeli; Israeli
4015	**discutido**-*adj*	controversial	4229	**noruego**-*adj; m*	Norwegian; Norwegian person
4020	**púrpura**-*adj*	purple	4232	**cubierto**-*adj; m*	covered; piece of cutlery
4021	**morado**-*adj*	purple	4238	**inminente**-*adj*	imminent
4046	**humillante**-*adj*	humiliating	4243	**indiferente**-*adj*	indifferent
4047	**eficiente**-*adj*	efficient	4244	**corporal**-*adj; m*	corporal; corporal
4059	**estadístico**-*adj; m*	statistical; statistician	4245	**egipcio**-*adj; m*	Egyptian; Egyptian person
4068	**presidencial**-*adj*	presidential	4254	**visible**-*adj*	visible
4073	**crudo**-*adj*	raw, tough (ES) (coll)	4256	**racional**-*adj*	rational
4076	**letal**-*adj*	lethal	4260	**sangriento**-*adj*	bloody
4079	**europeo**-*adj; m*	European; European	4261	**directivo**-*m; adj*	manager; managerial
4085	**insensible**-*adj*	insensitive	4263	**neutral**-*adj; m/f*	neutral; third party
4095	**transmisor**-*m; adj*	transmitter; transmitting	4271	**funerario**-*adj*	funeral
4098	**seguido**-*adj*	non-stop	4272	**grifo**-*m; adj*	water tap; curly (LA)
4100	**sabroso**-*adj*	tasty	4276	**corrupto**-*adj; m*	corrupt; corrupt person
4106	**neumático**-*m; adj*	tire; inflatable	4289	**irresistible**-*adj*	irresistible
4109	**africano**-*adj; m*	African; African person	4300	**atado**-*adj*	tied
4118	**apartado**-*m; adj*	section; remote	4304	**inquieto**-*adj*	restless
4128	**infernal**-*adj*	infernal	4307	**oral**-*adj*	oral
4130	**diplomático**-*adj; m*	diplomatic; diplomat	4312	**narcótico**-*adj; m*	narcotic; narcotic
4132	**exigente**-*adj*	demanding	4315	**amistoso**-*adj*	friendly
4133	**accidental**-*adj*	accidental	4316	**limitado**-*adj*	limited
4137	**irónico**-*adj*	ironic	4317	**adicional**-*adj*	additional
4146	**mineral**-*adj; m*	mineral; mineral	4327	**tacaño**-*adj*	miserly
4157	**anticuado**-*adj*	antiquated	4329	**comprensible**-*adj*	understandable
4165	**residente**-*adj; m/f*	resident; resident	4337	**inaceptable**-*adj*	unacceptable
4169	**infame**-*adj; m/f*	dreadful; villain	4339	**homicida**-*m/f; adj*	killer; murder
4171	**editorial**-*adj; m; f*	editorial; leading article; publishing house	4343	**cereal**-*adj; m*	grain-based; cereal
4176	**individual**-*adj*	single, personal	4355	**impecable**-*adj*	impeccable
4188	**audaz**-*adj*	bold	4358	**perverso**-*adj*	wicked
4189	**titular(se)**-*m; vb; adj*	headline; title; owner	4360	**observador**-*m; adj*	observer; observant
4192	**severo**-*adj*	stern	4364	**violeta**-*adj; f*	violet; violet
4193	**irrelevante**-*adj*	irrelevant	4374	**laboral**-*adj*	work
4196	**creciente**-*adj; f*	growing; swelling	4378	**estofado**-*m; adj*	stew; stewed
4198	**relleno**-*adj; m*	stuffed; stuff	4381	**civilizado**-*adj*	civilized
4204	**apurado**-*adj*	rushed	4382	**galo**-*adj*	Gallic
4208	**liberal**-*adj*	liberal			
4212	**invencible**-*adj*	invincible			

4401	**palestino**-*adj; m*	Palestinian; Palestinian person	
4409	**flojo**-*adj*	loose, slacker	
4420	**despiadado**-*adj*	ruthless	
4422	**psicológico**-*adj*	psychological	
4424	**circular**-*adj; vb*	circular; travel	
4429	**imprudente**-*adj*	reckless	
4430	**acelerador**-*m; adj*	accelerator; accelerant	
4435	**eficaz**-*adj*	effective	
4438	**siniestro**-*adj*	sinister	
4443	**inmoral**-*adj*	immoral	
4444	**convencional**-*adj*	conventional	
4450	**soberano**-*adj; m*	sovereign; sovereign	
4455	**cursi**-*adj; m/f*	corny; pretentious	
4463	**talentoso**-*adj*	talented	
4466	**inmigrante**-*adj; m/f*	immigrant; immigrant	
4470	**peludo**-*adj*	hairy	
4479	**presto**-*adj; adv*	ready; promptly	
4483	**callejero**-*adj; m*	stray; street map	
4484	**espeluznante**-*adj*	horrifying	
4486	**impotente**-*adj*	impotent	
4500	**entretenido**-*adj*	entertaining	
4501	**intacto**-*adj*	intact	
4509	**grueso**-*adj; m*	heavy; thickness	
4517	**acre**-*m; adj*	acre; acrid	
4518	**mediocre**-*adj*	mediocre	
4519	**contestador**-*adj*	cheeky, answering machine	
4522	**exquisito**-*adj*	exquisite	
4524	**considerable**-*adj*	considerable	
4525	**caluroso**-*adj*	hot	
4529	**lateral**-*adj*	side	
4534	**honorario**-*adj*	honorary	
4535	**defensivo**-*adj; m*	defensive; defense	
4537	**atroz**-*adj*	atrocious	
4538	**teatral**-*adj*	theatrical	
4539	**rosado**-*adj*	rose	
4542	**portátil**-*adj; m*	portable; laptop	
4552	**creíble**-*adj*	credible	
4556	**celeste**-*adj*	light blue, of heaven	
4559	**matrimonial**-*adj*	matrimonial	
4564	**vegetal**-*adj; m*	vegetal; vegetable	
4574	**coreano**-*adj; m*	Korean; Korean person
4575	**mero**-*adj*	mere
4582	**cruzado**-*adj*	cross
4584	**amplio**-*adj*	spacious
4596	**confortable**-*adj*	comfortable
4597	**anónimo**-*adj*	anonymous
4619	**precedente**-*adj; m*	previous; precedent
4632	**comprensivo**-*adj*	understanding, comprehensive
4637	**higiénico**-*adj*	hygienic
4644	**operativo**-*adj; m*	operational; operation
4651	**ruidoso**-*adj*	noisy
4658	**necio**-*m; adj*	fool; stupid
4663	**primitivo**-*adj*	primitive
4665	**alucinante**-*adj*	awesome
4670	**conservador**-*adj; m*	conservative; conservative
4672	**congelado**-*adj*	frozen
4673	**parcial**-*adj*	partial
4675	**interminable**-*adj*	endless
4682	**previo**-*adj*	previous
4685	**alejado**-*adj*	remote
4691	**distraído**-*adj; m*	distracted; scatterbrain
4693	**improbable**-*adj*	unlikely
4700	**agotador**-*adj*	exhausting
4703	**dominante**-*adj*	dominant
4707	**sobrenatural**-*adj*	supernatural
4708	**patriota**-*m/f; adj*	patriot; patriotic
4715	**boludo**-*adj; m*	silly (LA) (coll); moron (LA) (coll)
4717	**moribundo**-*adj; m*	dying; dying person
4718	**bancario**-*adj; m*	banking; bank employee
4726	**fiero**-*adj*	fierce
4733	**estudiantil**-*adj*	student (coll)
4739	**implacable**-*adj*	relentless
4747	**castaño**-*adj; m*	brown; chestnut
4750	**estimulante**-*adj; m*	stimulating; stimulant
4753	**posterior**-*adj*	rear, following
4760	**metálico**-*adj; m*	metal; cash
4762	**entrante**-*adj; m*	entering; appetizer (ES)

4773	**diabólico**-*adj*	diabolical
4779	**tropical**-*adj*	tropical
4787	**perezoso**-*adj; m*	lazy; sloth
4797	**adjunto**-*adj; m*	attached; attachment
4812	**indefenso**-*adj*	defenseless
4813	**polar**-*adj*	polar
4821	**portugués**-*adj; m*	Portuguese; Portuguese person
4822	**prometedor**-*adj*	promising
4824	**descarado**-*adj; m*	shameless; insolent person
4827	**cínico**-*adj; m*	shameless; shameless person
4844	**agudo**-*adj*	high-pitched
4847	**alérgico**-*adj; m*	allergic; person with allergies
4848	**parásito**-*m; adj*	parasite; parasitic
4851	**resistente**-*adj*	resistant
4852	**innecesario**-*adj*	unnecessary
4857	**preparatorio**-*adj; m*	preparatory; pre-university study
4859	**sonriente**-*adj*	smiling
4863	**pendejo**-*adj; m*	asshole (LA) (coll); fool (LA) (coll)
4866	**romo**-*adj*	blunt
4869	**ambulante**-*adj*	traveling
4871	**vencedor**-*adj; m*	winner; winner
4875	**inapropiado**-*adj*	inappropriate
4881	**descortés**-*adj*	impolite
4884	**tibio**-*adj*	warm
4887	**acogedor**-*adj*	cozy
4889	**viudo**-*m; adj*	widower; widow
4895	**horroroso**-*adj*	dreadful
4898	**equivalente**-*adj*	equivalent
4899	**relevante**-*adj*	outstanding
4909	**frontal**-*adj*	frontal
4913	**mundial**-*adj*	worldwide
4917	**hindú**-*adj; m/f*	Hindu; Hindu person
4919	**fúnebre**-*adj*	funeral
4922	**sublime**-*adj*	sublime
4925	**heterosexual**-*adj*	heterosexual
4933	**informal**-*adj; m/f*	informal; unreliable person
4942	**legendario**-*adj*	legendary
4947	**costero**-*adj*	coastal
4951	**volador**-*adj*	flying
4953	**imaginario**-*adj; m*	imaginary; imaginary
4962	**capitalista**-*adj; m/f*	capitalist; capitalist
4965	**enganchado**-*adj*	hooked (coll)
4968	**célebre**-*adj*	famous
4970	**monstruoso**-*adj*	monstrous
4974	**flexible**-*adj*	flexible
4975	**mafioso**-*adj; m*	mafia; mobster
4984	**acorde**-*m; adj*	chord; in accordance with
4986	**indispensable**-*adj*	indispensable
4987	**auxiliar**-*adj; vb*	assistant; assist
4989	**relativo**-*adj*	concerning
4994	**seductor**-*adj; m*	seductive; seducer
4998	**mayor**-*adj*	largest, elderly
5007	**numeroso**-*adj*	numerous
5013	**experimental**-*adj*	experimental
5018	**heroico**-*adj*	heroic
5022	**hebreo**-*adj; m*	Hebrew; Jew
5025	**nato**-*adj*	born

Adverbs

Rank	Spanish-PoS	Translation(s)
2734	**etc.**-*adv*	etc.
3054	**aprisa**-*adv*	quickly
3227	**maduro**-*adj; adv*	ripe; mature
3260	**nomás**-*adv*	just (LA)
3277	**cuan**-*adv*	as
3361	**eventualmente**-*adv*	occasionally
3368	**dondequiera**-*adv*	wherever
3433	**conforme**-*adj; adv*	in agreement; just as
3465	**anteriormente**-*adv*	previously
3954	**puntual**-*adj; adv*	punctual; on time
4099	**inclusive**-*adv*	inclusive
4479	**presto**-*adj; adv*	ready; promptly

Conjunctions

Rank	Spanish-*PoS*	Translation(s)
3393	**no obstante**-*con*	however

Prepositions

Rank	Spanish-*PoS*	Translation(s)
2845	**mediante**-*prp*	through
3609	**en torno a**-*prp*	about

Pronouns

Rank	Spanish-*PoS*	Translation(s)
3362	**quienquiera**-*prn*	whoever

Nouns

Rank	Spanish-PoS	Translation(s)
2501	episodio-*m*	episode
2505	músculo-*m*	muscle
2506	misil-*m*	missile
2507	obispo-*m*	bishop
2508	herencia-*f*	heritage, inheritance
2509	monje-*m*	monk
2512	tiroteo-*m*	gunfire
2513	cordero-*m*	lamb
2515	aplauso-*m*	applause
2516	píldora-*f*	pill
2517	puño-*m*	fist
2518	marea-*f*	tide
2520	disfraz-*m*	costume
2521	navaja-*f*	knife
2526	jungla-*f*	jungle
2529	bobo-*adj; m*	silly; fool
2530	descubrimiento-*m*	discovery
2531	mosca-*f*	fly
2534	heredero-*m*	heir
2535	cortina-*f*	curtain
2536	tonelada-*f*	ton
2537	adolescente-*m/f; adj*	teenager; teenage
2538	azar-*m*	fate
2539	postal-*adj; f*	postal; postcard
2540	hamburguesa-*f*	burger
2541	propietario-*m*	owner
2542	ficción-*f*	fiction
2545	pirata-*m/f; adj*	pirate; pirated
2547	goma-*f*	rubber
2548	obrero-*m*	worker
2549	encendido-*adj; m*	on; ignition
2550	tapa-*f*	cover
2552	lotería-*f*	lottery
2553	automóvil-*m*	car
2556	satélite-*m*	satellite
2557	perfil-*m*	profile
2558	veredicto-*m*	verdict
2559	manta-*f*	blanket
2560	polo-*m*	pole
2562	mansión-*f*	mansion
2563	pena-*f*	pity, punishment
2565	envidia-*f*	envy
2566	privilegio-*m*	privilege
2567	vago-*adj; m*	vague, lazy; slacker
2568	aguja-*f*	needle
2569	tortuga-*f*	tortoise
2570	obligación-*f*	obligation
2571	árabe-*adj; m/f*	Arabian; Arab
2572	cohete-*m*	rocket
2574	hilo-*m*	thread
2575	química-*f*	chemistry
2576	bandido-*m*	bandit
2578	conflicto-*m*	conflict
2581	conjunto-*m; adj*	combination; joint
2582	huésped-*m/f*	guest
2584	especialista-*m/f*	specialist
2585	forense-*adj; m/f*	forensic; forensic surgeon
2586	salvador-*m*	savior
2587	candidato-*m*	candidate
2588	literatura-*f*	literature
2589	rincón-*m*	corner
2591	volante-*m; adj*	steering wheel, referral (ES); flying
2592	solicitud-*f*	request
2593	marino-*adj; m*	marine; sailor
2594	febrero-*m*	February
2595	brigada-*f*	squad
2599	velada-*f*	soiree
2600	certificado-*m; adj*	certificate; registered
2602	homosexual-*adj; m/f*	homosexual; homosexual
2604	euro-*m*	euro
2607	vestuario-*m*	wardrobe, locker room
2608	ajedrez-*m*	chess
2609	perspectiva-*f*	perspective
2610	músico-*m; adj*	musician; musical
2611	semilla-*f*	seed
2612	reto-*m*	challenge
2614	descripción-*f*	description
2615	célula-*f*	cell
2616	sábana-*f*	bed sheet
2618	inocencia-*f*	innocence
2619	timbre-*m*	ring
2620	récord-*m*	record
2621	posesión-*f*	possession

2622	**ballet**-*m*	ballet
2623	**provisión**-*f*	provision
2624	**ayuntamiento**-*m*	local government
2625	**soga**-*f*	rope
2626	**jazz**-*m*	jazz
2629	**cafetería**-*f*	coffee shop
2637	**pila**-*f*	battery, sink, stack
2638	**cráneo**-*m*	skull
2639	**habitante**-*m/f*	inhabitant
2640	**volumen**-*m*	volume
2643	**romano**-*adj; m*	Roman; Roman person
2644	**pobreza**-*f*	poverty
2645	**pulmón**-*m*	lung
2646	**hueco**-*m; adj*	space; empty
2647	**hembra**-*f*	female
2650	**quinta**-*f; f*	country house (ES); mansion (LA)
2651	**brillo**-*m*	brightness
2653	**gorra**-*f*	cap
2654	**renta**-*f*	rent, income
2656	**turista**-*adj; m/f*	tourist; tourist
2657	**beca**-*f*	scholarship
2658	**novato**-*m; adj*	trainee; rookie
2659	**ascenso**-*m*	rise, promotion
2661	**facultad**-*f*	faculty
2662	**portero**-*m*	doorman, goalkeeper
2663	**dinamita**-*f*	dynamite
2665	**equilibrio**-*m*	balance
2667	**corte**-*m*	cut, court
2669	**signo**-*m*	sign
2670	**intercambio**-*m*	exchange
2672	**bañera**-*f*	bathtub
2674	**novedad**-*f*	novelty
2675	**individuo**-*m*	individual
2676	**cómico**-*adj; m*	comical; comedian
2678	**vientre**-*m*	belly
2679	**gol**-*m*	goal
2680	**inversión**-*f*	investment
2681	**cuñado**-*m*	brother-in-law
2682	**raya**-*f*	line
2684	**fotógrafo**-*m*	photographer
2685	**occidental**-*adj; m/f*	western; westerner
2686	**crítico**-*adj; m*	critical; critic
2687	**bruto**-*adj; m*	brutal; brute
2688	**cortesía**-*f*	courtesy
2689	**plataforma**-*f*	platform
2691	**probabilidad**-*f*	probability
2692	**torta**-*f*	cake, sandwich (LA)
2694	**cal**-*f*	lime
2695	**cirujano**-*m*	surgeon
2696	**tela**-*f*	fabric
2697	**furia**-*f*	fury
2698	**siesta**-*f*	nap
2699	**entusiasmo**-*m*	enthusiasm
2700	**coco**-*m*	coconut
2701	**afueras**-*fpl*	outskirts
2702	**ferrocarril**-*m*	railway
2703	**costo**-*m*	cost
2704	**margen**-*m*	margin
2705	**falda**-*f*	skirt
2707	**etapa**-*f*	stage
2708	**audición**-*f*	hearing, audition
2709	**mecánico**-*adj; m*	mechanical; mechanic
2710	**esencia**-*f*	essence
2711	**inicio**-*m*	beginning
2712	**cruce**-*m*	crossing
2713	**aliado**-*m; adj*	ally; allied
2714	**choque**-*m*	crash
2717	**inyección**-*f*	injection
2718	**hechizo**-*m*	spell
2719	**escopeta**-*f*	shotgun
2721	**gallo**-*m*	rooster
2722	**bárbaro**-*adj; m*	savage; Barbarian
2725	**caballería**-*f*	cavalry
2731	**linterna**-*f*	lantern
2732	**almohada**-*f*	pillow
2733	**vagina**-*f*	vagina
2735	**rama**-*f*	branch
2736	**bodega**-*f*	cellar
2739	**guardián**-*m*	guardian
2740	**gratitud**-*f*	gratitude
2741	**entierro**-*m*	burial
2742	**invasión**-*f*	invasion
2745	**escudo**-*m*	shield
2746	**masaje**-*m*	massage
2749	**césped**-*m*	lawn
2750	**lana**-*f*	wool
2752	**paisaje**-*m*	landscape

2753	**observación**-*f*	observation	2822	**inspiración**-*f*	inspiration
2754	**depresión**-*f*	depression	2823	**vicepresidente**-*m*	vice-president
2755	**artillería**-*f*	artillery	2825	**vagón**-*m*	carriage of a train
2756	**gemelo**-*adj; m*	twin; twin	2826	**mochila**-*f*	backpack
2757	**voluntario**-*adj; m*	voluntary; volunteer	2827	**atracción**-*f*	attraction
2758	**fallo**-*m*	failure	2828	**yen**-*m*	yen
2760	**cubo**-*m*	cube, bucket	2829	**apuro**-*m*	trouble
2761	**bus**-*m*	bus (coll)	2830	**cometa**-*m; f*	comet; kite
2763	**mariscal**-*m/f*	marshal	2831	**guardaespaldas**-*m/f*	bodyguard
2764	**caravana**-*f*	caravan	2832	**asistencia**-*f*	assistance
2765	**radiación**-*f*	radiation	2833	**manejo**-*m*	use
2766	**ácido**-*adj; m*	sour; acid	2834	**banquete**-*m*	banquet
2770	**bicho**-*m*	bug	2837	**fórmula**-*f*	formula
2771	**ubicación**-*f*	location	2839	**vena**-*f*	vein
2772	**sugerencia**-*f*	suggestion	2840	**especialidad**-*f*	specialty
2773	**tomate**-*m*	tomato	2841	**convención**-*f*	convention
2775	**prioridad**-*f*	priority	2842	**oriental**-*adj; m*	eastern; Asian
2781	**expedición**-*f*	expedition	2843	**álbum**-*m*	album
2782	**avance**-*m*	advance	2847	**flecha**-*f*	arrow
2784	**escondite**-*m*	hiding place, hide-and-seek	2848	**virtud**-*f*	virtue
2787	**respiro**-*m*	rest	2849	**curva**-*f*	curve
2789	**jamón**-*m*	ham	2850	**limón**-*m*	lemon
2790	**insecto**-*m*	insect	2852	**inferior**-*adj; m/f*	lower; subordinate
2791	**triunfo**-*m*	triumph	2854	**asilo**-*m*	asylum
2792	**manicomio**-*m*	asylum	2855	**desesperación**-*f*	despair
2793	**amabilidad**-*f*	kindness	2857	**ángulo**-*m*	angle
2794	**cicatriz**-*f*	scar	2861	**irlandés**-*adj; m*	Irish; Irish person
2795	**pipa**-*f*	pipe, seed	2863	**terrorismo**-*m*	terrorism
2801	**estreno**-*m*	premiere	2865	**ano**-*m*	anus
2803	**peste**-*f*	plague	2866	**rodaje**-*m*	filming
2804	**supervivencia**-*f*	survival	2870	**garantía**-*f*	guarantee
2805	**sierra**-*f*	mountains, saw	2871	**carnicero**-*m*	butcher
2806	**granero**-*m*	barn	2874	**salchicha**-*f*	sausage
2808	**ambición**-*f*	ambition	2875	**boxeo**-*m*	boxing
2810	**celebración**-*f*	celebration	2876	**intelectual**-*adj; m/f*	mental; intellectual
2811	**senado**-*m*	senate	2877	**rana**-*f*	frog
2812	**melodía**-*f*	melody	2879	**bienestar**-*m*	comfort
2813	**SIDA**-*m*	AIDS	2880	**taberna**-*f*	tavern
2814	**baúl**-*m*	trunk	2881	**impulso**-*m*	impulse
2815	**consejero**-*m*	counselor	2884	**ritual**-*adj; m*	ritual; ritual
2816	**demostración**-*f*	demonstration	2887	**perfección**-*f*	perfection
2819	**puñado**-*m*	handful	2888	**ejecutivo**-*adj; m*	executive; manager
2820	**batallón**-*m*	battalion	2889	**cuna**-*f*	cradle
2821	**coñac**-*m*	cognac			

2890	**dispositivo**-*m*	device	2959	**doncella**-*f*	maid
2892	**cómplice**-*m/f*	accomplice	2961	**renuncia**-*f*	resignation
2893	**caca**-*f*	poop (coll)	2963	**masacre**-*f*	massacre
2895	**sinvergüenza**-*m/f; adj*	wretch; rascal	2965	**lava**-*f*	lava
			2968	**altar**-*m*	altar
2897	**brisa**-*f*	breeze	2969	**pis**-*m*	piss (coll)
2898	**violín**-*m*	violin	2970	**ocupación**-*f*	occupation
2899	**menú**-*m*	menu	2972	**infarto**-*m*	heart
2901	**tirador**-*m*	shooter	2974	**triple**-*adj; m*	triple; triple
2903	**factura**-*f*	invoice	2975	**contenido**-*m; adj*	contents; reserved
2905	**billetera**-*f*	wallet	2976	**galaxia**-*f*	galaxy
2908	**síntoma**-*m*	symptom	2977	**eco**-*m*	echo
2910	**terremoto**-*m*	earthquake	2980	**claridad**-*f*	clarity
2911	**marqués**-*m*	marquis	2981	**desaparición**-*f*	disappearance
2912	**bata**-*f*	robe	2983	**difunto**-*m*	deceased
2913	**satisfacción**-*f*	satisfaction	2987	**cacería**-*f*	hunting
2914	**pacto**-*m*	pact	2988	**mozo**-*m*	lad
2917	**ignorante**-*adj; m*	ignorant; ignoramus	2989	**matrícula**-*f*	license plate, enrollment
2920	**categoría**-*f*	category	2991	**muñeco**-*m*	doll
2921	**bastón**-*m*	cane	2992	**mayordomo**-*m*	butler
2922	**luchador**-*m*	fighter	2993	**antepasado**-*m*	ancestor
2923	**rencor**-*m*	resentment	2994	**soda**-*f*	soda
2924	**zapatilla**-*f*	slipper	2998	**líquido**-*adj; m*	liquid; liquid
2925	**caramelo**-*m*	candy	3001	**protector**-*adj; m*	protective; protector
2928	**establo**-*m*	barn			
2929	**fan**-*m/f*	fan	3002	**casamiento**-*m*	marriage
2931	**invento**-*m*	invention	3004	**refrigerador**-*m*	refrigerator
2934	**supermercado**-*m*	supermarket	3005	**persecución**-*f*	persecution
2937	**promedio**-*m*	average	3007	**protesta**-*f*	protest
2938	**interrogatorio**-*m*	interrogation	3008	**montaje**-*m*	assembly
2939	**mito**-*m*	myth	3011	**cuadra**-*f*	stable, block (LA)
2940	**crucero**-*m*	cruise	3012	**crecimiento**-*m*	growth
2941	**independencia**-*f*	independence	3013	**obsesión**-*f*	obsession
2942	**crío**-*m*	child	3014	**institución**-*f*	institution
2943	**perla**-*f*	pearl	3015	**mulo**-*m*	mule
2944	**portada**-*f*	cover	3016	**aprobación**-*f*	approval
2947	**relámpago**-*m*	lightning	3018	**mariposa**-*f*	butterfly
2949	**set**-*m*	set	3019	**lunar**-*adj; m*	lunar; mole
2950	**baloncesto**-*m*	basketball	3020	**paloma**-*f*	dove
2951	**centímetro**-*m*	centimeter	3021	**sudor**-*m*	sweat
2953	**leña**-*f*	firewood	3023	**inicial**-*adj; f*	beginning; initial
2954	**ahorros**-*mpl*	savings	3024	**web**-*f*	web
2955	**autopsia**-*f*	autopsy	3025	**costilla**-*f*	rib
2956	**amo**-*m*	owner	3026	**vestíbulo**-*m*	lobby
2957	**cuerno**-*m*	horn	3027	**fundación**-*f*	foundation

3028	ingreso-*m*	entry, deposit
3030	enfermería-*f*	infirmary
3031	traficante-*m/f*	trafficker
3032	terraza-*f*	terrace
3033	sirena-*f*	siren
3034	judicial-*adj; m*	judicial; police officer
3035	sirviente-*m*	servant
3036	escritura-*f*	writing
3037	periodo-*m*	term
3038	etiqueta-*f*	label
3039	peso-*m*	weight
3040	religioso-*adj; m*	religious; priest
3042	resfriado-*adj; m*	have a cold; cold
3043	sumo-*m; adj*	sumo; supreme
3044	delincuente-*m/f; adj*	criminal; delinquent
3045	zar-*m*	tsar
3047	barriga-*f*	belly
3049	cerradura-*f*	lock
3050	pendiente-*m; f; adj*	earring; slope; pending
3051	barrera-*f*	barrier
3052	postura-*f*	posture
3053	provecho-*m*	benefit
3055	convento-*m*	convent
3056	infantería-*f*	infantry
3059	lavandería-*f*	laundry
3060	arroyo-*m*	stream
3062	reserva-*f*	reserve
3065	desprecio-*m*	disdain
3068	separación-*f*	separation
3071	peinado-*m*	hairstyle
3073	capilla-*f*	chapel
3074	agradecimiento-*m*	gratitude
3075	interpretación-*f*	interpretation
3076	cepillo-*m*	brush
3077	hábito-*m*	habit
3078	muro-*m*	wall
3079	consulta-*f*	inquiry
3082	constitución-*f*	constitution
3083	televisor-*m*	television
3085	despegue-*m*	takeoff
3086	varón-*m*	male
3087	halcón-*m*	hawk
3089	culto-*m; adj*	worship; educated
3090	merced-*f*	mercy
3091	calzón-*m*	shorts, knickers (LA)
3092	argumento-*m*	argument
3093	barril-*m*	barrel
3095	timón-*m*	rudder
3098	ballena-*f*	whale
3099	hacienda-*f*	estate
3100	órgano-*m*	organ
3102	socialism-*m*	socialism
3103	autógrafo-*m*	autograph
3104	víbora-*f*	viper
3105	anteojos-*mpl*	glasses
3106	transferencia-*f*	transfer
3109	reportero-*m*	reporter
3110	intimidad-*f*	privacy
3112	tentación-*f*	temptation
3113	haz-*m*	beam
3114	desconocido-*adj; m*	unknown; stranger
3116	técnica-*f*	technique
3117	denuncia-*f*	complaint
3119	farmacia-*f*	pharmacy
3121	gancho-*m*	hook
3122	furgoneta-*f*	van
3123	recuperación-*f*	recovery
3124	salido-*adj; m*	protruding; horny (coll)
3127	adicto-*m*	addict
3128	soviético-*adj; m*	Soviet; Soviet
3129	armadura-*f*	armor
3130	marcado-*adj; m*	noticeable; dialing (LA)
3132	embarazo-*m*	pregnancy
3133	medicamento-*m*	medicine
3134	ansiedad-*f*	anxiety
3135	cachorro-*m*	puppy
3136	arquitecto-*m*	architect
3137	lecho-*m*	bed
3138	pausa-*f*	pause
3140	tijeras-*fpl*	scissors
3141	cartero-*m*	postman
3144	latín-*m*	Latin
3145	verdura-*f*	vegetable
3151	tronco-*m*	trunk
3152	activo-*adj; m*	active; assets
3153	abuso-*m*	abuse
3154	católico-*adj; m*	Catholic; Catholic

3156	hormiga-*f*	ant
3158	rival-*adj; m/f*	rival; opponent
3159	asado-*adj; m*	roast; roast
3160	profeta-*m/f*	prophet
3161	inspección-*f*	inspection
3162	armonía-*f*	harmony
3163	paraguas-*m*	umbrella
3165	bandeja-*f*	tray
3169	sendero-*m*	path
3171	contraseña-*f*	password
3172	corrupción-*f*	corruption
3173	polaco-*adj; m*	Polish; Polish person
3174	kilogramo-*m*	kilogram
3175	generador-*m*	generator
3176	matanza-*f*	killing
3178	paja-*f*	stalk, masturbation (ES)
3179	abeja-*f*	bee
3180	infección-*f*	infection
3181	lata-*f*	can
3183	demora-*f*	delay
3184	referencia-*f*	reference
3185	alba-*m*	dawn
3186	pólvora-*f*	gunpowder
3188	coordenada-*f*	coordinate
3189	zoológico-*adj; m*	zoological; zoo
3190	paracaídas-*m*	parachute
3191	peluca-*f*	wig
3193	pabellón-*m*	pavilion
3199	botín-*m*	loot
3200	insulto-*m*	insult
3201	cifra-*f*	figure
3204	garra-*f*	claw
3205	exhibición-*f*	display
3206	detención-*f*	detention
3207	trueno-*m*	thunder
3209	contador-*m*	counter, accountant
3210	labor-*f*	work
3211	trigo-*m*	wheat
3212	cooperación-*f*	cooperation
3213	evolución-*f*	evolution
3215	entretenimiento-*m*	entertainment
3216	seno-*m*	breast, core
3218	régimen-*m*	regime
3220	mexicano-*adj; m*	Mexican; Mexican person
3221	marido-*m*	husband
3222	bombardeo-*m*	bombing
3223	vigilante-*adj; m/f*	attentive; guard
3224	reflejo-*m; adj*	reflection; reflex
3225	freno-*m*	brake
3226	lazo-*m*	bow, rope
3228	plomo-*m*	lead
3230	rabino-*m*	rabbi
3231	matón-*m*	thug
3232	boxeador-*m*	boxer
3233	recado-*m*	message
3236	mascota-*f*	pet
3238	mantenimiento-*m*	maintenance
3239	chatarra-*f*	scrap
3240	Pascua-*f*	Easter
3242	balcón-*m*	balcony
3244	privacidad-*f*	privacy
3246	barca-*f*	small boat
3247	investigador-*m*	researcher
3248	norteamericano-*adj; m*	North American; North American person
3249	chicle-*m*	gum
3250	supervisor-*m*	supervisor
3251	cobertura-*f*	coverage
3252	manga-*m/f; f*	manga; sleeve
3253	velo-*m*	veil
3256	argentino-*adj; m*	Argentinian; Argentinian person
3257	industrial-*adj; m*	industrial; industrialist
3258	comprensión-*f*	understanding
3259	ring-*m*	ring
3262	fruto-*m*	fruit
3264	aroma-*m*	scent
3265	perímetro-*m*	perimeter
3266	grandeza-*f*	greatness
3267	delantero-*adj; m*	front; forward
3268	propaganda-*f*	advertising
3269	yate-*m*	yacht
3271	atardecer-*m; vb*	twilight; get dark
3272	consideración-*f*	consideration
3275	rezo-*m*	prayer
3276	molino-*m*	mill

3280	cargamento-*m*	shipment	3344	carreta-*f*	wagon
3281	bloqueo-*m*	block	3345	reportaje-*m*	article
3283	jeep-*m*	jeep	3346	representación-*f*	representation
3284	bando-*m*	side	3347	CD-*m*	CD
3285	litro-*m*	liter	3349	nana-*f; f*	granny; lullaby
3286	sobreviviente-*m/f; adj*	survivor; surviving	3352	pellejo-*m*	skin
3287	chaleco-*m*	vest	3353	valentía-*f*	courage
3288	cualidad-*f*	quality	3354	baile-*m*	dance
3290	provincia-*f*	province	3355	afectado-*adj; m*	affected; victim
3291	mocoso-*m; adj*	snuffly; brat	3356	dominio-*m*	domain
3292	circuito-*m*	circuit	3358	tambor-*m*	drum
3296	pedo-*m*	fart	3359	mail-*m*	email (coll)
3299	tobillo-*m*	ankle	3360	refresco-*m*	soda
3300	jinete-*m/f*	rider	3363	crueldad-*f*	cruelty
3301	tango-*m*	tango	3364	pala-*f*	shovel
3303	billar-*m*	billiards	3365	instalación-*f*	installation
3304	nevada-*f*	snowfall	3366	mérito-*m*	merit
3305	buque-*m*	vessel	3367	admirador-*m*	fan
3306	descuento-*m*	discount	3369	nevera-*f*	fridge
3307	angustia-*f*	anguish	3372	infiel-*adj; m/f*	unfaithful; infidel
3308	cuervo-*m*	crow	3373	discreción-*f*	discretion
3309	documental-*adj; m*	documentary; documentary	3374	ajo-*m*	garlic
			3376	integridad-*f*	integrity
3312	estancia-*f*	stay	3378	revisión-*f*	review
3313	creador-*m*	creator	3380	santuario-*m*	sanctuary
3315	bloque-*m*	block	3381	corporación-*f*	corporation
3317	exceso-*m*	excess	3382	gripe-*f*	flu
3318	pulgar-*m*	thumb	3384	órbita-*f*	orbit
3320	terminal-*adj; m/f*	terminal; terminal	3385	agarre-*m*	grip
3322	ciclo-*m*	cycle	3387	tránsito-*m*	transit
3325	década-*f*	decade	3388	fugitivo-*adj; m*	fugitive; fugitive
3326	colapso-*m*	collapse	3389	calendario-*m*	calendar
3327	mejora-*f*	improvement	3390	pañal-*m*	diaper
3328	chantaje-*m*	blackmail	3391	cemento-*m*	cement
3329	turco-*adj; m*	Turkish; Turk	3392	morgue-*f*	morgue
3330	eminencia-*f*	eminence	3394	cancha-*f*	court
3331	golfo-*m; adj*	gulf; scoundrel	3395	fusión-*f*	fusion
3332	horizonte-*m*	horizon	3396	basurero-*m*	garbage dump, garbageman
3334	anochecer-*m; vb*	dusk; get dark	3397	suministro-*m*	supply
3336	reno-*m*	reindeer	3398	calibre-*m*	caliber
3337	harina-*f*	flour	3399	protocolo-*m*	protocol
3339	cardenal-*m*	cardinal	3400	agresión-*f*	aggression
3340	hermandad-*f*	brotherhood	3401	camello-*m*	camel
3341	tejido-*m*	tissue, fabric	3402	selección-*f*	selection
3342	escocés-*adj; m*	Scotch; Scot	3403	ancho-*m; adj*	width; wide

194

3404	**pijama**-*m*	pajamas
3406	**hospitalidad**-*f*	hospitality
3407	**burla**-*f*	taunt
3408	**captura**-*f*	capture
3409	**urgencia**-*f*	urgency
3410	**mara**-*f*	gang (LA)
3414	**nuez**-*f*	nut
3415	**láser**-*m*	laser
3416	**test**-*m*	test
3418	**niñez**-*f*	childhood
3420	**abandono**-*m*	neglect, desertion
3421	**jardinero**-*m*	gardener
3423	**facilidad**-*f*	ease
3425	**yarda**-*f*	yard
3426	**banquero**-*m*	banker
3427	**creencia**-*f*	belief
3428	**sólido**-*adj; m*	solid; solid
3429	**extraterrestre**-*adj; m/f*	alien; alien
3430	**ficha**-*f*	chip, ticket
3431	**hipoteca**-*f*	mortgage
3434	**cebolla**-*f*	onion
3435	**poste**-*m*	post
3436	**honestidad**-*f*	honesty
3437	**rebaño**-*m*	flock
3438	**acontecimiento**-*m*	event
3439	**financiero**-*adj; m*	financial; financier
3440	**excursión**-*f*	excursion
3442	**mejilla**-*f*	cheek
3443	**gasolinera**-*f*	gas station
3445	**psicología**-*f*	psychology
3446	**seguidor**-*m*	follower
3447	**palanca**-*f*	lever
3450	**nudo**-*m*	knot
3451	**iniciativa**-*f*	initiative
3453	**clavo**-*m*	nail
3454	**universitario**-*adj; m*	university; undergraduate
3457	**núcleo**-*m*	core
3458	**anfitrión**-*m*	host
3459	**hipócrita**-*adj; m/f*	hypocritical; hypocrite
3460	**rehabilitación**-*f*	rehabilitation
3461	**chile**-*m*	chili
3463	**codo**-*m*	elbow
3464	**ladrillo**-*m*	brick
3467	**amuleto**-*m*	amulet
3468	**revolucionario**-*adj; m*	revolutionary; revolutionary
3469	**alrededores**-*m*	surroundings
3470	**frijol**-*m*	bean
3472	**cuaderno**-*m*	notebook
3473	**rebelión**-*f*	rebellion
3475	**huracán**-*m*	hurricane
3476	**sinceridad**-*f*	sincerity
3478	**ancestro**-*m*	ancestor
3479	**mecanismo**-*m*	mechanism
3480	**cera**-*f*	wax
3481	**estanque**-*m*	pond
3482	**infinito**-*adj; m*	infinite; infinity
3483	**alojamiento**-*m*	accommodation
3484	**bono**-*m*	bonus, pass
3486	**rechazo**-*m*	rejection
3487	**comerciante**-*m*	merchant
3488	**blues**-*m*	blues
3489	**generosidad**-*f*	generosity
3490	**entorno**-*m*	environment
3493	**cintura**-*f*	waist
3494	**cálculo**-*m*	calculation
3495	**ignorancia**-*f*	ignorance
3496	**consentimiento**-*m*	consent
3500	**defensor**-*adj; m*	defense; defense attorney
3501	**concha**-*f*	shell, pussy (LA) (coll)
3502	**yerno**-*m*	son-in-law
3503	**tripa**-*f*	intestine, belly
3504	**puerco**-*m; adj*	pig; disgusting
3505	**espuma**-*f*	foam
3506	**taxista**-*m/f*	taxi driver
3507	**ausente**-*adj; m/f*	absent; absentee
3508	**despido**-*m*	dismissal
3509	**ingeniería**-*f*	engineering
3511	**adelanto**-*m*	advance
3512	**asamblea**-*f*	assembly
3513	**diputado**-*m*	deputy
3515	**descarga**-*f*	discharge
3516	**diálogo**-*m*	dialogue
3517	**stop**-*m*	stop sign
3518	**documentación**-*f*	documentation
3519	**administrador**-*m*	administrator
3520	**sillón**-*m*	armchair
3521	**faro**-*m*	lighthouse
3522	**enlace**-*m*	link

195

3523	semestre-*m*	semester	3589	lodo-*m*	mud
3524	oposición-*f*	opposition	3591	catástrofe-*f*	catastrophe
3525	alambre-*m*	wire	3592	precisión-*f*	precision
3527	participación-*f*	participation	3594	profecía-*f*	prophecy
3528	químico-*adj; m*	chemical; chemist	3595	pulgada-*f*	inch
3531	baba-*f*	slime	3597	normalidad-*f*	normalcy
3533	abismo-*m*	abyss	3598	retorno-*m*	return
3535	blusa-*f*	blouse	3600	preparación-*f*	preparation
3537	evacuación-*f*	evacuation	3601	cadera-*f*	hip
3539	fascista-*adj; m/f*	fascist; fascist	3603	contrabando-*m*	smuggling
3541	pescador-*m*	fisherman	3604	lloro-*m*	crying
3542	apertura-*f*	opening	3606	luto-*m*	mourning
3543	tomo-*m*	volume	3607	musulmán-*adj; m*	Muslim; Muslim
3544	caña-*f*	cane, rod	3608	servidor-*m*	server, servant
3545	pecador-*m; adj*	sinner; sinful	3614	fanático-*adj; m*	fan; fanatic
3546	suegro-*m*	father-in-law	3615	gramo-*m*	gram
3547	nuca-*f*	neck	3616	fax-*m*	fax
3548	valla-*f*	fence	3618	frasco-*m*	jar
3550	aborto-*m*	abortion	3619	interruptor-*m*	switch
3551	funcionario-*m*	public worker	3621	finca-*f*	ranch
3553	top-*m*	top	3622	esclavitud-*f*	slavery
3554	mostrador-*m*	counter	3623	precaución-*f*	caution
3556	cobre-*m*	copper	3624	correspondencia-*f*	correspondence
3557	lote-*m*	set	3625	lila-*adj; f*	lilac; lilac
3561	defecto-*m*	defect	3627	ciervo-*m*	deer
3563	bóveda-*f*	vault	3628	optimista-*adj; m/f*	optimistic; optimist
3564	casero-*adj; m*	home-made; landlord	3629	gimnasia-*f*	physical exercise
3565	chulo-*adj; m*	cocky (ES) (coll), great (ES) (coll); scumbag (coll)	3630	trofeo-*m*	trophy
			3632	villano-*m; adj*	villain; villain
			3633	monumento-*m*	monument
3568	nativo-*adj; m*	local; native	3634	obstáculo-*m*	obstacle
3569	estrado-*m*	podium	3636	reja-*f*	bar
3571	éxtasis-*m*	ecstasy	3637	cuarentena-*f*	quarantine
3572	iluminación-*f*	lighting	3638	gabinete-*m*	cabinet
3573	explorador-*m*	explorer	3639	software-*m*	software
3574	colchón-*m*	mattress	3640	lema-*m*	motto
3575	lavabo-*m*	sink, restroom	3641	cangrejo-*m*	crab
3576	forastero-*m; adj*	stranger; foreign	3642	porcentaje-*m*	percentage
3579	campus-*m*	campus	3643	cocodrilo-*m/f*	crocodile
3580	alias-*m*	alias	3644	llanto-*m*	crying
3584	votación-*f*	vote	3645	compadre-*m*	godfather, buddy (coll)
3585	inconveniente-*m; adj*	problem; inconvenient	3648	contable-*m/f; adj*	accountant; accounting
3586	apodo-*m*	nickname			
3587	rapidez-*f*	speed	3651	árbitro-*m/f*	referee
3588	ternura-*f*	tenderness			

3652	**creativo**-*adj; m*	creative; copywriter
3653	**arca**-*f*	ark
3654	**pasto**-*m*	pasture
3655	**arbusto**-*m*	bush
3656	**esperma**-*m*	sperm
3663	**buzón**-*m*	mailbox
3664	**fusil**-*m*	rifle
3667	**aburrimiento**-*m*	boredom
3668	**yanqui**-*m/f; adj*	Yankee (coll); Yankee (coll)
3670	**jet**-*m*	jet
3671	**capataz**-*m/f*	foreperson
3672	**sastre**-*m/f*	tailor
3673	**África**-*f*	Africa
3675	**injusticia**-*f*	injustice
3676	**penal**-*adj; m*	criminal; prison
3682	**definición**-*f*	definition
3683	**táctica**-*f*	tactic
3684	**portal**-*m*	portal
3686	**competición**-*f*	competition
3687	**langosta**-*f*	lobster
3688	**olla**-*f*	pot
3692	**Atlántico**-*m*	Atlantic
3693	**ingenio**-*m*	wit, ingenuity
3694	**recomendación**-*f*	recommendation
3695	**decepción**-*f*	disappointment
3696	**librería**-*f*	bookshop
3698	**racista**-*m/f; adj*	racist person; racist
3699	**sustancia**-*f*	substance
3700	**hongo**-*m*	fungus
3701	**ambicioso**-*adj; m*	ambitious; greedy
3703	**protagonista**-*m/f*	protagonist
3704	**aparición**-*f*	appearance, apparition
3705	**reglamento**-*m*	regulation
3706	**conserje**-*m/f*	janitor
3707	**homenaje**-*m*	tribute
3709	**morfina**-*f*	morphine
3711	**traslado**-*m*	move
3712	**ejemplar**-*m; adj*	model; exemplary
3714	**ganso**-*m; adj*	goose; foolish (ES) (coll)
3715	**trompeta**-*f*	trumpet
3716	**mostaza**-*f*	mustard
3717	**picante**-*adj; m*	spicy; spiciness
3720	**maniobra**-*f*	maneuver
3721	**hemorragia**-*f*	hemorrhage
3722	**humedad**-*f*	moisture
3723	**banca**-*f*	banking
3724	**notable**-*adj; m*	notable; dignitary
3726	**acera**-*f*	sidewalk
3727	**distracción**-*f*	distraction
3728	**estafa**-*f*	scam
3729	**tesis**-*f*	thesis
3730	**pureza**-*f*	purity
3732	**monasterio**-*m*	monastery
3734	**burbuja**-*f*	bubble
3735	**zumo**-*m*	juice
3736	**empresario**-*m*	businessman
3741	**margarita**-*f*	daisy
3742	**himno**-*m*	hymn
3743	**tocino**-*m*	bacon
3744	**enojo**-*m*	anger
3745	**panza**-*f*	belly
3746	**cólera**-*f*	anger
3747	**ostra**-*f*	oyster
3748	**humillación**-*f*	humiliation
3750	**flora**-*f*	flora
3752	**medicación**-*f*	medication
3753	**lancha**-*f*	boat
3754	**uva**-*f*	grape
3756	**huérfano**-*adj; m*	orphaned; orphan
3759	**muda**-*f*	change
3760	**terrestre**-*adj; m*	land; terrestrial
3761	**género**-*m*	gender
3764	**grúa**-*f*	crane
3765	**flujo**-*m*	flow
3767	**factor**-*m*	factor
3769	**tramposo**-*m; adj*	trickster; dishonest
3770	**motocicleta**-*f*	motorcycle
3771	**hostia**-*f; int*	blow (coll); damn (coll)
3775	**intuición**-*f*	intuition
3776	**chispa**-*f*	spark
3777	**congresista**-*m/f*	delegate
3778	**aislamiento**-*m*	isolation
3779	**intervención**-*f*	intervention
3781	**tos**-*f*	cough
3783	**tinieblas**-*fpl*	darkness
3784	**simpatía**-*f*	friendliness

3786	**tacto**-*m*	touch
3788	**síndrome**-*m*	syndrome
3789	**legión**-*f*	legion
3791	**fresa**-*f*	strawberry
3792	**asesor**-*m; adj*	adviser; advisory
3793	**canasta**-*f*	basket
3794	**radical**-*adj; m/f*	radical; radical person
3796	**manifestación**-*f*	manifestation
3797	**veterinario**-*m*	veterinarian
3798	**promoción**-*f*	promotion
3799	**oponente**-*m/f; adj*	opponent; opposing
3801	**pasado**-*adj; m*	past; past
3803	**salmón**-*m*	salmon
3804	**fraternidad**-*f*	fraternity
3805	**sensibilidad**-*f*	sensitivity
3806	**mermelada**-*f*	jam
3807	**puñetazo**-*m*	punch
3808	**pimienta**-*f*	pepper
3811	**suéter**-*m*	sweater
3812	**búfalo**-*m*	buffalo
3813	**resaca**-*f*	hangover
3814	**tregua**-*f*	truce
3815	**vanidad**-*f*	vanity
3816	**vino**-*m*	wine
3820	**tumor**-*m*	tumor
3822	**flanco**-*m*	flank
3824	**viajero**-*m*	traveler
3826	**carnaval**-*m*	carnival
3827	**holandés**-*adj; m*	Dutch; Dutch person
3831	**jurisdicción**-*f*	jurisdiction
3832	**comprador**-*m*	buyer
3834	**escoba**-*f*	broom
3835	**extensión**-*f*	extension
3838	**calefacción**-*f*	heating
3839	**devoción**-*f*	devotion
3842	**colaboración**-*f*	collaboration
3843	**ramo**-*m*	bouquet
3844	**aguante**-*m*	endurance
3845	**proposición**-*f*	proposition
3846	**pino**-*m*	pine
3847	**canadiense**-*adj; m/f*	Canadian; Canadian person
3848	**mención**-*f*	mention
3850	**partícula**-*f*	particle
3851	**genética**-*f*	genetics
3852	**elevador**-*m*	elevator
3854	**confirmación**-*f*	confirmation
3855	**comparación**-*f*	comparison
3856	**diagnóstico**-*m; adj*	diagnosis; diagnostic
3857	**trama**-*f*	plot
3858	**látigo**-*m*	whip
3859	**complicación**-*f*	complication
3861	**hoguera**-*f*	bonfire
3862	**domicilio**-*m*	address
3863	**expreso**-*adj; m*	express; express
3864	**pelirrojo**-*adj; m*	redheaded; redhead
3866	**crítica**-*f*	review
3867	**honra**-*f*	honor
3868	**consumo**-*m*	consumption
3869	**histérico**-*adj; m*	hysterical; hysteric
3870	**caviar**-*m*	caviar
3871	**sobredosis**-*f*	overdose
3874	**mendigo**-*m*	beggar
3875	**escalofrío**-*m*	chill
3878	**volcán**-*m*	volcano
3879	**letrero**-*m*	sign
3880	**tercio**-*m*	third
3881	**epidemia**-*f*	epidemic
3882	**decano**-*m*	dean
3883	**dimensión**-*f*	dimension
3884	**estándar**-*adj; m*	standard; standard
3885	**culpabilidad**-*f*	culpability
3887	**deriva**-*f*	drift
3888	**psiquiátrico**-*adj; m*	psychiatric; psychiatric hospital
3890	**trauma**-*m*	trauma
3891	**negociación**-*f*	negotiation
3892	**lujuria**-*f*	lust
3893	**menta**-*f*	mint
3895	**altitud**-*f*	altitude
3896	**correa**-*f*	strap
3897	**aspirina**-*f*	aspirin
3898	**finanzas**-*fpl*	treasury
3899	**occidente**-*m*	west
3900	**esqueleto**-*m*	skeleton
3901	**formulario**-*m*	form
3902	**pianista**-*m/f*	pianist

3903	**sereno**-*adj; m*	calm; dew
3904	**carpa**-*f*	marquee, carp
3905	**mandíbula**-*f*	jaw
3906	**aprendiz**-*m/f*	apprentice
3908	**padrastro**-*m*	stepfather
3909	**encendedor**-*m*	lighter
3910	**zoo**-*m*	zoo
3911	**atún**-*m*	tuna
3914	**ametralladora**-*f*	machine gun
3916	**suciedad**-*f*	dirt
3917	**decencia**-*f*	decency
3919	**tutor**-*m*	tutor
3920	**agrado**-*m*	liking
3921	**retrete**-*m*	toilet
3923	**vale**-*m; int*	voucher; ok
3924	**disturbio**-*m*	disturbance
3926	**gorro**-*m*	hat
3927	**tablero**-*m*	board
3928	**sede**-*f*	headquarters
3929	**noroeste**-*m*	northwest
3930	**puntería**-*f*	aim
3932	**caminata**-*f*	walk
3933	**diccionario**-*m*	dictionary
3935	**agonía**-*f*	agony
3937	**calentamiento**-*m*	heating
3938	**expectativas**-*fpl*	expectations
3939	**horca**-*f*	gallows
3940	**sueco**-*adj; m*	Swedish; Swedish person
3942	**cobertizo**-*m*	shed
3943	**acompañante**-*m/f*	companion
3944	**variedad**-*f*	variety
3947	**armada**-*f*	navy
3948	**fiscalía**-*f*	district attorney's officer
3949	**cebo**-*m*	bait
3950	**antigüedad**-*f*	antiquity
3951	**jarra**-*f*	mug
3952	**artefacto**-*m*	artifact
3957	**alcohólico**-*adj; m*	alcoholic; alcoholic person
3959	**penique**-*m*	penny
3960	**plegaria**-*f*	prayer
3965	**atleta**-*m/f*	athlete
3966	**cantina**-*f*	cafeteria
3967	**tour**-*m*	tour
3970	**chisme**-*m*	rumor, junk (coll)
3971	**corrección**-*f*	correction
3972	**gitano**-*adj; m*	gypsy; gypsy
3974	**convicto**-*adj; m*	convicted; convict
3975	**rol**-*m*	role
3976	**estafador**-*m*	swindler
3978	**jornada**-*f*	day
3980	**cuadrado**-*adj; m*	square; square
3981	**veterano**-*adj; m*	veteran; veteran
3982	**saque**-*m*	kickoff
3983	**choza**-*f*	hut
3984	**minero**-*m*	miner
3985	**instructor**-*m*	instructor
3990	**aprieto**-*m*	predicament
3992	**buey**-*m*	ox
3993	**murciélago**-*m/f*	bat
3994	**calabaza**-*f*	pumpkin
3996	**antídoto**-*m*	antidote
3998	**jaleo**-*m*	fuss (coll)
3999	**manteca**-*f*	butter
4000	**canciller**-*m/f*	chancellor
4001	**escalón**-*m*	step
4003	**ternero**-*m*	calf
4004	**telón**-*m*	curtain
4005	**vara**-*f*	rod
4006	**carpintero**-*m*	carpenter
4007	**cucaracha**-*f*	cockroach
4008	**arranque**-*m*	start, outburst
4009	**corral**-*m*	farmyard
4010	**Vaticano**-*m*	Vatican
4012	**soporte**-*m*	support
4013	**tenedor**-*m*	fork
4016	**sensor**-*m*	sensor
4017	**compositor**-*m*	composer
4018	**pasatiempo**-*m*	pastime
4019	**organismo**-*m*	organism
4022	**admiración**-*f*	admiration
4023	**pilar**-*m*	pillar
4024	**operador**-*m*	operator
4025	**espionaje**-*m*	espionage
4027	**inauguración**-*f*	opening
4028	**nostalgia**-*f*	nostalgia
4029	**sustituto**-*m*	substitute
4030	**momia**-*f*	mummy
4031	**conmoción**-*f*	shock
4032	**ría**-*f*	estuary
4035	**suero**-*m*	serum

4037	**espina**-*f*	thorn
4038	**determinación**-*f*	determination
4039	**sapo**-*m*	toad
4041	**pezón**-*m*	nipple
4043	**navegación**-*f*	navigation
4044	**filmación**-*f*	shooting
4045	**guardería**-*f*	daycare center
4050	**laberinto**-*m*	maze
4052	**jaque**-*m*	check
4053	**madrina**-*f*	godmother
4054	**víspera**-*f*	eve
4055	**Nochebuena**-*f*	Christmas Eve
4056	**noción**-*f*	notion
4057	**balsa**-*f*	raft
4058	**tendencia**-*f*	trend
4059	**estadístico**-*adj; m*	statistical; statistician
4060	**carbono**-*m*	carbon
4061	**bocado**-*m*	bite
4062	**cóctel**-*m*	cocktail
4063	**Panamá**-*m*	Panama
4064	**vicio**-*m*	vice
4065	**manguera**-*f*	hose
4067	**antena**-*f*	antenna
4071	**astronauta**-*m/f*	astronaut
4074	**circulación**-*f*	circulation
4075	**drogadicto**-*m*	junkie
4077	**náusea**-*f*	nausea
4078	**soborno**-*m*	bribery
4079	**europeo**-*adj; m*	European; European
4080	**sardina**-*f*	sardine
4082	**igualdad**-*f*	equality
4083	**maquinaria**-*f*	machinery
4084	**subtítulo**-*m*	subtitle
4088	**pirámide**-*f*	pyramid
4089	**convoy**-*m*	convoy
4090	**maní**-*m*	peanut
4091	**fidelidad**-*f*	fidelity
4092	**trapo**-*m*	cloth
4093	**arquitectura**-*f*	architecture
4094	**preparativos**-*mpl*	preparations
4095	**transmisor**-*m; adj*	transmitter; transmitting
4096	**cumbre**-*f*	summit
4101	**patrulla**-*f*	patrol
4103	**barbero**-*m*	barber
4104	**revelación**-*f*	revelation
4105	**lanza**-*f*	spear
4106	**neumático**-*m; adj*	tire; inflatable
4107	**rap**-*m*	rap
4109	**africano**-*adj; m*	African; African person
4110	**tranvía**-*m*	tram
4112	**nalga**-*f*	buttock
4113	**aviación**-*f*	aviation
4114	**nobleza**-*f*	nobility
4115	**broche**-*m*	brooch
4117	**panel**-*m*	panel
4118	**apartado**-*m; adj*	section; remote
4119	**peluquería**-*f*	hairdresser
4120	**bocadillo**-*m*	sandwich
4121	**bofetada**-*f*	slap
4122	**talón**-*m*	heel
4123	**porción**-*f*	portion
4124	**acta**-*f*	record
4125	**ironía**-*f*	irony
4126	**filósofo**-*m*	philosopher
4129	**escombro**-*m*	rubbish
4130	**diplomático**-*adj; m*	diplomatic; diplomat
4131	**muslo**-*m*	thigh
4134	**lima**-*f*	lime, file
4135	**espectador**-*m*	viewer
4136	**diseñador**-*m*	designer
4138	**equivocación**-*f*	mistake
4140	**riñón**-*m*	kidney
4141	**asno**-*m*	donkey
4144	**panda**-*m*	panda
4145	**pertenencia**-*f*	belonging
4146	**mineral**-*adj; m*	mineral; mineral
4147	**cesta**-*f*	basket
4148	**distribución**-*f*	distribution
4149	**destructor**-*m*	destroyer
4150	**prosperidad**-*f*	prosperity
4151	**contabilidad**-*f*	accounting
4152	**porro**-*m*	joint
4153	**orientación**-*f*	orientation
4156	**comunismo**-*m*	communism
4158	**intensidad**-*f*	intensity
4159	**seminario**-*m*	seminary
4160	**percepción**-*f*	perception
4161	**arsenal**-*m*	arsenal

4162	**contribución**-*f*	contribution
4163	**verdugo**-*m*	executioner
4164	**funcionamiento**-*m*	functioning
4165	**residente**-*adj; m/f*	resident; resident
4167	**cuota**-*f*	fee
4168	**liderazgo**-*m*	leadership
4169	**infame**-*adj; m/f*	dreadful; villain
4170	**testículo**-*m*	testicle
4171	**editorial**-*adj; m; f*	editorial; leading article; publishing house
4172	**cagado**-*m*	wimpy (coll)
4173	**resurrección**-*f*	Resurrection
4174	**brujería**-*f*	witchcraft
4175	**saliva**-*f*	saliva
4177	**bronce**-*m*	bronze
4178	**barbacoa**-*f*	barbecue
4180	**guarida**-*f*	hideout
4181	**opio**-*m*	opium
4182	**faraón**-*m*	pharaoh
4183	**cagada**-*f*	shit (coll), screw-up (coll)
4185	**puré**-*m*	purée
4186	**paradero**-*m*	whereabouts
4187	**vínculo**-*m*	link
4189	**titular(se)**-*m; vb; adj*	headline; title; owner
4190	**cerilla**-*f*	match
4191	**utilidad**-*f*	utility
4195	**morada**-*f*	dwelling
4196	**creciente**-*adj; f*	growing; swelling
4197	**informante**-*m/f*	informant
4198	**relleno**-*adj; m*	stuffed; stuff
4200	**enfoque**-*m*	approach
4201	**cartucho**-*m*	cartridge
4202	**banana**-*f*	banana
4203	**carnicería**-*f; f*	butcher's shop; slaughter
4205	**caracol**-*m*	snail
4206	**vacuna**-*f*	vaccine
4207	**tazón**-*m*	bowl
4209	**cápsula**-*f*	capsule
4210	**marcador**-*m*	marker
4211	**bancarrota**-*f*	bankruptcy
4213	**rompecabezas**-*m*	puzzle
4214	**federación**-*f*	federation
4215	**reposo**-*m*	rest
4217	**descenso**-*m*	descent
4219	**adopción**-*f*	adoption
4220	**falla**-*f*	fault
4221	**temperamento**-*m*	temperament
4223	**presidencia**-*f*	presidency
4224	**intruso**-*m; adj*	intruder; out of place
4225	**israelí**-*adj; m/f*	Israeli; Israeli
4226	**bufanda**-*f*	scarf
4228	**relato**-*m*	tale
4229	**noruego**-*adj; m*	Norwegian; Norwegian person
4230	**flauta**-*f*	flute
4231	**suceso**-*m*	event
4232	**cubierto**-*adj; m*	covered; piece of cutlery
4233	**vitamina**-*f*	vitamin
4234	**bombardero**-*m*	bomber
4235	**alucinación**-*f*	hallucination
4236	**ruptura**-*f*	rupture
4237	**tractor**-*m*	tractor
4239	**tributo**-*m*	tribute
4240	**manuscrito**-*m*	manuscript
4241	**carroza**-*f*	carriage
4242	**biología**-*f*	biology
4244	**corporal**-*adj; m*	corporal; corporal
4245	**egipcio**-*adj; m*	Egyptian; Egyptian person
4246	**ingle**-*f*	groin
4247	**fragmento**-*m*	fragment
4248	**silbato**-*m*	whistle
4249	**delfín**-*m*	dolphin
4252	**eje**-*m*	shaft
4253	**carnet**-*m*	license
4255	**Sudáfrica**-*f*	South Africa
4258	**psicólogo**-*m*	psychologist
4259	**estufa**-*f*	stove
4261	**directivo**-*m; adj*	manager; managerial
4262	**esfera**-*f*	sphere
4263	**neutral**-*adj; m/f*	neutral; third party
4264	**prejuicio**-*m*	prejudice
4266	**verso**-*m*	verse
4267	**destacamento**-*m*	detachment
4269	**jarrón**-*m*	vase
4270	**cofre**-*m*	chest

4272	**grifo**-*m; adj*	water tap; curly (LA)
4274	**abundancia**-*f*	abundance
4275	**incumbencia**-*f*	incumbency
4276	**corrupto**-*adj; m*	corrupt; corrupt person
4277	**contexto**-*m*	context
4278	**cónsul**-*m/f*	consul
4279	**libreta**-*f*	notebook
4280	**topo**-*m*	mole
4281	**interrupción**-*f*	interruption
4282	**pistolero**-*m*	gunman
4283	**consulado**-*m*	consulate
4284	**característica**-*f*	feature
4285	**esteroide**-*m*	steroid
4286	**tortilla**-*f*	omelette
4287	**balance**-*m*	balance
4288	**Atenas**-*f*	Athens
4290	**antro**-*m*	den
4291	**pulga**-*f*	flea
4292	**establecimiento**-*m*	establishment
4293	**gelatina**-*f*	jelly
4295	**periodismo**-*m*	journalism
4296	**madrastra**-*f*	stepmother
4297	**ceja**-*f*	eyebrow
4298	**loro**-*m*	parrot
4299	**trayectoria**-*f*	trajectory
4302	**capricho**-*m*	whim
4303	**póquer**-*m*	poker
4305	**válvula**-*f*	valve
4309	**proyección**-*f*	projection
4310	**monitor**-*m*	monitor
4311	**discípulo**-*m*	disciple
4312	**narcótico**-*adj; m*	narcotic; narcotic
4313	**evaluación**-*f*	evaluation
4314	**lector**-*m*	reader
4318	**arrogancia**-*f*	arrogance
4319	**agencia**-*f*	agency
4320	**bolígrafo**-*m*	pen
4321	**milicia**-*f*	militia
4322	**imitación**-*f*	imitation
4323	**delegación**-*f*	delegation
4324	**catarata**-*f*	cataract
4325	**rabo**-*m*	tail
4326	**laguna**-*f*	lagoon
4331	**exilio**-*m*	exile
4333	**simio**-*m*	ape
4334	**contaminación**-*f*	contamination
4338	**leopardo**-*m*	leopard
4339	**homicida**-*m/f; adj*	killer; murder
4342	**motín**-*m*	riot
4343	**cereal**-*adj; m*	grain-based; cereal
4344	**pulsera**-*f*	bracelet
4346	**vómito**-*m*	vomit
4347	**remo**-*m*	oar
4348	**cordón**-*m*	cord
4349	**remate**-*m*	ending
4350	**reverencia**-*f*	reverence
4351	**fósforo**-*m*	match
4352	**inmortalidad**-*f*	immortality
4353	**vocación**-*f*	vocation
4354	**coral**-*m*	coral
4356	**recreo**-*m*	break
4359	**encanto**-*m*	charm
4360	**observador**-*m; adj*	observer; observant
4361	**plantación**-*f*	plantation
4362	**prado**-*m*	meadow
4364	**violeta**-*adj; f*	violet; violet
4365	**calificación**-*f*	qualification
4366	**transformación**-*f*	transformation
4368	**cansancio**-*m*	fatigue
4369	**ventilación**-*f*	ventilation
4370	**mosquito**-*m*	mosquito
4371	**codicia**-*f*	greed
4373	**póliza**-*f*	policy
4375	**lesión**-*f*	injury
4376	**esponja**-*f*	sponge
4377	**bocina**-*f*	horn
4378	**estofado**-*m; adj*	stew; stewed
4379	**transbordador**-*m*	ferry
4380	**portón**-*m*	gate
4383	**heno**-*m*	hay
4384	**compensación**-*f*	compensation
4386	**cierre**-*m*	closing
4387	**trío**-*m*	trio
4388	**barbilla**-*f*	chin
4389	**bachillerato**-*m*	A levels
4390	**índice**-*m*	index
4391	**mártir**-*m/f*	martyr
4392	**foco**-*m*	focus, spotlight

4393	**fastidio**-*m*	nuisance
4394	**reemplazo**-*m*	replacement
4395	**inscripción**-*f*	registration
4396	**adrenalina**-*f*	adrenalin
4398	**hormona**-*f*	hormone
4399	**herrero**-*m*	blacksmith
4401	**palestino**-*adj; m*	Palestinian; Palestinian person
4402	**limosna**-*f*	alms
4403	**duende**-*m*	spirit
4405	**pegamento**-*m*	glue
4406	**prostitución**-*f*	prostitution
4407	**agricultura**-*f*	agriculture
4410	**mango**-*m*	mango
4411	**nuera**-*f*	daughter-in-law
4413	**tasa**-*f*	valuation
4414	**reactor**-*m*	reactor
4416	**brújula**-*f*	compass
4417	**cereza**-*f*	cherry
4418	**apelación**-*f*	appeal
4421	**natación**-*f*	swimming
4425	**arzobispo**-*m*	archbishop
4426	**inventario**-*m*	inventory
4430	**acelerador**-*m; adj*	accelerator; accelerant
4431	**ardilla**-*f*	squirrel
4432	**composición**-*f*	composition
4433	**decoración**-*f*	decoration
4434	**peluquero**-*m*	hairdresser
4437	**retaguardia**-*f*	rearguard
4439	**elegancia**-*f*	elegance
4442	**roble**-*m*	oak
4445	**zanahoria**-*f*	carrot
4446	**masajista**-*m/f*	massage therapist
4447	**semen**-*m*	semen
4448	**boletín**-*m*	bulletin
4449	**enseñanza**-*f*	teaching
4450	**soberano**-*adj; m*	sovereign; sovereign
4452	**Caribe**-*m*	the Caribbean
4454	**mudanza**-*f*	move
4455	**cursi**-*adj; m/f*	corny; pretentious
4456	**donación**-*f*	donation
4457	**suburbio**-*m*	suburb
4459	**disputa**-*f*	dispute
4460	**resolución**-*f*	resolution
4462	**humildad**-*f*	humility
4465	**teja**-*f*	tile
4466	**inmigrante**-*adj; m/f*	immigrant; immigrant
4468	**corteza**-*f*	crust
4469	**avena**-*f*	oats
4471	**seña**-*f*	sign
4472	**corazonada**-*f*	hunch
4473	**buitre**-*m*	vulture
4474	**remordimiento**-*m*	remorse
4475	**laurel**-*m*	laurel
4477	**parroquia**-*f*	parish
4478	**tarifa**-*f*	rate
4480	**peón**-*m*	pawn
4481	**perdición**-*f*	perdition
4483	**callejero**-*adj; m*	stray; street map
4485	**albergue**-*m*	hostel
4488	**aula**-*f*	classroom
4489	**criterio**-*m*	opinion, guideline
4490	**hipótesis**-*f*	hypothesis
4492	**mármol**-*m*	marble
4493	**diploma**-*m*	diploma
4494	**anestesia**-*f*	anesthesia
4495	**joyería**-*f*	jewelry
4497	**secuestrador**-*m*	kidnapper
4499	**sucesor**-*m*	successor
4502	**decreto**-*m*	decree
4503	**superviviente**-*m/f*	survivor
4504	**yeso**-*m*	plaster
4505	**peine**-*m*	comb
4506	**prenda**-*f*	garment
4507	**azotea**-*f*	rooftop
4508	**armamento**-*m*	armament
4509	**grueso**-*adj; m*	heavy; thickness
4510	**foro**-*m*	forum
4512	**capitalismo**-*m*	capitalism
4513	**respaldo**-*m*	back
4515	**ídolo**-*m/f*	idol
4516	**suspiro**-*m*	sigh
4517	**acre**-*m; adj*	acre; acrid
4521	**republicano**-*m*	republican
4526	**entendimiento**-*m*	understanding
4527	**quemadura**-*f*	burn
4531	**taco**-*m*	taco, peg
4533	**jabalí**-*m/f*	wild boar
4535	**defensivo**-*adj; m*	defensive; defense

4542	**portátil**-*adj; m*	portable; laptop	4606	**metáfora**-*f*	metaphor
4544	**col**-*f*	cabbage	4608	**vejez**-*f*	old age
4545	**triángulo**-*m*	triangle	4609	**tirano**-*m*	tyrant
4546	**asma**-*m*	asthma	4610	**catálogo**-*m*	catalog
4547	**mayonesa**-*f*	mayonnaise	4611	**mediana**-*f*	median
4548	**uña**-*f*	nail	4612	**liebre**-*f*	hare
4549	**gen**-*m*	gene	4613	**realeza**-*f*	royalty
4553	**céntimo**-*m*	cent	4614	**cascada**-*f*	waterfall
4554	**condolencia**-*f*	condolence	4615	**comunión**-*f*	communion
4555	**charlatán**-*m*	fraudster, chatterbox	4616	**inundación**-*f*	flood
4557	**cartón**-*m*	cardboard	4617	**rendición**-*f*	surrender
4558	**comediante**-*m/f*	comedian	4619	**precedente**-*adj; m*	previous; precedent
4560	**piojo**-*m*	louse	4621	**tubería**-*f*	pipeline
4561	**consciencia**-*f*	consciousness	4622	**Holanda**-*f*	Holland
4562	**bobada**-*f*	nonsense, trifle	4625	**cisne**-*m*	swan
4564	**vegetal**-*adj; m*	vegetal; vegetable	4626	**sello**-*m*	seal
4565	**canguro**-*m; m/f*	kangaroo; babysitter	4627	**dinosaurio**-*m*	dinosaur
4567	**media**-*f*	stocking	4629	**grabadora**-*f*	recorder
4569	**módulo**-*m*	module	4630	**franqueza**-*f*	frankness
4570	**grieta**-*f*	crack	4631	**compatriota**-*m/f*	compatriot
4571	**concejal**-*m*	councilor	4633	**suposición**-*f*	assumption
4572	**amnesia**-*f*	amnesia	4634	**suspensión**-*f*	suspension
4573	**comodidad**-*f*	comfort	4636	**revancha**-*f*	rematch
4574	**coreano**-*adj; m*	Korean; Korean person	4638	**turismo**-*m*	tourism
4576	**aparcamiento**-*m*	parking	4639	**sable**-*m*	saber
4577	**ofensa**-*f*	offense	4640	**enigma**-*m*	enigma
4578	**extinción**-*f*	extinction	4642	**accionista**-*m/f*	shareholder
4580	**ticket**-*m*	ticket	4643	**estante**-*m*	shelf
4581	**actualidad**-*f*	currently	4644	**operativo**-*adj; m*	operational; operation
4583	**taquilla**-*f*	ticket window	4645	**arrecife**-*m*	reef
4585	**pizarra**-*f*	blackboard	4646	**aluminio**-*m*	aluminum
4588	**emisora**-*f*	broadcasting station	4647	**fachada**-*f*	facade
4589	**prefecto**-*m*	prefect	4650	**sobretodo**-*m*	overcoat
4591	**creyente**-*m/f*	believer	4652	**rollo**-*m*	roll, bore (coll)
4592	**farol**-*m*	lantern, bluff	4653	**señorito**-*m*	young gentleman
4594	**ajuste**-*m*	adjustment	4655	**inquilino**-*m*	tenant
4595	**obsequio**-*m*	gift	4656	**huerto**-*m*	orchard
4598	**consultorio**-*m*	office, consultancy	4657	**celebridad**-*f*	celebrity
4599	**dedicación**-*f*	dedication	4658	**necio**-*m; adj*	fool; stupid
4601	**tiranía**-*f*	tyranny	4659	**olfato**-*m*	smell
4602	**tornillo**-*m*	screw	4660	**moralidad**-*f*	morality
4603	**interferencia**-*f*	interference	4661	**fibra**-*f*	fiber
4605	**rosario**-*m*	rosary	4662	**cultivo**-*m*	farming
			4666	**ponche**-*m*	punch

4667	**inmersión**-*f*	immersion
4668	**preciosidad**-*f*	preciousness
4670	**conservador**-*adj; m*	conservative; conservative
4674	**juerga**-*f*	good time
4678	**decena**-*f*	ten
4679	**terciopelo**-*m*	velvet
4680	**reparación**-*f*	repair
4681	**longitud**-*f*	length
4683	**telescopio**-*m*	telescope
4684	**cordura**-*f*	sanity
4687	**dilema**-*m*	dilemma
4688	**panadería**-*f*	bakery
4689	**sexualidad**-*f*	sexuality
4691	**distraído**-*adj; m*	distracted; scatterbrain
4692	**antorcha**-*f*	torch
4694	**vainilla**-*f*	vanilla
4695	**camisón**-*m*	nightgown
4696	**párrafo**-*m*	paragraph
4697	**inmunidad**-*f*	immunity
4698	**ración**-*f*	ration
4701	**tic**-*m*	tic
4702	**escorpión**-*m*	scorpion
4704	**charla**-*f*	chat
4705	**invención**-*f*	invention
4706	**noticiero**-*m*	news (LA)
4708	**patriota**-*m/f; adj*	patriot; patriotic
4709	**aduana**-*f*	customs
4710	**dinastía**-*f*	dynasty
4712	**desempleo**-*m*	unemployment
4713	**formalidad**-*f*	formality
4715	**boludo**-*adj; m*	silly (LA) (coll); moron (LA) (coll)
4716	**discoteca**-*f*	disco
4717	**moribundo**-*adj; m*	dying; dying person
4718	**bancario**-*adj; m*	banking; bank employee
4719	**detector**-*m*	detector
4720	**microondas**-*mpl*	microwave
4721	**ancla**-*f*	anchor
4722	**escultura**-*f*	sculpture
4724	**jerez**-*m*	sherry
4727	**exploración**-*f*	exploration
4728	**alimentación**-*f*	food, supply
4729	**can**-*m*	hound
4730	**pradera**-*f*	meadow
4731	**rublo**-*m*	ruble
4735	**adversario**-*m*	adversary
4737	**cimiento**-*m*	foundation
4738	**adicción**-*f*	addiction
4741	**donante**-*m/f*	donor
4742	**moción**-*f*	motion
4743	**paranoia**-*f*	paranoia
4745	**programación**-*f*	programming
4746	**esposo**-*m*	husband
4747	**castaño**-*adj; m*	brown; chestnut
4748	**redacción**-*f*	essay, editorial office
4750	**estimulante**-*adj; m*	stimulating; stimulant
4754	**motivación**-*f*	motivation
4755	**localización**-*f*	location
4756	**caldo**-*m*	broth
4757	**guarnición**-*f*	trimming, garnish
4758	**complot**-*m*	conspiracy
4759	**recorte**-*m*	cutback
4760	**metálico**-*adj; m*	metal; cash
4761	**apocalipsis**-*m*	apocalypse
4762	**entrante**-*adj; m*	entering; appetizer (ES)
4764	**clemencia**-*f*	clemency
4766	**rocío**-*m*	dew
4767	**diarrea**-*f*	diarrhea
4768	**cargador**-*m*	charger
4769	**vocabulario**-*m*	vocabulary
4770	**mugre**-*f*	grime
4772	**esmeralda**-*f*	emerald
4774	**obediencia**-*f*	obedience
4775	**umbral**-*m*	threshold
4777	**brecha**-*f*	gap
4778	**acuario**-*m*	aquarium
4780	**desertor**-*m*	deserter
4781	**transición**-*f*	transition
4783	**acoso**-*m*	harassment
4786	**magistrado**-*m*	magistrate
4787	**perezoso**-*adj; m*	lazy; sloth
4791	**anhelo**-*m*	longing
4792	**hocico**-*m*	snout
4793	**jefatura**-*f*	leadership
4794	**caldera**-*f*	boiler
4795	**chivo**-*m*	kid, young goat

4797	**adjunto**-*adj; m*	attached; attachment
4798	**sultán**-*m*	sultan
4800	**pingüino**-*m*	penguin
4801	**mandato**-*m*	mandate
4803	**sabotaje**-*m*	sabotage
4804	**esplendor**-*m*	splendor
4805	**faz**-*f*	face
4806	**búho**-*m*	owl
4808	**empeño**-*m*	determination, pawn
4809	**delicadeza**-*f*	delicacy
4810	**fondos**-*mpl*	funds
4811	**matadero**-*m*	slaughterhouse
4815	**panorama**-*m*	landscape
4816	**sanatorio**-*m*	sanatorium
4817	**proveedor**-*m*	supplier
4818	**mentalidad**-*f*	mentality
4820	**prototipo**-*m*	prototype
4821	**portugués**-*adj; m*	Portuguese; Portuguese person
4823	**aperitivo**-*m*	appetizer
4824	**descarado**-*adj; m*	shameless; insolent person
4826	**neumonía**-*f*	pneumonia
4827	**cínico**-*adj; m*	shameless; shameless person
4828	**ganga**-*f*	bargain
4829	**siervo**-*m*	serf
4830	**convicción**-*f*	conviction
4831	**palco**-*m*	box seat
4832	**hedor**-*m*	stench
4833	**mercurio**-*m*	mercury
4834	**secta**-*f*	sect
4835	**desacuerdo**-*m*	disagreement
4836	**excitación**-*f*	excitement
4837	**hidrógeno**-*m*	hydrogen
4838	**jubilación**-*f*	retirement
4839	**autoestima**-*f*	self-esteem
4840	**directorio**-*m*	directory
4841	**vivienda**-*f*	apartment
4842	**rastreo**-*m*	search
4843	**parrilla**-*f*	grill
4845	**renacimiento**-*m*	rebirth, Renaissance
4846	**portaaviones**-*m*	aircraft carrier
4847	**alérgico**-*adj; m*	allergic; person with allergies
4848	**parásito**-*m; adj*	parasite; parasitic
4849	**sincronización**-*f*	synchronization
4853	**cenicero**-*m*	ashtray
4854	**superintendente**-*m/f*	superintendent
4855	**senda**-*f*	track
4857	**preparatorio**-*adj; m*	preparatory; pre-university study
4861	**homosexualidad**-*f*	homosexuality
4862	**intérprete**-*m/f*	interpreter
4863	**pendejo**-*adj; m*	asshole (LA) (coll); fool (LA) (coll)
4865	**pésame**-*m*	condolence
4867	**popularidad**-*f*	popularity
4868	**reservación**-*f*	reservation (LA)
4871	**vencedor**-*adj; m*	winner; winner
4872	**tormento**-*m*	torment
4873	**folleto**-*m*	brochure
4876	**tacón**-*m*	heel
4877	**trinchera**-*f*	trench
4878	**destreza**-*f*	skill
4879	**demócrata**-*m/f*	democrat
4880	**rienda**-*f*	rein
4882	**muchedumbre**-*f*	crowd
4885	**manto**-*m*	mantle
4886	**dictadura**-*f*	dictatorship
4888	**cobra**-*f*	cobra
4889	**viudo**-*m; adj*	widower; widow
4890	**credibilidad**-*f*	credibility
4891	**especia**-*f*	spice
4892	**aro**-*m*	ring
4893	**evangelio**-*m*	gospel
4896	**disgusto**-*m*	disgust
4897	**acercamiento**-*m*	approach
4900	**emisión**-*f*	emission
4902	**alga**-*f*	seaweed
4903	**atuendo**-*m*	attire
4904	**descendiente**-*m/f*	descendant
4905	**mareo**-*m*	dizziness
4907	**rasgo**-*m*	feature
4908	**lagarto**-*m*	lizard
4910	**lechuga**-*f*	lettuce
4911	**charco**-*m*	puddle
4914	**histeria**-*f*	hysteria
4915	**balazo**-*m*	shot

4916	**navío**-*m*	ship
4917	**hindú**-*adj; m/f*	Hindu; Hindu person
4918	**quirófano**-*m*	operating room
4921	**compás**-*m*	compass
4923	**portador**-*m*	carrier
4924	**tempestad**-*f*	storm
4928	**súbdito**-*m*	subject
4929	**ingrediente**-*m*	ingredient
4930	**reconstrucción**-*f*	reconstruction
4931	**cadete**-*m/f*	cadet
4932	**recuento**-*m*	count
4933	**informal**-*adj; m/f*	informal; unreliable person
4934	**alza**-*f*	rise
4935	**compartimento**-*m*	compartment
4936	**espectro**-*m*	spectrum, ghost
4937	**pulpo**-*m*	octopus
4938	**comuna**-*f*	commune
4939	**servilleta**-*f*	napkin
4940	**porcelana**-*f*	porcelain
4943	**prójimo**-*m*	neighbor, friend (LA)
4944	**brutalidad**-*f*	brutality
4948	**tolerancia**-*f*	tolerance
4950	**escrúpulo**-*m*	scruple
4952	**trucha**-*f*	trout
4953	**imaginario**-*adj; m*	imaginary; imaginary
4954	**soja**-*f*	soy
4955	**aprendizaje**-*m*	learning
4956	**recinto**-*m*	enclosure
4957	**lavadora**-*f*	washing machine
4958	**ruleta**-*f*	roulette
4959	**filtro**-*m*	filter
4960	**superstición**-*f*	superstition
4961	**Colombia**-*f*	Colombia
4962	**capitalista**-*adj; m/f*	capitalist; capitalist
4964	**arcilla**-*f*	clay
4966	**desvío**-*m*	detour
4967	**fogata**-*f*	bonfire
4969	**anarquía**-*f*	anarchy
4971	**lona**-*f*	canvas
4972	**Mediterráneo**-*m*	Mediterranean
4975	**mafioso**-*adj; m*	mafia; mobster
4976	**holocausto**-*m*	holocaust
4978	**chorrada**-*f*	nonsense, knick-knack (ES) (coll)
4979	**rugby**-*m*	rugby
4981	**útero**-*m*	uterus
4982	**contenedor**-*m*	container
4984	**acorde**-*m; adj*	chord; in accordance with
4985	**estatura**-*f*	stature
4988	**noreste**-*m*	northeast
4990	**encaje**-*m*	lace, fitting
4991	**vibración**-*f*	vibration
4992	**residuo**-*m*	residue
4993	**camarón**-*m*	prawn
4994	**seductor**-*adj; m*	seductive; seducer
4997	**rampa**-*f*	ramp
5001	**indicio**-*m*	indication
5002	**piña**-*f*	pineapple
5004	**trayecto**-*m*	journey
5005	**linaje**-*m*	lineage
5006	**manantial**-*m*	spring
5008	**negligencia**-*f*	negligence
5009	**coyote**-*m*	coyote
5011	**fulano**-*m*	some guy (coll)
5012	**milenio**-*m*	millennium
5015	**analista**-*m/f*	analyst
5016	**hermosura**-*f*	beauty
5017	**erupción**-*f*	eruption
5019	**marfil**-*m*	ivory
5020	**malaria**-*f*	malaria
5021	**precipicio**-*m*	cliff
5022	**hebreo**-*adj; m*	Hebrew; Jew
5023	**hipnosis**-*f*	hypnosis
5024	**persiana**-*f*	blind

Numerals

Rank	Spanish-*PoS*	Translation(s)
2720	**sexto**-*num*	sixth
2894	**sesenta**-*num*	sixty
3000	**trece**-*num*	thirteen
3111	**séptimo**-*num*	seventh
3164	**doscientos**-*num*	two hundred
3229	**catorce**-*num*	fourteen
3371	**setenta**-*num*	seventy
3499	**ochenta**-*num*	eighty
3613	**veinticinco**-*num*	twenty-five
3650	**dieciséis**-*num*	sixteen
3731	**noventa**-*num*	ninety
3818	**dieciocho**-*num*	eighteen
3821	**quinientos**-*num*	five hundred
3987	**octavo**-*num*	eighth
4116	**diecisiete**-*num*	seventeen
4676	**décimo**-*num*	tenth
4690	**noveno**-*num*	ninth
4711	**trescientos**-*num*	three hundred

Verbs

Rank	Spanish-PoS	Translation(s)
2502	durar-*vb*	last
2503	organizar-*vb*	organize
2510	atravesar-*vb*	cross
2514	sellar-*vb*	seal, stamp
2519	estimar-*vb*	estimate, respect
2522	indicar-*vb*	indicate
2523	fracasar-*vb*	fail
2528	confesar(se)-*vb*	confess
2532	pretender-*vb*	pretend
2533	derrotar-*vb*	defeat
2544	contratar-*vb*	hire
2546	lidiar-*vb*	deal with
2551	avergonzar(se)-*vb*	embarrass
2554	garantizar-*vb*	guarantee
2555	corear-*vb*	chant
2561	grabar-*vb*	record
2573	llover-*vb*	rain
2577	curar(se)-*vb*	heal
2579	corresponder-*vb*	be appropriate, return
2583	admirar-*vb*	admire
2597	proponer(se)-*vb; vbr*	suggest; decide
2598	impresionar(se)-*vb*	impress
2605	descuidar(se)-*vb; vbr*	neglect; not worry
2606	adelantar(se)-*vb*	overtake
2613	traducir-*vb*	translate
2617	decepcionar(se)-*vb*	disappoint
2627	atar-*vb*	tie
2630	reunir(se)-*vb*	get together
2631	agotar(se)-*vb*	exhaust
2632	producir-*vb*	produce
2634	tallar-*vb*	engrave
2635	versar-*vb*	be about
2636	destrozar-*vb*	shatter
2641	girar(se)-*vb*	turn
2642	tardar(se)-*vb*	be late
2649	suicidarse-*vbr*	commit suicide
2655	educar-*vb*	educate
2666	insistir-*vb*	insist
2668	multar-*vb*	fine
2671	divertir(se)-*vb*	amuse
2673	conservar-*vb*	keep
2677	retroceder-*vb*	go back
2690	malentender-*vb*	misunderstand
2706	competir-*vb*	compete
2723	arder-*vb*	burn
2724	recorrer-*vb*	go across, run your eyes over
2727	arriesgar(se)-*vb*	risk
2728	perseguir-*vb*	chase
2729	retirar(se)-*vb*	remove
2730	apuntar-*vb*	make a note, aim
2738	relacionar-*vb*	connect
2748	caber-*vb*	fit
2751	emocionar(se)-*vb*	thrill
2759	respetar-*vb*	respect
2767	identificar-*vb*	identify
2769	propinar-*vb*	inflict
2774	prever-*vb*	foresee
2777	mear(se)-*vb*	piss
2780	cagar(se)-*vb; vbr*	shit (coll); be terrified
2783	sostener-*vb*	hold
2785	basar(se)-*vb*	base on
2786	mojar-*vb*	wet
2788	atraer-*vb*	attract
2796	asistir-*vb*	attend
2799	traicionar-*vb*	betray
2800	expresar(se)-*vb*	express
2802	entrenar(se)-*vb*	train
2807	coartar-*vb*	restrict
2809	declarar-*vb*	declare
2817	concernir-*vb*	concern
2818	avanzar-*vb*	advance
2835	establecer-*vb*	establish
2838	aprovechar-*vb*	take advantage of
2844	ahorrar-*vb*	save
2856	poseer-*vb*	possess
2858	reparar-*vb*	repair
2859	cancelar-*vb*	cancel
2860	soltar-*vb*	free, drop
2862	castigar-*vb*	punish
2868	desesperar-*vb*	despair
2872	asumir-*vb*	assume
2873	alborotar-*vb*	disturb
2878	inventar-*vb*	invent
2882	comprometer(se)-*vb; vbr*	implicate; get engaged

2883	**obedecer**-*vb*	obey	3131	**describir**-*vb*	describe
2891	**conectar**-*vb*	connect	3139	**orinar**-*vb*	urinate
2896	**capturar**-*vb*	capture	3142	**desperdiciar**-*vb*	waste
2900	**conquistar**-*vb*	conquer	3143	**iniciar**-*vb*	start
2906	**combatir**-*vb*	combat	3146	**morder(se)**-*vb*	bite
2907	**madrugar**-*vb*	rise early	3148	**donar**-*vb*	donate
2909	**deprimir(se)**-*vb*	depress	3149	**registrar**-*vb*	register
2916	**temblar**-*vb*	shake	3150	**exigir**-*vb*	require
2919	**navegar**-*vb*	sail	3155	**entrever**-*vb*	glimpse
2926	**apretar**-*vb*	tighten	3167	**explorar**-*vb*	explore
2930	**batir**-*vb*	beat, whip	3170	**mudar(se)**-*vb*	move
2932	**comparar**-*vb*	compare	3177	**brindar**-*vb*	toast, provide
2933	**aumentar**-*vb*	increase	3182	**envidiar**-*vb*	envy
2935	**autorizar**-*vb*	authorize	3194	**borrar**-*vb*	delete
2945	**contactar**-*vb*	contact	3195	**congelar**-*vb*	freeze
2958	**flotar**-*vb*	float	3196	**hacer cosquillas**-*vb*	tickle
2962	**estallar**-*vb*	burst			
2966	**colocar**-*vb*	put	3203	**localizar**-*vb*	locate
2967	**soplar**-*vb*	blow	3214	**surgir**-*vb*	appear
2971	**confirmar**-*vb*	confirm	3219	**regular**-*vb*	regulate
2978	**debatir**-*vb*	discuss	3234	**resumir**-*vb*	summarize
2982	**encajar**-*vb*	fit	3235	**apoyar**-*vb*	support
2985	**añadir**-*vb*	add	3237	**provocar**-*vb*	provoke
2986	**ilusionar(se)**-*vb*	inspire hope	3243	**acelerar**-*vb*	accelerate
2990	**rendir(se)**-*vb; vbr*	perform; surrender	3254	**empacar**-*vb*	pack (LA)
			3255	**completar**-*vb*	complete
2996	**solucionar**-*vb*	solve	3261	**estropear**-*vb*	spoil
2997	**revelar**-*vb*	reveal	3263	**ensayar**-*vb*	rehearse
3003	**manar**-*vb*	flow	3271	**atardecer**-*m; vb*	twilight; get dark
3006	**apartar**-*vb*	set aside	3273	**palmar**-*vb*	die (ES) (coll)
3041	**repartir**-*vb*	distribute	3274	**interpretar**-*vb*	play, perform
3048	**ofender**-*vb*	offend	3278	**refugiar(se)**-*vb*	shelter
3058	**doler**-*vb*	hurt	3279	**verificar**-*vb*	verify
3061	**aconsejar**-*vb*	advise	3282	**atascar**-*vb*	jam
3064	**cavar**-*vb*	dig	3293	**atajar**-*vb*	take a shortcut, tackle
3066	**plagar**-*vb*	infest			
3069	**regalar**-*vb*	gift	3294	**juntar**-*vb*	put together
3070	**escoltar**-*vb*	escort	3295	**examinar**-*vb*	examine
3072	**marcar**-*vb*	mark	3297	**alabar**-*vb*	praise
3080	**anunciar**-*vb*	announce	3298	**reducir**-*vb*	reduce
3084	**pillar**-*vb*	catch up	3302	**implicar(se)**-*vb*	involve
3097	**posar**-*vb*	pose	3310	**consistir**-*vb*	consist
3101	**rechazar**-*vb*	reject	3314	**operar**-*vb*	work
3107	**despegar**-*vb*	take off	3316	**emboscar**-*vb*	ambush
3108	**alquilar**-*vb*	rent	3323	**determinar**-*vb*	determine
3115	**fallecer**-*vb*	die	3324	**cesar**-*vb*	cease

3334	**anochecer**-*m; vb*	dusk; get dark
3335	**obsesionar(se)**-*vb*	obsess
3343	**publicar**-*vb*	publish
3350	**dibujar**-*vb*	draw
3379	**amenazar**-*vb*	threaten
3383	**patear**-*vb*	kick
3405	**comunicar**-*vb*	communicate
3411	**acondicionar(se)**-*vb*	prepare
3413	**ignorar**-*vb*	ignore
3417	**protestar**-*vb*	protest
3419	**presuponer**-*vb*	assume
3422	**destinar**-*vb*	destine
3424	**dominar**-*vb*	master
3456	**alterar**-*vb*	alter
3466	**tensar(se)**-*vb*	tense
3474	**distinguir**-*vb*	distinguish
3491	**tramar**-*vb*	plot
3497	**apreciar**-*vb*	appreciate
3510	**expulsar**-*vb*	expel
3514	**agregar**-*vb*	add
3526	**envolver**-*vb*	wrap
3529	**atrasar(se)**-*vb*	delay
3536	**violar**-*vb*	violate
3562	**proceder**-*vb*	come from, proceed
3570	**aficionar**-*vb*	become interested
3582	**gobernar**-*vb*	rule
3583	**doblar**-*vb*	bend, double
3590	**yacer**-*vb*	lie
3596	**provenir**-*vb*	proceed
3599	**chupar**-*vb*	suck, absorb (coll)
3610	**extender**-*vb*	extend
3612	**desarrollar**-*vb*	develop
3617	**aprobar**-*vb*	approve
3626	**latir**-*vb*	beat
3631	**conceder**-*vb*	grant
3646	**invertir**-*vb*	invest
3657	**exagerar**-*vb*	exaggerate
3658	**bordar**-*vb*	embroider, do excellently (coll)
3659	**ahogar(se)**-*vb*	drown
3662	**legar**-*vb*	bequeath
3669	**acostar(se)**-*vb*	lay down
3674	**trucar**-*vb*	rig
3677	**sincronizar**-*vb*	synchronize
3678	**subastar**-*vb*	auction
3679	**nombrar**-*vb*	name
3689	**tolerar**-*vb*	tolerate
3690	**diseñar**-*vb*	design
3697	**variar**-*vb*	vary
3708	**ejecutar**-*vb*	implement, execute
3713	**solicitar**-*vb*	request
3737	**quebrar**-*vb*	break
3738	**portar(se)**-*vb; vbr*	carry; behave
3739	**sacrificar**-*vb*	sacrifice
3740	**testificar**-*vb*	testify
3749	**presentir**-*vb*	have a feeling
3751	**respectar**-*vb*	concern
3755	**experimentar**-*vb*	experiment
3757	**escalar**-*vb*	climb
3758	**excitar**-*vb*	excite
3762	**afrontar**-*vb*	face
3766	**internar**-*vb*	send in
3768	**complacer**-*vb*	please
3773	**cooperar**-*vb*	cooperate
3774	**rastrear**-*vb*	track
3780	**bloquear**-*vb*	block
3785	**afirmar**-*vb*	affirm, maintain
3802	**suspender**-*vb*	hang, cancel, fail
3809	**aislar**-*vb*	isolate
3810	**dorar**-*vb*	brown
3823	**imitar**-*vb*	imitate
3825	**anotar**-*vb*	write down
3828	**afeitar(se)**-*vb*	shave
3833	**dañar**-*vb*	damage
3836	**comportarse**-*vbr*	behave
3837	**derribar**-*vb*	knock down
3840	**remolcar**-*vb*	tow
3853	**presionar**-*vb*	press
3865	**coser**-*vb*	sew
3872	**atracar(se)**-*vb; vbr*	rob, dock; stuff yourself
3873	**enterar(se)**-*vb; vbr*	pay (LA); find out
3886	**fichar**-*vb*	sign, clock in
3889	**acudir**-*vb*	go to
3907	**transmitir**-*vb*	transmit
3913	**intervenir**-*vb*	take part, operate
3915	**hundir(se)**-*vb*	sink
3918	**maquinar**-*vb*	plot
3922	**calentar**-*vb*	heat

3925	**interferir**-*vb*	interfere	4179	**tostar**-*vb*	toast
3931	**topar(se)**-*vb*	run into	4184	**patinar**-*vb*	skate
3936	**marear(se)**-*vb*	make someone dizzy, annoy (coll)	4189	**titular(se)**-*m; vb; adj*	headline; title; owner
3941	**reclamar**-*vb*	demand	4194	**aproximar(se)**-*vb*	bring closer
3946	**concentrar(se)**-*vb*	assemble, focus	4199	**forzar**-*vb*	force
3956	**adoptar**-*vb*	adopt	4216	**interrogar**-*vb*	question
3958	**reventar**-*vb*	burst	4218	**dividir**-*vb*	divide
3961	**acceder**-*vb*	agree, access	4222	**exponer**-*vb*	expose
3963	**espiar**-*vb*	spy	4227	**tender(se)**-*vb; vbr*	tend, hang up; lie down
3964	**entrañar**-*vb*	involve	4250	**descifrar**-*vb*	decipher
3968	**analizar**-*vb*	analyze	4251	**burlar(se)**-*vb; vbr*	evade; mock
3988	**editar**-*vb*	edit	4257	**acampar**-*vb*	camp
3991	**rasguñar**-*vb*	scratch	4265	**mezclar**-*vb*	mix
3997	**ingresar**-*vb*	hospitalize, join	4268	**piar**-*vb*	tweet
4011	**animar**-*vb*	encourage	4273	**corregir**-*vb*	correct
4026	**asignar**-*vb*	assign	4294	**estrellar(se)**-*vb*	crash
4033	**ceder**-*vb*	give	4301	**entusiasmar(se)**-*vb; vbr*	delight; be thrilled
4034	**evacuar**-*vb*	evacuate	4306	**triunfar**-*vb*	triumph
4036	**plantar(se)**-*vb; vbr*	plant, stand up (coll); stand firm	4308	**abordar**-*vb*	tackle
4042	**reemplazar**-*vb*	replace	4328	**secuestrar**-*vb*	kidnap
4048	**enfermar(se)**-*vb*	get sick	4330	**desmayarse**-*vbr*	faint
4049	**envenenar**-*vb*	poison	4332	**procurar**-*vb*	attempt
4051	**pisar**-*vb*	step	4335	**cultivar**-*vb*	cultivate
4066	**disfrazar(se)**-*vb*	disguise	4336	**reflexionar**-*vb*	reflect
4069	**cabalgar**-*vb*	ride	4340	**encubrir**-*vb*	cover
4070	**bastar(se)**-*vb; vbr*	be enough; be capable of	4341	**alzar**-*vb*	raise
4072	**ofertar**-*vb*	offer	4345	**reponer**-*vb*	replenish
4081	**decorar**-*vb*	decorate	4357	**divorciar(se)**-*vb*	divorce
4086	**apasionar(se)**-*vb; vbr*	inspire; be crazy about	4363	**evidenciar**-*vb*	demonstrate
4087	**reconstruir**-*vb*	rebuild	4367	**inspirar**-*vb*	inspire
4097	**sudar**-*vb*	sweat	4372	**dotar**-*vb*	supply
4102	**reaccionar**-*vb*	react	4385	**compensar**-*vb*	compensate
4108	**incumbir**-*vb*	concern	4397	**fabricar**-*vb*	manufacture
4111	**fiar(se)**-*vb; vbr*	sell on credit; trust	4400	**programar**-*vb*	program
4127	**mamar**-*vb*	nurse	4404	**esquiar**-*vb*	ski
4139	**colmar**-*vb*	fulfill	4408	**aplastar**-*vb*	crush
4142	**arrojar**-*vb*	throw	4412	**chocar**-*vb*	hit
4143	**componer**-*vb*	compose	4415	**consultar**-*vb*	consult
4154	**fluir**-*vb*	flow	4419	**disgustar**-*vb*	disgust
4155	**prevenir(se)**-*vb; vbr*	warn; get ready	4423	**empeorar**-*vb*	worsen
			4424	**circular**-*adj; vb*	circular; travel
4166	**vengar(se)**-*vb*	avenge	4427	**honrar**-*vb*	honor
			4428	**hervir**-*vb*	boil
			4436	**atentar**-*vb*	attack

4440	**templar**-*vb*	cool down
4441	**pronunciar**-*vb*	pronounce
4451	**aliviar**-*vb*	relieve
4453	**agitar**-*vb*	shake
4458	**rajar(se)**-*vb; vbr*	slice; back out (coll)
4461	**coincidir**-*vb*	coincide
4464	**deshacer**-*vb*	undo
4467	**delegar**-*vb*	delegate
4476	**descargar**-*vb*	download
4482	**recurrir**-*vb*	appeal, resort
4487	**envejecer**-*vb*	age
4491	**desarmar**-*vb*	disarm
4496	**acertar**-*vb*	get right
4498	**denunciar**-*vb*	report
4511	**demandar**-*vb*	sue, demand
4514	**clavar**-*vb*	nail
4520	**ejercer**-*vb*	practice
4523	**empapar(se)**-*vb*	soak
4528	**graduar(se)**-*vb; vbr*	adjust; graduate
4530	**enmendar**-*vb*	amend
4532	**fracturar(se)**-*vb*	fracture
4536	**tornar(se)**-*vb*	change
4540	**justificar**-*vb*	justify
4541	**predecir**-*vb*	predict
4543	**reformar**-*vb*	reform
4550	**transferir**-*vb*	transfer
4551	**estacionar**-*vb*	park
4563	**escupir**-*vb*	spit
4566	**vagar**-*vb*	wander
4568	**transformar(se)**-*vb*	transform
4579	**insultar**-*vb*	insult
4586	**invadir**-*vb*	invade
4587	**preservar**-*vb*	preserve
4590	**morar**-*vb*	dwell
4593	**castrar**-*vb*	castrate
4600	**reflejar(se)**-*vb*	reflect
4604	**festejar**-*vb*	celebrate
4607	**pujar**-*vb*	bid
4618	**aplicar**-*vb*	apply
4620	**instalar**-*vb*	install
4623	**mascar**-*vb*	chew
4624	**cuadrar**-*vb*	square
4628	**transportar**-*vb*	transport
4635	**intercambiar**-*vb*	exchange
4641	**calcular**-*vb*	calculate
4648	**torcer(se)**-*vb*	twist
4649	**colaborar**-*vb*	collaborate
4654	**reportar(se)**-*vb; vbr*	bring, report (LA); report in (LA)
4664	**activar**-*vb*	activate
4669	**arrastrar(se)**-*vb*	drag
4671	**paralizar**-*vb*	paralyze
4677	**librar(se)**-*vb; vbr*	fight, have free time; escape from
4686	**humillar**-*vb*	humiliate
4699	**seducir**-*vb*	seduce
4714	**colar(se)**-*vb; vbr*	strain, leak; sneak in
4723	**empatar**-*vb*	tie
4725	**abortar**-*vb*	abort
4732	**limitar(se)**-*vb*	restrict
4734	**oponer(se)**-*vb*	oppose
4736	**ajustar**-*vb*	adjust
4740	**definir**-*vb*	define
4744	**pender**-*vb*	hang over
4749	**retener**-*vb*	retain
4751	**degenerar**-*vb*	degenerate
4752	**broncear(se)**-*vb*	tan
4763	**plasmar**-*vb*	express
4765	**derramar**-*vb*	spill
4771	**embarcar**-*vb*	embark
4776	**iluminar**-*vb*	illuminate
4782	**frustrar(se)**-*vb; vbr*	hinder; become frustrated
4784	**atropellar**-*vb*	run over
4785	**infectar(se)**-*vb*	infect
4788	**ahorcar(se)**-*vb*	hang
4789	**torturar(se)**-*vb*	torture
4790	**guiar**-*vb*	guide
4796	**zanjar**-*vb*	dig, settle
4799	**frenar**-*vb*	brake
4802	**elevar**-*vb*	raise
4807	**enloquecer**-*vb*	madden
4814	**trasladar(se)**-*vb*	move
4819	**chequear**-*vb*	check
4825	**planchar**-*vb*	iron
4850	**desafiar**-*vb*	challenge
4856	**razonar**-*vb*	reason
4858	**perturbar(se)**-*vb*	disturb, disorient
4860	**sentenciar**-*vb*	sentence
4864	**señalar**-*vb*	mark
4870	**penetrar**-*vb*	penetrate

4874	**doctorar(se)**-*vb*	award a doctorate
4883	**insinuar**-*vb*	insinuate
4894	**descender**-*vb*	descend
4901	**asociar**-*vb*	associate
4906	**asaltar**-*vb*	assault
4912	**ojear**-*vb*	glance over
4920	**manchar**-*vb*	stain
4926	**anular(se)**-*vb; vbr*	cancel; destroy
4927	**abusar**-*vb*	abuse
4941	**manipular**-*vb*	manipulate
4945	**ascender**-*vb*	ascend
4946	**cuestionar**-*vb*	question
4949	**retorcer**-*vb*	twist
4963	**ligar(se)**-*vb*	tie, flirt (coll)
4973	**criticar**-*vb*	criticize
4977	**zarpar**-*vb*	set sail
4980	**constar**-*vb*	feature, appear
4983	**adquirir**-*vb*	acquire
4987	**auxiliar**-*adj; vb*	assistant; assist
4995	**largar(se)**-*vb; vbr*	tell, give; leave (coll)
4996	**carecer**-*vb*	lack
4999	**madurar**-*vb*	mature
5000	**enorgullecer(se)**-*vb; vbr*	please; feel proud
5003	**reclutar**-*vb*	recruit
5010	**presenciar**-*vb*	witness
5014	**encarcelar**-*vb*	imprison

Alphabetical Order

Rank	Spanish-*PoS*	Translation(s)
	A	
3420	**abandono**-*m*	neglect, desertion
3179	**abeja**-*f*	bee
3533	**abismo**-*m*	abyss
4308	**abordar**-*vb*	tackle
4725	**abortar**-*vb*	abort
3550	**aborto**-*m*	abortion
4274	**abundancia**-*f*	abundance
3667	**aburrimiento**-*m*	boredom
4927	**abusar**-*vb*	abuse
3153	**abuso**-*m*	abuse
4257	**acampar**-*vb*	camp
3961	**acceder**-*vb*	agree, access
4133	**accidental**-*adj*	accidental
4642	**accionista**-*m/f*	shareholder
4430	**acelerador**-*m; adj*	accelerator; accelerant
3243	**acelerar**-*vb*	accelerate
3849	**aceptable**-*adj*	acceptable
3726	**acera**-*f*	sidewalk
4897	**acercamiento**-*m*	approach
4496	**acertar**-*vb*	get right
2766	**ácido**-*adj; m*	sour; acid
4887	**acogedor**-*adj*	cozy
3943	**acompañante**-*m/f*	companion
3411	**acondicionar(se)**-*vb*	prepare
3061	**aconsejar**-*vb*	advise
3438	**acontecimiento**-*m*	event
4984	**acorde**-*m; adj*	chord; in accordance with
4783	**acoso**-*m*	harassment
3669	**acostar(se)**-*vb*	lay down
4517	**acre**-*m; adj*	acre; acrid
4124	**acta**-*f*	record
4664	**activar**-*vb*	activate
3152	**activo**-*adj; m*	active; assets
4581	**actualidad**-*f*	currently
4778	**acuario**-*m*	aquarium
3889	**acudir**-*vb*	go to
2606	**adelantar(se)**-*vb*	overtake
3511	**adelanto**-*m*	advance
4738	**adicción**-*f*	addiction
4317	**adicional**-*adj*	additional
3127	**adicto**-*m*	addict
4797	**adjunto**-*adj; m*	attached; attachment
3519	**administrador**-*m*	administrator
3492	**admirable**-*adj*	admirable
4022	**admiración**-*f*	admiration
3367	**admirador**-*m*	fan
2583	**admirar**-*vb*	admire
2537	**adolescente**-*m/f; adj*	teenager; teenage
4219	**adopción**-*f*	adoption
3956	**adoptar**-*vb*	adopt
4983	**adquirir**-*vb*	acquire
4396	**adrenalina**-*f*	adrenalin
4709	**aduana**-*f*	customs
4735	**adversario**-*m*	adversary
3355	**afectado**-*adj; m*	affected; victim
3828	**afeitar(se)**-*vb*	shave
3570	**aficionar**-*vb*	become interested
3785	**afirmar**-*vb*	affirm, maintain
3800	**afirmativo**-*adj; int*	affirmative; sure
3673	**África**-*f*	Africa
4109	**africano**-*adj; m*	African; African person
3762	**afrontar**-*vb*	face
2701	**afueras**-*fpl*	outskirts
3385	**agarre**-*m*	grip
4319	**agencia**-*f*	agency
4453	**agitar**-*vb*	shake
3935	**agonía**-*f*	agony
4700	**agotador**-*adj*	exhausting
2631	**agotar(se)**-*vb*	exhaust
3074	**agradecimiento**-*m*	gratitude
3920	**agrado**-*m*	liking
3514	**agregar**-*vb*	add
3400	**agresión**-*f*	aggression
3566	**agresivo**-*adj*	aggressive
4407	**agricultura**-*f*	agriculture
3844	**aguante**-*m*	endurance
4844	**agudo**-*adj*	high-pitched
2568	**aguja**-*f*	needle
3659	**ahogar(se)**-*vb*	drown
4788	**ahorcar(se)**-*vb*	hang
2844	**ahorrar**-*vb*	save

2954	**ahorros**-*mpl*	savings	
3778	**aislamiento**-*m*	isolation	
3809	**aislar**-*vb*	isolate	
2608	**ajedrez**-*m*	chess	
3374	**ajo**-*m*	garlic	
4736	**ajustar**-*vb*	adjust	
4594	**ajuste**-*m*	adjustment	
3297	**alabar**-*vb*	praise	
3525	**alambre**-*m*	wire	
3185	**alba**-*m*	dawn	
4485	**albergue**-*m*	hostel	
2873	**alborotar**-*vb*	disturb	
2843	**álbum**-*m*	album	
3957	**alcohólico**-*adj; m*	alcoholic; alcoholic person	
4685	**alejado**-*adj*	remote	
2596	**aleluya**-*int*	hallelujah	
4847	**alérgico**-*adj; m*	allergic; person with allergies	
4902	**alga**-*f*	seaweed	
2713	**aliado**-*m; adj*	ally; allied	
3580	**alias**-*m*	alias	
4728	**alimentación**-*f*	food, supply	
4451	**aliviar**-*vb*	relieve	
2732	**almohada**-*f*	pillow	
3067	**aló**-*int*	hello (LA)	
3483	**alojamiento**-*m*	accommodation	
3108	**alquilar**-*vb*	rent	
3469	**alrededores**-*m*	surroundings	
2968	**altar**-*m*	altar	
3456	**alterar**-*vb*	alter	
3895	**altitud**-*f*	altitude	
4235	**alucinación**-*f*	hallucination	
4665	**alucinante**-*adj*	awesome	
4646	**aluminio**-*m*	aluminum	
4934	**alza**-*f*	rise	
4341	**alzar**-*vb*	raise	
2793	**amabilidad**-*f*	kindness	
3977	**amargo**-*adj*	bitter	
2808	**ambición**-*f*	ambition	
3701	**ambicioso**-*adj; m*	ambitious; greedy	
4869	**ambulante**-*adj*	traveling	
3379	**amenazar**-*vb*	threaten	
3914	**ametralladora**-*f*	machine gun	
3934	**amigable**-*adj*	friendly	
4315	**amistoso**-*adj*	friendly	

4572	**amnesia**-*f*	amnesia
2956	**amo**-*m*	owner
3647	**amoroso**-*adj*	loving
4584	**amplio**-*adj*	spacious
3467	**amuleto**-*m*	amulet
2985	**añadir**-*vb*	add
5015	**analista**-*m/f*	analyst
3968	**analizar**-*vb*	analyze
4969	**anarquía**-*f*	anarchy
3478	**ancestro**-*m*	ancestor
3403	**ancho**-*m; adj*	width; wide
4721	**ancla**-*f*	anchor
4494	**anestesia**-*f*	anesthesia
3458	**anfitrión**-*m*	host
2857	**ángulo**-*m*	angle
3307	**angustia**-*f*	anguish
4791	**anhelo**-*m*	longing
4011	**animar**-*vb*	encourage
3334	**anochecer**-*m; vb*	dusk; get dark
2865	**ano**-*m*	anus
4597	**anónimo**-*adj*	anonymous
3567	**anormal**-*adj*	unusual
3825	**anotar**-*vb*	write down
3134	**ansiedad**-*f*	anxiety
2683	**ansioso**-*adj*	eager, worried
4067	**antena**-*f*	antenna
3105	**anteojos**-*mpl*	glasses
2993	**antepasado**-*m*	ancestor
3465	**anteriormente**-*adv*	previously
4157	**anticuado**-*adj*	antiquated
3996	**antídoto**-*m*	antidote
3950	**antigüedad**-*f*	antiquity
4692	**antorcha**-*f*	torch
4290	**antro**-*m*	den
3081	**anual**-*adj*	annual
4926	**anular(se)**-*vb; vbr*	cancel; destroy
3080	**anunciar**-*vb*	announce
2915	**apagado**-*adj*	off
4576	**aparcamiento**-*m*	parking
3704	**aparición**-*f*	appearance, apparition
4118	**apartado**-*m; adj*	section; remote
3006	**apartar**-*vb*	set aside
4086	**apasionar(se)**-*vb; vbr*	inspire; be crazy about
4418	**apelación**-*f*	appeal

4823	aperitivo-*m*	appetizer	2778	arrogante-*adj*	arrogant
3542	apertura-*f*	opening	4142	arrojar-*vb*	throw
4408	aplastar-*vb*	crush	3060	arroyo-*m*	stream
2515	aplauso-*m*	applause	4161	arsenal-*m*	arsenal
4618	aplicar-*vb*	apply	3952	artefacto-*m*	artifact
4761	apocalipsis-*m*	apocalypse	3057	artificial-*adj*	artificial
3586	apodo-*m*	nickname	2755	artillería-*f*	artillery
3235	apoyar-*vb*	support	3485	artístico-*adj*	artistic
3497	apreciar-*vb*	appreciate	4425	arzobispo-*m*	archbishop
4955	aprendizaje-*m*	learning	3159	asado-*adj; m*	roast; roast
3906	aprendiz-*m/f*	apprentice	4906	asaltar-*vb*	assault
2926	apretar-*vb*	tighten	3512	asamblea-*f*	assembly
3990	aprieto-*m*	predicament	4945	ascender-*vb*	ascend
3054	aprisa-*adv*	quickly	2659	ascenso-*m*	rise, promotion
3016	aprobación-*f*	approval	3792	asesor-*m; adj*	adviser; advisory
3617	aprobar-*vb*	approve	4026	asignar-*vb*	assign
2838	aprovechar-*vb*	take advantage of	2854	asilo-*m*	asylum
4194	aproximar(se)-*vb*	bring closer	2832	asistencia-*f*	assistance
2730	apuntar-*vb*	make a note, aim	2796	asistir-*vb*	attend
4204	apurado-*adj*	rushed	4546	asma-*m*	asthma
2829	apuro-*m*	trouble	4141	asno-*m*	donkey
2571	árabe-*adj; m/f*	Arabian; Arab	4901	asociar-*vb*	associate
3651	árbitro-*m/f*	referee	3897	aspirina-*f*	aspirin
3655	arbusto-*m*	bush	4071	astronauta-*m/f*	astronaut
3653	arca-*f*	ark	2872	asumir-*vb*	assume
4964	arcilla-*f*	clay	4300	atado-*adj*	tied
2723	arder-*vb*	burn	3293	atajar-*vb*	take a shortcut, tackle
2904	ardiente-*adj*	burning			
4431	ardilla-*f*	squirrel	3271	atardecer-*m; vb*	twilight; get dark
3256	argentino-*adj; m*	Argentinian; Argentinian person	2627	atar-*vb*	tie
			3282	atascar-*vb*	jam
			4288	Atenas-*f*	Athens
3092	argumento-*m*	argument	4436	atentar-*vb*	attack
3947	armada-*f*	navy	2886	atento-*adj*	attentive
3129	armadura-*f*	armor	3166	aterrador-*adj*	frightening
4508	armamento-*m*	armament	3692	Atlántico-*m*	Atlantic
3162	armonía-*f*	harmony	3965	atleta-*m/f*	athlete
4892	aro-*m*	ring	3560	atómico-*adj*	atomic
3264	aroma-*m*	scent	3872	atracar(se)-*vb; vbr*	rob, dock; stuff yourself
3136	arquitecto-*m*	architect			
4093	arquitectura-*f*	architecture	2827	atracción-*f*	attraction
4008	arranque-*m*	start, outburst	2788	atraer-*vb*	attract
4669	arrastrar(se)-*vb*	drag	3529	atrasar(se)-*vb*	delay
4645	arrecife-*m*	reef	2510	atravesar-*vb*	cross
2727	arriesgar(se)-*vb*	risk	4784	atropellar-*vb*	run over
4318	arrogancia-*f*	arrogance	4537	atroz-*adj*	atrocious

4903	**atuendo**-*m*	attire
3911	**atún**-*m*	tuna
4188	**audaz**-*adj*	bold
2708	**audición**-*f*	hearing, audition
3540	**au**-*int*	ouch
4488	**aula**-*f*	classroom
2933	**aumentar**-*vb*	increase
3507	**ausente**-*adj; m/f*	absent; absentee
4839	**autoestima**-*f*	self-esteem
3103	**autógrafo**-*m*	autograph
2995	**automático**-*adj*	automatic
2553	**automóvil**-*m*	car
2955	**autopsia**-*f*	autopsy
2935	**autorizar**-*vb*	authorize
4987	**auxiliar**-*adj; vb*	assistant; assist
2782	**avance**-*m*	advance
2818	**avanzar**-*vb*	advance
4469	**avena**-*f*	oats
2551	**avergonzar(se)**-*vb*	embarrass
4113	**aviación**-*f*	aviation
2624	**ayuntamiento**-*m*	local government
2538	**azar**-*m*	fate
4507	**azotea**-*f*	rooftop

B

3531	**baba**-*f*	slime
4389	**bachillerato**-*m*	A levels
4040	**bah**-*int*	bah
3354	**baile**-*m*	dance
4287	**balance**-*m*	balance
4915	**balazo**-*m*	shot
3242	**balcón**-*m*	balcony
3098	**ballena**-*f*	whale
2622	**ballet**-*m*	ballet
2950	**baloncesto**-*m*	basketball
4057	**balsa**-*f*	raft
4202	**banana**-*f*	banana
3723	**banca**-*f*	banking
4718	**bancario**-*adj; m*	banking; bank employee
4211	**bancarrota**-*f*	bankruptcy
3165	**bandeja**-*f*	tray
2576	**bandido**-*m*	bandit
3284	**bando**-*m*	side
2672	**bañera**-*f*	bathtub

3426	**banquero**-*m*	banker
2834	**banquete**-*m*	banquet
4178	**barbacoa**-*f*	barbecue
2722	**bárbaro**-*adj; m*	savage; Barbarian
4103	**barbero**-*m*	barber
4388	**barbilla**-*f*	chin
3246	**barca**-*f*	small boat
3051	**barrera**-*f*	barrier
3047	**barriga**-*f*	belly
3093	**barril**-*m*	barrel
2785	**basar(se)**-*vb*	base on
4070	**bastar(se)**-*vb; vbr*	be enough; be capable of
2921	**bastón**-*m*	cane
3396	**basurero**-*m*	garbage dump, garbageman
2912	**bata**-*f*	robe
2820	**batallón**-*m*	battalion
2930	**batir**-*vb*	beat, whip
2814	**baúl**-*m*	trunk
2657	**beca**-*f*	scholarship
2770	**bicho**-*m*	bug
2879	**bienestar**-*m*	comfort
3303	**billar**-*m*	billiards
2905	**billetera**-*f*	wallet
4242	**biología**-*f*	biology
3819	**blando**-*adj*	soft
3780	**bloquear**-*vb*	block
3315	**bloque**-*m*	block
3281	**bloqueo**-*m*	block
3488	**blues**-*m*	blues
3535	**blusa**-*f*	blouse
4562	**bobada**-*f*	nonsense, trifle
2529	**bobo**-*adj; m*	silly; fool
4120	**bocadillo**-*m*	sandwich
4061	**bocado**-*m*	bite
4377	**bocina**-*f*	horn
2736	**bodega**-*f*	cellar
4121	**bofetada**-*f*	slap
4448	**boletín**-*m*	bulletin
4320	**bolígrafo**-*m*	pen
4715	**boludo**-*adj; m*	silly (LA) (coll); moron (LA) (coll)
3222	**bombardeo**-*m*	bombing
4234	**bombardero**-*m*	bomber
3484	**bono**-*m*	bonus, pass

#	Word	Meaning
3658	bordar-*vb*	embroider, do excellently (coll)
3194	borrar-*vb*	delete
3199	botín-*m*	loot
3563	bóveda-*f*	vault
3232	boxeador-*m*	boxer
2875	boxeo-*m*	boxing
4777	brecha-*f*	gap
2595	brigada-*f*	squad
2651	brillo-*m*	brightness
3177	brindar-*vb*	toast, provide
2897	brisa-*f*	breeze
4115	broche-*m*	brooch
4752	broncear(se)-*vb*	tan
4177	bronce-*m*	bronze
4174	brujería-*f*	witchcraft
4416	brújula-*f*	compass
3096	brutal-*adj*	brutal
4944	brutalidad-*f*	brutality
2687	bruto-*adj; m*	brutal; brute
3992	buey-*m*	ox
3812	búfalo-*m*	buffalo
4226	bufanda-*f*	scarf
4806	búho-*m*	owl
4473	buitre-*m*	vulture
3305	buque-*m*	vessel
3734	burbuja-*f*	bubble
3407	burla-*f*	taunt
4251	burlar(se)-*vb; vbr*	evade; mock
2761	bus-*m*	bus (coll)
3663	buzón-*m*	mailbox

C

#	Word	Meaning
4069	cabalgar-*vb*	ride
2725	caballería-*f*	cavalry
2748	caber-*vb*	fit
2893	caca-*f*	poop (coll)
2987	cacería-*f*	hunting
3135	cachorro-*m*	puppy
3601	cadera-*f*	hip
4931	cadete-*m/f*	cadet
2629	cafetería-*f*	coffee shop
4183	cagada-*f*	shit (coll), screw-up (coll)
4172	cagado-*m*	wimpy (coll)
2780	cagar(se)-*vb; vbr*	shit (coll); be terrified
3994	calabaza-*f*	pumpkin
4641	calcular-*vb*	calculate
3494	cálculo-*m*	calculation
4794	caldera-*f*	boiler
4756	caldo-*m*	broth
3838	calefacción-*f*	heating
3389	calendario-*m*	calendar
3937	calentamiento-*m*	heating
3922	calentar-*vb*	heat
2694	cal-*f*	lime
3398	calibre-*m*	caliber
3412	cálido-*adj*	warm
4365	calificación-*f*	qualification
4483	callejero-*adj; m*	stray; street map
4525	caluroso-*adj*	hot
3091	calzón-*m*	shorts, knickers (LA)
4993	camarón-*m*	prawn
3401	camello-*m*	camel
3932	caminata-*f*	walk
4695	camisón-*m*	nightgown
3579	campus-*m*	campus
3847	canadiense-*adj; m/f*	Canadian; Canadian person
3544	caña-*f*	cane, rod
3793	canasta-*f*	basket
2859	cancelar-*vb*	cancel
3394	cancha-*f*	court
4000	canciller-*m/f*	chancellor
2587	candidato-*m*	candidate
3641	cangrejo-*m*	crab
4565	canguro-*m; m/f*	kangaroo; babysitter
4729	can-*m*	hound
4368	cansancio-*m*	fatigue
3966	cantina-*f*	cafeteria
3671	capataz-*m/f*	foreperson
3073	capilla-*f*	chapel
4512	capitalismo-*m*	capitalism
4962	capitalista-*adj; m/f*	capitalist; capitalist
4302	capricho-*m*	whim
4209	cápsula-*f*	capsule
3408	captura-*f*	capture
2896	capturar-*vb*	capture

4205	caracol-*m*	snail
4284	característica-*f*	feature
2925	caramelo-*m*	candy
2764	caravana-*f*	caravan
4060	carbono-*m*	carbon
3339	cardenal-*m*	cardinal
3649	cardíaco-*adj*	cardiac
4996	carecer-*vb*	lack
3046	cargado-*adj*	strong
4768	cargador-*m*	charger
3280	cargamento-*m*	shipment
4452	Caribe-*m*	the Caribbean
4014	cariñoso-*adj*	affectionate
3826	carnaval-*m*	carnival
4253	carnet-*m*	license
4203	carnicería-*f; f*	butcher's shop; slaughter
2871	carnicero-*m*	butcher
3904	carpa-*f*	marquee, carp
4006	carpintero-*m*	carpenter
3344	carreta-*f*	wagon
4241	carroza-*f*	carriage
3141	cartero-*m*	postman
4557	cartón-*m*	cardboard
4201	cartucho-*m*	cartridge
3002	casamiento-*m*	marriage
4614	cascada-*f*	waterfall
3564	casero-*adj; m*	home-made; landlord
4747	castaño-*adj; m*	brown; chestnut
2862	castigar-*vb*	punish
4593	castrar-*vb*	castrate
4610	catálogo-*m*	catalog
4324	catarata-*f*	cataract
3591	catástrofe-*f*	catastrophe
2920	categoría-*f*	category
3154	católico-*adj; m*	Catholic; Catholic
3229	catorce-*num*	fourteen
3064	cavar-*vb*	dig
3870	caviar-*m*	caviar
3347	CD-*m*	CD
3434	cebolla-*f*	onion
3949	cebo-*m*	bait
4033	ceder-*vb*	give
4297	ceja-*f*	eyebrow
2810	celebración-*f*	celebration
4968	célebre-*adj*	famous
4657	celebridad-*f*	celebrity
4556	celeste-*adj*	light blue, of heaven
3321	celestial-*adj*	celestial
2615	célula-*f*	cell
3391	cemento-*m*	cement
4853	cenicero-*m*	ashtray
2951	centímetro-*m*	centimeter
4553	céntimo-*m*	cent
3076	cepillo-*m*	brush
3480	cera-*f*	wax
4343	cereal-*adj; m*	grain-based; cereal
2590	cerebral-*adj*	cerebral
4417	cereza-*f*	cherry
4190	cerilla-*f*	match
3049	cerradura-*f*	lock
2600	certificado-*m; adj*	certificate; registered
3324	cesar-*vb*	cease
2749	césped-*m*	lawn
4147	cesta-*f*	basket
3287	chaleco-*m*	vest
3328	chantaje-*m*	blackmail
3197	chao-*int*	ciao
4911	charco-*m*	puddle
4704	charla-*f*	chat
4555	charlatán-*m*	fraudster, chatterbox
3239	chatarra-*f*	scrap
2867	che-*int*	hey, dude (LA)
4819	chequear-*vb*	check
3249	chicle-*m*	gum
3461	chile-*m*	chili
3970	chisme-*m*	rumor, junk (coll)
3776	chispa-*f*	spark
2946	chistoso-*adj*	funny
4795	chivo-*m*	kid, young goat
4412	chocar-*vb*	hit
2714	choque-*m*	crash
4978	chorrada-*f*	nonsense, knick-knack (ES) (coll)
3983	choza-*f*	hut
3565	chulo-*adj; m*	cocky (ES) (coll), great (ES) (coll); scumbag (coll)

3599	**chupar**-*vb*	suck, absorb (coll)
2794	**cicatriz**-*f*	scar
3322	**ciclo**-*m*	cycle
4386	**cierre**-*m*	closing
3627	**ciervo**-*m*	deer
3201	**cifra**-*f*	figure
4737	**cimiento**-*m*	foundation
4827	**cínico**-*adj; m*	shameless; shameless person
3493	**cintura**-*f*	waist
3292	**circuito**-*m*	circuit
4074	**circulación**-*f*	circulation
4424	**circular**-*adj; vb*	circular; travel
2695	**cirujano**-*m*	surgeon
4625	**cisne**-*m*	swan
4381	**civilizado**-*adj*	civilized
2980	**claridad**-*f*	clarity
4514	**clavar**-*vb*	nail
3453	**clavo**-*m*	nail
4764	**clemencia**-*f*	clemency
2807	**coartar**-*vb*	restrict
3942	**cobertizo**-*m*	shed
3251	**cobertura**-*f*	coverage
4888	**cobra**-*f*	cobra
3556	**cobre**-*m*	copper
3643	**cocodrilo**-*m/f*	crocodile
2700	**coco**-*m*	coconut
4062	**cóctel**-*m*	cocktail
4371	**codicia**-*f*	greed
3463	**codo**-*m*	elbow
4270	**cofre**-*m*	chest
2572	**cohete**-*m*	rocket
4461	**coincidir**-*vb*	coincide
3842	**colaboración**-*f*	collaboration
4649	**colaborar**-*vb*	collaborate
3326	**colapso**-*m*	collapse
4714	**colar(se)**-*vb; vbr*	strain, leak; sneak in
3574	**colchón**-*m*	mattress
3746	**cólera**-*f*	anger
4544	**col**-*f*	cabbage
4139	**colmar**-*vb*	fulfill
2966	**colocar**-*vb*	put
4961	**Colombia**-*f*	Colombia
3063	**colorado**-*adj*	red
2906	**combatir**-*vb*	combat

4558	**comediante**-*m/f*	comedian
3487	**comerciante**-*m*	merchant
2830	**cometa**-*m; f*	comet; kite
2676	**cómico**-*adj; m*	comical; comedian
4573	**comodidad**-*f*	comfort
3645	**compadre**-*m*	godfather, buddy (coll)
3855	**comparación**-*f*	comparison
2932	**comparar**-*vb*	compare
4935	**compartimento**-*m*	compartment
4921	**compás**-*m*	compass
4631	**compatriota**-*m/f*	compatriot
4384	**compensación**-*f*	compensation
4385	**compensar**-*vb*	compensate
3686	**competición**-*f*	competition
2706	**competir**-*vb*	compete
3768	**complacer**-*vb*	please
3255	**completar**-*vb*	complete
3859	**complicación**-*f*	complication
2892	**cómplice**-*m/f*	accomplice
4758	**complot**-*m*	conspiracy
4143	**componer**-*vb*	compose
3836	**comportarse**-*vbr*	behave
4432	**composición**-*f*	composition
4017	**compositor**-*m*	composer
3832	**comprador**-*m*	buyer
4329	**comprensible**-*adj*	understandable
3258	**comprensión**-*f*	understanding
4632	**comprensivo**-*adj*	understanding, comprehensive
2882	**comprometer(se)**-*vb; vbr*	implicate; get engaged
4938	**comuna**-*f*	commune
3405	**comunicar**-*vb*	communicate
4615	**comunión**-*f*	communion
4156	**comunismo**-*m*	communism
2821	**coñac**-*m*	cognac
3631	**conceder**-*vb*	grant
4571	**concejal**-*m*	councilor
3946	**concentrar(se)**-*vb*	assemble, focus
2817	**concernir**-*vb*	concern
3501	**concha**-*f*	shell, pussy (LA) (coll)
3094	**concreto**-*adj*	specific
4554	**condolencia**-*f*	condolence
2891	**conectar**-*vb*	connect

2528	**confesar(se)**-*vb*	confess	4519	**contestador**-*adj*	cheeky, answering machine
3894	**confiable**-*adj*	reliable	4277	**contexto**-*m*	context
2846	**confidencial**-*adj*	confidential	2979	**continente**-*adj*	continent
3854	**confirmación**-*f*	confirmation	3603	**contrabando**-*m*	smuggling
2971	**confirmar**-*vb*	confirm	3171	**contraseña**-*f*	password
2578	**conflicto**-*m*	conflict	2544	**contratar**-*vb*	hire
3433	**conforme**-*adj; adv*	in agreement; just as	4162	**contribución**-*f*	contribution
4596	**confortable**-*adj*	comfortable	4444	**convencional**-*adj*	conventional
3357	**confundido**-*adj*	confused	2841	**convención**-*f*	convention
2902	**confuso**-*adj*	confusing	2743	**conveniente**-*adj*	convenient
4672	**congelado**-*adj*	frozen	3055	**convento**-*m*	convent
3195	**congelar**-*vb*	freeze	4830	**convicción**-*f*	conviction
3777	**congresista**-*m/f*	delegate	3974	**convicto**-*adj; m*	convicted; convict
2581	**conjunto**-*m; adj*	combination; joint	3549	**convincente**-*adj*	convincing
4031	**conmoción**-*f*	shock	4089	**convoy**-*m*	convoy
3986	**conmovedor**-*adj*	touching	3212	**cooperación**-*f*	cooperation
2900	**conquistar**-*vb*	conquer	3773	**cooperar**-*vb*	cooperate
4561	**consciencia**-*f*	consciousness	3188	**coordenada**-*f*	coordinate
2815	**consejero**-*m*	counselor	4354	**coral**-*m*	coral
3496	**consentimiento**-*m*	consent	4472	**corazonada**-*f*	hunch
3706	**conserje**-*m/f*	janitor	2513	**cordero**-*m*	lamb
4670	**conservador**-*adj; m*	conservative; conservative	4348	**cordón**-*m*	cord
			4684	**cordura**-*f*	sanity
2673	**conservar**-*vb*	keep	4574	**coreano**-*adj; m*	Korean; Korean person
4524	**considerable**-*adj*	considerable			
3272	**consideración**-*f*	consideration	2555	**corear**-*vb*	chant
3310	**consistir**-*vb*	consist	3381	**corporación**-*f*	corporation
4980	**constar**-*vb*	feature, appear	4244	**corporal**-*adj; m*	corporal; corporal
3082	**constitución**-*f*	constitution	4009	**corral**-*m*	farmyard
4283	**consulado**-*m*	consulate	3896	**correa**-*f*	strap
4278	**cónsul**-*m/f*	consul	3971	**corrección**-*f*	correction
3079	**consulta**-*f*	inquiry	4273	**corregir**-*vb*	correct
4415	**consultar**-*vb*	consult	3624	**correspondencia**-*f*	correspondence
4598	**consultorio**-*m*	office, consultancy	2579	**corresponder**-*vb*	be appropriate, return
3868	**consumo**-*m*	consumption	3172	**corrupción**-*f*	corruption
4151	**contabilidad**-*f*	accounting	4276	**corrupto**-*adj; m*	corrupt; corrupt person
3648	**contable**-*m/f; adj*	accountant; accounting	2667	**corte**-*m*	cut, court
2945	**contactar**-*vb*	contact	3782	**cortés**-*adj*	courteous
3209	**contador**-*m*	counter, accountant	2688	**cortesía**-*f*	courtesy
			4468	**corteza**-*f*	crust
4334	**contaminación**-*f*	contamination	2535	**cortina**-*f*	curtain
4982	**contenedor**-*m*	container	3865	**coser**-*vb*	sew
2975	**contenido**-*m; adj*	contents; reserved	4947	**costero**-*adj*	coastal
			3025	**costilla**-*f*	rib

2703	**costo**-*m*	cost
5009	**coyote**-*m*	coyote
2638	**cráneo**-*m*	skull
3313	**creador**-*m*	creator
3652	**creativo**-*adj; m*	creative; copywriter
4196	**creciente**-*adj; f*	growing; swelling
3012	**crecimiento**-*m*	growth
4890	**credibilidad**-*f*	credibility
3427	**creencia**-*f*	belief
4552	**creíble**-*adj*	credible
4591	**creyente**-*m/f*	believer
2942	**crío**-*m*	child
4489	**criterio**-*m*	opinion, guideline
3866	**crítica**-*f*	review
4973	**criticar**-*vb*	criticize
2686	**crítico**-*adj; m*	critical; critic
2712	**cruce**-*m*	crossing
2940	**crucero**-*m*	cruise
3829	**crucial**-*adj*	crucial
4073	**crudo**-*adj*	raw, tough (ES) (coll)
3363	**crueldad**-*f*	cruelty
4582	**cruzado**-*adj*	cross
3472	**cuaderno**-*m*	notebook
3980	**cuadrado**-*adj; m*	square; square
3011	**cuadra**-*f*	stable, block (LA)
4624	**cuadrar**-*vb*	square
3288	**cualidad**-*f*	quality
3277	**cuan**-*adv*	as
3637	**cuarentena**-*f*	quarantine
4232	**cubierto**-*adj; m*	covered; piece of cutlery
2760	**cubo**-*m*	cube, bucket
4007	**cucaracha**-*f*	cockroach
2957	**cuerno**-*m*	horn
3308	**cuervo**-*m*	crow
4946	**cuestionar**-*vb*	question
2936	**cuidadoso**-*adj*	careful
3885	**culpabilidad**-*f*	culpability
4335	**cultivar**-*vb*	cultivate
4662	**cultivo**-*m*	farming
3089	**culto**-*m; adj*	worship; educated
3455	**cultural**-*adj*	cultural
4096	**cumbre**-*f*	summit
2681	**cuñado**-*m*	brother-in-law
2889	**cuna**-*f*	cradle
4167	**cuota**-*f*	fee
2577	**curar(se)**-*vb*	heal
4455	**cursi**-*adj; m/f*	corny; pretentious
2849	**curva**-*f*	curve

D

3833	**dañar**-*vb*	damage
2978	**debatir**-*vb*	discuss
3325	**década**-*f*	decade
3882	**decano**-*m*	dean
4678	**decena**-*f*	ten
3917	**decencia**-*f*	decency
2617	**decepcionar(se)**-*vb*	disappoint
3695	**decepción**-*f*	disappointment
4676	**décimo**-*num*	tenth
2809	**declarar**-*vb*	declare
4433	**decoración**-*f*	decoration
4081	**decorar**-*vb*	decorate
4502	**decreto**-*m*	decree
4599	**dedicación**-*f*	dedication
3561	**defecto**-*m*	defect
4535	**defensivo**-*adj; m*	defensive; defense
3500	**defensor**-*adj; m*	defense; defense attorney
3682	**definición**-*f*	definition
4740	**definir**-*vb*	define
4751	**degenerar**-*vb*	degenerate
3267	**delantero**-*adj; m*	front; forward
4323	**delegación**-*f*	delegation
4467	**delegar**-*vb*	delegate
4249	**delfín**-*m*	dolphin
4002	**deliberado**-*adj*	deliberate
4809	**delicadeza**-*f*	delicacy
3044	**delincuente**-*m/f; adj*	criminal; delinquent
4511	**demandar**-*vb*	sue, demand
4879	**demócrata**-*m/f*	democrat
3183	**demora**-*f*	delay
2816	**demostración**-*f*	demonstration
3979	**dental**-*adj*	dental
3117	**denuncia**-*f*	complaint
4498	**denunciar**-*vb*	report
3719	**deportivo**-*adj*	sports
2754	**depresión**-*f*	depression

3555	**deprimente**-*adj*	depressing	4966	**desvío**-*m*	detour
2909	**deprimir(se)**-*vb*	depress	4719	**detector**-*m*	detector
3887	**deriva**-*f*	drift	3206	**detención**-*f*	detention
4765	**derramar**-*vb*	spill	4038	**determinación**-*f*	determination
3837	**derribar**-*vb*	knock down	3969	**determinado**-*adj*	determined
2533	**derrotar**-*vb*	defeat	3323	**determinar**-*vb*	determine
4835	**desacuerdo**-*m*	disagreement	3839	**devoción**-*f*	devotion
4850	**desafiar**-*vb*	challenge	4773	**diabólico**-*adj*	diabolical
2981	**desaparición**-*f*	disappearance	3856	**diagnóstico**-*m; adj*	diagnosis; diagnostic
4491	**desarmar**-*vb*	disarm			
3612	**desarrollar**-*vb*	develop	3516	**diálogo**-*m*	dialogue
4824	**descarado**-*adj; m*	shameless; insolent person	4767	**diarrea**-*f*	diarrhea
			3350	**dibujar**-*vb*	draw
3515	**descarga**-*f*	discharge	3933	**diccionario**-*m*	dictionary
4476	**descargar**-*vb*	download	4886	**dictadura**-*f*	dictatorship
4894	**descender**-*vb*	descend	3818	**dieciocho**-*num*	eighteen
4904	**descendiente**-*m/f*	descendant	3650	**dieciséis**-*num*	sixteen
4217	**descenso**-*m*	descent	4116	**diecisiete**-*num*	seventeen
4250	**descifrar**-*vb*	decipher	2983	**difunto**-*m*	deceased
3114	**desconocido**-*adj; m*	unknown; stranger	3462	**digital**-*adj*	digital
			4687	**dilema**-*m*	dilemma
4881	**descortés**-*adj*	impolite	3883	**dimensión**-*f*	dimension
3131	**describir**-*vb*	describe	2663	**dinamita**-*f*	dynamite
2614	**descripción**-*f*	description	4710	**dinastía**-*f*	dynasty
2530	**descubrimiento**-*m*	discovery	4627	**dinosaurio**-*m*	dinosaur
3306	**descuento**-*m*	discount	4493	**diploma**-*m*	diploma
3989	**descuidado**-*adj*	careless	4130	**diplomático**-*adj; m*	diplomatic; diplomat
2605	**descuidar(se)**-*vb; vbr*	neglect; not worry			
			3513	**diputado**-*m*	deputy
4712	**desempleo**-*m*	unemployment	4261	**directivo**-*m; adj*	manager; managerial
4780	**desertor**-*m*	deserter			
2855	**desesperación**-*f*	despair	4840	**directorio**-*m*	directory
2868	**desesperar**-*vb*	despair	4311	**discípulo**-*m*	disciple
4464	**deshacer**-*vb*	undo	4716	**discoteca**-*f*	disco
4330	**desmayarse**-*vbr*	faint	3373	**discreción**-*f*	discretion
3107	**despegar**-*vb*	take off	3702	**discreto**-*adj*	discreet
3085	**despegue**-*m*	takeoff	4015	**discutido**-*adj*	controversial
3142	**desperdiciar**-*vb*	waste	4136	**diseñador**-*m*	designer
4420	**despiadado**-*adj*	ruthless	3690	**diseñar**-*vb*	design
3508	**despido**-*m*	dismissal	4066	**disfrazar(se)**-*vb*	disguise
3192	**despreciable**-*adj*	despicable	2520	**disfraz**-*m*	costume
3065	**desprecio**-*m*	disdain	4419	**disgustar**-*vb*	disgust
4267	**destacamento**-*m*	detachment	4896	**disgusto**-*m*	disgust
3422	**destinar**-*vb*	destine	2890	**dispositivo**-*m*	device
4878	**destreza**-*f*	skill	4459	**disputa**-*f*	dispute
2636	**destrozar**-*vb*	shatter	3581	**distante**-*adj*	distant
4149	**destructor**-*m*	destroyer	3474	**distinguir**-*vb*	distinguish

3727	**distracción**-*f*	distraction
4691	**distraído**-*adj; m*	distracted; scatterbrain
4148	**distribución**-*f*	distribution
3924	**disturbio**-*m*	disturbance
2671	**divertir(se)**-*vb*	amuse
4218	**dividir**-*vb*	divide
4357	**divorciar(se)**-*vb*	divorce
3583	**doblar**-*vb*	bend, double
4874	**doctorar(se)**-*vb*	award a doctorate
3518	**documentación**-*f*	documentation
3309	**documental**-*adj; m*	documentary; documentary
3058	**doler**-*vb*	hurt
3862	**domicilio**-*m*	address
4703	**dominante**-*adj*	dominant
3424	**dominar**-*vb*	master
3356	**dominio**-*m*	domain
4456	**donación**-*f*	donation
4741	**donante**-*m/f*	donor
2959	**doncella**-*f*	maid
3368	**dondequiera**-*adv*	wherever
3810	**dorar**-*vb*	brown
3164	**doscientos**-*num*	two hundred
4372	**dotar**-*vb*	supply
3552	**dramático**-*adj*	dramatic
4075	**drogadicto**-*m*	junkie
4403	**duende**-*m*	spirit
2502	**durar**-*vb*	last

E

2737	**ebrio**-*adj*	drunk
2977	**eco**-*m*	echo
3532	**económico**-*adj*	economic
3988	**editar**-*vb*	edit
4171	**editorial**-*adj; m; f*	editorial; leading article; publishing house
2655	**educar**-*vb*	educate
4435	**eficaz**-*adj*	effective
4047	**eficiente**-*adj*	efficient
4245	**egipcio**-*adj; m*	Egyptian; Egyptian person
3708	**ejecutar**-*vb*	implement, execute

2888	**ejecutivo**-*adj; m*	executive; manager
4252	**eje**-*m*	shaft
3712	**ejemplar**-*m; adj*	model; exemplary
4520	**ejercer**-*vb*	practice
3795	**electrónico**-*adj*	electronic
4439	**elegancia**-*f*	elegance
3955	**elevado**-*adj*	high
3852	**elevador**-*m*	elevator
4802	**elevar**-*vb*	raise
3132	**embarazo**-*m*	pregnancy
3593	**embarazoso**-*adj*	embarrassing
4771	**embarcar**-*vb*	embark
3316	**emboscar**-*vb*	ambush
3330	**eminencia**-*f*	eminence
4900	**emisión**-*f*	emission
4588	**emisora**-*f*	broadcasting station
2744	**emocional**-*adj*	emotional
2751	**emocionar(se)**-*vb*	thrill
3254	**empacar**-*vb*	pack (LA)
4523	**empapar(se)**-*vb*	soak
4723	**empatar**-*vb*	tie
4808	**empeño**-*m*	determination, pawn
4423	**empeorar**-*vb*	worsen
3736	**empresario**-*m*	businessman
3609	**en torno a**-*prp*	about
2982	**encajar**-*vb*	fit
4990	**encaje**-*m*	lace, fitting
4359	**encanto**-*m*	charm
5014	**encarcelar**-*vb*	imprison
3909	**encendedor**-*m*	lighter
2549	**encendido**-*adj; m*	on; ignition
4340	**encubrir**-*vb*	cover
4048	**enfermar(se)**-*vb*	get sick
3030	**enfermería**-*f*	infirmary
4200	**enfoque**-*m*	approach
4965	**enganchado**-*adj*	hooked (coll)
4640	**enigma**-*m*	enigma
3522	**enlace**-*m*	link
4807	**enloquecer**-*vb*	madden
4530	**enmendar**-*vb*	amend
3744	**enojo**-*m*	anger
5000	**enorgullecer(se)**-*vb; vbr*	please; feel proud
3263	**ensayar**-*vb*	rehearse

4449	enseñanza-*f*	teaching	4772	esmeralda-*f*	emerald
4526	entendimiento-*m*	understanding	4891	especia-*f*	spice
3873	enterar(se)-*vb; vbr*	pay (LA); find out	2840	especialidad-*f*	specialty
2741	entierro-*m*	burial	2584	especialista-*m/f*	specialist
3490	entorno-*m*	environment	3787	específico-*adj*	specific
3964	entrañar-*vb*	involve	2527	espectacular-*adj*	spectacular
4762	entrante-*adj; m*	entering; appetizer (ES)	4135	espectador-*m*	viewer
			4936	espectro-*m*	spectrum, ghost
2802	entrenar(se)-*vb*	train	4484	espeluznante-*adj*	horrifying
4500	entretenido-*adj*	entertaining	3656	esperma-*m*	sperm
3215	entretenimiento-*m*	entertainment	3963	espiar-*vb*	spy
			4037	espina-*f*	thorn
3155	entrever-*vb*	glimpse	4025	espionaje-*m*	espionage
4301	entusiasmar(se)-*vb; vbr*	delight; be thrilled	2564	espléndido-*adj*	splendid
			4804	esplendor-*m*	splendor
2699	entusiasmo-*m*	enthusiasm	4376	esponja-*f*	sponge
4487	envejecer-*vb*	age	4746	esposo-*m*	husband
4049	envenenar-*vb*	poison	3505	espuma-*f*	foam
2565	envidia-*f*	envy	3900	esqueleto-*m*	skeleton
3182	envidiar-*vb*	envy	4404	esquiar-*vb*	ski
3526	envolver-*vb*	wrap	2776	estable-*adj*	stable
3881	epidemia-*f*	epidemic	2835	establecer-*vb*	establish
2501	episodio-*m*	episode	4292	establecimiento-*m*	establishment
2665	equilibrio-*m*	balance	2928	establo-*m*	barn
4898	equivalente-*adj*	equivalent	4551	estacionar-*vb*	park
4138	equivocación-*f*	mistake	4059	estadístico-*adj; m*	statistical; statistician
5017	erupción-*f*	eruption			
3757	escalar-*vb*	climb	3976	estafador-*m*	swindler
3875	escalofrío-*m*	chill	3728	estafa-*f*	scam
4001	escalón-*m*	step	2962	estallar-*vb*	burst
3622	esclavitud-*f*	slavery	3312	estancia-*f*	stay
3834	escoba-*f*	broom	3884	estándar-*adj; m*	standard; standard
3342	escocés-*adj; m*	Scotch; Scot			
3070	escoltar-*vb*	escort	3481	estanque-*m*	pond
4129	escombro-*m*	rubbish	4643	estante-*m*	shelf
2784	escondite-*m*	hiding place, hide-and-seek	4985	estatura-*f*	stature
			3348	estelar-*adj*	stellar
2719	escopeta-*f*	shotgun	4285	esteroide-*m*	steroid
4702	escorpión-*m*	scorpion	2519	estimar-*vb*	estimate, respect
3036	escritura-*f*	writing	4750	estimulante-*adj; m*	stimulating; stimulant
4950	escrúpulo-*m*	scruple			
2745	escudo-*m*	shield	4378	estofado-*m; adj*	stew; stewed
4722	escultura-*f*	sculpture	3569	estrado-*m*	podium
4563	escupir-*vb*	spit	3945	estrecho-*adj*	narrow
2710	esencia-*f*	essence	4294	estrellar(se)-*vb*	crash
2762	esencial-*adj*	essential	2801	estreno-*m*	premiere
4262	esfera-*f*	sphere	3432	estricto-*adj*	strict

3261	estropear-vb	spoil		3835	extensión-f	extension
4733	estudiantil-adj	student (coll)		4578	extinción-f	extinction
4259	estufa-f	stove		3429	extraterrestre-adj; m/f	alien; alien
2707	etapa-f	stage				
2734	etc.-adv	etc.				
3538	ético-adj	ethical			**F**	
3038	etiqueta-f	label				
2604	euro-m	euro		4397	fabricar-vb	manufacture
4079	europeo-adj; m	European; European		4647	fachada-f	facade
				3423	facilidad-f	ease
3537	evacuación-f	evacuation		3767	factor-m	factor
4034	evacuar-vb	evacuate		2903	factura-f	invoice
4313	evaluación-f	evaluation		2661	facultad-f	faculty
4893	evangelio-m	gospel		2705	falda-f	skirt
3361	eventualmente-adv	occasionally		4220	falla-f	fault
				3115	fallecer-vb	die
4363	evidenciar-vb	demonstrate		2758	fallo-m	failure
3213	evolución-f	evolution		3614	fanático-adj; m	fan; fanatic
3657	exagerar-vb	exaggerate		2929	fan-m/f	fan
3295	examinar-vb	examine		4182	faraón-m	pharaoh
3010	excepcional-adj	exceptional		3119	farmacia-f	pharmacy
3317	exceso-m	excess		4592	farol-m	lantern, bluff
4836	excitación-f	excitement		3521	faro-m	lighthouse
2601	excitante-adj	exciting		3539	fascista-adj; m/f	fascist; fascist
3758	excitar-vb	excite		4393	fastidio-m	nuisance
3611	exclusivo-adj	exclusive		3616	fax-m	fax
3440	excursión-f	excursion		4805	faz-f	face
3205	exhibición-f	display		2594	febrero-m	February
4132	exigente-adj	demanding		4214	federación-f	federation
3150	exigir-vb	require		2726	femenino-adj	female
4331	exilio-m	exile		2869	fenomenal-adj	phenomenal
3830	exitoso-adj	successful		3534	feroz-adj	fierce
3938	expectativas-fpl	expectations		2702	ferrocarril-m	railway
2781	expedición-f	expedition		4604	festejar-vb	celebrate
5013	experimental-adj	experimental		4111	fiar(se)-vb; vbr	sell on credit; trust
3755	experimentar-vb	experiment				
4727	exploración-f	exploration		4661	fibra-f	fiber
3573	explorador-m	explorer		2542	ficción-f	fiction
3167	explorar-vb	explore		3430	ficha-f	chip, ticket
4222	exponer-vb	expose		3886	fichar-vb	sign, clock in
2800	expresar(se)-vb	express		4091	fidelidad-f	fidelity
3863	expreso-adj; m	express; express		4726	fiero-adj	fierce
3510	expulsar-vb	expel		2885	fijo-adj	fixed
4522	exquisito-adj	exquisite		4044	filmación-f	shooting
3571	éxtasis-m	ecstasy		4126	filósofo-m	philosopher
3610	extender-vb	extend		4959	filtro-m	filter

3439	**financiero**-*adj; m*	financial; financier
3898	**finanzas**-*fpl*	treasury
3621	**finca**-*f*	ranch
3088	**fino**-*adj*	fine
3948	**fiscalía**-*f*	district attorney's officer
3448	**flaco**-*adj*	skinny
3822	**flanco**-*m*	flank
4230	**flauta**-*f*	flute
2847	**flecha**-*f*	arrow
4974	**flexible**-*adj*	flexible
4409	**flojo**-*adj*	loose, slacker
3750	**flora**-*f*	flora
2958	**flotar**-*vb*	float
4154	**fluir**-*vb*	flow
3765	**flujo**-*m*	flow
4392	**foco**-*m*	focus, spotlight
4967	**fogata**-*f*	bonfire
4873	**folleto**-*m*	brochure
4810	**fondos**-*mpl*	funds
3576	**forastero**-*m; adj*	stranger; foreign
2585	**forense**-*adj; m/f*	forensic; forensic surgeon
3009	**formal**-*adj*	formal
4713	**formalidad**-*f*	formality
3245	**formidable**-*adj*	formidable
2837	**fórmula**-*f*	formula
3901	**formulario**-*m*	form
4510	**foro**-*m*	forum
3605	**forzado**-*adj*	forced
4199	**forzar**-*vb*	force
4351	**fósforo**-*m*	match
2684	**fotógrafo**-*m*	photographer
2523	**fracasar**-*vb*	fail
4532	**fracturar(se)**-*vb*	fracture
3017	**frágil**-*adj*	fragile
4247	**fragmento**-*m*	fragment
4630	**franqueza**-*f*	frankness
3618	**frasco**-*m*	jar
3804	**fraternidad**-*f*	fraternity
4799	**frenar**-*vb*	brake
3225	**freno**-*m*	brake
3791	**fresa**-*f*	strawberry
3470	**frijol**-*m*	bean
2864	**frito**-*adj*	fried
4909	**frontal**-*adj*	frontal

4782	**frustrar(se)**-*vb; vbr*	hinder; become frustrated
3262	**fruto**-*m*	fruit
3388	**fugitivo**-*adj; m*	fugitive; fugitive
5011	**fulano**-*m*	some guy (coll)
4164	**funcionamiento**-*m*	functioning
3551	**funcionario**-*m*	public worker
3027	**fundación**-*f*	foundation
3498	**fundamental**-*adj*	fundamental
4919	**fúnebre**-*adj*	funeral
4271	**funerario**-*adj*	funeral
3122	**furgoneta**-*f*	van
2697	**furia**-*f*	fury
3664	**fusil**-*m*	rifle
3395	**fusión**-*f*	fusion

G

3638	**gabinete**-*m*	cabinet
2976	**galaxia**-*f*	galaxy
2721	**gallo**-*m*	rooster
4382	**galo**-*adj*	Gallic
3121	**gancho**-*m*	hook
4828	**ganga**-*f*	bargain
3714	**ganso**-*m; adj*	goose; foolish (ES) (coll)
2870	**garantía**-*f*	guarantee
2554	**garantizar**-*vb*	guarantee
3204	**garra**-*f*	claw
3443	**gasolinera**-*f*	gas station
4293	**gelatina**-*f*	jelly
2756	**gemelo**-*adj; m*	twin; twin
3175	**generador**-*m*	generator
3761	**género**-*m*	gender
3489	**generosidad**-*f*	generosity
3851	**genética**-*f*	genetics
4549	**gen**-*m*	gene
3629	**gimnasia**-*f*	physical exercise
2641	**girar(se)**-*vb*	turn
3972	**gitano**-*adj; m*	gypsy; gypsy
3620	**glorioso**-*adj*	glorious
3582	**gobernar**-*vb*	rule
3331	**golfo**-*m; adj*	gulf; scoundrel
2679	**gol**-*m*	goal
2547	**goma**-*f*	rubber
2653	**gorra**-*f*	cap

3926	**gorro**-*m*	hat
4629	**grabadora**-*f*	recorder
2561	**grabar**-*vb*	record
4528	**graduar(se)**-*vb; vbr*	adjust; graduate
3615	**gramo**-*m*	gram
3266	**grandeza**-*f*	greatness
2806	**granero**-*m*	barn
2740	**gratitud**-*f*	gratitude
4570	**grieta**-*f*	crack
4272	**grifo**-*m; adj*	water tap; curly (LA)
3382	**gripe**-*f*	flu
3764	**grúa**-*f*	crane
4509	**grueso**-*adj; m*	heavy; thickness
2831	**guardaespaldas**-*m/f*	bodyguard
4045	**guardería**-*f*	daycare center
2739	**guardián**-*m*	guardian
4180	**guarida**-*f*	hideout
4757	**guarnición**-*f*	trimming, garnish
2952	**guay**-*adj; int*	great; great (ES) (coll)
4790	**guiar**-*vb*	guide

H

3147	**hábil**-*adj*	skilled
2639	**habitante**-*m/f*	inhabitant
3077	**hábito**-*m*	habit
3196	**hacer cosquillas**-*vb*	tickle
3099	**hacienda**-*f*	estate
3087	**halcón**-*m*	hawk
2540	**hamburguesa**-*f*	burger
3337	**harina**-*f*	flour
3113	**haz**-*m*	beam
5022	**hebreo**-*adj; m*	Hebrew; Jew
2718	**hechizo**-*m*	spell
4832	**hedor**-*m*	stench
2647	**hembra**-*f*	female
3721	**hemorragia**-*f*	hemorrhage
4383	**heno**-*m*	hay
2534	**heredero**-*m*	heir
2508	**herencia**-*f*	heritage, inheritance
3340	**hermandad**-*f*	brotherhood

5016	**hermosura**-*f*	beauty
5018	**heroico**-*adj*	heroic
4399	**herrero**-*m*	blacksmith
4428	**hervir**-*vb*	boil
4925	**heterosexual**-*adj*	heterosexual
4837	**hidrógeno**-*m*	hydrogen
4637	**higiénico**-*adj*	hygienic
2574	**hilo**-*m*	thread
3742	**himno**-*m*	hymn
4917	**hindú**-*adj; m/f*	Hindu; Hindu person
5023	**hipnosis**-*f*	hypnosis
3459	**hipócrita**-*adj; m/f*	hypocritical; hypocrite
3431	**hipoteca**-*f*	mortgage
4490	**hipótesis**-*f*	hypothesis
4914	**histeria**-*f*	hysteria
3869	**histérico**-*adj; m*	hysterical; hysteric
3351	**histórico**-*adj*	historical
4792	**hocico**-*m*	snout
3861	**hoguera**-*f*	bonfire
4622	**Holanda**-*f*	Holland
3827	**holandés**-*adj; m*	Dutch; Dutch person
4976	**holocausto**-*m*	holocaust
3707	**homenaje**-*m*	tribute
4339	**homicida**-*m/f; adj*	killer; murder
2602	**homosexual**-*adj; m/f*	homosexual; homosexual
4861	**homosexualidad**-*f*	homosexuality
3125	**hondo**-*adj*	deep
3436	**honestidad**-*f*	honesty
3700	**hongo**-*m*	fungus
4534	**honorario**-*adj*	honorary
3867	**honra**-*f*	honor
4427	**honrar**-*vb*	honor
3939	**horca**-*f*	gallows
3332	**horizonte**-*m*	horizon
3156	**hormiga**-*f*	ant
4398	**hormona**-*f*	hormone
4895	**horroroso**-*adj*	dreadful
3406	**hospitalidad**-*f*	hospitality
3771	**hostia**-*f; int*	blow (coll); damn (coll)
3681	**hostil**-*adj*	hostile
2646	**hueco**-*m; adj*	space; empty

3756	**huérfano**-*adj; m*	orphaned; orphan
4656	**huerto**-*m*	orchard
2582	**huésped**-*m/f*	guest
3722	**humedad**-*f*	moisture
3733	**húmedo**-*adj*	wet
4462	**humildad**-*f*	humility
3748	**humillación**-*f*	humiliation
4046	**humillante**-*adj*	humiliating
4686	**humillar**-*vb*	humiliate
3915	**hundir(se)**-*vb*	sink
3475	**huracán**-*m*	hurricane

I

2767	**identificar**-*vb*	identify
4515	**ídolo**-*m/f*	idol
3495	**ignorancia**-*f*	ignorance
2917	**ignorante**-*adj; m*	ignorant; ignoramus
3413	**ignorar**-*vb*	ignore
4082	**igualdad**-*f*	equality
3572	**iluminación**-*f*	lighting
4776	**iluminar**-*vb*	illuminate
2986	**ilusionar(se)**-*vb*	inspire hope
4953	**imaginario**-*adj; m*	imaginary; imaginary
4322	**imitación**-*f*	imitation
3217	**impaciente**-*adj*	impatient
4355	**impecable**-*adj*	impeccable
2853	**imperial**-*adj*	imperial
4739	**implacable**-*adj*	relentless
3302	**implicar(se)**-*vb*	involve
4486	**impotente**-*adj*	impotent
2598	**impresionar(se)**-*vb*	impress
4693	**improbable**-*adj*	unlikely
4429	**imprudente**-*adj*	reckless
2881	**impulso**-*m*	impulse
4337	**inaceptable**-*adj*	unacceptable
4875	**inapropiado**-*adj*	inappropriate
4027	**inauguración**-*f*	opening
4099	**inclusive**-*adv*	inclusive
2660	**incómodo**-*adj*	uncomfortable
3585	**inconveniente**-*m; adj*	problem; inconvenient
3666	**incorrecto**-*adj*	incorrect
4275	**incumbencia**-*f*	incumbency

4108	**incumbir**-*vb*	concern
4812	**indefenso**-*adj*	defenseless
2941	**independencia**-*f*	independence
2522	**indicar**-*vb*	indicate
4390	**índice**-*m*	index
5001	**indicio**-*m*	indication
4243	**indiferente**-*adj*	indifferent
4986	**indispensable**-*adj*	indispensable
4176	**individual**-*adj*	single, personal
2675	**individuo**-*m*	individual
3257	**industrial**-*adj; m*	industrial; industrialist
3377	**inesperado**-*adj*	unexpected
3962	**inestable**-*adj*	unstable
2715	**inevitable**-*adj*	inevitable
4169	**infame**-*adj; m/f*	dreadful; villain
3056	**infantería**-*f*	infantry
2972	**infarto**-*m*	heart
3180	**infección**-*f*	infection
4785	**infectar(se)**-*vb*	infect
2852	**inferior**-*adj; m/f*	lower; subordinate
4128	**infernal**-*adj*	infernal
3372	**infiel**-*adj; m/f*	unfaithful; infidel
3482	**infinito**-*adj; m*	infinite; infinity
4933	**informal**-*adj; m/f*	informal; unreliable person
4197	**informante**-*m/f*	informant
3509	**ingeniería**-*f*	engineering
3693	**ingenio**-*m*	wit, ingenuity
3270	**ingenioso**-*adj*	witty
3718	**ingenuo**-*adj*	ingenuous
4246	**ingle**-*f*	groin
4929	**ingrediente**-*m*	ingredient
3997	**ingresar**-*vb*	hospitalize, join
3028	**ingreso**-*m*	entry, deposit
3023	**inicial**-*adj; f*	beginning; initial
3143	**iniciar**-*vb*	start
3451	**iniciativa**-*f*	initiative
2711	**inicio**-*m*	beginning
3675	**injusticia**-*f*	injustice
2524	**injusto**-*adj*	unfair
3860	**inmenso**-*adj*	immense
4667	**inmersión**-*f*	immersion
4466	**inmigrante**-*adj; m/f*	immigrant; immigrant
4238	**inminente**-*adj*	imminent

4443	**inmoral**-*adj*	immoral
3187	**inmortal**-*adj*	immortal
4352	**inmortalidad**-*f*	immortality
4697	**inmunidad**-*f*	immunity
4852	**innecesario**-*adj*	unnecessary
2618	**inocencia**-*f*	innocence
3680	**inofensivo**-*adj*	harmless
4304	**inquieto**-*adj*	restless
4655	**inquilino**-*m*	tenant
4395	**inscripción**-*f*	registration
2790	**insecto**-*m*	insect
4085	**insensible**-*adj*	insensitive
2984	**insignificante**-*adj*	insignificant
4883	**insinuar**-*vb*	insinuate
2666	**insistir**-*vb*	insist
2824	**insoportable**-*adj*	unbearable
3161	**inspección**-*f*	inspection
2822	**inspiración**-*f*	inspiration
4367	**inspirar**-*vb*	inspire
3365	**instalación**-*f*	installation
4620	**instalar**-*vb*	install
3014	**institución**-*f*	institution
3985	**instructor**-*m*	instructor
4579	**insultar**-*vb*	insult
3200	**insulto**-*m*	insult
4501	**intacto**-*adj*	intact
3376	**integridad**-*f*	integrity
2876	**intelectual**-*adj; m/f*	mental; intellectual
4158	**intensidad**-*f*	intensity
3118	**intenso**-*adj*	powerful
4635	**intercambiar**-*vb*	exchange
2670	**intercambio**-*m*	exchange
4603	**interferencia**-*f*	interference
3925	**interferir**-*vb*	interfere
4675	**interminable**-*adj*	endless
3766	**internar**-*vb*	send in
3157	**interno**-*adj*	internal
3075	**interpretación**-*f*	interpretation
3274	**interpretar**-*vb*	play, perform
4862	**intérprete**-*m/f*	interpreter
4216	**interrogar**-*vb*	question
2938	**interrogatorio**-*m*	interrogation
4281	**interrupción**-*f*	interruption
3619	**interruptor**-*m*	switch
3779	**intervención**-*f*	intervention
3913	**intervenir**-*vb*	take part, operate
3110	**intimidad**-*f*	privacy
3876	**íntimo**-*adj*	intimate
4224	**intruso**-*m; adj*	intruder; out of place
3775	**intuición**-*f*	intuition
4616	**inundación**-*f*	flood
2648	**inusual**-*adj*	unusual
4586	**invadir**-*vb*	invade
2742	**invasión**-*f*	invasion
4212	**invencible**-*adj*	invincible
4705	**invención**-*f*	invention
4426	**inventario**-*m*	inventory
2878	**inventar**-*vb*	invent
2931	**invento**-*m*	invention
2680	**inversión**-*f*	investment
3973	**invertido**-*adj*	inverted
3646	**invertir**-*vb*	invest
3247	**investigador**-*m*	researcher
2717	**inyección**-*f*	injection
2861	**irlandés**-*adj; m*	Irish; Irish person
4125	**ironía**-*f*	irony
4137	**irónico**-*adj*	ironic
4193	**irrelevante**-*adj*	irrelevant
4289	**irresistible**-*adj*	irresistible
3995	**irresponsable**-*adj*	irresponsible
4225	**israelí**-*adj; m/f*	Israeli; Israeli

J

4533	**jabalí**-*m/f*	wild boar
3998	**jaleo**-*m*	fuss (coll)
2789	**jamón**-*m*	ham
4052	**jaque**-*m*	check
3421	**jardinero**-*m*	gardener
3951	**jarra**-*f*	mug
4269	**jarrón**-*m*	vase
2626	**jazz**-*m*	jazz
3283	**jeep**-*m*	jeep
4793	**jefatura**-*f*	leadership
4724	**jerez**-*m*	sherry
3670	**jet**-*m*	jet
3300	**jinete**-*m/f*	rider
3978	**jornada**-*f*	day
4495	**joyería**-*f*	jewelry
4838	**jubilación**-*f*	retirement

3034	**judicial**-*adj; m*	judicial; police officer
4674	**juerga**-*f*	good time
2526	**jungla**-*f*	jungle
3294	**juntar**-*vb*	put together
3831	**jurisdicción**-*f*	jurisdiction
4540	**justificar**-*vb*	justify
3710	**juvenil**-*adj*	youth

K

3174	**kilogramo**-*m*	kilogram

L

4050	**laberinto**-*m*	maze
4374	**laboral**-*adj*	work
3210	**labor**-*f*	work
3464	**ladrillo**-*m*	brick
4908	**lagarto**-*m*	lizard
4326	**laguna**-*f*	lagoon
2851	**lamentable**-*adj*	unfortunate, pathetic
2750	**lana**-*f*	wool
3753	**lancha**-*f*	boat
3687	**langosta**-*f*	lobster
4105	**lanza**-*f*	spear
4995	**largar(se)**-*vb; vbr*	tell, give; leave (coll)
3415	**láser**-*m*	laser
3181	**lata**-*f*	can
4529	**lateral**-*adj*	side
3858	**látigo**-*m*	whip
3144	**latín**-*m*	Latin
3626	**latir**-*vb*	beat
4475	**laurel**-*m*	laurel
3575	**lavabo**-*m*	sink, restroom
4957	**lavadora**-*f*	washing machine
2965	**lava**-*f*	lava
3059	**lavandería**-*f*	laundry
3226	**lazo**-*m*	bow, rope
3137	**lecho**-*m*	bed
4910	**lechuga**-*f*	lettuce
4314	**lector**-*m*	reader
3662	**legar**-*vb*	bequeath
4942	**legendario**-*adj*	legendary
3789	**legión**-*f*	legion

3691	**legítimo**-*adj*	legitimate
2747	**lejano**-*adj*	distant
3640	**lema**-*m*	motto
2953	**leña**-*f*	firewood
4338	**leopardo**-*m*	leopard
4375	**lesión**-*f*	injury
4076	**letal**-*adj*	lethal
3879	**letrero**-*m*	sign
3817	**leve**-*adj*	mild
2927	**liberado**-*adj*	free
4208	**liberal**-*adj*	liberal
4677	**librar(se)**-*vb; vbr*	fight, have free time; escape from
3696	**librería**-*f*	bookshop
4279	**libreta**-*f*	notebook
4168	**liderazgo**-*m*	leadership
2546	**lidiar**-*vb*	deal with
4612	**liebre**-*f*	hare
4963	**ligar(se)**-*vb*	tie, flirt (coll)
2504	**ligero**-*adj*	light
3625	**lila**-*adj; f*	lilac; lilac
4134	**lima**-*f*	lime, file
4316	**limitado**-*adj*	limited
4732	**limitar(se)**-*vb*	restrict
2850	**limón**-*m*	lemon
4402	**limosna**-*f*	alms
5005	**linaje**-*m*	lineage
2731	**linterna**-*f*	lantern
2998	**líquido**-*adj; m*	liquid; liquid
2588	**literatura**-*f*	literature
3285	**litro**-*m*	liter
3644	**llanto**-*m*	crying
3604	**lloro**-*m*	crying
2573	**llover**-*vb*	rain
4755	**localización**-*f*	location
3203	**localizar**-*vb*	locate
3589	**lodo**-*m*	mud
4971	**lona**-*f*	canvas
4681	**longitud**-*f*	length
4298	**loro**-*m*	parrot
3557	**lote**-*m*	set
2552	**lotería**-*f*	lottery
2922	**luchador**-*m*	fighter
3892	**lujuria**-*f*	lust
3019	**lunar**-*adj; m*	lunar; mole
3606	**luto**-*m*	mourning

M

4296	**madrastra**-*f*	stepmother
3102	**socialismo**-*m*	socialism
4053	**madrina**-*f*	godmother
2907	**madrugar**-*vb*	rise early
4999	**madurar**-*vb*	mature
3227	**maduro**-*adj; adv*	ripe; mature
4975	**mafioso**-*adj; m*	mafia; mobster
4786	**magistrado**-*m*	magistrate
3359	**mail**-*m*	email (coll)
5020	**malaria**-*f*	malaria
2690	**malentender**-*vb*	misunderstand
4127	**mamar**-*vb*	nurse
5006	**manantial**-*m*	spring
3003	**manar**-*vb*	flow
4920	**manchar**-*vb*	stain
4801	**mandato**-*m*	mandate
3905	**mandíbula**-*f*	jaw
2833	**manejo**-*m*	use
3252	**manga**-*m/f; f*	manga; sleeve
4410	**mango**-*m*	mango
4065	**manguera**-*f*	hose
2792	**manicomio**-*m*	asylum
3796	**manifestación**-*f*	manifestation
4090	**maní**-*m*	peanut
3720	**maniobra**-*f*	maneuver
4941	**manipular**-*vb*	manipulate
2562	**mansión**-*f*	mansion
2559	**manta**-*f*	blanket
3999	**manteca**-*f*	butter
3238	**mantenimiento**-*m*	maintenance
4885	**manto**-*m*	mantle
4240	**manuscrito**-*m*	manuscript
4083	**maquinaria**-*f*	machinery
3918	**maquinar**-*vb*	plot
3410	**mara**-*f*	gang (LA)
3130	**marcado**-*adj; m*	noticeable; dialing (LA)
4210	**marcador**-*m*	marker
3072	**marcar**-*vb*	mark
3126	**marcial**-*adj*	martial
2518	**marea**-*f*	tide
3936	**marear(se)**-*vb*	make someone dizzy, annoy (coll)
4905	**mareo**-*m*	dizziness
5019	**marfil**-*m*	ivory
3741	**margarita**-*f*	daisy
2704	**margen**-*m*	margin
3221	**marido**-*m*	husband
2593	**marino**-*adj; m*	marine; sailor
3018	**mariposa**-*f*	butterfly
2763	**mariscal**-*m/f*	marshal
4492	**mármol**-*m*	marble
2911	**marqués**-*m*	marquis
2798	**marrón**-*adj*	brown
4391	**mártir**-*m/f*	martyr
2963	**masacre**-*f*	massacre
2746	**masaje**-*m*	massage
4446	**masajista**-*m/f*	massage therapist
4623	**mascar**-*vb*	chew
3236	**mascota**-*f*	pet
3477	**masculino**-*adj*	masculine
3661	**masivo**-*adj*	massive
4811	**matadero**-*m*	slaughterhouse
3176	**matanza**-*f*	killing
3231	**matón**-*m*	thug
2989	**matrícula**-*f*	license plate, enrollment
4559	**matrimonial**-*adj*	matrimonial
4547	**mayonesa**-*f*	mayonnaise
4998	**mayor**-*adj*	largest, elderly
2992	**mayordomo**-*m*	butler
2777	**mear(se)**-*vb*	piss
2709	**mecánico**-*adj; m*	mechanical; mechanic
3479	**mecanismo**-*m*	mechanism
4567	**media**-*f*	stocking
4611	**mediana**-*f*	median
2845	**mediante**-*prp*	through
3752	**medicación**-*f*	medication
3133	**medicamento**-*m*	medicine
4518	**mediocre**-*adj*	mediocre
4972	**Mediterráneo**-*m*	Mediterranean
3442	**mejilla**-*f*	cheek
3327	**mejora**-*f*	improvement
2812	**melodía**-*f*	melody
3848	**mención**-*f*	mention
3874	**mendigo**-*m*	beggar
3893	**menta**-*f*	mint
4818	**mentalidad**-*f*	mentality

2899	**menú**-*m*	menu	4342	**motín**-*m*	riot
3090	**merced**-*f*	mercy	4754	**motivación**-*f*	motivation
4833	**mercurio**-*m*	mercury	3770	**motocicleta**-*f*	motorcycle
3366	**mérito**-*m*	merit	2988	**mozo**-*m*	lad
3806	**mermelada**-*f*	jam	4882	**muchedumbre**-*f*	crowd
4575	**mero**-*adj*	mere	3759	**muda**-*f*	change
4606	**metáfora**-*f*	metaphor	4454	**mudanza**-*f*	move
4760	**metálico**-*adj; m*	metal; cash	3170	**mudar(se)**-*vb*	move
3220	**mexicano**-*adj; m*	Mexican; Mexican person	2999	**mudo**-*adj*	mute
			4770	**mugre**-*f*	grime
4265	**mezclar**-*vb*	mix	3015	**mulo**-*m*	mule
4720	**microondas**-*mpl*	microwave	2668	**multar**-*vb*	fine
5012	**milenio**-*m*	millennium	3725	**múltiple**-*adj*	multiple
4321	**milicia**-*f*	militia	4913	**mundial**-*adj*	worldwide
4146	**mineral**-*adj; m*	mineral; mineral	2991	**muñeco**-*m*	doll
3984	**minero**-*m*	miner	3823	**imitar**-*vb*	imitate
2506	**misil**-*m*	missile	3993	**murciélago**-*m/f*	bat
2939	**mito**-*m*	myth	3078	**muro**-*m*	wall
2826	**mochila**-*f*	backpack	2505	**músculo**-*m*	muscle
4742	**moción**-*f*	motion	2610	**músico**-*m; adj*	musician; musical
3291	**mocoso**-*m; adj*	snuffly; brat	4131	**muslo**-*m*	thigh
3471	**modesto**-*adj*	modest	3607	**musulmán**-*adj; m*	Muslim; Muslim
4569	**módulo**-*m*	module	3029	**mutuo**-*adj*	mutual
2786	**mojar**-*vb*	wet			
3276	**molino**-*m*	mill		**N**	
4030	**momia**-*f*	mummy			
3732	**monasterio**-*m*	monastery	4112	**nalga**-*f*	buttock
4310	**monitor**-*m*	monitor	3349	**nana**-*f; f*	granny; lullaby
2509	**monje**-*m*	monk	4312	**narcótico**-*adj; m*	narcotic; narcotic
4970	**monstruoso**-*adj*	monstrous	4421	**natación**-*f*	swimming
3008	**montaje**-*m*	assembly	3202	**natal**-*adj*	native
3633	**monumento**-*m*	monument	3568	**nativo**-*adj; m*	local; native
4195	**morada**-*f*	dwelling	5025	**nato**-*adj*	born
4021	**morado**-*adj*	purple	4077	**náusea**-*f*	nausea
4660	**moralidad**-*f*	morality	2521	**navaja**-*f*	knife
4590	**morar**-*vb*	dwell	3577	**naval**-*adj*	naval
3146	**morder(se)**-*vb*	bite	4043	**navegación**-*f*	navigation
3685	**moreno**-*adj*	dark skinned, brunette	2919	**navegar**-*vb*	sail
			4916	**navío**-*m*	ship
3709	**morfina**-*f*	morphine	4658	**necio**-*m; adj*	fool; stupid
3392	**morgue**-*f*	morgue	5008	**negligencia**-*f*	negligence
4717	**moribundo**-*adj; m*	dying; dying person	3891	**negociación**-*f*	negotiation
			4106	**neumático**-*m; adj*	tire; inflatable
2531	**mosca**-*f*	fly	4826	**neumonía**-*f*	pneumonia
4370	**mosquito**-*m*	mosquito	4263	**neutral**-*adj; m/f*	neutral; third party
3716	**mostaza**-*f*	mustard			
3554	**mostrador**-*m*	counter			

3304	**nevada**-*f*	snowfall
3369	**nevera**-*f*	fridge
3418	**niñez**-*f*	childhood
3393	**no obstante**-*con*	however
4114	**nobleza**-*f*	nobility
4055	**Nochebuena**-*f*	Christmas Eve
4056	**noción**-*f*	notion
3260	**nomás**-*adv*	just (LA)
3679	**nombrar**-*vb*	name
4988	**noreste**-*m*	northeast
3597	**normalidad**-*f*	normalcy
3929	**noroeste**-*m*	northwest
3248	**norteamericano**-*adj; m*	North American; North American person
4229	**noruego**-*adj; m*	Norwegian; Norwegian person
4028	**nostalgia**-*f*	nostalgia
3724	**notable**-*adj; m*	notable; dignitary
4706	**noticiero**-*m*	news (LA)
2658	**novato**-*m; adj*	trainee; rookie
2674	**novedad**-*f*	novelty
4690	**noveno**-*num*	ninth
3731	**noventa**-*num*	ninety
3547	**nuca**-*f*	neck
3457	**núcleo**-*m*	core
3450	**nudo**-*m*	knot
4411	**nuera**-*f*	daughter-in-law
3414	**nuez**-*f*	nut
5007	**numeroso**-*adj*	numerous

O

2883	**obedecer**-*vb*	obey
4774	**obediencia**-*f*	obedience
2507	**obispo**-*m*	bishop
2570	**obligación**-*f*	obligation
2548	**obrero**-*m*	worker
4595	**obsequio**-*m*	gift
2753	**observación**-*f*	observation
4360	**observador**-*m; adj*	observer; observant
3335	**obsesionar(se)**-*vb*	obsess
3013	**obsesión**-*f*	obsession
3634	**obstáculo**-*m*	obstacle
2685	**occidental**-*adj; m/f*	western; westerner

3899	**occidente**-*m*	west
3499	**ochenta**-*num*	eighty
3987	**octavo**-*num*	eighth
2836	**oculto**-*adj*	hidden
2970	**ocupación**-*f*	occupation
3048	**ofender**-*vb*	offend
4577	**ofensa**-*f*	offense
3241	**ofensivo**-*adj*	offensive
4072	**ofertar**-*vb*	offer
4912	**ojear**-*vb*	glance over
4659	**olfato**-*m*	smell
3688	**olla**-*f*	pot
4024	**operador**-*m*	operator
3314	**operar**-*vb*	work
4644	**operativo**-*adj; m*	operational; operation
4181	**opio**-*m*	opium
3799	**oponente**-*m/f; adj*	opponent; opposing
4734	**oponer(se)**-*vb*	oppose
3558	**oportuno**-*adj*	timely
3524	**oposición**-*f*	opposition
3628	**optimista**-*adj; m/f*	optimistic; optimist
3386	**opuesto**-*adj*	opposite
4307	**oral**-*adj*	oral
3384	**órbita**-*f*	orbit
3953	**ordinario**-*adj*	ordinary
4019	**organismo**-*m*	organism
2652	**organizado**-*adj*	tidy
2503	**organizar**-*vb*	organize
3100	**órgano**-*m*	organ
4153	**orientación**-*f*	orientation
2842	**oriental**-*adj; m*	eastern; Asian
3139	**orinar**-*vb*	urinate
3747	**ostra**-*f*	oyster

P

3193	**pabellón**-*m*	pavilion
2914	**pacto**-*m*	pact
3908	**padrastro**-*m*	stepfather
2752	**paisaje**-*m*	landscape
3178	**paja**-*f*	stalk, masturbation (ES)
3364	**pala**-*f*	shovel
3447	**palanca**-*f*	lever

4831	**palco**-*m*	box seat	4434	**peluquero**-*m*	hairdresser
4401	**palestino**-*adj; m*	Palestinian; Palestinian person	2563	**pena**-*f*	pity, punishment
3333	**pálido**-*adj*	pale	3676	**penal**-*adj; m*	criminal; prison
3273	**palmar**-*vb*	die (ES) (coll)	4863	**pendejo**-*adj; m*	asshole (LA) (coll); fool (LA) (coll)
3020	**paloma**-*f*	dove	4744	**pender**-*vb*	hang over
4688	**panadería**-*f*	bakery	3050	**pendiente**-*m; f; adj*	earring; slope; pending
3390	**pañal**-*m*	diaper	4870	**penetrar**-*vb*	penetrate
4063	**Panamá**-*m*	Panama	3959	**penique**-*m*	penny
4144	**panda**-*m*	panda	3148	**donar**-*vb*	donate
4117	**panel**-*m*	panel	4480	**peón**-*m*	pawn
4815	**panorama**-*m*	landscape	4160	**percepción**-*f*	perception
3745	**panza**-*f*	belly	4481	**perdición**-*f*	perdition
3190	**paracaídas**-*m*	parachute	4787	**perezoso**-*adj; m*	lazy; sloth
4186	**paradero**-*m*	whereabouts	2887	**perfección**-*f*	perfection
3163	**paraguas**-*m*	umbrella	2557	**perfil**-*m*	profile
4671	**paralizar**-*vb*	paralyze	3265	**perímetro**-*m*	perimeter
4743	**paranoia**-*f*	paranoia	4295	**periodismo**-*m*	journalism
4848	**parásito**-*m; adj*	parasite; parasitic	3037	**periodo**-*m*	term
4673	**parcial**-*adj*	partial	2943	**perla**-*f*	pearl
4696	**párrafo**-*m*	paragraph	3449	**perpetuo**-*adj*	perpetual
4843	**parrilla**-*f*	grill	3005	**persecución**-*f*	persecution
4477	**parroquia**-*f*	parish	2728	**perseguir**-*vb*	chase
3527	**participación**-*f*	participation	5024	**persiana**-*f*	blind
3850	**partícula**-*f*	particle	2609	**perspectiva**-*f*	perspective
3801	**pasado**-*adj; m*	past; past	4145	**pertenencia**-*f*	belonging
4018	**pasatiempo**-*m*	pastime	4858	**perturbar(se)**-*vb*	disturb, disorient
3240	**Pascua**-*f*	Easter	4358	**perverso**-*adj*	wicked
3654	**pasto**-*m*	pasture	4865	**pésame**-*m*	condolence
3383	**patear**-*vb*	kick	3541	**pescador**-*m*	fisherman
4184	**patinar**-*vb*	skate	3530	**pésimo**-*adj*	awful
4708	**patriota**-*m/f; adj*	patriot; patriotic	3039	**peso**-*m*	weight
4101	**patrulla**-*f*	patrol	2803	**peste**-*f*	plague
3138	**pausa**-*f*	pause	4041	**pezón**-*m*	nipple
3545	**pecador**-*m; adj*	sinner; sinful	3902	**pianista**-*m/f*	pianist
3841	**peculiar**-*adj*	peculiar	4268	**piar**-*vb*	tweet
3296	**pedo**-*m*	fart	3717	**picante**-*adj; m*	spicy; spiciness
4405	**pegamento**-*m*	glue	3404	**pijama**-*m*	pajamas
3071	**peinado**-*m*	hairstyle	2637	**pila**-*f*	battery, sink, stack
4505	**peine**-*m*	comb	4023	**pilar**-*m*	pillar
3864	**pelirrojo**-*adj; m*	redheaded; redhead	2516	**píldora**-*f*	pill
3352	**pellejo**-*m*	skin	3084	**pillar**-*vb*	catch up
3191	**peluca**-*f*	wig	3808	**pimienta**-*f*	pepper
4470	**peludo**-*adj*	hairy	5002	**piña**-*f*	pineapple
4119	**peluquería**-*f*	hairdresser	4800	**pingüino**-*m*	penguin

3846	**pino**-*m*	pine		2856	**poseer**-*vb*	possess
4560	**piojo**-*m*	louse		2621	**posesión**-*f*	possession
2795	**pipa**-*f*	pipe, seed		2539	**postal**-*adj; f*	postal; postcard
4088	**pirámide**-*f*	pyramid		3435	**poste**-*m*	post
2545	**pirata**-*m/f; adj*	pirate; pirated		4753	**posterior**-*adj*	rear, following
4051	**pisar**-*vb*	step		3052	**postura**-*f*	posture
2969	**pis**-*m*	piss (coll)		3912	**potente**-*adj*	powerful
4282	**pistolero**-*m*	gunman		4730	**pradera**-*f*	meadow
4585	**pizarra**-*f*	blackboard		4362	**prado**-*m*	meadow
3066	**plagar**-*vb*	infest		3623	**precaución**-*f*	caution
4825	**planchar**-*vb*	iron		4619	**precedente**-*adj; m*	previous; precedent
4361	**plantación**-*f*	plantation				
4036	**plantar(se)**-*vb; vbr*	plant, stand up (coll); stand firm		4668	**preciosidad**-*f*	preciousness
				5021	**precipicio**-*m*	cliff
4763	**plasmar**-*vb*	express		3592	**precisión**-*f*	precision
2689	**plataforma**-*f*	platform		4541	**predecir**-*vb*	predict
3960	**plegaria**-*f*	prayer		4589	**prefecto**-*m*	prefect
3228	**plomo**-*m*	lead		4264	**prejuicio**-*m*	prejudice
2644	**pobreza**-*f*	poverty		4506	**prenda**-*f*	garment
3168	**podrido**-*adj*	rotten		3600	**preparación**-*f*	preparation
3173	**polaco**-*adj; m*	Polish; Polish person		4094	**preparativos**-*mpl*	preparations
				4857	**preparatorio**-*adj; m*	preparatory; pre-university study
4813	**polar**-*adj*	polar				
4373	**póliza**-*f*	policy		5010	**presenciar**-*vb*	witness
2560	**polo**-*m*	pole		3749	**presentir**-*vb*	have a feeling
3186	**pólvora**-*f*	gunpowder		4587	**preservar**-*vb*	preserve
4666	**ponche**-*m*	punch		4223	**presidencia**-*f*	presidency
4867	**popularidad**-*f*	popularity		4068	**presidencial**-*adj*	presidential
4303	**póquer**-*m*	poker		3853	**presionar**-*vb*	press
4940	**porcelana**-*f*	porcelain		4479	**presto**-*adj; adv*	ready; promptly
3642	**porcentaje**-*m*	percentage		3419	**presuponer**-*vb*	assume
4123	**porción**-*f*	portion		2532	**pretender**-*vb*	pretend
4152	**porro**-*m*	joint		4155	**prevenir(se)**-*vb; vbr*	warn; get ready
4846	**portaaviones**-*m*	aircraft carrier				
2944	**portada**-*f*	cover		2774	**prever**-*vb*	foresee
4923	**portador**-*m*	carrier		4682	**previo**-*adj*	previous
3684	**portal**-*m*	portal		3441	**primario**-*adj*	primary
3738	**portar(se)**-*vb; vbr*	carry; behave		4663	**primitivo**-*adj*	primitive
4542	**portátil**-*adj; m*	portable; laptop		2775	**prioridad**-*f*	priority
2662	**portero**-*m*	doorman, goalkeeper		3244	**privacidad**-*f*	privacy
				2566	**privilegio**-*m*	privilege
4380	**portón**-*m*	gate		2691	**probabilidad**-*f*	probability
4821	**portugués**-*adj; m*	Portuguese; Portuguese person		3562	**proceder**-*vb*	come from, proceed
				4332	**procurar**-*vb*	attempt
3311	**pos(t)**-*pfx*	post		2632	**producir**-*vb*	produce
3097	**posar**-*vb*	pose		3594	**profecía**-*f*	prophecy

3160	**profeta**-*m/f*	prophet
4745	**programación**-*f*	programming
4400	**programar**-*vb*	program
3559	**prohibido**-*adj*	prohibited
4943	**prójimo**-*m*	neighbor, friend (LA)
2937	**promedio**-*m*	average
4822	**prometedor**-*adj*	promising
3798	**promoción**-*f*	promotion
4441	**pronunciar**-*vb*	pronounce
3268	**propaganda**-*f*	advertising
2541	**propietario**-*m*	owner
2769	**propinar**-*vb*	inflict
2597	**proponer(se)**-*vb; vbr*	suggest; decide
3845	**proposición**-*f*	proposition
4150	**prosperidad**-*f*	prosperity
4406	**prostitución**-*f*	prostitution
3703	**protagonista**-*m/f*	protagonist
3001	**protector**-*adj; m*	protective; protector
3007	**protesta**-*f*	protest
3417	**protestar**-*vb*	protest
3399	**protocolo**-*m*	protocol
4820	**prototipo**-*m*	prototype
3053	**provecho**-*m*	benefit
4817	**proveedor**-*m*	supplier
3596	**provenir**-*vb*	proceed
3290	**provincia**-*f*	province
2623	**provisión**-*f*	provision
3237	**provocar**-*vb*	provoke
4309	**proyección**-*f*	projection
2973	**prudente**-*adj*	prudent
3445	**psicología**-*f*	psychology
4422	**psicológico**-*adj*	psychological
4258	**psicólogo**-*m*	psychologist
3888	**psiquiátrico**-*adj; m*	psychiatric; psychiatric hospital
3343	**publicar**-*vb*	publish
3504	**puerco**-*m; adj*	pig; disgusting
4607	**pujar**-*vb*	bid
3595	**pulgada**-*f*	inch
4291	**pulga**-*f*	flea
3318	**pulgar**-*m*	thumb
2645	**pulmón**-*m*	lung
4937	**pulpo**-*m*	octopus
4344	**pulsera**-*f*	bracelet
2819	**puñado**-*m*	handful
3807	**puñetazo**-*m*	punch
2517	**puño**-*m*	fist
3930	**puntería**-*f*	aim
3954	**puntual**-*adj; adv*	punctual; on time
4185	**puré**-*m*	purée
3730	**pureza**-*f*	purity
4020	**púrpura**-*adj*	purple

Q

3737	**quebrar**-*vb*	break
4527	**quemadura**-*f*	burn
3362	**quienquiera**-*prn*	whoever
2575	**química**-*f*	chemistry
3528	**químico**-*adj; m*	chemical; chemist
3821	**quinientos**-*num*	five hundred
2650	**quinta**-*f; f*	country house (ES); mansion (LA)
4918	**quirófano**-*m*	operating room

R

3230	**rabino**-*m*	rabbi
4325	**rabo**-*m*	tail
4256	**racional**-*adj*	rational
4698	**ración**-*f*	ration
3698	**racista**-*m/f; adj*	racist person; racist
2765	**radiación**-*f*	radiation
3794	**radical**-*adj; m/f*	radical; radical person
4458	**rajar(se)**-*vb; vbr*	slice; back out (coll)
2735	**rama**-*f*	branch
3843	**ramo**-*m*	bouquet
4997	**rampa**-*f*	ramp
2877	**rana**-*f*	frog
3587	**rapidez**-*f*	speed
4107	**rap**-*m*	rap
4907	**rasgo**-*m*	feature
3991	**rasguñar**-*vb*	scratch
3774	**rastrear**-*vb*	track
4842	**rastreo**-*m*	search
2682	**raya**-*f*	line
4856	**razonar**-*vb*	reason

4102	**reaccionar**-*vb*	react
4414	**reactor**-*m*	reactor
4613	**realeza**-*f*	royalty
3437	**rebaño**-*m*	flock
3473	**rebelión**-*f*	rebellion
3233	**recado**-*m*	message
3101	**rechazar**-*vb*	reject
3486	**rechazo**-*m*	rejection
4956	**recinto**-*m*	enclosure
3941	**reclamar**-*vb*	demand
5003	**reclutar**-*vb*	recruit
3694	**recomendación**-*f*	recommendation
4930	**reconstrucción**-*f*	reconstruction
4087	**reconstruir**-*vb*	rebuild
2620	**récord**-*m*	record
2724	**recorrer**-*vb*	go across, run your eyes over
4759	**recorte**-*m*	cutback
4356	**recreo**-*m*	break
2543	**recto**-*adj*	straight
4932	**recuento**-*m*	count
3123	**recuperación**-*f*	recovery
4482	**recurrir**-*vb*	appeal, resort
4748	**redacción**-*f*	essay, editorial office
3790	**redondo**-*adj*	round
3298	**reducir**-*vb*	reduce
4042	**reemplazar**-*vb*	replace
4394	**reemplazo**-*m*	replacement
3184	**referencia**-*f*	reference
4600	**reflejar(se)**-*vb*	reflect
3224	**reflejo**-*m; adj*	reflection; reflex
4336	**reflexionar**-*vb*	reflect
4543	**reformar**-*vb*	reform
3360	**refresco**-*m*	soda
3004	**refrigerador**-*m*	refrigerator
3278	**refugiar(se)**-*vb*	shelter
3069	**regalar**-*vb*	gift
3218	**régimen**-*m*	regime
3149	**registrar**-*vb*	register
3705	**reglamento**-*m*	regulation
3219	**regular**-*vb*	regulate
3460	**rehabilitación**-*f*	rehabilitation
3636	**reja**-*f*	bar
2738	**relacionar**-*vb*	connect
2947	**relámpago**-*m*	lightning
4989	**relativo**-*adj*	concerning
4228	**relato**-*m*	tale
4899	**relevante**-*adj*	outstanding
3040	**religioso**-*adj; m*	religious; priest
4198	**relleno**-*adj; m*	stuffed; stuff
4349	**remate**-*m*	ending
3840	**remolcar**-*vb*	tow
4347	**remo**-*m*	oar
4474	**remordimiento**-*m*	remorse
3375	**remoto**-*adj*	distant
4845	**renacimiento**-*m*	rebirth, Renaissance
2923	**rencor**-*m*	resentment
4617	**rendición**-*f*	surrender
2990	**rendir(se)**-*vb; vbr*	perform; surrender
3336	**reno**-*m*	reindeer
2654	**renta**-*f*	rent, income
2961	**renuncia**-*f*	resignation
4680	**reparación**-*f*	repair
2858	**reparar**-*vb*	repair
3041	**repartir**-*vb*	distribute
3602	**repentino**-*adj*	sudden
4345	**reponer**-*vb*	replenish
3345	**reportaje**-*m*	article
4654	**reportar(se)**-*vb; vbr*	bring, report (LA); report in (LA)
3109	**reportero**-*m*	reporter
4215	**reposo**-*m*	rest
3346	**representación**-*f*	representation
4521	**republicano**-*m*	republican
3813	**resaca**-*f*	hangover
4868	**reservación**-*f*	reservation (LA)
3062	**reserva**-*f*	reserve
3042	**resfriado**-*adj; m*	have a cold; cold
4165	**residente**-*adj; m/f*	resident; resident
4992	**residuo**-*m*	residue
4851	**resistente**-*adj*	resistant
4460	**resolución**-*f*	resolution
4513	**respaldo**-*m*	back
3751	**respectar**-*vb*	concern
2768	**respetable**-*adj*	respectable
2759	**respetar**-*vb*	respect
2787	**respiro**-*m*	rest
3234	**resumir**-*vb*	summarize
4173	**resurrección**-*f*	Resurrection
4437	**retaguardia**-*f*	rearguard

4749	retener-*vb*	retain	4639	sable-*m*	saber
2729	retirar(se)-*vb*	remove	4803	sabotaje-*m*	sabotage
2612	reto-*m*	challenge	4100	sabroso-*adj*	tasty
4949	retorcer-*vb*	twist	3739	sacrificar-*vb*	sacrifice
3598	retorno-*m*	return	2874	salchicha-*f*	sausage
3921	retrete-*m*	toilet	3124	salido-*adj; m*	protruding; horny (coll)
2677	retroceder-*vb*	go back			
3635	reunido-*adj*	gathered	4175	saliva-*f*	saliva
2630	reunir(se)-*vb*	get together	3803	salmón-*m*	salmon
4636	revancha-*f*	rematch	2586	salvador-*m*	savior
4104	revelación-*f*	revelation	4816	sanatorio-*m*	sanatorium
2997	revelar-*vb*	reveal	4260	sangriento-*adj*	bloody
3958	reventar-*vb*	burst	3380	santuario-*m*	sanctuary
4350	reverencia-*f*	reverence	4039	sapo-*m*	toad
3378	revisión-*f*	review	3982	saque-*m*	kickoff
3468	revolucionario-*adj; m*	revolutionary; revolutionary	4080	sardina-*f*	sardine
			3672	sastre-*m/f*	tailor
3275	rezo-*m*	prayer	2556	satélite-*m*	satellite
4032	ría-*f*	estuary	2913	satisfacción-*f*	satisfaction
4880	rienda-*f*	rein	3763	satisfecho-*adj*	satisfied
2589	rincón-*m*	corner	4834	secta-*f*	sect
3259	ring-*m*	ring	3120	secuestrado-*adj*	kidnapped
4140	riñón-*m*	kidney	4497	secuestrador-*m*	kidnapper
2884	ritual-*adj; m*	ritual; ritual	4328	secuestrar-*vb*	kidnap
3158	rival-*adj; m/f*	rival; opponent	3928	sede-*f*	headquarters
4442	roble-*m*	oak	4699	seducir-*vb*	seduce
4766	rocío-*m*	dew	4994	seductor-*adj; m*	seductive; seducer
2866	rodaje-*m*	filming	4098	seguido-*adj*	non-stop
4652	rollo-*m*	roll, bore (coll)	3446	seguidor-*m*	follower
3975	rol-*m*	role	3402	selección-*f*	selection
2643	romano-*adj; m*	Roman; Roman person	2514	sellar-*vb*	seal, stamp
			4626	sello-*m*	seal
4866	romo-*adj*	blunt	4447	semen-*m*	semen
4213	rompecabezas-*m*	puzzle	3523	semestre-*m*	semester
4539	rosado-*adj*	rose	2611	semilla-*f*	seed
4605	rosario-*m*	rosary	4159	seminario-*m*	seminary
4731	rublo-*m*	ruble	2811	senado-*m*	senate
2633	rudo-*adj*	rough, rude	4471	seña-*f*	sign
4979	rugby-*m*	rugby	4864	señalar-*vb*	mark
4651	ruidoso-*adj*	noisy	4855	senda-*f*	track
4958	ruleta-*f*	roulette	3169	sendero-*m*	path
4236	ruptura-*f*	rupture	3216	seno-*m*	breast, core
			4653	señorito-*m*	young gentleman
	S		2628	sensacional-*adj*	sensational
			3578	sensato-*adj*	sensible
2616	sábana-*f*	bed sheet	3805	sensibilidad-*f*	sensitivity

4016	sensor-*m*	sensor	2625	soga-*f*	rope
3338	sensual-*adj*	sensual	4954	soja-*f*	soy
4860	sentenciar-*vb*	sentence	3713	solicitar-*vb*	request
2779	sentimental-*adj*	sentimental	2592	solicitud-*f*	request
3068	separación-*f*	separation	3428	sólido-*adj; m*	solid; solid
3111	séptimo-*num*	seventh	2860	soltar-*vb*	free, drop
3903	sereno-*adj; m*	calm; dew	2996	solucionar-*vb*	solve
3608	servidor-*m*	server, servant	4859	sonriente-*adj*	smiling
4939	servilleta-*f*	napkin	2967	soplar-*vb*	blow
2894	sesenta-*num*	sixty	4012	soporte-*m*	support
3371	setenta-*num*	seventy	2783	sostener-*vb*	hold
2949	set-*m*	set	3128	soviético-*adj; m*	Soviet; Soviet
4192	severo-*adj*	stern	3517	stop-*m*	stop sign
2720	sexto-*num*	sixth	3678	subastar-*vb*	auction
4689	sexualidad-*f*	sexuality	4928	súbdito-*m*	subject
2813	SIDA-*m*	AIDS	4922	sublime-*adj*	sublime
2805	sierra-*f*	mountains, saw	3660	subterráneo-*adj*	underground
4829	siervo-*m*	serf	4084	subtítulo-*m*	subtitle
2698	siesta-*f*	nap	4457	suburbio-*m*	suburb
2669	signo-*m*	sign	4231	suceso-*m*	event
4248	silbato-*m*	whistle	4499	sucesor-*m*	successor
3198	silencioso-*adj*	silent	3916	suciedad-*f*	dirt
3520	sillón-*m*	armchair	4255	Sudáfrica-*f*	South Africa
2664	similar-*adj*	similar	4097	sudar-*vb*	sweat
4333	simio-*m*	ape	3021	sudor-*m*	sweat
3784	simpatía-*f*	friendliness	3940	sueco-*adj; m*	Swedish; Swedish person
3476	sinceridad-*f*	sincerity			
4849	sincronización-*f*	synchronization	3546	suegro-*m*	father-in-law
3677	sincronizar-*vb*	synchronize	4035	suero-*m*	serum
3788	síndrome-*m*	syndrome	3811	suéter-*m*	sweater
4438	siniestro-*adj*	sinister	2772	sugerencia-*f*	suggestion
2908	síntoma-*m*	symptom	2649	suicidarse-*vbr*	commit suicide
2895	sinvergüenza-*m/f; adj*	wretch; rascal	4798	sultán-*m*	sultan
			3397	suministro-*m*	supply
3033	sirena-*f*	siren	3043	sumo-*m; adj*	sumo; supreme
3035	sirviente-*m*	servant	3877	superficial-*adj*	superficial
4450	soberano-*adj; m*	sovereign; sovereign	4854	superintendente-*m/f*	superintendent
4078	soborno-*m*	bribery	2934	supermercado-*m*	supermarket
3871	sobredosis-*f*	overdose	4960	superstición-*f*	superstition
4707	sobrenatural-*adj*	supernatural	3250	supervisor-*m*	supervisor
4650	sobretodo-*m*	overcoat	2804	supervivencia-*f*	survival
3286	sobreviviente-*m/f; adj*	survivor; surviving	4503	superviviente-*m/f*	survivor
			4633	suposición-*f*	assumption
3208	sobrio-*adj*	sober	2918	supremo-*adj*	supreme
2994	soda-*f*	soda	3214	surgir-*vb*	appear
3639	software-*m*	software			

3802	**suspender**-*vb*	hang, cancel, fail
4634	**suspensión**-*f*	suspension
4516	**suspiro**-*m*	sigh
3699	**sustancia**-*f*	substance
4029	**sustituto**-*m*	substitute
3665	**sutil**-*adj*	subtle

T

2880	**taberna**-*f*	tavern
3927	**tablero**-*m*	board
4327	**tacaño**-*adj*	miserly
4531	**taco**-*m*	taco, peg
4876	**tacón**-*m*	heel
3683	**táctica**-*f*	tactic
3786	**tacto**-*m*	touch
4463	**talentoso**-*adj*	talented
2634	**tallar**-*vb*	engrave
4122	**talón**-*m*	heel
3358	**tambor**-*m*	drum
3301	**tango**-*m*	tango
2550	**tapa**-*f*	cover
4583	**taquilla**-*f*	ticket window
2642	**tardar(se)**-*vb*	be late
4478	**tarifa**-*f*	rate
4413	**tasa**-*f*	valuation
3506	**taxista**-*m/f*	taxi driver
4207	**tazón**-*m*	bowl
4538	**teatral**-*adj*	theatrical
3116	**técnica**-*f*	technique
4465	**teja**-*f*	tile
3341	**tejido**-*m*	tissue, fabric
2696	**tela**-*f*	fabric
2580	**telefónico**-*adj*	telephonic
4683	**telescopio**-*m*	telescope
3083	**televisor**-*m*	television
4004	**telón**-*m*	curtain
2916	**temblar**-*vb*	shake
4221	**temperamento**-*m*	temperament
4924	**tempestad**-*f*	storm
4440	**templar**-*vb*	cool down
4058	**tendencia**-*f*	trend
4227	**tender(se)**-*vb; vbr*	tend, hang up; lie down
4013	**tenedor**-*m*	fork
3466	**tensar(se)**-*vb*	tense

3112	**tentación**-*f*	temptation
3880	**tercio**-*m*	third
4679	**terciopelo**-*m*	velvet
3320	**terminal**-*adj; m/f*	terminal; terminal
4003	**ternero**-*m*	calf
3588	**ternura**-*f*	tenderness
3032	**terraza**-*f*	terrace
2910	**terremoto**-*m*	earthquake
3760	**terrestre**-*adj; m*	land; terrestrial
2863	**terrorismo**-*m*	terrorism
3729	**tesis**-*f*	thesis
4170	**testículo**-*m*	testicle
3740	**testificar**-*vb*	testify
3416	**test**-*m*	test
4884	**tibio**-*adj*	warm
4580	**ticket**-*m*	ticket
4701	**tic**-*m*	tic
2716	**tierno**-*adj*	tender
3140	**tijeras**-*fpl*	scissors
2619	**timbre**-*m*	ring
3095	**timón**-*m*	rudder
3783	**tinieblas**-*fpl*	darkness
2948	**tinto**-*adj*	red wine
2901	**tirador**-*m*	shooter
4601	**tiranía**-*f*	tyranny
4609	**tirano**-*m*	tyrant
2512	**tiroteo**-*m*	gunfire
4189	**titular(se)**-*m; vb; adj*	headline; title; owner
3299	**tobillo**-*m*	ankle
3743	**tocino**-*m*	bacon
4948	**tolerancia**-*f*	tolerance
3689	**tolerar**-*vb*	tolerate
2773	**tomate**-*m*	tomato
3543	**tomo**-*m*	volume
2536	**tonelada**-*f*	ton
3931	**topar(se)**-*vb*	run into
3553	**top**-*m*	top
4280	**topo**-*m*	mole
4648	**torcer(se)**-*vb*	twist
4872	**tormento**-*m*	torment
4536	**tornar(se)**-*vb*	change
4602	**tornillo**-*m*	screw
2692	**torta**-*f*	cake, sandwich (LA)
4286	**tortilla**-*f*	omelette

2569	**tortuga**-*f*	tortoise
4789	**torturar(se)**-*vb*	torture
3781	**tos**-*f*	cough
4179	**tostar**-*vb*	toast
3967	**tour**-*m*	tour
4237	**tractor**-*m*	tractor
2960	**tradicional**-*adj*	traditional
2613	**traducir**-*vb*	translate
3031	**traficante**-*m/f*	trafficker
3022	**trágico**-*adj*	tragic
2799	**traicionar**-*vb*	betray
3857	**trama**-*f*	plot
3491	**tramar**-*vb*	plot
3769	**tramposo**-*m; adj*	trickster; dishonest
4379	**transbordador**-*m*	ferry
3106	**transferencia**-*f*	transfer
4550	**transferir**-*vb*	transfer
4366	**transformación**-*f*	transformation
4568	**transformar(se)**-*vb*	transform
4781	**transición**-*f*	transition
3387	**tránsito**-*m*	transit
4095	**transmisor**-*m; adj*	transmitter; transmitting
3907	**transmitir**-*vb*	transmit
4628	**transportar**-*vb*	transport
4110	**tranvía**-*m*	tram
4092	**trapo**-*m*	cloth
4814	**trasladar(se)**-*vb*	move
3711	**traslado**-*m*	move
3890	**trauma**-*m*	trauma
5004	**trayecto**-*m*	journey
4299	**trayectoria**-*f*	trajectory
3000	**trece**-*num*	thirteen
3814	**tregua**-*f*	truce
2525	**tremendo**-*adj*	tremendous
4711	**trescientos**-*num*	three hundred
4545	**triángulo**-*m*	triangle
4239	**tributo**-*m*	tribute
3211	**trigo**-*m*	wheat
4877	**trinchera**-*f*	trench
4387	**trío**-*m*	trio
3503	**tripa**-*f*	intestine, belly
2974	**triple**-*adj; m*	triple; triple
4306	**triunfar**-*vb*	triumph
2791	**triunfo**-*m*	triumph
3630	**trofeo**-*m*	trophy
3715	**trompeta**-*f*	trumpet
3151	**tronco**-*m*	trunk
4779	**tropical**-*adj*	tropical
3674	**trucar**-*vb*	rig
4952	**trucha**-*f*	trout
3207	**trueno**-*m*	thunder
4621	**tubería**-*f*	pipeline
3820	**tumor**-*m*	tumor
3329	**turco**-*adj; m*	Turkish; Turk
4638	**turismo**-*m*	tourism
2656	**turista**-*adj; m/f*	tourist; tourist
3919	**tutor**-*m*	tutor

U

2771	**ubicación**-*f*	location
4775	**umbral**-*m*	threshold
4548	**uña**-*f*	nail
2797	**universal**-*adj*	universal
3454	**universitario**-*adj; m*	university; undergraduate
3409	**urgencia**-*f*	urgency
3452	**usual**-*adj*	usual
4981	**útero**-*m*	uterus
4191	**utilidad**-*f*	utility
3754	**uva**-*f*	grape
3444	**uy**-*int*	whoah, ouch

V

4206	**vacuna**-*f*	vaccine
4566	**vagar**-*vb*	wander
2733	**vagina**-*f*	vagina
2567	**vago**-*adj; m*	vague, lazy; slacker
2825	**vagón**-*m*	carriage of a train
4694	**vainilla**-*f*	vanilla
3923	**vale**-*m; int*	voucher; ok
3353	**valentía**-*f*	courage
2511	**valioso**-*adj*	valuable
3548	**valla**-*f*	fence
4305	**válvula**-*f*	valve
3815	**vanidad**-*f*	vanity
4005	**vara**-*f*	rod
3697	**variar**-*vb*	vary

3944	**variedad**-*f*	variety
3086	**varón**-*m*	male
4010	**Vaticano**-*m*	Vatican
4564	**vegetal**-*adj; m*	vegetal; vegetable
3613	**veinticinco**-*num*	twenty-five
4608	**vejez**-*f*	old age
2599	**velada**-*f*	soiree
3253	**velo**-*m*	veil
3370	**veloz**-*adj*	fast
2839	**vena**-*f*	vein
4871	**vencedor**-*adj; m*	winner; winner
4166	**vengar(se)**-*vb*	avenge
4369	**ventilación**-*f*	ventilation
4163	**verdugo**-*m*	executioner
3145	**verdura**-*f*	vegetable
2558	**veredicto**-*m*	verdict
2693	**vergonzoso**-*adj*	shameful
3279	**verificar**-*vb*	verify
2635	**versar**-*vb*	be about
4266	**verso**-*m*	verse
3026	**vestíbulo**-*m*	lobby
2607	**vestuario**-*m*	wardrobe, locker room
3981	**veterano**-*adj; m*	veteran; veteran
3797	**veterinario**-*m*	veterinarian
3824	**viajero**-*m*	traveler
3104	**víbora**-*f*	viper
4991	**vibración**-*f*	vibration
2823	**vicepresidente**-*m*	vice-president
4064	**vicio**-*m*	vice
2678	**vientre**-*m*	belly
3223	**vigilante**-*adj; m/f*	attentive; guard
3319	**vil**-*adj*	vile
3632	**villano**-*m; adj*	villain; villain
4187	**vínculo**-*m*	link
3816	**vino**-*m*	wine
3536	**violar**-*vb*	violate
4364	**violeta**-*adj; f*	violet; violet
2898	**violín**-*m*	violin
2848	**virtud**-*f*	virtue
4254	**visible**-*adj*	visible
4054	**víspera**-*f*	eve
2964	**visual**-*adj*	visual
2603	**vital**-*adj*	vital
4233	**vitamina**-*f*	vitamin
4889	**viudo**-*m; adj*	widower; widow
4841	**vivienda**-*f*	apartment
3289	**viviente**-*adj*	living
4769	**vocabulario**-*m*	vocabulary
4353	**vocación**-*f*	vocation
4951	**volador**-*adj*	flying
2591	**volante**-*m; adj*	steering wheel, referral (ES); flying
3878	**volcán**-*m*	volcano
2640	**volumen**-*m*	volume
2757	**voluntario**-*adj; m*	voluntary; volunteer
4346	**vómito**-*m*	vomit
3584	**votación**-*f*	vote
3772	**vulnerable**-*adj*	vulnerable

V

3024	**web**-*f*	web

Y

3590	**yacer**-*vb*	lie
3668	**yanqui**-*m/f; adj*	Yankee (coll); Yankee (coll)
3425	**yarda**-*f*	yard
3269	**yate**-*m*	yacht
2828	**yen**-*m*	yen
3502	**yerno**-*m*	son-in-law
4504	**yeso**-*m*	plaster

Z

4445	**zanahoria**-*f*	carrot
4796	**zanjar**-*vb*	dig, settle
2924	**zapatilla**-*f*	slipper
3045	**zar**-*m*	tsar
4977	**zarpar**-*vb*	set sail
3189	**zoológico**-*adj; m*	zoological; zoo
3910	**zoo**-*m*	zoo
3735	**zumo**-*m*	juice

Contact, Further Reading and Resources

For more tools, tips & tricks visit our site www.mostusedwords.com. We publish various language learning resources. If you have a great idea you want to pitch us, please send an e-mail to info@mostusedwords.com.

Frequency Dictionaries

In this series:

Spanish Frequency Dictionary 1 – Essential Vocabulary – 2500 Most Common Spanish Words
Spanish Frequency Dictionary 2 - Intermediate Vocabulary – 2501-5000 Most Common Spanish Words
Spanish Frequency Dictionary 3 - Advanced Vocabulary – 5001-7500 Most Common Spanish Words
Spanish Frequency Dictionary 4 - Master Vocabulary – 7501-10000 Most Common Spanish Words

Our mission is to provide language learners worldwide with frequency dictionaries for every major and minor language. We are working hard to accomplish this goal. You can view our selection on https://store.mostusedwords.com/frequency-dictionaries

Bilingual books

We're creating a selection of parallel texts. We decided to rework timeless classics, such as Alice in Wonderland, Sherlock Holmes, Dracula, The Picture of Dorian Gray, etc.

Our books are paragraph aligned: on the left side of the page you will find the English version of the story, and on the right side the Spanish version..

To help you in your language learning journey, all our bilingual books come with a dictionary included, created for that particular book.

Current bilingual books available are English, Spanish, Portuguese, Italian, German, and Spanish.

For more information, check https://store.mostusedwords.com/bilingual-books . Check back regularly for new books and languages.

Other language learning methods

You'll find reviews of other 3rd party language learning applications, software, audio courses, and apps. There are so many available, and some are (much) better than others.

Check out our reviews at www.mostusedwords.com/reviews.

Contact

If you have any questions, you can contact us through e-mail info@mostusedwords.com.

Made in the USA
Las Vegas, NV
05 February 2024

85331925R00136